PENGI

Jim Cusack is the *Sunday Independent*'s security correspondent. Henry McDonald is Ireland correspondent for the *Observer* and author of *INLA* and *David Trimble*. Cusack and McDonald previously co-authored *The UVF*.

UDA

Inside the Heart of Loyalist Terror

HENRY McDONALD AND JIM CUSACK

PENGUIN BOOKS

PENGUIN BOOKS

Published by the Penguin Group
Penguin Ireland, 25 St Stephen's Green, Dublin 2, Ireland
a division of Penguin Books Ltd
Penguin Books Ltd, 80 Strand, London WC2R ORL, England
Penguin Group (USA) Inc., 375 Hudson Street, New York, New York 10014, USA
Penguin Group (Canada), 10 Alcorn Avenue, Toronto, Ontario, Canada M4V 3B2
(a division of Pearson Penguin Canada Inc.)
Penguin Group (Australia), 250 Camberwell Road,
Camberwell, Victoria 3124, Australia (a division of Pearson Australia Group Pty Ltd)
Penguin Books India Pvt Ltd, 11 Community Centre,
Panchsheel Park, New Delhi – 110 017, India
Penguin Group (NZ), cnr Airborne and Rosedale Roads, Albany,
Auckland 1310, New Zealand (a division of Pearson New Zealand Ltd)
Penguin Books (South Africa) (Pty) Ltd, 24 Sturdee Avenue,
Rosebank 2196, South Africa

Penguin Books Ltd, Registered Offices: 80 Strand, London WC2R ORL, England

www.penguin.com

First published by Penguin Ireland 2004
Published with updated epilogue material in Penguin Books 2005
1

Printed in England by Clays Ltd, St Ives plc

Contents

List of Illustrations

Photo credits
1–5, 7 and 11–14: from a private collection; 6: *Belfast Telegraph*; 8: Pacemaker Press; 9–10: Kelvin Boyes Photography.

Prologue – Top Gun

Every year during the last decade of Northern Ireland's Troubles the Ulster Defence Association held its very own ghoulish version of the Oscars. 'Volunteer of the Year' was an award ceremony for top assassins, usually staged in bars and drinking dens in the loyalist stronghold of Belfast's Lower Shankill. The star turn for almost the entire period was a young Protestant from the Greater Shankill known to friend and foe alike as 'Top Gun'.

Hundreds of men and women would gather to hear speakers, usually members of the UDA leadership, announce who had won the year's big award. Inevitably Top Gun's name would be called out over the PA and the crowd, worse for wear from drink and drugs, would cheer wildly as on to the stage stepped one of the Shankill's own – Stephen McKeag. His prize was usually a plaque or plinth, manufactured by loyalist prisoners locked up inside the top security Maze prison, with a mini-handgun or assault rifle mounted on top, and his nickname, Top Gun, engraved underneath.

From 1990 until his ignominious death ten years later, McKeag was one of the most fearsome and ruthless murderers inside the UDA. Detectives who dedicated endless hours and resources to putting him behind bars estimate that Top Gun killed at least a dozen men and women in the greater Belfast area. Former comrades insist that the body-count is probably much higher.

Of the twelve or so killings in which McKeag took part, former Royal Ulster Constabulary (RUC) officers highlight two particularly callous assassinations. On 28 April 1992 McKeag shot dead Philomena Hanna, a young Catholic shop assistant working at a chemist's close to an arterial route which links the loyalist Shankill with the nationalist Springfield Road. McKeag walked into the premises shortly after it opened. He fired on Philomena Hanna as she worked on a window display and, when she fell to the ground, he fired several more shots into her body. Then he strolled out of the shop and mounted the back of a stolen motorcycle that did a U-turn and sped off towards Lanark Way, the favoured route of loyalist killers returning from West Belfast to the Shankill. Eyewitnesses who saw the two-man gang escape from the scene reported that as they left the killers were singing: 'Follow the Yellow Brick Road'. Years later one of his close associates said that when he fled a killing McKeag always sang the same refrain from 'The Wizard of Oz', the 'joke' being that he and his fellow assassins regarded Lanark Way, and other arterial routes into the Shankill, as their 'yellow brick roads' to safety.

Top Gun's intended target had been the sister of a Sinn Fein publicity director and close associate of Gerry Adams, Richard McAuley. The UDA wrongly believed she worked in the pharmacy. Instead its hit-man got Philomena Hanna. But such a mistake would not have bothered the viscerally sectarian ranks of the West Belfast UDA.

A year later, on a bright Saturday morning in September, McKeag and two accomplices drove up the Donegall Road from the loyalist village area. Their destination was a hairdressing salon at the junction of the Donegall and Falls Road. McKeag and one of his gang walked into the hairdresser's and confronted its owner, forty-year-old Sean Hughes. McKeag fired just once from a handgun. As their victim lay on the ground both UDA men opened fire again, this time using an automatic weapon as well as the pistol. For good measure, McKeag and his accomplice also shot at the terrified receptionist who had seen her boss gunned down before her eyes. Though he was charged with the Hughes murder, McKeag walked free from court after the judge cast doubt on eyewitness evidence. Police officers pursuing him were furious at the decision.

McKeag's short but violent life typifies the vicious sectarian world of the second generation of working-class Protestants that emerged from loyalist ghettos during the Troubles. He had graduated alongside an old friend and comrade, Johnny 'Mad Dog' Adair, from the nihilistic street violence of the skinheads into the Ulster Young Militants, the junior wing of the UDA, before joining the parent organization. These young men lived, breathed and slept violence and sectarianism. Even their clothes and jewellery exuded menace: around McKeag's neck a mini golden gun dangled from a solid gold chain.

Shaven-headed, muscular and tattooed McKeag was the model for what Adair later evolved into. He was fond of fast motorbikes, body-building, drink, drugs and, most of all, women. With scores of lovers, he confirmed the cliché that power is an aphrodisiac. On one occasion the man who took away so many lives, managed to bring one into the world. At the height of the UDA's murder campaign one of his girlfriends, who was heavily pregnant, asked McKeag to take her to hospital from her home in the County Down market town of Newtonards. In McKeag's four-wheel-drive Jeep the woman's waters broke. McKeag pulled into the concourse of a local petrol station, telephoned for an ambulance and helped to deliver the child after the paramedics arrived. The story of Top Gun the emergency midwife became as legendary on the Lower Shankill as his exploits as a killing machine. He fathered four children by different women whose devotion to him was outweighed only by their lack of imagination: the two girls were called Stephanie, the two boys, Stephen.

However, in the Ulster loyalist underworld legends are idols with feet of clay and there is always someone trying to topple them. McKeag fell victim to intense jealousy. He belonged to the most notorious and militant loyalist terror unit in Northern Ireland – the UDA's 'C' company from the Lower Shankill. 'C' company was divided into teams – C1, C2, C3 and so on. It first emerged as the cutting edge of the resurgent UDA terror campaign in 1989. McKeag's team was a hit squad; others organized prison welfare and fund-raising (bank robberies, extortion, money-lending and, latterly, drug-dealing). His team's exploits, and his hands-on role in murder, threatened to undermine the macho image of other loyalist commanders on the Shankill.

In the summer of 1999 McKeag was invited to a fund-raising concert at the Royal Antediluvian Buffaloes' club on the Corcrain estate in Portadown. McKeag was mobbed by admirers from the Loyalist Volunteer Force and he was invited on to the stage to receive another plaque in honour of his role in 'C' company. Loyalists who attended the function noted that the only ones not cheering were members of his own UDA unit who had travelled with him from Belfast. They included Johnny Adair and his close friend, Gary 'Smickers' Smyth. Smyth was known to be incensed about Top Gun's celebrity status. At the annual UDA West Belfast Brigade award ceremony a few months later he caused a scene as McKeag was called up to receive another 'Volunteer of the Year' trophy. At the top of his voice he cried out in protest: 'What about me? What about me?' McKeag now had a powerful enemy inside 'C' company. Smyth exerted influence over Adair and had become overall commander of the unit while Adair was back in jail. Moreover, McKeag was seen as somewhat of an outsider in 'C' company. He had been recruited into the unit long after Adair asserted himself on the Shankill.

Things fell apart for McKeag in early 2000 after he intervened in a series of violent disputes involving women at loyalist shebeens in the Shankill. He was ordered off the Shankill and 'exiled' to his native Lower Oldpark for fighting in UDA-controlled drinking dens. By now McKeag had become addicted to cocaine and reliant on extremely powerful morphine-based painkillers which he had started taking after a motorbike accident in June 1998 when he was knocked 50 feet into the air in a collision with a car driven by a member of the rival Ulster Volunteer Force (UVF). The accident left him with a broken leg and arm and he underwent several operations, at one stage being put on a life support machine. Pins were put into his limbs and due to his injuries he was in constant pain. He was dubbed the 'Bionic man' for having survived the crash but his mental and physical state began to deteriorate.

Top Gun's purdah ended in the summer of 2000 when Johnny Adair allowed him to return to the Lower Shankill. By this stage Adair was laying plans to foment a feud with the UVF in the area. When the blood-letting erupted in August McKeag infuriated Adair and his coterie by informing them that he would take no part in the internecine fighting and they beat him up. Hearing this, the UVF told its units that McKeag was not a target and should be left alone. The UDA's number one killer of the 1990s was now an isolated and depressed figure.

McKeag died on the night of Sunday 24 September, at his home at Florence Court off the Crumlin Road, in the most sordid and inglorious of circumstances. His family found him lying face-down on his living-room floor, his face heavily bruised from the fall. Inexplicably, a crossbow bolt was wedged into the wall above his body. At first the McKeag family believed their son had been murdered, either by the UVF or, more likely, in some family members' minds at least, by his former comrades in 'C' company. However, the inquest into his death found that he had died from a drug overdose, having consumed a lethal cocktail of cocaine and the painkillers he had been on since his car crash two years earlier.

About one thousand mourners turned up for McKeag's funeral at Roselawn Cemetery in East Belfast. Among them were 'C' company figures, including his new enemies, Adair and Smyth, as well as a large delegation from the Mid-Ulster Loyalist Volunteer Force (LVF). Among the hundreds of wreaths left at his graveside were tiny silver and gold guns – a token of his other addiction, murder. The Ulster Young Militants and each constituent part of 'C' company left floral tributes. So did Combat 18, the neo-Nazi terror group. The most striking wreaths made up a tribute a foot high and ten feet long, spelling out the name 'Top Gun'.

Top Gun's short and brutal life illustrates the UDA's thirty-year evolution from a mass movement of the Protestant working class to a collection of closely knit armed street gangs. What was once an organization with 40,000 members and a large reservoir of support within the loyalist community changed into a series of self-serving fiefdoms controlled mainly by men interested in profits first and pro-British patriotism second.

This book is the story of how a once-powerful popular Protestant army transformed itself into an alliance of criminal factions. Stephen McKeag embodies that journey. His life and death inside the UDA are a warning not only to young Protestant men seeking to follow his murderous path, but also to the society that produced him. McKeag has been immortalized in Northern Irish paramilitary death cult: his image now adorns the walls of the Lower Shankill, while Johnny Adair's has been defaced or erased. In death the legend of 'Top Gun' has outlived that of 'Mad Dog'. And while the eulogizing of republicanism's equivalents of McKeag and his counterparts goes unchallenged, the potential remains for a new generation of sectarian assassins to emerge on that side too.

1. Bloody Beginnings

Victorian buildings with load-bearing walls were not designed to withstand bombs. The horizontal pressure created by an explosion simply blows in the brick walls that hold up the joists supporting the upper floors and roof. With the supporting wall gone, gravity takes over and the upper floors are pulled down. The world was reminded of that fact on September 11 2001, when the intense heat caused by the exploding fuel from two airliners melted the upper floor struts of the Twin Towers in New York causing an accelerating downward domino effect and catastrophic collapse.

Thirty years earlier people on the Shankill Road in Belfast had witnessed this devastating sequence of blast, heat and implosion of a building. On the afternoon of 11 December 1971 a bomb planted by the IRA exploded without warning at the doorway of the Balmoral Furniture Store, a typically red brick-fronted shop between Peter's Hill and Agnes Street. The pressure from the blast smashed down the ground-floor front wall. The first floor caved in, pulling the floor above it down and then the rest of the building. Several tons of brick from the façade fell on to the pavement outside on top of the pre-Christmas Saturday-afternoon shoppers. A cloud of mortar and brick dust engulfed the street.

After the huge bang of the explosion and the rumble of the collapsing building there was a brief silence before people began screaming. Hundreds of people who heard the explosion poured out of the side streets along the Shankill, tearing at the rubble for survivors. Under the ruins they found the decapitated body of two-year-old Tracy Munn and the limp and crushed remains of another child, Colin Nichol, only seventeen months old. The two children had died the instant the shop front had fallen on to their tiny defenceless bodies. Harold King, a twenty-year-old store man at the shop, was also killed, along with Hugh Bruce, a fifty-year-old ex-soldier and member of the Royal Corps of Commissionaires, who was the doorman. He had been standing beside the bomb and was killed instantly. More than twenty people, including Tracy Munn's mother who had been out shopping on the Shankill, were badly injured. As the bodies of the children were lifted from the debris silence again descended on the Shankill, broken only by men and women sobbing.

Bleak scenes like this were being played out across Northern Ireland from late 1971 onwards as the IRA stepped up its campaign to terrorize the Protestant community and drive British rule out of Ireland. By December over 200 people had already died in the Troubles, mainly in rioting and gun battles, but as winter set in, they began to be killed in attacks by republicans and loyalist bombers. By the time the Troubles came to an end the death toll from terrorism was roughly the same total as that on September 11 – but in Northern Ireland the terror was drawn out over a sickening thirty years.

The IRA attack on Moffatt's, as the store was more commonly called on the Shankill, was directed by the leadership of the Provisional IRA in Belfast against Protestant civilians as retaliation for the loyalist bombing of McGurk's Bar on North Queen Street a week earlier. McGurk's, a quiet family pub with no republican or paramilitary connections, was also a Victorian building with load-bearing walls somewhat older and with even less structural protection than Moffatt's. A bomb planted by the Protestant Ulster Volunteer Force exploded in the doorway causing the entire building to collapse in on itself. Fifteen Catholics were killed.

The attack on McGurk's was in retaliation for a series of bomb attacks on Protestant pubs by the Provisional IRA over the previous months. In May several people were injured when an IRA bomb exploded without warning at the Mountainview Tavern on the Shankill. And at the end of September two men had been killed in the Four Step Inn, also on the Shankill Road. Hundreds of men from the Shankill had torn away the rubble of the Four Step with their bare hands, finding the bodies of two men, Alexander Andrews, sixty, and 38-year-old Ernie Bates, who had been among a crowd watching a local soccer match on the pub television. 'Joker' Andrews was laid out in the local Orange Hall with a uniformed honour guard of Ulster Volunteer Force men standing at attention beside his coffin. The bombings continued. Three more people were killed in another IRA attack on the Red Lion on the Ormeau Road in November.

The city where this was taking place had long been accustomed to communal sectarian strife but the ferocity of this IRA assault on its people and its commercial centre was unprecedented. Why was this happening now? Generally speaking, Belfast was a city of stable working-class neighbourhoods with an outer ring of middle-class suburbs and new housing estates. Its nineteenth-century working-class housing, however, was falling into severe decline and dilapidation, partly due to laws that prevented land-lords increasing rents, which meant that it was uneconomic to carry out repairs. By the 1960s bad housing was the most impor-tant issue in working-class politics in Belfast, particularly on the Shankill, where tens of thousands of working-class Protestants were tightly packed in rows of terraced streets over an area of less than 200 acres. In the Shankill, as late as 1960, 90 per cent of houses had no bath, inside toilet or hot water. An early 1970s report on the Shankill's housing conditions, commissioned by the Northern Ireland government, found they were so bad that it recommended the purchase and demolition of 5,000 houses. The constant crit-icism levelled against the Stormont unionist regime was that it misruled and discriminated against Catholics. It did so, but it also misruled and discriminated against the Protestant working classes of Belfast.

And the Shankill was the heartland of Ulster loyalism. This was supposed to be the home of the aristocracy of Protestant labour. The Shankill was a tightly knit community, cautious about outsiders and regularly at odds with its Catholic neighbours from the Falls Road along its southern flank and in Ardoyne to the north. But, by the mid-1960s it was generally a community at ease with itself, despite the terrible housing situation. There was even something of a natural social hierarchy. The lower Shankill area had very bad housing, probably the worst of the city's slums. People who lived further up the road in somewhat newer housing referred to the lower Shankill as 'Apache' territory – both a derogatory reference to the poor conditions and a reflection of the 'tuppence ha'penny looking down on tuppence' view that the people who lived there were shiftless and indolent. They also referred to Catholic working-class areas of the city as 'Apache' or 'Indian' territory.

The Shankill had subdivisions with local names: the Hammer, Nick, Pad, Banjo and Little Hammer. These areas all had gangs of teenagers and younger boys who sparked off each other, usually on their way to soccer matches on Saturdays. However, until the late 1960s brought major slum clearance and 'redevelopment', the population was highly stable. Children played in the streets outside their homes under the watchful eye of aunties, grannies and neighbours. When they reached adulthood and married, a high proportion continued to live in houses near their parents, who could be depended on to look after grandchildren if their mother was away at work.

When the 1960s demands for civil rights for Catholics raised the issue of housing conditions for poor Catholics, many Protestants on the Shankill Road were surprised to see that it was exactly as bad as their own housing. Protestants and Catholics had common cause on this issue, but in divided Belfast there was no chance of them joining forces – the political dynamics of both sides saw to that.

Before the bombing started, the city had already undergone two summers of street warfare. On the Catholic and Protestant sides, new terrorist groups of naked sectarian ferocity were being created. On the Catholic side this took the form of the Provisional IRA; on the Protestant side the picture was far less clear. There was the Ulster Volunteer Force – a small but, as the McGurk's bar bombing showed, deadly group. It was highly secretive and slight in numbers and though many Protestants knew it existed few knew how to join.

There were literally dozens of other groups operating across the Protestant working-class parts of the city carrying out vigilante patrols to keep Catholics from invading their areas. A paramilitary group, the Ulster Protestant Volunteers (UPV) was active in the Shankill and in several other loyalist areas and played a significant part in the early riots and upheavals in West Belfast. Initially the UPV had been the paramilitary wing of the extremist Protestant group led by the firebrand preacher Ian Paisley. However, once the UPV became associated with violent agitation and was found by the RUC to be acquiring arms and explosives, Paisley dissociated himself from it. His relationship with the UPV leader and his one-time bodyguard, John McKeague, grew cold and the two separated acrimoniously. Both were vying for leadership of Ulster loyalism but, unlike Paisley, McKeague was prepared to get his hands dirty. Following his split from the UPV, McKeague addressed a meeting in Tennent Street Hall in the Shankill in May 1969 at which it was decided to form the Shankill Defence Association (SDA). The SDA was intended to act as a vigilante organization and also, because housing and the redevelopment of the Shankill slums were such critical issues in the community, to agitate for improved housing. Outside its small core of leaders, the SDA was something of a mystery for most Protestants. Many thought the SDA was the UPV because of McKeague's previous involvement with that association; others unwittingly believed the SDA was a housing action committee.

There were several of these action committees on the Shankill. Included in these groups were many of the men and women with organizational skills derived from their involvement in trade unionism who would later go on to form the largest citizen army raised in Northern Ireland since Carson's UVF had stood against Home Rule in 1912. It would become the most powerful paramilitary force in the British Isles, prepared to stand up to the might of the British army and bring Northern Ireland's first power-sharing Assembly crashing to the ground. It would also murder more than 400 Catholics and quite a few of its own members.

The roots of the Ulster Defence Association were in the rioting that flared across Belfast between 1968 and 1970. Rioting in Belfast was traditionally sectarian and when the violence broke out it did so on both flanks of the Shankill. Pitched battles were fought on the streets that crossed the sectarian divide. Catholics who found themselves isolated in Protestant streets had their houses burned. But, although this period is often portrayed as a one-sided pogrom against Catholics the blame goes both ways, and Protestants were also burned out in significant numbers in the surrounding Catholic areas.

Virtually the first person to be shot dead by republicans in the Troubles was Herbert Roy, one of a large crowd of Shankill Protestants who had gathered at the Dover Street interface between the Shankill and Falls on the night of 14 August 1969. He was hit by a bullet fired by an IRA gunman. The following night a shot fired from the Shankill killed a young IRA man on the Falls. The IRA fired back into the Shankill, killing another Protestant, David Linton, the same evening.

The sense of outrage spread to the Protestants in Northern Ireland's second city, Londonderry. There, Protestants watched the intense rioting in the Bogside, which raged around the city's famous walls, *the* symbol of Ulster loyalism since they were successfully defended against the Jacobite forces of King James in 1689, a year before King William's victory at the Boyne. In September 1969 the Catholic rioters successfully beat back the RUC and its part-time militia, the Ulster Special Constabulary – the 'B' Specials – and appeared to be winning; the Jacobites were threatening to overthrow the Reformation 280 years on. Protestants living on the predominantly Catholic Bogside of the city were now the besieged. The Catholic rioters beat to death a local Protestant, William King – a murder that is rarely mentioned in the Catholic version of events in Derry that year.

The catalyst that set the two working-class communities against each other in deadly earnest had been the organized spread of Catholic rioting from the Bogside in mid-August 1969, with a call from the Civil Rights Association for Catholics around Northern Ireland to rise up to take pressure off the rioters in Derry. This was a *de facto* signal for rebellion. The intention was that the already overstretched 3,200 men of the RUC and its badly trained reserve arm would collapse as rioting erupted in

Belfast, Dungannon, Dungiven, Armagh and Newry. As violence gripped Belfast the plan appeared to be succeeding.

On the evening of 14 August Catholic rioters formed up in strength along Cupar Street, which ran between the Shankill and Falls and where, until this point, Catholics and Protestants had lived, if not on friendly, at least on peaceful terms. Johnny McKeague formed his SDA men up alongside Ulster Protestant Volunteers and both were soon joined by hundreds of men from the Shankill. Attempts by the RUC and 'B' Specials to separate the sides were hopeless and fierce fighting broke out. Four hundred houses were torched and families – mainly Catholics living on the Shankill side of the street – were forced to move. During the early hours shooting broke out. Almost every house in Bombay Street was destroyed. Vicious fighting erupted between the upper Shankill streets and Ardoyne and a Protestant man was shot dead by an IRA sniper. IRA men opened fire in at least four streets from the Falls side and 'B' Specials, who were now mixed with the Protestants from the Shankill, returned fire. Newspaper pictures of the 'B' men mingling with the Protestant crowds and firing into the Falls sealed the fate of the Specials as an unacceptable force of law and order.

By midday on Friday the police were defeated and the British army was called in. A battalion of soldiers from the Queen's Regiment, followed by the Royal Regiment of Wales, moved in to separate the two sides. Catholics were relieved that the soldiers had arrived and held the Protestants back from wiping them out. McKeague infamously declared that if his men had had 'another forty-eight hours' they would have wiped the Catholics out of the maze of side streets around the Clonard Monastery which many of the loyalists would have liked to raze. As the soldiers had arrived without adequate supplies, relieved Catholics brought them cups of tea and sandwiches at the barricades that separated them from the Shankill. The news pictures of Catholics welcoming the troops infuriated the loyalists, who went on rioting the following night.

By the time the summer ended and the city settled, 1,820 families had been forced to leave their homes, 1,500 of them Catholics.

A great number of the Protestants who had left Catholic areas, particularly in the upper Springfield, Ardoyne and Oldpark areas had been given assistance by the same men from McKeague's organization who had been forcibly evicting Catholics from the Protestant areas. The effects of the August rioting on the Catholic–Protestant interfaces were cataclysmic. These parts of the city now resembled war zones. Belfast had a refugee crisis as thousands of people fled their homes to relative safety among their co-religionists. At least 300 Protestant families forced out of their houses on the wrong side of the sectarian divide moved back into the already crowded Shankill area looking for accommodation.

In all, more than 700 people were injured in the Belfast rioting, most of which took place on the southern and northern flanks of the Shankill. There was a deep and growing sense there of being a community under siege. Attempts to defuse matters in September were thrown into disarray when another Shankill man, Jack Todd, was shot dead by an IRA gunman as he left a meeting with Catholic vigilantes in Ardoyne to discuss ways of calming the situation down.

What happened next did nothing to ease tension in the Shankill. Spurred by two judicial reports – one that condemned the discrim- inatory record of the Stormont government and the other the conduct of the RUC and 'B' Specials in their handling of the October 1968 civil rights marches in Derry – the Westminster government announced the disbanding of the 'B' Specials, the disarming of the RUC and the formation of a locally raised militia to be called the Ulster Defence Regiment (UDR), whose membership was to be open to Catholics. The Shankill erupted again. On Saturday 11 October 1969 several thousand men advanced towards the Catholic Unity Flats complex at Peter's Hill, where teenagers had stoned a passing Orange parade the previous June. The rioting flared again. When they were confronted by lines of police and soldiers, members of the Ulster Volunteer Force opened fire, killing Constable Victor Arbuckle, the first of over 300 RUC officers to die in the Troubles. Soldiers from the Light Infantry returned twenty-six shots, killing two Protestants. So it was that the first British army engagement in the Troubles, in which it was to lose 500 soldiers to IRA attacks, was with Protestants from the Shankill, and the first people it killed were Protestants.

The SDA's John McKeague was out of the picture on the Shankill from July 1969 to January 1970 after he was arrested and held on remand for possession of firearms. The charges were dropped for lack of evidence, but when he returned to the Shankill others had filled his place and, as an outsider who lived in East Belfast, he was already mistrusted. His attempts to reactivate the SDA failed. When he attempted to set up similar bodies elsewhere he ran up against opposition from rivals, and Ian Paisley had turned completely against his one-time bodyguard. When McKeague tried to organize a defence association in the Donegall Road area, the local Defence Committee, loyal to Paisley, issued a statement telling people not to associate with him. The official institutions of unionism – the Ulster Unionist Party and the Orange Order – were deeply nervous about McKeague, and joined Paisley in denouncing him. There was also an effective whispering campaign about McKeague's homosexuality. The word was put around the Shankill that he was a 'fruit'. As a result of this, from early 1970 McKeague kept to the east side of Belfast where he set up his own private army, called the Red Hand Commando (RHC), which was small but well armed and dangerous.

In May 1971 loyalists from the Shankill travelled across the city to the shop McKeague ran on the Albertbridge Road and threw a petrol bomb through the window. He lived upstairs with his 67-year-old mother, Isabella. An arthritis sufferer, she was unable to escape from the building and perished. McKeague, a devoted son, was devastated. After 1970 he stayed firmly away from the Shankill and his small group remained located in East Belfast and the north of County Down. He was jailed for armed robbery in 1973 and detained in all for three years. He never regained the prominence he had enjoyed in the heat of battle on the Shankill. Nine years later he was shot dead in his shop by a republican splinter group. McKeague had contributed significantly to spreading the views that Protestants needed to organize; that they could not trust their own government; and that the Catholics, backed by the forces of Rome and the government in Dublin, were intent on driving Protestants out of Ulster. His ideas of working-class organization would be taken up by others.

Maybe because of McKeague's absence the situation calmed somewhat during early 1970. However, with the first demonstration of the Orange marching season matters worsened again. When members of the Springfield Road Orange Lodge attempted to march past the now segregated Springfield Road they were attacked by Catholic youths. The Orangemen's traditional Easter outing involved marching down into the city centre and then proceeding by train to the seaside resort of Bangor for the day, where there would be some more marching, tea and sandwiches or a few pints before the return in the evening to march back home. By teatime, however, the IRA had gathered a large crowd at Ballymurphy and again they attacked the Orange marchers. The confrontation was staged by the IRA, alarmed at the friendly reception Catholics on the Falls had given the British army the previous August, and had the desired effect – from the IRA's point of view – of forcing the British army to turn away from the Protestants, who had been causing them problems up to this point, and against the Catholic rioters.

In June rioting returned to North Belfast, orchestrated on the Catholic side by the IRA in time to coincide with the Orange marches, and designed specifically to draw Protestant rioters out on to the streets. During the trouble, IRA snipers opened fire on the Shankill, killing three Protestants – eighteen-year-old Alexander Gould, 28-year-old William Kincaid and Daniel Loughlins who was thirty-two. The same night, when a huge Protestant crowd tried to storm the Catholic Short Strand enclave in East Belfast, IRA snipers opened fire, killing four of the Protestant rioters. UVF gunmen returned fire and a Catholic man was killed.

The government imposed a ban on all demonstrations. Undeterred, the Shankill loyalists defied the ban and mounted an Apprentice Boys' demonstration in defiance of the law. (The Apprentice Boys are an Orange Order offshoot with thousands of members who annually celebrate the 105-day siege of Derry by King James's army in which thousands of Protestant inhabitants were killed before James was finally forced to withdraw. He was defeated by King William the following year at the Battle of the Boyne.) Six men, including a 23-year-old, David Payne, from the Woodvale area of the Shankill, appeared in Belfast Magistrates' Court on charges of illegal assembly. The army already knew that Payne was up to his neck in organizing resistance in the Shankill. During an army raid on a house in which he was staying in Brussels Street, he had brandished a ceremonial sword from the bedroom window and shouted at soldiers that they would 'get that' if they came in. The soldiers had forced their way in but had found no guns. Payne was at the beginning of a career that would mark him out as one of the most vicious figures to emerge in the Northern Ireland Troubles.

In 1971 the IRA bombing campaign began in earnest. Five BBC engineers were killed early in the year by an IRA landmine in Country Tyrone. Nightly gun battles between the IRA and the army broke out in Catholic areas across Belfast. A car bomb at the Northern Ireland Electricity offices in South Belfast injured more than 100 staff, many of them young women, who suffered terrible disfiguring injuries when the large plate-glass windows blew in on them. The number of army and civilian deaths was climbing rapidly.

Violence on this scale had not been encountered in Ireland since the tumultuous period of partition in the early 1920s. More than 140 bombs, mostly IRA devices, exploded between April and July. Against the advice of the army Brian Faulkner, the new prime minister at Stormont, decided to introduce internment. When the army mounted Operation Demetrius, breaking into hundreds of homes in a huge early-morning operation on 9 August, all hell broke loose in the Catholic areas of the city. During the night of internment, as well as firing on the army, the IRA again opened fire into Protestant areas.

However, having experienced two years of rioting and shooting, most Protestant areas now had organized groups of vigilantes – some of them armed – who were drilled by men with military service behind them. The response from the Protestants, was more measured and rioting was no longer directed at the security forces. Local vigilante leaders, many ex-soldiers, began fostering good relations with the soldiers. In turn, the army appreciated not being shot at from the back as it faced into increasingly hostile Catholic territory.

As the death toll from gun battles and the IRA bombing campaign dramatically increased in August 1971 the calls for mass mobilization of Protestants became more urgent. Typical of the kind of exhortations to action was a leaflet distributed throughout the Protestant districts by former associates of McKeague, proclaiming:

Being convinced that the enemies of the Faith and Freedom are determined to destroy the State of Northern Ireland and thereby enslave the people of God, we call on all members of our loyalist institutions, and other responsible citizens, to organise themselves immediately into platoons of twenty under the command of someone capable of acting as sergeant. Every effort must be made to arm these platoons with whatever weapons are available. The first duty of each platoon will be to formulate a plan for the defence of its own street or road in co-operation with platoons in adjoining areas. A structure of command is already in existence and the various platoons will eventually be linked in a co-ordinated effort.

The claim of 'a structure of command' was far-fetched. There was no central coordination of the local vigilante and paramilitary groups springing up across the North. However, the impression of a growing movement was taking hold on the Shankill and in other loyalist working-class areas of the North. Groups of men wearing ex-army issue fatigues became a familiar sight across the city. One of the first and biggest of these groups was calling itself the Woodvale Defence Association (WDA).

One of the first figures to lead one of these groups was Charles Harding Smith, a burly local ex-soldier who lived in Rosebank Street on the upper Shankill. He called a meeting in July 1971 at the Pigeon Fanciers' Club in Leopold Street to discuss an organized response to the threat of Catholic incursions from the neighbouring

Ardoyne and the shooting dead of three local men. The meeting was attended by only around thirty men, some middle-aged, who all shared his view that the Woodvale needed to defend itself against attack. Among them was 'Big' Dave Fogel, a Londoner and ex-soldier who had done his service in Northern Ireland, and met and married a Shankill girl. They had only recently settled in Palmer Street, one of the side streets badly affected by the rioting and attacks from Ardoyne. At the meeting Fogel proposed that men should start training in military activity. Harding Smith agreed and Fogel took responsibility for drilling a small group of local men. An initial troop of about forty, including local teenage boys, was assembled and Fogel oversaw their training on a farm north of Belfast. By the end of 1971 the Woodvale Defence Association had more than seventy men, and as word spread hundreds more flooded in to be trained and kitted out with combat uniforms. Fogel was appointed second-in-command to Harding Smith, with his close friend and drinking partner Ernie Elliott as his 'lieutenant'.

Other figures were emerging from other 'defence associations' across the city. Further down the Shankill in Aberdeen Street, a lorry driver, Alan Moon, was doing the same as Harding Smith and Fogel. In the Highfield and Glencairn areas of the upper Shankill a young Andy Tyrie, who had just been evicted from his home in the Ballymurphy area, was organizing men in his district. One of the more respected organizers in the mid-Shankill was Jim Anderson, who owned a glazier's shop on the Crumlin Road. Billy Hull, over 20 stone in weight and a well-known shop steward, worked closely with Anderson.

In June, Alan Moon had convened the first of a series of meetings in the hall of the Aberdeen Street Primary School at which the idea of coordinating all these defence groups was floated. Only a handful of people attended the first meeting but they decided the idea was worth pursuing and spread the word. Another meeting, in late August, attracted over a hundred men. For the third meeting, in early September, it is estimated that over 3,000 men turned up. The caretaker had forgotten to leave the gates open so they poured over the rails. The hall was quickly packed and over 2,000 stood outside waiting for word from inside. Despite the old rivalries between the different districts of the Shankill, and between the Shankill and other large Protestant areas of East, South and North Belfast, what emerged from the meeting was the idea that there needed to be a single, centrally coordinated organization. (The Protestants had done this before, in Carson's time, to stop Home Rule from sweeping Ulster into a Catholic, Dublin-ruled independent state.) The meeting agreed to appoint the formidable Billy Hull, already the convenor of thousands of shipyard workers, as chairman of this new organization, and Moon as vice-chairman. (However, from the beginning there was rivalry and mutual distrust, and within a couple of months Moon found himself edged out in favour of Jim Anderson.) At the end of the meeting, almost as an afterthought, someone in the hall asked what the new organization should be called. A 'wee man' no one seemed to know, but who was thought to have travelled into the Shankill from one of the housing estates in East Antrim, suggested the name Ulster Defence Association. There was general agree-ment. The UDA was born.

Shortly before his murder at the hands of the IRA in 1976, the UDA's first public spokesman, Sammy Smyth, recalled this as the moment it was decided that Protestants had to organize them-selves outside the traditional party political unionist and Orange Order structures.

The [nationalist] propaganda was devastating and the Unionist Party was consistently ineffective in its attempts at combating this. Lord only knows why. Wilting under this propaganda, the role of governing Northern Ireland passed to Westminster who gave the orders. The RUC was completely demoralized, the USC [Ulster Special Constabulary, the old 'B' Special part-time Protestant police force] was disbanded and the British army called in. The army also succumbed to this vicious prop-aganda and assumed that the loyalists were fascists, that the Catholics had always been subjected to the grossest of abuse, that they couldn't walk about the streets with their heads held high and that they just couldn't get work if a Protestant could be found to do the job. The result of all this was that in the working-class areas — and I emphasize working class like Louisa Street, Oldpark Road, Bryson Street, Roden

Street, New Barnsley, Heathfield and so on – our people were under sustained attack by the IRA, the nationalists giving sympathy, succour and support to the IRA. The front-line areas became more isolated and people living there more demoralized by the fact that people in the better-class areas – Cregagh, Upper Newtownards Road, West Belfast – just didn't want to know, thinking that this situation was only a temporary phenomenon and it would soon subside. They didn't want to get involved or get their hands dirtied.

Part of my own family lived in the Oldpark area, Louisa Street. The army were there in Louisa Street, which borders on the Bone. This is a sort of peripheral area of Ardoyne. The army posts faced the loyalists and their backs were to the hinterland of the Ardoyne. The IRA men came down through Mayfair Street into Louisa Street where they shot at the people and threw nail bombs, week after week. In the Bone you had the bin lid bashing from 10 p.m. to midnight, from midnight to 2 a.m. you had sniper fire and from 2 to 4 a.m. you had nail-bomb attacks. The only respite we had was the introduction of internment. For the first time in eighteen months the people of Louisa Street could get a night's sleep.

People in these front-line areas were desperate. This situation was repeated in all the interface areas. In New Barnsley the army stood by and watched the wee church there being burned down. It's called the Taggart Memorial Hall but it is a church nevertheless. When the parishioners came to recover the communion table and other valuables they were stoned by Catholics from Ballymurphy and there were shots fired but the army again stood by and gave them no assistance. They couldn't go to the police as they were demoralized. There was no USC and the army just stood there letting the terrorists come through their ranks, commit their depredations and allowing them to go back from where they came without stopping them.

In Louisa Street and other areas we decided we would have to stop them ourselves. So we pursued them, but only up to the army post, then the army stopped us and said if we went any further we would be shot. At that time we were unarmed and if we were to chase after those who shot at us the army would shoot us.

The situation got worse and worse. Groups of individuals got together and put up barriers and manned them from 7 p.m. to 7 a.m. on a rota.

This worked for a couple of nights, then the army knocked them down. We complained bitterly but were told that nobody could block the streets of Belfast.

Groups of vigilantes from different areas got together in the school at Aberdeen Street. Alan Moon convened the meeting and he and I addressed it. A collection was held and some of us stayed behind to discuss the formation of what is now the UDA.

It is my considered opinion that if the UDA had not come into being at that particular time there would have been a civil war. And at that time the loyalists would not have stood a chance for they were unarmed.

From the outset Harding Smith's Woodvale Defence Association was the most prominent group within the body. As it had the highest profile it began to be blamed for the increasing number of loyalist bombings and shootings that started in 1971, although most of these were the work of the shadowy Ulster Volunteer Force. The UVF was the only loyalist group that had bomb-making skills and was a tightly controlled terrorist group not based on neighbourhood defence groups. Its members were told to infiltrate and monitor the nascent mass loyalist movement but, despite efforts to do so, they could not control it.

Despite all the talking, it took the bombing of the Balmoral Furniture Store in December to really spur all those involved into action. By January 1972 the UDA had acquired a structure: it had a thirteen-member 'Security Council', with Harding Smith, Jim Anderson and Tommy Herron from East Belfast already established as leading figures. Harding Smith claimed the chairmanship over the less pugnacious Jim Anderson.

It was a paramilitary organization, democratic to a degree, recognizing merit in men's abilities to fight, or organize or commit offences for which they could expect long terms of imprisonment. It was also exclusively working class. A fairly frequent criticism of the UDA in later years, as details of its activities emerged in court cases, was that it had sprung from a Protestant underclass, the corner boys who had no jobs and nothing to do all day, and this was used to reason away some of the horrors that ensued – that they were the work of morally indigent Protestants not representative of the mass. In Protestant working-class society the unemployed were regarded as somehow feckless, 'Apaches' or 'Indians', who were as bad as Catholics. Indeed, some unemployed Protestants were made to feel unwanted within their own community, like the outsiders – the Catholics.

Shortly before his death in 1976, Sammy Smyth explained in an interview with a *Newsletter* journalist how the early leaders went about shaping the organization. He saw its strengths and weaknesses as coming from the same source:

The first thing the UDA did was to build up discipline and seek arms to defend their community. The operative word being defence and this is where they made their mistake, in being a defensive organization.

If you have an organization with a name, a goal, you have something to maintain the motivation and hold people together and keep the spirit to carry on and make the movement worthwhile. Defence is not a name, it's not a goal, it is simply a situation you take up. You can only remain forceful and motivated while you are under attack. In periods of inactivity most except the totally dedicated men will filter back to their normal way of life.

But the UDA is the one organization that permeates every section of working-class life. This has been its strength, is its strength and will always be its strength. But the people who drift away during a lull will quickly come back as soon as an attack is threatened. They know why the UDA was formed and that loyalty is still there even though they may be some of the organization's most ardent critics.

The UDA was open to all physically able males and promotion within it was based on some of the same rules that applied in the city's street gangs: tough, clever opportunists would rise to the top; hardened street fighters were clearly going to do well too. In several areas men who had reputations as tough street fighters took hold of UDA groups. One early leading figure, Ingram Beckitt, was constantly getting involved in disputes and was killed after a fight in a pub. Anyone who had done military service and knew how to handle a gun was also a candidate for promotion. 'Chancers' – such as one early WDA leader who was quickly ousted after making over-inflated claims about his ability to get hold of weapons – were unlikely to last.

Although from the start leaders gave themselves absurd military titles, aping the British army, it was an army largely without an officer class. In some places the leaders were there because the men agreed that they were the leaders. Some 'officers' were elected via a kind of democratic process – sometimes even by a relatively free vote; in Rathcoole and East Antrim this seemed to be the method. In other places the hard men seized power and threatened anyone to challenge. Men who had organized the first vigilante groups graduated to larger commands as the numbers grew.

The structure that emerged by 1972, and was to stay largely intact, was based on the broad Protestant working-class communal divisions of the city. The four Belfast 'Battalions', eventually renamed 'Brigades' as they grew in size, were based in the north, south, east and west of the city. 'North Belfast' was spread over a number of Protestant enclaves from Shore Road westwards to the Ballysillan estate which was built on a steep incline at the bottom of Cave Hill and north to the Whitewell Estate. 'South Belfast' began just off the city centre at Sandy Row and gradually spread out to contain the units in Lisburn and towns like Dromara and Ballynahinch. The area of control within 'East Belfast' stretched from the shipyards on the Lagan eventually out as far as Bangor and Newtownards. 'West Belfast' was centred in the Shankill Road and had companies 'B' in the central Shankill area, 'C' in the lower Shankill and 'A' further up the road, around the Shankill estates of Glencairn and Highfield and the West Circular Road area.

There was also the 'East Antrim', which stretched from the northern outskirts of the city, the Rathcoole estate, and contained the loyalist towns and working-class estates from Greenisland to Carrickfergus and west to Antrim and Ballymena. The 'Londonderry Brigade' was based in the mainly Protestant Waterside of the eastern banks of the Foyle and continued out to Limavady and Coleraine. The UDA in Derry and the north-west part of Northern Ireland was numerically the largest group outside Belfast. The small 'Mid-Ulster Battalion' was unable to develop in its mainly rural environment. There were further pockets of UDA organization centred around loyalist villages in County Down.

The most frequently self-claimed size of the UDA at the height of its strength was 70,000 – even 80,000. Jim Anderson, the first overall leader, with the title of 'Major General', claimed in the early days that he could summon between 25,000 to 100,000 men, half of them armed. Tens of thousands of men did take part in some of the larger demonstrations organized under umbrella loyalist titles, but many of these were purely part-timers who had jobs and family commitments – wives or girlfriends who took a dim view of time spent hanging around with other local men playing at being soldiers. The working core of the UDA – those who could devote more than the odd evening or Saturday afternoon to the organization – was much smaller. Many of the companies existed only on the two nights a week when drilling went on in locally commandeered halls or when night-time 'patrolling' was taking place during the 'no-go' era in 1971–2. The available daily strength of the UDA was in the low thousands. A British army estimate at the time was that it could lay hands only on around 6,000 full-time volunteers at any given time. This may have been a deliberate underestimate, and it is probable that there were at least 25,000 UDA men in Belfast at the end of 1972.

A permanent cadre of foot-soldiers began to hang around makeshift drinking clubs and public houses abandoned when their Catholic proprietors had been forcibly evicted. They made arrangements with drink companies to continue the supply of beer and spirits and from the outset the 'clubs' became central to UDA culture. Officers usually directed the local company from an office at the back or over the pub – just as the SDA's first office had been over the Bricklayer's Arms in Wilton Street. The WDA, which could not lay its hands on a decent arsenal, still managed to spend £4,000 on building an impressive social club in 1972. Across the city local UDA companies built clubs and a whole new unlicensed trade in drink began which fed large sums of money into the paramilitary coffers. Members hijacked drink lorries. The foot-soldiers who hung around the clubs and pubs ran errands, moved guns and equipment and also collected 'donations' from local shops and businesses. This very quickly took on the air of extortion as pubs were expected to pay at least £50 a week and businesses were made to pay 'subscriptions' commensurate with their size and estimated turnover.

The UDA targeted and recruited teenage gang members throughout Belfast. In East Belfast a UDA company commander, Billy Elliott, was named in court as having set up a group in a local secondary school which had come to light when the headmaster found a revolver and took the sixteen-year-old culprit to the local police. They subsequently found out that the UDA boss had set up a unit of nineteen youths, aged from thirteen to seventeen. At the time 'Tartan' gangs, which derived their name from their habit of wearing tartan scarves or patches on denims, were ubiquitous in Belfast. The tartan colours were adopted by young loyalists after the IRA murdered three young Scottish soldiers in a 'honeytrap' killing in March 1971. These huge gangs – some in the east and south had hundreds of members – provided the new UDA with a massive recruitment resource. In the Shankill the Tartans were subsumed into a junior wing of the new UDA, but there was a failure to control the gangs in the east, which led to trouble during rioting in 1972, when they were persistently out of control.

Some of the UDA leadership was not only loyalist but socialist in outlook, reflecting the post-war politics of the United Kingdom. Protestant Belfast was a working-class stronghold and, if it had been integrated fully in the British electoral system, would have voted Labour. The first UDA man to achieve public prominence was North Belfast Protestant community activist Sammy Smyth, who became the UDA's first public relations officer. In 1972 a masked Smyth appeared on a television debate with the civil rights leader and nationalist politician John Hume, and launched an attack on the new Social Democratic and Labour Party, of which Hume was a founding member, during which he used the term 'Protestant backlash'. His contribution delighted loyalists but was seen as sinister by Catholics. Although a dedicated community worker involved in projects on both sides of the sectarian divide in Belfast, Smyth made some ferocious statements. In response to an interview given by the IRA leader Daithi Ó Conaill to a Dublin newspaper, he said: 'At that moment in time I could have, without a twinge of conscience, bombed every well-filled chapel in Belfast.' He also edited an extreme underground news-sheet, *Ulster Militant*, which preached all-out war against republicans and their 'passive sympathizers'.

Some remember Smyth as being a great motivator who travelled throughout Belfast and to country towns to recruit and set up UDA companies. Others thought much less of him. As his many detractors in the UDA would later say, Smyth could talk. But although an important founding figure and organizer, he was never a military man or a figure of power in the organization. As he became increasingly marginalized he began to plough his own furrow. Before the UDA, Smyth had been a housing and community activist in the Shankill, and after he was sidelined he became one of Belfast's leading cross-community housing activists. He was assassinated by a young IRA gunman as he visited his sister at her home near Ardoyne in March 1976.

With his interest in broader ideological issues, Sammy Smyth was in a minority among the early UDA leadership. What motivated most of the emerging leaders was obtaining money and guns. Harding Smith's predecessor as head of the WDA was accused of pocketing cash from the twenty-five pence dues paid each week by its members. He had also failed to find any worthwhile firearms and was ousted within a couple of months. Thousands of Martini Henry rifles had been run into Ulster in 1914 to arm Carson's Ulster Volunteers and many were still serviceable, although there was little suitable ammunition. The WDA lost half its arsenal in an army raid in October 1972 when a .303 rifle and four revolvers, all of pre-Second World War vintage, were seized. However, weapons had started to arrive in Protestant areas from men who had gone to Scotland or England on holidays. Many ex-soldiers living in Belfast had held on to weapons after leaving the army and also picked up handguns or shotguns from old military contacts.

The organization was also quickly building up a war chest for buying guns. The main source of weapons was Britain, where small support groups sprang up, the largest in Scotland where there was strong support in Protestant working-class areas. The Scottish police, alerted to the increasing illegal arms trade into Northern Ireland, set up undercover Special Branch operations to tackle it.

The Woodvale boss, Harding Smith, assumed the role of weapons buyer-in-chief. In early 1972 he got in touch with a Belfast businessman, who, in turn, made contact with a middle-man, who was told there was £50,000 to buy arms for the new organization. The intermediary put the businessman in touch with a Scottish arms dealer. In fact this 'dealer' was a Special Branch officer. An arrangement was made to meet the 'dealer' in a pub in London's West End and Harding Smith, the businessman and three other WDA men — one a serving RUC member — walked into a trap. On 29 April the Special Branch officer, referred to only as 'B' during the subsequent trial for conspiracy, led the businessman and the three WDA men — John White, Bobby Dalzell and Robert Lusty (the member of the RUC) — to a room at London's Hilton Hotel where another Branch officer was waiting. Details of the proposed arms deal were discussed and secretly taped. The three were arrested and taken to Scotland Yard. Harding Smith had not gone to the hotel but oddly went to the Metropolitan Police's headquarters later the same evening to ask about the four. He, too, was arrested and charged. Two other UDA men were in London at the same time but evaded arrest and returned to Belfast.

The UDA smarted badly at Harding Smith's arrest. On 14 May Fogel organized a 'no-go' area in the Woodvale. They hijacked some thirty lorries and blocked streets around the area. Other UDA battalions followed suit. The situation in East Belfast deteriorated when confrontations with the army, trying to tear down the barricades, erupted into all-out rioting by the Tartans. A gun battle with the army broke out on 21 May. At the end of the month an estimated 15,000 UDA men in combat uniform, most wearing masks or sunglasses, marched through the centre of Belfast, shouting the loyalist war cry: 'No surrender'.

The UDA began staging 'no-go' areas across Northern Ireland.

They took place at weekends so as to cause as little disruption as possible to the areas concerned but they were widespread and effective. The UDA 'no-go' exercise, however, created a real sense of fear among the remaining Catholics in some of the affected streets.

On 3 July Fogel wanted to seal off the western corner of Woodvale at Ainsworth Avenue, near its intersection with the mainly Catholic Springfield Road, but this meant that fifty Catholic families living in Ainsworth Avenue would be effectively held hostage inside the UDA barricades. Catholic community leaders called on the secretary of state, William Whitelaw, to stop the UDA men. The army blocked the street and the Woodvale men were held back for several hours. The UDA leaders found themselves negotiating the stand-off – first with the Belfast Commanding Officer, Brigadier Sandy Boswell, and later with the head of the British army's entire garrison in Northern Ireland, General Officer Commanding, Major General Robert Ford. Throughout the day the army – with a rank of armoured personnel carriers pulled up to form a barrier – and the 700 UDA men faced each other. Herron and Anderson sent out word for reinforcements and soon thousands of UDA men flocked into the area from around the city. At one point at least 6,000 were drawn up in ranks stretching down Ainsworth and up the Shankill to Ballygomartin. The Shankill was in the full grip of the UDA.

The UDA men in the front ranks facing the soldiers had batons and shields, just like the army. They beat their shields and shouted, 'UDA . . . UDA'. The army offered compromises to Jim Anderson, Davy Fogel, Tommy Herron and Sammy Doyle from the Shankill, which were discussed and rejected. They raised the idea of having joint army and UDA patrols. Ford was against this but left to consult Whitelaw. He returned about two hours later and conceded that the UDA could erect small barriers across the road, but it could not seal off the area. As the day drew to an end, the UDA victors called a midnight press conference in the Europa Hotel. They announced that from then on there would be joint UDA–army patrols in parts of the Shankill.

The UDA leaders saw this as a fantastic coup. Their men were working-class Protestants with no previous prospect of political or other advancement. Their Orange and unionist leaders had failed to stop the collapse of Stormont and the abolition of the 'B' Specials, and they had watched as the RUC and the British army had failed to stop the IRA. Now they were negotiating with the head of the British army and the political administration and getting their way. When the army finally launched Operation Motorman in July to break down the IRA barricades and breach the Catholic 'no-go' areas, the UDA could claim that they had forced the government into taking stiffer action against the republicans. After a succession of setbacks to loyalism and concessions to republicanism, the Ainsworth Avenue stand-off was seen as the first major victory for the Protestants – and the UDA had pulled it off.

The suspension of the Stormont government on 30 March 1972 had significantly altered relationships of power in Northern Ireland. The Ulster Unionist Party (UUP) was badly split and no longer entirely representative of the Protestant community and unionism fragmented further. Power shifted to Westminster where the priorities were security and solving the 'Northern Ireland problem'. The UDA was, effectively, stepping into the power vacuum in unionism. The British government, through William Whitelaw, had no option but to talk to those who gave the impression of having power. In fact, two weeks before the Ainsworth Avenue events he had already invited the UDA men Tommy Herron, Billy Hull and Dave Fogel to see him at Stormont using the cover of being part of a trade union and community vigilante group. In mid-June he had held meetings with the full thirteen-member UDA Security Council as he tried to talk them out of creating 'no-go' areas.

Similarly, in the absence of anyone with power to talk to on the Catholic side, the government was talking to the IRA. On 22 June 1972 the IRA announced a ceasefire, beginning from the 26th. Gerry Adams was freed from Long Kesh, and together with his fellow Army Council members – Seán MacStiofáin, Daithi Ó Conaill, Martin McGuinness, Ivor Bell and Seamus Twomey – was flown to London on an RAF aircraft for talks with Whitelaw. The talks were unsuccessful though no one in the unionist community knew this and the IRA ceasefire began as announced. Alarm bells were ringing in the Protestant community – what kind of deal was being done with the Provos? The UDA determined to break the truce and stop London talking to the IRA.

Its opportunity arose from a dispute over housing allocation at Horn Drive in the Lenadoon estate in south-west Belfast where the IRA had forced out local Protestants and wanted to install Catholic families who had been intimidated out of other parts of the city. The South Belfast UDA commander, Sammy Murphy, drew his men up in Horn Drive and refused to let the Catholics in. A major stand-off developed, with the army again caught between the UDA on one side and increasingly angry Catholics on the other. Two weeks into the IRA ceasefire, the stand-off at Horn Drive came to a head and the Catholics began stoning the army. The soldiers replied with tear gas and rubber bullets. Within a short while IRA snipers took up position. When a burst of fire was heard the snipers and the soldiers began shooting. The ceasefire was over. The UDA had staged another deliberate stand-off. And it claimed to have fired the burst of shots that precipitated the IRA–army gun battle. The UDA had won another battle.

The UDA could not contain its over-enthusiastic members who continued to riot in Protestant areas. The army on the Shankill had a difficult time and at the end of the summer Ford made the decision to send in the Parachute Regiment. It was soldiers of the Parachute Regiment who had shot dead twelve Catholic demonstrators during a civil rights march in Derry on 30 January 1972 in what came to be known as 'Bloody Sunday'. The most serious clash with the army occurred in September when there was extensive rioting and running gun battles on the Shankill during which two local men, Robert McKinney and Robert Johnston, were shot dead in hotly disputed circumstances. The UDA reacted furiously to the tough response of the paratroopers sent to quell the Shankill riots. During rioting in East Belfast in October two UDA men, 26-year-old John Clarke and William Warnock, aged only fifteen, were crushed to death by one of the army's Saracen armoured personnel carriers breaking through barricades thrown up across side streets. The same night, in the upper Shankill, a young woman was killed by a bullet believed to have been fired by a UDA man during a gun battle with the army, and a UDA gunman, John Todd, was also shot dead in an exchange of fire with troops. The East Belfast commander, Tommy Herron, began issuing unilateral statements declaring the UDA was 'at war' with the army.

One of the first UDA members to be killed by the IRA was shot dead on 22 August 1972. The IRA abducted forty-year-old James Johnston, a leading UDA member, from the Grosvenor Road haulage company where he worked, and shot him in an alleyway in the lower Falls area. Johnston was also a prominent figure in the Loyalist Association of Workers (LAW) a UDA-controlled vehicle for industrial action that attracted trade unionists who were less enthusiastic about the 'military' side of the organization. Hundreds of men in combat uniform lined the Shankill Road for his funeral – including forty in dark blue fatigues with LAW–UDA insignia.

While the UDA tried to give the impression of being a united and centrally controlled army, the truth was that power was vested in the hands of the local brigadiers, as they were now terming themselves, and the leadership was riven with rivalry. Not only that, but the organization had not yet articulated any set of political or other objectives. A conference of some fifty leading figures in the movement was called in November. They met at the Girton Lodge Hotel in East Belfast and issued an eight-point declaration on 8 November 1972:

1. We demand the return of a democratically elected government to Stormont with a full status quo.
2. We state that there is no place for Eire in any discussions pertaining to the affairs of Northern Ireland other than trade.
3. Northern Ireland must remain part of the United Kingdom for all time, for the benefit of all the people of Northern Ireland and any person or persons working for or on behalf of a hostile nation to the detriment of Northern Ireland should be regarded as committing an act of treason and should be treated as such.

4. We oppose the imposition of any electoral system other than that currently in vogue in the rest of the United Kingdom.

5. We strongly urge that the Roman Catholic people free themselves from the shackles that bind them to the IRA and all impediments, and participate in the future development within Northern Ireland, and work to that end.

6. We demand that the economic contribution by Northern Ireland to the British economy be given, taking into consideration the invisible earnings from shipping, airline insurance and British investment, in order that the true position be realized by the whole of the United Kingdom.

7. We call on the British Government to guarantee to the new Government of Northern Ireland full financial backing and a free hand to press ahead with the provision of new industries and development of existing Ulster industries, to provide full employment and a better living standard for all people.

8. We request that social amenities be made readily available for the people of Northern Ireland thereby eliminating any impediment to a good social environment. The UDA will strive to achieve these objectives with its full resources on behalf of the people of Northern Ireland.

Herron and – on his return from London in December – Harding Smith, were the most powerful figures in the Security Council, which had grown from a core of thirteen and become unwieldy, but they turned up at its regular Wednesday meetings only intermittently. Others followed suit so that eventually Anderson was reduced to calling an attendance roll. There were frequent squabbles.

In December the UDA men's trial for the attempted arms deal at the Hilton took place. The prosecution – rather implausibly – claimed that the UDA had £350,000 for guns. The defence claim that the businessman with Harding Smith believed he was working for the RUC, which was trying to entrap an IRA arms dealer, was accepted. The conspiracy charge could not be proved and the case collapsed. Harding Smith had missed all the action in Belfast during his sojourn in prison awaiting trial in London and in his absence the WDA had been run by Davy Fogel, whose star had risen considerably. On his return Harding Smith quickly ousted Fogel and threatened to kill him if he didn't accept that Harding Smith was back in charge. Fogel claimed later that when Harding Smith arrived back from the airport he had declared to his men: 'I'm the boss. I take orders from no one.'

Fogel had reason to be nervous. His closest aide, Ernie Elliott, had been shot dead in early December. At first the UDA concocted a story that he had been abducted and murdered by the IRA. Another bizarre tale, possibly circulated by a British army press officer, suggested that Elliott was killed because he was discovered to be a member of a secret loyalist group called the Ulster Citizens Army which held Marxist views. (The purpose of this rumour – which is believed to be one of the British army's first attempts at 'psychological operations', 'psyops', in Northern Ireland – remains difficult to fathom. Perhaps the imaginary organization might have become some kind of vehicle for under-cover intelligence-gathering or 'black' propaganda.) Fogel later claimed that Elliott was a socialist and read Che Guevara. During the Shankill 'no-go' episode all sorts of people had turned up to talk to the UDA, including a delegation from the United States Congress, and approaches were made by left-wing groups, includ-ing one called Two Nations which purported to espouse both Marxist and unionist policies. Some right-wing unionists had also begun accusing the UDA of being communists.

In fact, Elliott's death was a much more prosaic affair. He was a prominent and founding figure in the WDA but was a heavy drinker and prone to fighting with other members. In early December he travelled from the Shankill to Sandy Row to retrieve a gun that had been lent to the Sandy Row men and was overdue back in his arsenal. He walked into the UDA drinking club in Sandy Row and allegedly pointed a gun at drinkers. One of them grabbed the gun and a struggle ensued during which Elliott was punched. The row moved outside and one of the Sandy Row men pointed a shotgun at Elliott. It went off, killing Elliott. There was, according to all reliable accounts, no ideological discussion, but a great deal of drinking, prior to Elliott's death, and he had started the row himself. The truth eventually emerged in May 1983, when a local UDA man, who left for England shortly after the killing, returned, apparently suffering from remorse, and confessed his part in the episode.

Within a couple of weeks of his arrival in Belfast Harding Smith moved against Fogel, accusing him of stealing UDA funds. Harding Smith's men held Fogel captive in a UDA club for three hours during which they made it clear that he had no option but to leave the Shankill. Harding Smith's people also put it about that a senior British army officer had let the UDA leadership know that Fogel was in some way a danger to the organization and that he had tipped off the army about guns in the Woodvale club. When Fogel was asked to go to East Belfast for a second 'meeting' with other UDA men he decided it was time to leave. He caused a minor sensation when he gave an interview on 28 January 1973 to *Sunday Times* journalists from his new home in the south of England. Among other things he told them that the UDA had already imported guns into Northern Ireland and that one shipment had come through the port of Dublin. The interview alarmed the UDA leaders, who worried that it would bring them under investigation or have the organization declared illegal. From the outset, the leadership had deliberately fostered the impression that the UDA adhered to purely legal defence activities. The arrests of Harding Smith and the others in London, followed by Fogel's revelations, suggested that it was an altogether more sinister operation.

2. UDA by Day, UFF by Night

For the overworked and hardened police, staff and journalists who covered the City Commission (later Belfast Crown Court) there were days of testimony that would remain imprinted decades later. The cases that dealt with the murders, terrorism and criminality that were engulfing normal life in Northern Ireland were heart-breaking and appalling in turn. Some of the very worst of these involved the UDA. Few of those who were present will forget the testimony of a North Belfast woman who recounted the details of the loyalists' bonfire night, 11–12 July 1972, when four drunk and armed UDA men broke into her home in the Oldpark area at three o'clock in the morning. Mrs McClenaghan, a Catholic widow with three children, was in the house with her fourteen-year-old son, David, a boy who had learning difficulties and was described as loving and trusting. The alleged reason for the break-in was that the family was 'fenian' (a derogatory term) and had 'guns in the house'. The McClenaghans were Catholic but nothing could be further from the truth than claiming they had guns. It was a drunken, murderous escapade.

Mrs McClenaghan was woken from her sleep by the sound of breaking glass. She went downstairs and was grabbed by the four men, one wearing a balaclava, two with pillowslips over their heads, and one unmasked. They asked her religion and said neighbours had told them that she was in the IRA. Two of the intruders went upstairs and dragged David from his bed and downstairs to his mother and made him open her handbag and take out her rosary beads and a missal. The boy was taken back up to his bedroom while the two older UDA men – the others were in their teens – raped his mother. Then she was taken up to David's bedroom where he was shot three times. His mother tried to shield him and was also shot and left for dead. She survived to testify.

Introducing the evidence against the men at the trial in May

1973, prosecuting counsel said: 'I venture to suggest that the details of this case will create in your minds a new dimension. The restraints of civilization on evil human passion are in this case totally non-existent. It is said that violence begets violence and you may well think that in this case we have reached the lowest level of human depravity.'

Sentencing them, the judge said: 'I do not believe that anyone, however extreme, could view the ruthless killing of this poor retarded boy, while his violated mother tried to shield him, with anything but revulsion.' Sent down for life, the four joined a growing number of UDA prisoners – in all, 200 would receive life sentences. On their arrival in prison they were beaten up – not for murdering a fourteen-year-old boy or shooting his mother, but for the rape. Eventually they were allowed into the UDA wings of the Maze to serve their time alongside the other UDA prisoners.

The horrific murder of David McClenaghan occurred against a backdrop of terrorism and violence in which there was little humanity or restraint on either side. By the end of 1972 more than 800 people had already been killed in the Troubles. The UDA killings had started after the IRA bombing of the Balmoral Furnishing Company in December 1971, at a time when there were daily IRA atrocities. The indiscriminate IRA bombings had begun in earnest early in 1972 with an attack on 4 March on the popular and usually crowded Abercorn Restaurant in the city centre, in which two young Catholic women were killed and dozens of others injured, several of whom needed amputations. The IRA campaign had grown in intensity in the summer of 1972 with a cascade of no-warning bombs that had provided the fuel for loyalist hatred of all things republican and Catholic. Colour TVs were arriving in homes and pubs for the first time and everyone, save the perpetrators, watched in horror the film footage of soldiers gathering up body parts from outside the Oxford Street bus station on 'Bloody Friday', 21 July. The IRA had unleashed an all-out assault on Belfast that day, detonating twenty-two bombs in as many minutes.

The IRA bombing emanated from behind the barriers erected to create the republican 'no-go' areas of West Belfast and Derry's

Bogside. Similarly, the upsurge in the loyalist assassinations coincided with the establishment of the UDA 'no-go' areas. The barricading of streets around UDA clubs and pubs provided the gangs with the opportunity to capture Catholics and bring them to the clubs for torture, interrogation and inevitable assassination. These killings became known as 'rompering' – a sick joke referring to the popular Ulster Television children's programme *Romper Room*. The UDA gangs were treating their victims – not just Catholics but their own people – like playthings. Rompering became a byword for the basest behaviour imaginable and was synonymous with Belfast UDA violence.

In mid to late 1972 relations between the UDA and the British army deteriorated. In mid-October the army turned up the throttle, moving against the loyalist 'no-go' areas in the Shankill and East Belfast to bulldoze UDA barricades. Serious rioting ensued and shooting broke out – to the horror of many loyalists who began to think the UDA had completely lost its way by attacking the British army. There was a strong belief that the army had been sent in to soften up the UDA prior to foisting on unionists an unwanted and unpopular political settlement.

After two nights of rioting in East Belfast Tommy Herron, the East Belfast UDA brigadier who had taken to styling himself deputy, or second-in-command to Jim Anderson, announced that their relationship with the British army – which had been cordial enough in places – was finished. And he lumped the RUC in with the army. Roy Bradford, Ulster Unionist MP for the Victoria ward in East Belfast, intervened and things calmed down. The army commander in Belfast, Colonel Sandy Boswell, said that he would do all in his power to take the heat out of the situation. Herron and Anderson ordered their men off the streets, ensuring that the rioting stopped and were praised by Bradford and hardline Unionist politician, Bill Craig.

Herron and Anderson were beginning to come under pressure from people within their own communities who were disgusted at the looting, hijacking and arson that had broken out among the undisciplined UDA ranks. Eight prominent Protestant clergymen in West Belfast issued a joint statement attacking the UDA's 'wanton destruction' of their areas. There was alarm among the Protestant middle classes at UDA statements that the British army and British government were Ulster's 'enemies'. In a sly piece of black propaganda – as part of the growing stream of propaganda and misinformation issuing from the army's press office at Thiepval barracks in Lisburn – journalists were briefed that the army had come across 'links' between the UDA and the Provisional IRA. The lie was designed to turn ordinary Protestants against the UDA and may have momentarily worked, as Herron and the rest of the leadership sought to bring the locally unpopular uprising in Protestant areas to a speedy end. It was actually a relief for Herron to send a message to Colonel Boswell on 20 October saying the trouble was over and adding: 'Now that we have re-established cooperation with the army I earnestly hope you will continue to exercise that control to support the rule of law and in the interest of all the citizens of Ulster.'

At the end of November 1972 Herron and fellow leader Billy Hull left Northern Ireland for a 'publicity tour' of Canada to raise awareness of Ulster's plight and to 'counter' IRA propaganda. There was actually very little republican propaganda in Canada to counter. Herron and Hull's visit was to establish links with Ulster Protestant *émigrés* who could be counted on to supply the UDA with money and weapons.

Behind these public events the UDA was increasingly engaged in a campaign of sickening sectarian murder, details of which would begin filtering out in reports from Belfast's City Commission Court. One of the first concerned the Mersey Street UDA club in East Belfast where three prominent members took umbrage at a young barman who they believed had said that they had been drinking in a Catholic-owned hotel in Belfast. The 27-year-old was taken to the 'romper room' at the back of the club and bound to a bedstead. His attackers slashed him repeatedly with a cutthroat razor and attempted to castrate him. His fingernails and four of his teeth were pulled out with pliers. Then they took him out through the back of the club to the bank of a small river and beat him with a jack handle. One of the men fired a shotgun at him. Then they left, satisfied they had done enough to finish him off.

He was barely alive when he was found by children the next morning. A compensation hearing heard that he was permanently and severely disabled as a result and he received one of the largest awards made by the courts.

The establishment of a 'no-go' area in the Shankill and Woodvale at the start of July 1972 had coincided with the murders of five Catholics in night-time assassinations between 1 and 3 July. The 'no-go' areas provided the UDA torture and murder gangs with an additional level of security while they carried out their activities. Two men, Gerard McCrea and Jim Howell, abducted by Shankill UDA men in North Belfast, were both tortured and then shot before being left in a car which was set on fire. At the end of the month a popular young Catholic folk singer, Rose McCartney, and her fiancé, Patrick O'Neill, were stopped as they made their way home from a folk concert in Ardoyne and taken to the UDA club in the Woodvale. Davy Payne led the gang that took charge of the young Catholic couple, taunting them in front of other UDA men in the club before taking them to a lock-up garage. O'Neill was beaten, then both were shot in the head. Rumours spread throughout Catholic North Belfast that the killers were mutilating their victims but not, as it happened, in this case.

Mutilation was taking place and Davy Payne, a psychopath, was torturer-in-chief. The weekend of 11–13 August 1972 was not a good time for Catholics to be wandering the streets of North Belfast, particularly at night. Payne and the Woodvale UDA gang, including figures who would later become prominent loyalists, had a thirst for Catholic blood. Two innocent Catholic men, Frank Wynne and Thomas Madden, both sociable bachelors who enjoyed a drink, met grisly deaths at the hands of the gang.

Wynne, who was thirty-seven and unemployed, was first to die. He had been drinking with friends in North Belfast and was walking home along the Crumlin Road when he was waylaid, bundled into a car and driven a short distance to a lock-up garage. He was beaten and tortured and was almost certainly unconscious before being shot and dumped in an alleyway. Loyalists later confirmed that Wynne, as far as can be ascertained, was tortured in an effort to find out if he was involved with the IRA or, coming from the Falls area, knew any IRA people.

The following night the gang kidnapped 48-year-old Thomas Madden, by all accounts a quiet man with no enemies, who lived with his mother, worked as a nightwatchman and almost certainly knew nothing about the IRA. He was last seen leaving a pub in the city centre at around 8.45 p.m. to walk home. He was grabbed by the gang and taken to a lock-up off the Oldpark Road, believed to be the one where Frank Wynne was tortured and killed. Madden, it was later adduced from post-mortem examination, was tied by the wrists and strung up to a roof beam so that he had to stand on the tips of his toes – a recognized and agonizing torture used by many brutal regimes. The UDA gang, eager in its work, also subjected their victim to a protracted and grotesque additional torture, inflicting shallow stab wounds all over his body. The pathologist counted some 110 punctures. People living in the Oldpark, near the lock-up, later told police they had heard a man screaming 'kill me, kill me' – Thomas Madden beseeching his tormentors to end his agony. Eventually they tired of torturing this innocent man and shot him in the head, dumping his body in a nearby doorway.

The East Belfast gang's first assassination victim was Philip Faye, a young Catholic barman who worked at the popular Stormont Hotel in East Belfast, opposite the gates of the Stormont parliament building. On the evening of 18 August a UDA assassin, the former soldier Albert 'Ginger' Baker, knocked on the front door of the house Faye rented off Dee Street in the centre of loyalist East Belfast. Faye, a young country man originally from County Cavan, seemed to have no idea he was at risk. He answered the door and when Baker asked him if he was a Catholic replied that he was. Baker shot him five times.

Baker, who was only twenty-one, carried out at least three more assassinations and participated in torturing, but after a year it all became too much for him. He returned to his regiment in England, where he was court-martialled and dishonourably discharged. Wracked with remorse he went to the police and confessed his part in the sectarian murders in East Belfast, agreeing to testify against some of his associates including Ned McCreery, another East Belfast UDA man, who was later to be killed during internal feuding. Baker pleaded guilty to four murders and was sentenced to twenty-five years' imprisonment, serving a total of eighteen years before his release in 1992.

Ned McCreery described himself as a 'Colonel' in the organization and sat on its Security or Inner Council. He killed at least six Catholics in 1972 and was responsible for an incident in which a grenade was thrown into a bus carrying Catholic workmen, killing one and injuring several. McCreery was one of the first loyalists to be interned in 1973. He was charged with murder when his former associate, Baker, chose to turn Queen's evidence. Baker implicated McCreery and six others in the torture and murder of a 21-year-old Catholic, James McCartan, on 3 October 1972. However, Baker's testimony was inconsistent and he tried to minimize his role in some of the crimes. The judge found his evidence unsafe, dismissed the case and the seven UDA men were freed.

Another Catholic, Patrick Devaney, suffered prolonged torture before he was killed by the Sandy Row UDA on 30 August. He was hung upside-down from a beam and beaten with batons and a hammer before being shot in the back of the head. Devaney, who was twenty-seven, had been discharged out of the British army two years earlier after suffering an eye injury which caused partial paralysis. He was another of those innocent victims who were prone to taking late-night walks around Belfast and thus were easy prey for the UDA. One of Patrick Devaney's torturers was Ernie Elliott, second-in-command to Dave Fogel, who would be dead himself three months later.

An unusual proportion of the men stopped, and in several instances killed, by the paramilitary patrols were middle-aged bachelors. Years later a member of Belfast's gay community pointed out to one of the authors that some of these men found wandering the streets late at night were almost certainly part of Belfast's male homosexual community who had no specific meeting place and tended to cruise the city's bars or hoped to meet other men in the quiet streets around the city centre. The lifestyle of Catholic homosexuals made them doubly vulnerable in an unforgiving city.

Some victims of the travelling gunmen had emigrated to England to find work and been away for years, then returned and adopted their old habits, unaware of the new dangers posed by walking the streets at night. After the body of a gay Catholic man was found hanging from iron window bars in a street near the docks, there were even fears among gay men in the city that there was a purge specifically aimed at them.

A particularly dangerous route from the city centre was northwards up Clifton Street to Carlisle Circus and up the Crumlin or Antrim Roads. Newspapers later dubbed this stretch of Belfast the 'murder mile' and this the era of the 'travelling gunmen', when the UDA murder campaign was in full swing across the north of the city. The Shankill, Woodvale, Oldpark and Tigers Bay UDA were active in this area. The Woodvale was probably the most active and was responsible for fifteen or more murders. Everyone who lived there knew what was going on – that loyalist gunmen were on a nightly hunt for victims to kill in retaliation for IRA murders and bombings. But strangely the local and British national media tended to believe that the legal and outwardly open loyalist militia was not fully engaged in this campaign – that 'extreme' and unknown loyalist groups were at work. In a city where weird beliefs flourish – many republicans claimed the IRA no-warning bombing campaign in the city was the work of undercover British agents trying to tarnish the reputation of the republican movement – some Protestants even expressed the view that it was the IRA that was killing Catholics in order to terrorize its own community for some unfathomable reason. The reality was that an ill-trained but vicious terrorist group – the UDA – was targeting vulnerable Catholics as a simple, brutal way of getting at the community that it believed was harbouring Ulster's enemies.

The fact that the UDA was involved in murder became a public issue only in the autumn of 1972 when Albert Brown, a well-known UDA man in North Belfast, murdered a policeman. That October Constable Gordon Harron, an RUC traffic officer, had the misfortune to stop a car hijacked by UDA gunmen as it travelled along the M2 motorway in North Belfast. The front-seat passenger fired a burst at Constable Harron as he approached the

car, killing him instantly – the second RUC officer to be killed
by loyalists. (The first was 29-year-old Constable Victor Arbuckle,
shot dead during rioting in the Shankill in August 1969.) It was
still a capital offence to kill a policeman or soldier in Northern
Ireland and Brown, who was arrested shortly afterwards, was
sentenced to death. He was held in the condemned cell in Crumlin
Road Prison before his sentence was commuted to life imprisonment. Brown was the last person to be sentenced to death in
Northern Ireland and his period in the condemned cell led to the
creation of a consensus between the UDA leadership on the outside,
the civil rights movement and the SDLP who were opposed to
the death penalty on moral grounds, while the main unionist parties
were for it. It was abolished a short time later.

Whereas during 1971 and 1972 the UDA leadership could depend
on the general confusion of events in Northern Ireland to cover
its tracks, the veil was beginning to slip in early 1973. In June, after
bad rioting in East Belfast, the RUC raided the UDA's headquarters, recovered a .38 revolver, a sawn-off shotgun and 540 rounds
of ammunition and arrested two men. The raid was particularly
badly timed for the UDA leaders, including Tommy Herron, who
at this stage were standing for election mostly under the political
banner of the new Vanguard Unionist Progressive Party (VUPP),
as it provided clear evidence that gun culture was at the heart of
the UDA.

The activities of the British army with regard to the UDA
become interesting at this point. In the early days of the army it
and the British government definitely did not want confrontation
with a mass movement of Protestants. There was frequent liaison
with the UDA leaders and this was public knowledge. Officers
were often pictured talking to UDA bosses at barricades. Prior to
Herron's declarations of war, the UDA regularly informed the press
that it was working with the army to establish peace and communal harmony, and the loyalist 'no-go' issue was eventually resolved
mainly through negotiation.

However, the British army had for at least the previous two
decades been engaged in 'counter insurgency' operations in the

remnants of the empire and had developed ideas and strategies that were to come into play with mixed effect in Northern Ireland which, in military parlance, and despite the horrors depicted in the media, was a 'low-intensity conflict'. The army was looking for an indigenous terrorist group that broadly sided with its point of view and could be useful in distracting or even fighting the IRA.

In the early part of the Troubles the IRA was inflicting heavy casualties on a conventional army which was not fully prepared for a terrorist campaign fought within the boundaries of the British Isles. Although – as Bloody Sunday infamously showed – the army did shoot to kill suspected rioters, it could find itself in trouble when troops overreacted. After the killings in the Bogside, soldiers were directed to adhere to stricter rules of engagement and fire only when under threat themselves, or at an identified gunman or bomber who posed a threat to other people's lives. Urban terrorism of the type being conducted in Belfast and Derry was a relatively new phenomenon and the army was facing a new type of insurgency. In earlier times the army's response to such insurrection as that under way in Northern Ireland would have been swift, unequivocal and very brutal. But the natural instinct of the military – to shoot the opposition – could not be given free rein in a late twentieth-century urban setting, especially with the press around. The army had to adopt different means to protect itself.

One of these was the use of undercover units to counter the threat from the IRA and to gather intelligence. A special unit of soldiers trained in undercover work called the Mobile Reserve Force (MRF) was responsible for some highly dubious activities in the early 1970s. On 12 May 1972 soldiers shot dead a leading Catholic community activist, Patrick Joseph McVeigh, in a disputed incident in West Belfast. Witnesses said soldiers in plain clothes shot McVeigh, near the junction of Riverdale Park South and Finaghy Road North, and then sped off in an unmarked car.

On 27 September 1972 another undercover unit, believed to be from the same MRF group, shot dead Daniel Rooney, a nineteen-year-old Catholic, at St James Parade on the upper Falls Road. Army headquarters in Lisburn issued a statement saying a patrol had been fired on and had returned fire. The army also claimed Rooney was a known gunman. The six soldiers involved did not give evidence at Rooney's inquest in December 1973, but had their statements read out by an RUC officer. They claimed Rooney and his companion had a rifle and a handgun. The inquest heard that forensic tests on Rooney's clothing showed no signs that he had been either carrying or using a gun. There was now uncertainty as to whether these were loyalist or undercover military operations. It was, in the confusion of the time, very difficult to differentiate.

The activities of the undercover unit were exposed on 2 October 1972 during another MRF operation when a laundry van, used to spy on republican areas, was intercepted by the IRA and one of the undercover soldiers shot dead. The 'Four Square Laundry' scheme, in which undercover soldiers drove around Catholic areas collecting laundry and gathering whatever snippets of information they could, revealed how desperate the army was to build up intelligence – any intelligence – on the IRA. The RUC's intelligence wing, the Special Branch, had almost completely broken down and lost its lead role in gathering and assessing intelligence. The army had little idea who was shooting its members. The RUC and the army simply could not keep up with the growing numbers of young men and women swelling the ranks of all the paramilitary groups.

Soldiers in plain clothes tried to establish contact with loyalists and to recruit spies in the new UDA. Their attempts were sometimes amateurish – in some instances turning up quite conspicuously at the big public rallies and even at non-paramilitary and non-political community action events, particularly in the Shankill. One man who was highly active in campaigning for housing rights on the Shankill as the battles raged around him remembers a poorly attended housing action meeting at which two men wearing tweed jackets joined the five or six local people in the audience. They sat quietly, not contributing to the discussion, until a senior British officer, whose job involved liaising with the local community, walked in unannounced. To the amusement of the local activists, the two men at the back of the hall snapped to attention.

Much would be made later of army and RUC collusion with loyalists, but the fact was that by 1972 the violence in Northern Ireland was out of control and collusion was not an issue. Even with more than 25,000 troops stationed in the North, the urban terrain of Belfast, with its weave of side streets and 'no-go' areas, made it impossible to control the terrorist groups who were on a rampage. Police stations were fortresses under constant attack. And the bombers and travelling gunmen had an edge they had never previously enjoyed: improved living conditions had allowed many families to buy saloon cars which were reliable, fairly fast, great for commuting and family outings – and equally efficient at transporting armed men or bombs. This was a tremendous advantage to the terrorist of the early 1970s.

The UDA's relations with the army were still badly strained and New Year 1973 brought the first detentions of loyalists – two Woodvale UDA members. This resulted from strong evidence that the UDA had been involved in murder, including that of Constable Harron. There were already loyalists on remand and the two detainees joined them, along with the 300-plus republicans, in the billets of the wartime Royal Air Force base at Long Kesh, just south of Lisburn. The UDA, together with splinter groups Down Orange Welfare, the Orange Volunteers, Ulster Special Constabulary and Vanguard Defence Volunteers, issued a statement saying they would not be daunted by this move. 'This strategy [internment of loyalists] will fail because these organizations are led by working-class Protestants and the leaders are replaceable.'

Despite the sanguine public statement, however, the UDA determined that it could use mass muscle to force the British to back down on the internment of loyalists. It decided on a loyalist strike, or 'day of action', bringing the North to a standstill to make its point. That it coincided with calls from a loyalist coalition, involving politicians Craig and Paisley, seeking to reverse the political dismantling of Stormont by the British government was fortuitous. The protest was, ostensibly, part of a combined front, including Billy Hull's Loyalist Association of Workers, Bill Craig's Vanguard and a variety of others under the banner of the United Loyalist

Council. Some of these groups had separate memberships and identities but for the most part they operated in or around the two main loyalist groups, the UDA and the UVF.

The stated agenda for the stoppage was a protest about the deteriorating security position and British plans for the future of the North. Unionism's worsening political situation at the start of 1973 had led many loyalists to decide on industrial and protest action on as large a scale as possible. This was, or should have been, constitutional action, something broadly supported by the majority of law-abiding Protestants who would have nothing to do with paramilitary and terrorist groups. The strike call was heeded by the power workers who brought electricity supplies down to a critical level causing factory closures across the Belfast region during the day.

The idea backfired, however, when rioting broke out again in loyalist areas particularly in East and South Belfast. The drunkenness and general lack of control of the Sandy Row UDA was particularly marked on the 7 February day of action. Few people stayed away from work and there was widespread intimidation by UDA men who burned cars and assaulted workers. During the day, amid widespread disruption, the Sandy Row UDA set fire to a number of shops, including a boutique at the corner of Sandy Row and Donegall Pass. The fire brigade was called and, as firemen tried to douse the flames, a UDA man emerged from a nearby club with a sub-machine gun and opened fire on them. Brian Douglas, a 23-year-old Protestant fireman who lived with his blind widowed father, was killed. Four others were also killed and dozens of buildings – many belonging to Catholics – were burned; Catholic churches and premises were attacked. During the night Herron's East Belfast units exchanged fire with the army. This was the absolute opposite of what most law-abiding Protestants wanted to see. It was a shambles and a sectarian rampage and did considerable damage to the notion of organized loyalist resistance to police change.

Another Vanguard/LAW rally, planned for the city centre on 24 March, flopped largely as a result of concern among the politicians involved in the previous fiasco, the UDA's violence and

Herron's bombastic outpourings. Dissent among the organizers emerged days earlier when a good portion of the Ulster Unionists who were supposed to support the rally, pulled out because of what they termed the involvement of 'sinister elements'. Protestant workers stayed away in droves. As it happened, the UDA had been lukewarm about the rally anyway, and there were internal disputes about the growing association with Paisley and Craig. The rally was touted to attract an estimated 60,000 loyalists in support of a renamed umbrella 'Ulster Loyalist Front' but only 2,000 turned up.

As expected, at the end of March Craig announced the formation of his new party, Vanguard Unionist Progressive Party (VUPP) and said it would work in unity with a previously unheard-of group, the Loyalist Action Group, another cover name for the men in the forage caps and dark glasses. Tommy Herron immediately declared that he was 'very, very pleased' at Mr Craig's new party. He said: 'We will be supporting the new party 100 per cent and using every means within our power to ensure its success.' One of the rocks on which the UDA had been built – no political association – was gone. Despite a statement issued by the VUPP that members of the UDA would not be selected as candidates, in time Herron's name was on the nomination list in East Belfast.

The UDA's attempts to promote itself as the embodiment of loyalist and unionist opposition – and the power behind Vanguard – were further damaged on 10 June when a UDA gunman, firing on soldiers in the Beersbridge Road in East Belfast, killed the driver of a passing bus. The UDA had earlier issued a statement saying it would 'shoot down' police and soldiers. The death of Samuel Rush was seized on by the moderate unionist leader, Brian Faulkner, who branded the UDA 'cut-throats' and 'ruthless conspirators'; Herron lashed back at these 'so-called politicians'. Vanguard issued a grudging statement saying that, regrettably, the death had resulted from the 'collapse of authority'.

Although possibly the most powerful figure in the UDA, Charles Harding Smith had avoided the limelight – probably because he was, basically, an inarticulate hard man from the Shankill. The man who became increasingly synonymous with the UDA was Tommy

Herron. Herron was catapulted to public prominence from humble origins since becoming a founder member of the UDA in East Belfast, where he worked in a filling station. When the UDA was created in 1971 Herron had grafted himself on to the top of the huge East Belfast UDA contingent where fund-raising became a high priority. Their area of operations was not seriously affected by IRA bombings, and at night it was safe from attacks as it included only a tiny Catholic enclave – Short Strand – which was pushed up against the eastern bank of the Lagan.

East Belfast prided itself in its mercantile culture and many people living in the more affluent suburbs were proud of their rise from working-class origins through hard work. That strong entrepreneurial ethos was at the heart of its burgeoning UDA brigade. Herron and his men set up a huge illegal money-raising operation. Pub owners were advised that a donation of £50 a week was the minimum payment acceptable and, depending on the size of their businesses, shopkeepers could be expected to pay around £25. According to a local shopkeeper it was very difficult for some of the smaller ones, but most paid up and kept quiet. Offices and businesses were visited by young UDA men who made extortionate demands with obvious menace, knocking over furniture or merely standing around outside in a threatening manner. There were frequent robberies and hijackings – as there were all over the city. The number of robberies – carried out by all terrorist groups and not just the UDA – rocketed from 50 in 1968 to 490 in 1971 and over 1,000 in 1972. The UDA in East Belfast organized major raffles, in one instance offering a new car as a prize. It later emerged the car had been 'donated' by a local dealer after a visit by UDA heavies who made it abundantly clear what he needed to do to stop his business from being burned down. As one favourite extortion line at the time put it: 'Either a hundred pounds or a hundred-pound bomb.'

Herron was a hopeless liability to any political cause. He was, in the eyes of most people in East Belfast, little more than a gangster. There was also clear evidence that the UDA was setting up illegal unlicensed drinking clubs across the east of the city, many selling stolen drink taken from hijacked delivery lorries. In a laughable attempt to address the large number of complaints about UDA extortion and racketeering in East Belfast he rounded up a number of frightened local pub owners and held a press conference. With Herron listening at the back of the room the unfortunate publicans told sceptical reporters that they had not encountered any extortion and were only too glad to donate 'nominal' sums for loyalist prisoner welfare. One helpfully added that when his entire stock was stolen the UDA had got it back for him; another that the UDA had dealt with one of its own senior members who was causing a nuisance on his premises. Herron was a big man in the pub and club world in the East Belfast UDA but he would soon get his come-uppance, first from the electorate of East Belfast.

At the same time as it was establishing its structures in Belfast and the eastern counties of Northern Ireland, the UDA was also establishing itself in the poor housing estates of the Waterside (east of the Foyle River) of Londonderry city, and with representation in small towns from the border with East Donegal to the bigger provincial towns of Limavady and Coleraine. The UVF had a presence in the same places, and in the future there would be tensions and violence between the two groups. However, in the 1970s there were signs of a working relationship between parts of the otherwise rival organizations.

The Top of the Hill, a rare Catholic-owned bar on the mainly Protestant Waterside of Derry, offered a particularly inviting target for UDA gunmen. It was a small cosy place, easily accessible and with a guaranteed ready escape into the Protestant estates around it. On the evening of 20 December 1972 two UDA gunmen walked in and calmly shot dead 31-year-old Charles Moore, thirty-year-old Christopher McClafferty, 26-year-old Bernard Kelly, 58-year-old Francis McCarron and Michael McGinley who was thirty-seven. It was the worst shooting atrocity in Northern Ireland until then. No claim was made by the killers but few people in Derry had any doubts about who was responsible. The name of the gang leader was on many people's lips over the coming months and years. The Top of the Hill set a new benchmark for UDA gangs which until then had simply carried out random drive-by shootings or abductions and executions of vulnerable, individual Catholics.

The Derry UDA also set its eyes on the 'Free State', a few miles away across the border in Donegal. In the early hours of New Year's Day 1973 a young Catholic couple, 21-year-old Briege Porter from Buncrana, and her 25-year-old fiancé, Oliver Boyce, were stabbed and then shot and left outside the Donegal village of Burnfoot. They were random victims of a UDA squad that had crossed the border, intent on murder. An eighteen-year-old UDA member, Robert Taylor, from Derry was subsequently arrested and made an alleged admission to the RUC. Taylor was extradited to the Republic – despite ugly but empty threats from the UDA about exacting a bloody price on the Republic – and brought before the Special Criminal Court in Dublin, charged with murdering Boyce and Porter. The statement he had given the RUC was thrown out and he was acquitted.

On St Patrick's Day 1973 a UDA man from Derry's Waterside was killed as he attempted to perpetrate what could have been a major massacre at Cloughfin, County Donegal. Lindsay Mooney was a nineteen-year-old clerk with strong loyalist views who had joined the UDA as soon as it had been established in Derry. He was killed as he tried to prime a bomb which he was taking to Kirk's Lounge Bar where people were celebrating St Patrick's night. Ivan Cooper, the local SDLP representative who lived and had business interests in the border area, said he recognized Mooney from previous cross-border bombing attacks in Donegal. Mooney became a celebrated figure in UDA folklore and had a flute band and ballad dedicated to his memory.

On New Year's Day, as the murder scene of the young Donegal couple was being examined by local gardaí, on the other side of the province a Catholic engineering worker on his way to the Rolls-Royce factory in Dundonald was gunned down by the UDA. Jack Mooney was thirty-one, married with two children. He was shot as he arrived with five workmates, including his father, Hugh, who also worked at the factory and was less than a year away from retirement. Mooney, one of only sixty Catholics in a workforce of 800 at the factory, was set up by loyalists who worked alongside him and knew his religion.

On 29, 30 and 31 January the South Belfast brigade of the UDA shot dead four young Catholics from West Belfast aged between fourteen and twenty-two. Peter Joseph Watterson, a fifteen-year-old schoolboy, lived with his younger brother and widowed mother who owned a newsagent's shop on the Falls Road, opposite Donegall Road. A gang of UDA men from the Village area, under the command of the South Belfast brigade, travelled up Donegall Road towards the Falls, and Watterson's shop was directly in front of them. Peter was standing outside with friends when they were fired on from the UDA men's car. He was killed.

A short while later, less than a mile away, at the Speedline filling station on Kennedy Way in the upper Falls area, three men pulled up in a car and a gunman fired shots at another soft target. James Trainor, a 22-year-old petrol pump attendant, was hit four times at close range and died instantly.

That evening the IRA in West Belfast sent one of its squads across the sectarian divide to the Village, where it shot dead one of the UDA's leading figures in South Belfast, 28-year-old Francis 'Hatchet' Smith. Smith was rumoured to have led the gang that had shot the schoolboy and petrol pump attendant earlier in the day. He was well known in South Belfast and had possibly already been identified by the IRA. At his inquest his widow said he had returned home about 1.20 a.m. on 30 January, apparently drunk. He had kissed her and their infant child and said he had to go out again. The IRA, in a statement admitting his killing, said he had been captured as he fired shots into the Catholic Roden Street area, a short distance from his home. He was found later that morning in an alleyway at the back of his house. He had been shot in the head.

Smith's killing spurred the South Belfast UDA into further action. The following day it kidnapped a Catholic boy, Philip Rafferty, from his home in the heart of Andersonstown. The UDA men took him to the Giant's Ring, a large Neolithic monument at Shaws Bridge on the southern outskirts of the city, which was to become a familiar dumping ground for the victims of the South Belfast brigade. Philip, who had celebrated his fourteenth birthday only two weeks earlier, was described as small, slight and asthmatic. They made him kneel on the grass at the Giant's Ring, pulled his coat over his head and shot him at point-blank range.

The South Belfast UDA appears to have then returned to Andersonstown and abducted another youth who was standing outside the Busy Bee shopping centre. Seventeen-year-old Gabriel Savage was hooded and shot at an unknown location, probably in the Village. His killers then drove to the nearby M1 motorway and dumped the body on the verge, where it was found the next morning.

In the middle of the nineteenth century when Belfast comprised a set of slum villages around mills built on the Lagan tributaries surrounding a commercial centre, there were already sectarian fights and murders between labourers. Most of these had arrived from the countryside, bringing with them the factional hatreds that were rife outside the city. One of the worst traditional clash points was between the Protestant slums of Sandy Row and the Catholic Pound Loney on the site of today's lower Falls and Durham Street. In the early 1970s this old tradition was being resurrected by the UDA in Sandy Row. As is the custom in working-class areas, groups of people often gathered to chat at street corners. In vulnerable locations like Durham Street in Belfast such people provided good targets for gunmen travelling in cars. Sixteen-year-old Bernard McErlain was one such target when he was shot close to his home in Durham Street on the evening of 20 March 1973. There had been a commotion in the area a short while earlier when an army armoured personnel carrier (APC) had burst through a small barricade of beer barrels. Minutes later UDA men drove past McErlain and his friends and opened fire.

On the evening of 24 March 1973 28-year-old John Huddleston was bringing chicken and chips to his widowed mother in their home in Durham Street when a car drove up and shots were fired. Huddleston was found dying on his neighbour's front-door step. The killers sped off across Grosvenor Road and over the Boyne Bridge and were back in Sandy Row in a few seconds. Two others were killed in the Sandy Row/Falls interface in the following month.

The UDA – still a legal organization with a high media profile, prominently involved in several loyalist umbrella groups alongside respectable unionists – had managed to hide the fact that after its men left the mass rallies and demonstrations many of them were going about the business of plotting, organizing and carrying out some of the worst atrocities of the Troubles.

But in many people's minds, particularly around the Woodvale Defence Association's stronghold, there was no doubt that the UDA was conducting a sectarian murder campaign. Davy Payne and John White's involvement in sectarian murder was an open secret in north-west Belfast. By early 1973 well-known UDA members were already in prison because they were suspected of conducting the campaign, and there were three UDA compounds in Long Kesh filled with UDA internees who were held with men on remand for serious charges, including murder.

As more and more – mainly young – men appeared in Northern Ireland's courts accused of increasingly serious offences, the judiciary made increasingly pointed comments challenging the government's policy of allowing the UDA to stay legal. Sentencing a young UDA man for firebombing Catholic houses in East Belfast, one senior judge described the events as 'obscene acts of naked sectarianism'. Others called such activity 'diabolical' and acts of 'criminal bigotry at its crudest'. A young man received some leniency for firearms offences by a judge who remarked that, had it not been for 'the sinister influence of the UDA', he might not have become involved in terrorism. In a judgement directed at the government, Lord Justice McGonigle said: 'Although it is not an unlawful organization it has led many people to turn to crime and violence.' Sentencing six UDA men to life imprisonment for the murder of Constable Michael Logue, shot dead by the UDA on the Shankill in 1973, the judge observed that more and more of those coming before the courts charged with crimes of violence were 'said to be members of the UDA'.

The terms 'rompering' and the 'romper room' first emerged in public during the trial of seven UDA men from the Lower Newtownards Road for the murder of a 21-year-old East Belfast Catholic, James Patrick McCartan. He had been pointed out to the UDA on a number of occasions as he lived in Holywood, outside East Belfast, and socialized with Protestant friends in discos and pubs in the east end of the city. When word reached the UDA men on the night of 2 October 1972 that he was at a disco at the Park Avenue Hotel on the Holywood Road, they set out. Three men grabbed McCartan, dragged him, screaming, away from the crowded hotel foyer and drove him to the UDA club in nearby Finmore Street. At their trial in September 1973, prosecuting counsel said that in Finmore Street there was an argument as to whether or not he should be shot dead on the spot or taken to the Clermont Street UDA club. 'This,' counsel told the court, 'is a room where members of the UDA are disciplined, where interrogations are carried out on persons suspected by the UDA and which, in this case, turned out to be a place of torture for Mr McCartan.'

For the sake of his family what James McCartan had to suffer was not fully revealed to the court, although it was said in evidence that he endured spells in two romper rooms – both at Finmore Street and Clermont Lane. He was beaten and stabbed a number of times before a rope was found and he was tied up. He was then strung up, upside-down, from the roof. 'He was interrogated about alleged association with the IRA and at one time [name of one of the accused] made to cut off his private parts but he was restrained by [Edward 'Ned'] McCreery who appears to have been in charge of the operation.' At this stage, according to loyalist sources, there were quite a few UDA men in the club, which had been reopened after its usual closing time for the purpose of the murder. The bar reopened and UDA men were helping themselves to drink. According to some accounts a number had brought their girlfriends with them. At the end of his torture McCartan was cut down and dropped on his head. He was hooded and left in the hands of a young army deserter, Albert Baker, who was told to take him away and shoot him. This he did. McCreery, the head of the gang, and the others went on drinking.

The murder of John Boyd, a 33-year-old Protestant from East Belfast who had accidentally incurred the anger of some local UDA bosses, illustrated the casual barbarity of which the organization was capable. Boyd was taken to a club off Severn Street on 4 February 1973 and subjected to prolonged torture before being finally stabbed to death. He was stripped, burned, beaten and stabbed in the heart and in the head. His body was found the following morning dumped in the Connswater River, which flows through East Belfast behind the rows of houses.

Possibly the worst of all the romper room stories concerned the murder of a young Protestant single mother who had moved to Belfast from the country with her daughter and who had allegedly succumbed to the advances of a Sandy Row UDA man. The man's wife, a UDA woman 'commander' in Sandy Row, suspected this whether it was true or not. The Sandy Row and Donegall Pass UDA was barely in control of itself, its members inured to murder and violence and wallowing in drunkenness from cheap or stolen liquor consumed in rough shebeens. Women as well as men were caught up in this downward spiral from civilized behaviour. On a summer afternoon in 1974 the UDA women of Sandy Row passed sentence on the 31-year-old single mother. Jealousy and blood lust seem to be the reasons for what then happened.

Ann Ogilby was taken to the romper room some days before her death and subjected to rough questioning but released. The women then changed their minds and, as she was about to board a bus near Sandy Row, she was grabbed with her six-year-old daughter and bundled into a car. The vehicle was stopped by an RUC patrol who suspected something was wrong. But Ann Ogilby was too frightened to make a complaint and the UDA women were released. A couple of days later she was taken back to the shebeen in Hunter Street and, while her child was held in the next room, she was beaten to death with a number of implements including a brick and a club. At one point the women stopped for a smoke before resuming their work; when she was dead, they dolled themselves up and went to a disco. The child wailed in the next room as her mother died. The body was taken away and dumped by the side of the M1 motorway by men who had been drinking downstairs.

Catholics were by no means the only people who needed to avoid the UDA. The brutish male culture of both republican and loyalist terrorism was a particular danger to vulnerable women. Two years after Ann Ogilby was clubbed to death, another unfortunate woman with a drink problem found herself the subject of unwarranted attention in another UDA drinking den in Sandy Row. She was taken upstairs to a room usually kept for beatings and raped by more than twenty men including well-known UDA figures in the area. Rape and the beating and humiliation of women in working-class Belfast was as routine as gunfire but was subsumed in the maelstrom of violence engulfing the North.

'Listen carefully. I represent the Ulster Freedom Fighters. We have assassinated an IRA man on the way to Larne. We gave him two in the back of the head. He is dead. This is in retaliation for Wilson.'

It was the second time in two days that the newsdesks of Belfast newspapers had been telephoned by men claiming to be from a 'new' Ulster terror group. The calls created a sensation in the local media which was well aware of the campaign of sectarian assassination aimed at Catholics and the nightly bomb attacks on, and desecration of, Catholic churches. But with the killings and bombings there were no claims of admission, no one to pin the blame on. Now they had a name and a voice, if no faces.

The calls started on the weekend of 16–17 June 1973. The 'IRA man' referred to in the statement was an innocent Catholic with no connections to the IRA. He had actually been one of the relatively small number of Catholics who had answered the government's call for Catholics to join the new Ulster Defence Regiment. Ninety minutes before the phone call to the *Newsletter*'s newsroom, the RUC had discovered his body. Jim Kelly, a 25-year-old County Larne man, was returning to the town after visiting his girlfriend in the Whitewell area of North Belfast. It was a hazardous journey for a Catholic. Kelly had to make his way along the Whitewell Road, which was fringed with the loyalist White City estate where the UDA was active. He then had to get past the UDA stronghold of Rathcoole, and he was again in dangerous territory on the outskirts of the city as there were further UDA pockets out towards Templepatrick and Larne. Kelly was well known to the loyalists in Larne as he had grown up in a predominantly Protestant neighbourhood. The night before his murder, men meeting in the Larne UDA club claimed Kelly was an IRA spy and agreed that he had to be done away with. They drew straws to decide who would kill him. A relation of Kelly's and another UDA man – neither of whom had ever committed a serious crime before – were about to become sectarian murderers. They knew Kelly's schedule and that he would be hitching a lift home after visiting his girlfriend. It was an easy matter for the four-man snatch team to overpower him. He was beaten into submission, driven a couple of miles out into the country, made to kneel in the grassy roadside and was shot through the head.

The same evening the South Belfast UDA's Taughmonagh company was also in action. Their random target was an equally blameless Catholic teenager. The *Belfast Telegraph*'s newsdesk was the first to receive a call from a man claiming to represent the 'UFF', for the murder of Daniel Rouse, a seventeen-year-old youth from the Riverdale area of West Belfast. The neat estate where he lived was within easy reach of the loyalist housing estates at Taughmonagh, Seymour Hill and Dunmurry, and he was snatched as he walked home. He was driven a short distance to Upper Dunmurry Lane, where he was savagely beaten and shot dead. One of the 'UFF' team, later sentenced to life imprisonment for the murder, was the commander of the UDA company at Taughmonagh and a member of the UDA's Inner Council.

It was the increasing evidence of UDA involvement in assassinations and terrorism that spurred the UDA leadership, concerned at being publicly blamed for the murders, to come up with the UFF cover name. The creation of the Ulster Freedom Fighters *nom de guerre* – which started out as a joke – was a simple but effective expedient to divert political and media attention away from the fact that the hands of UDA leaders were stained with innocent blood. Senior figures from the time say the idea of assassinating Catholics was never raised at Inner Council meetings, that instead it was something that arose from the actions of individuals from the ranks. This may well be, but there was widespread knowledge within the UDA about the murders taking place from 1972 onwards.

After the first UFF phone calls in 1973 there was a media fixation with the new group and various commentators and politicians tried to put a fix on it. Was it a group of Protestant extremists? Or the IRA in disguise assassinating Catholics? Or communists? No, the UFF was the UDA's young murder gangs. Before Rouse and Kelly there had been something like seventy-nine sectarian assassinations by the UDA, beginning in March 1972, with the murder of Patrick McCrory, a seventeen-year-old shot dead outside his home in the Ravenhill area by members of a Tartan gang from south-east Belfast who almost certainly knew the Catholic teenager. There were a further twenty killings involving the UDA – murders of their own members and people killed by accident or in riots.

Nine days later the 'UFF' struck again and set another landmark in cruelty. The bodies of Senator Paddy Wilson and his companion Irene Andrews were found in a quarry off the Hightown Road on the western slopes of the Cave Hill. He had been stabbed thirty-two times, she nineteen. It was the work of the Woodvale UDA.

Irene Andrews was a 25-year-old civil servant and was well known as a ballroom dancer. She had been socializing in the city centre and was being given a lift home by Senator Wilson, a prominent and respected nationalist politician, election agent for the SDLP leader and West Belfast MP, Gerry Fitt, and a member of the Northern Ireland Senate. He and Irene Andrews had been together in McGlade's Bar on Donegall Street, a popular pub with journalists and politicians, and had left at around 11.25 p.m. Two hours later a 'Captain Black' telephoned the *Newsletter*: 'Tonight we have got Senator Paddy Wilson and a lady friend. Their bodies are lying in Hightown Road. After the IRA murdered a retarded boy we are not going to stand any longer for what those animals have done to us for the past four years. There will be more deaths in reprisal.' The 'retarded boy' was David Walker, a sixteen-year-old Protestant who had been abducted from near his home in East Belfast by members of the Official IRA, and shot dead in the lower Falls Road area.

'Captain Black' was a pun on the name of the UDA's top assassin in West Belfast, John White, who was one of the killers and may have actually made the call. White and a number of his associates were the creators of the Ulster Freedom Fighters cover name which was used successfully in the following years to strike terror into the Catholic community and to divert media attention away from the UDA.

On the evening of 25 June, the Shankill assassination unit led by Davy Payne and John White, both close associates of the West Belfast Woodvale UDA leadership, had set off in search of victims. Any Catholic would do. White later admitted they had had no intention to seek out the senator but had come across him in Donegall Street outside the bar, one of the locations where it was likely they would pick up Catholics.

The previous night, 24 June, the UDA had killed a 36-year-old man living in a Protestant part of North Belfast. Joseph Cunningham had been a practising Protestant in the Oldpark area for years, but he had been born a Catholic and that was sufficient reason for his murder. He was shot dead as he answered a knock at his front door. The UDA gang – the same group responsible for torture killings – claimed responsibility in a telephone call to a newspaper. The UDA caller described himself as 'Captain Black' of the Ulster Freedom Fighters.

A masked UDA/UFF member gave an interview to a British newspaper stating that all nineteen SDLP members elected to the new Northern Ireland Assembly were on a death list. 'Their day has not yet come but when it does come, we'll get them,' he threatened. Asked about his motivation he said it was the tele-vised pictures of soldiers scraping body parts off Oxford Street after the IRA's Bloody Friday bombings the previous year. 'The world is condemning us as murderers – we call ourselves patri-ots. We are fighting for Ulster's freedom. During the past four years we have waited for the authorities to take positive action against the gangsters who have ravaged and raped our country. We have, alas, waited in vain. We are now fighting for our very survival. Our backs are against the wall.' He ended the statement with a warning to Catholics: 'We would appeal to the RC popu-lace: throw these gangsters out of your midst. Until you do this, you must bear the agony. Our fight is not with you but the animals you shelter.' This was followed by a public threat to kill six Catholics for every Protestant murdered.

White and Payne were interned on suspicion of carrying out

the UFF murders. After their release they were regularly rearrested
and questioned about them. White, police officers recall, was cocky
during interrogations and appeared to feel no remorse for his
actions. But the gradual process of 'pulling him in' – subjecting
him to prolonged questioning over days and confronting him with
the atrocities he had committed – succeeded. Rearrested in 1978,
White eventually broke down, at last genuinely suffering from guilt,
and admitted his role in the Andrews and Wilson murders. The
confession was sufficient; he was sentenced to life imprisonment
in October 1978.

In prison White studied for and gained an Open University
degree in social sciences and criminology and on his release in
1992 returned to the UDA in West Belfast, projecting himself as a
political activist and eventually a spokesman. He played a part in
the peace process leading to the Belfast Agreement in April 1994.
In 1995 he was elected to the Northern Ireland Forum, but he
failed to be elected to the Northern Ireland Assembly in 1996. On
22 July 1996 he was one of four members of the UDA's political
wing who met the British prime minister, John Major, at Downing
Street. His presence at the talks shocked Catholics who recalled
his role as a UDA butcher. Gerry Fitt, now Lord Fitt, and Senator
Wilson's family were critical of the British prime minister's decision to allow White into his official residence. Protestants felt the
same when they saw Gerry Adams welcomed into Number 10
Downing Street.

Between 1970 and 1973 the terrorists on both sides ran rings round
the security forces. Army casualties were the highest since the
Second World War – 108 in 1972 alone – and, what's more, the
UDA remained a legal organization. It took the British government until mid-November 1973 to issue an order proscribing even
the Ulster Freedom Fighters – an organization that, along with
McKeague's Red Hand Commando, did not really exist. And this
happened only after it had been decided that the UFF was stepping up its sectarian assassinations in an attempt to undermine
political talks and attempts to set up a power-sharing Executive at
Stormont and a Council of Ireland. This pointless move caused

almost no reaction in the UDA, which took the opportunity to urge loyalists to support the anti-Devolution White Paper unionists. It said: 'We want to make it clear that there will never be a Council of Ireland and there is only one party in Northern Ireland today that we can give our 100 per cent support to and that is the Democratic Unionist Party and the Loyalist Coalition. We would ask all Loyalists to support Mr Paisley and Mr Craig against the Council of Ireland.'

The SDLP leader, Gerry Fitt, was fully aware of the UDA's true nature and called on the government to ban it, urging Secretary of State Whitelaw to take all necessary steps to stop the loyalist assassins. In one of his usual pithy turns of phrase, Fitt said: 'We take the view that a man would be a member of the UDA by day and a member of the UFF by night.'

There were good political reasons from a British government perspective for not banning an organization it knew was up to its eyes in atrocities. At the same time as it 'banned' the UFF and Red Hand Commando, it removed Sinn Féin from the list of organizations proscribed under the old 'emergency' laws of Northern Ireland. The reason was simple: the government was secretly speaking to gunmen and needed to legitimize its interlocutors so it could not be accused of dealing with terrorists. Decriminalizing Sinn Féin enabled the British government to speak to republicans who held power in Catholic areas. Keeping the UDA legal gave it the chance to speak to those who held power in Protestant areas.

3. The Strike

The most humiliating defeat suffered by a British government since Suez could be construed as having begun with an innocuous decision by the UDA to call a conference in March 1973 to review where it stood. The organization had many issues to discuss, including the replacement of Jim Anderson who had announced his resignation. Anderson was already a marginal figure, uneasy with the hard men around him, who now had a grip on an organization which, broadly speaking, law-abiding figures like him had formed as a legitimate defence association for the Ulster working classes. Ironically, its first motto had been 'Law before Violence', before changing to the fancier '*Quis Separabit*' ('Who Shall Separate Us) – stolen from the Irish Guards' Regiment. Sammy Smyth had been pushed out. Power lay firmly in the grasp of two men: Tommy Herron in East Belfast and Charles Harding Smith in West Belfast. They looked and dressed like a Scots–Irish version of *mafiosi* and, like two mafia dons, they had carved up the city between themselves and felt unassailable.

The conference was a meeting of the two bosses (deputy chairmen), eleven brigadiers and their forty or so variously titled colonels or company commanders – the men who headed the subdivisions of the brigade areas. The conference agenda included the selection of a chairman; it was, in fact, the only issue of any importance to be decided. The title, whoever held it, meant that that person could claim to be 'supreme commander', the *cappo di tutti cappi*. The prospect of either Herron or Harding Smith holding the title spelt trouble. If Harding Smith grabbed it there could be war with Herron, and vice versa. Everyone realized the consequences of internecine warfare. It was only a few months since Ernie Elliott had ended up in a cardboard box in Sandy Row with a big hole in him. A compromise candidate had to be found – someone who was no threat to either of the two big bosses and who was broadly acceptable to the rest of the UDA. As a bonus, he might have some organizational skills. Someone like Andy Whatsisname from Highfield – aye, Andy Tyrie.

Until the spring of 1973 Andy Tyrie had never figured on the radar of anyone outside the UDA. He was barely known outside the Shankill. According to Tyrie and his supporters his selection was pure accident. He had been appointed to chair the conference and had done an acceptable job and someone – no one can remember who – suggested that *he* should become chairman. Herron and Harding Smith looked at the nobody from the Shankill estates, and agreed. He was no threat to either of them. Or so they thought.

Within six months Herron would be dead and within two years Harding Smith would flee Belfast for his life after being shot a total of six times in two assassination attempts. And Tyrie – a man who eschewed the flash lifestyle of the other bosses, who drank moderately, if at all, and didn't smoke – would have as near overall control as was possible in the UDA. He would lead it to its greatest victory and stay on top for sixteen years. The two big mafia chumps had just let Prince Machiavelli in the door to help run their affairs.

The man to whose presence politicians, personalities and journalists would later flock was one of seven children of a poor Shankill Road family. He attended Brown Square School, one of the toughest in the city, went to church and Sunday school and left school at fourteen to become a gardener with Belfast City Corporation. When he was eleven the family moved to a corporation house in the Ballymurphy estate, and then to a slightly better one in New Barnsley – both areas later to become Provisional IRA strongholds. Tyrie became a machinist for an animal feed company and did what was traditional at the time: married young and found a house in New Barnsley near his own family. And that would have been the last the world would have heard of him if it were not for the riots and intimidation of 1969. There were only around fifty Protestant families living in New Barnsley and the Tyries were thrown out, passing the Catholics fleeing the Shankill estates going the other way. He found his family a house in Glencairn, one of the new estates at the top of the Shankill. Some friends and neighbours held on for another two years in New Barnsley and Tyrie continued to visit despite the obvious dangers involved. When they were finally evicted he returned with lorries to help their evacuation.

At the start of the Troubles Tyrie was a member of the UVF, having been sworn in sometime in 1967. However, like quite a few displaced Protestants, he was disappointed at the UVF's failure to have any impact in the riots and mass violence of 1969. It was members of McKeague's UPV/SDA who helped the Protestants out of New Barnsley. So he joined the UDA from its outset. He was by then an experienced shop steward and had the organizational skill to come to the fore locally. Quite quickly he was appointed head of the UDA in the Shankill estates area covering Glencairn, Highfield and Springmartin, under the control of the West Belfast boss, Harding Smith.

The consensus among the thinking UDA leaders was that Herron was a serious irritant and had to go. He had faced censure in January 1973 after issuing a statement apparently condemning loyalist violence. He was what journalists at the time termed a 'rent-a-quote', and was seen as 'shooting off at the mouth' by other leaders, several of whom, including Harding Smith, were said to resent his media profile. Herron preened himself at the head of big UDA displays for Bill Craig's Vanguard rallies in South and East Belfast and accepted a nomination to stand for Vanguard in the June 1973 Assembly elections. He was enraged at being rebuffed by the electorate and argued that the vote had been rigged against him. After he and Billy Snoddy, the other Belfast UDA commander who stood in the election, lost their deposits, Herron threatened to stop the nightly patrolling by his men in East Antrim. Other UDA leaders – Tommy Lyttle in North Belfast and Billy Hull in West Belfast – received derisory votes. Only one man openly associated with the UDA, the North-West brigadier Glen Barr, was elected.

In August 1973 soldiers stopped Herron's car and arrested him under the Emergency Powers Act. When they took him to their barracks they found he had a considerable wad of cash in his jacket. The story was leaked to the press who variously described the sum as being between £3,000 and £9,000. According to Herron the money, which he said was only £2,000, was to pay for the trial in Dublin of the Derry UDA man Robert Taylor, who was facing extradition for murdering a young County Donegal couple on New Year's night 1972. Herron had been the key speaker at UDA rallies across Northern Ireland to raise money for Taylor's defence.

Herron was the first full-time salaried member of the UDA and he made a point of letting reporters know that he had taken a drop in wages from his well-paid garage manager's job. Others in East Belfast had a different version of his earnings. They watched in growing annoyance as Herron and his family began to show signs of having suddenly become rich. Some UDA men knew Herron had a Catholic mother and put it about that he had a cousin in the IRA. After his arrest and the disclosure about the money he was carrying – almost certainly done to damage him – he began to feel under pressure.

Herron had had plenty of warning that the rest of the UDA in East Belfast was closing in on him when gunmen burst into his house in the Braniel area three months earlier. He was not at home and so they shot dead Michael Wilson, the brother of his young wife, Hillary, and one of Herron's trusted lieutenants. Hillary told the inquest into her brother's death that as the gunman left, he had said: 'We will get him some time and you would get it too only for the children.' The official line from the UDA at the time of Wilson's murder was that it was the work of the IRA – despite the fact that the car used had been hijacked and later abandoned in the heart of loyalist East Belfast. In spite of the rumours, Wilson was given a funeral with full paramilitary honours and an oration from Ian Paisley. As though to reinforce its claim that the IRA had done it, by way of 'retaliation' the East Belfast UDA killed two young Catholic men, Daniel Rouse and Jim Kelly, the following day.

As the summer wore on Herron gave the impression of being a distracted man. His family recalled that on a visit to Portrush he seemed to be in a trance and accidentally walked off the pier.

The end came on 16 September when he left a meeting in the UDA headquarters in East Belfast. There were conflicting reports that he got into a red car or a van. His body was found two mornings later, lying in a ditch on a quiet road on the southern outskirts of the city. There were plenty of stories about army and RUC involvement in his death but, according to well-placed loyalist sources, it was his own people who did him in. One of the figures involved still lives in East Belfast and is described as an 'honourable' man. Interestingly, there was still a large roll of banknotes left in Herron's pocket, along with his legally held pistol. His killers did not want his money or his gun.

Herron's 'mysterious' death and his replacement as East Belfast commander by the less headstrong Sammy McCormick – the opposite of Herron: not in the least showy and clearly not on the take – allowed the UDA to impose some form of discipline on East Belfast, something that was absolutely necessary if a loyalist movement wished to appeal to the Protestant masses.

With Herron out of the way, organizing in earnest for Ulster loyalism's big challenge could begin. Westminster had moved remarkably quickly to end the dangerous political vacuum left in the North since the proroguing of Stormont the previous year. The White Paper on devolution had been published on 20 March 1973 and Assembly elections called for the end of May. The complete redefinition of political structures in Northern Ireland was now under way: from a position of unionist hegemony in the early 1960s, and in the face of a republican onslaught, the British government had closed Stormont, disbanded the 'B' Specials and disarmed the RUC, and was now proposing radical new measures to include nationalists in government at Stormont and to give Dublin a role in the government of Northern Ireland.

The cracks in the Ulster Unionist Party became splits and then a chasm. On one side were the anti-White Paper unionists, including Bill Craig, who had been sacked from his job as home affairs minister by Terence O'Neill for his handling of the police during the 1968 civil rights demonstration in Derry, and was now outside the party fold with his Vanguard organization; and Ian Paisley, who had run O'Neill very close in his Antrim constituency in 1971 and had set up the Democratic Unionist Loyalist Party – later simply the DUP. Anti-White Paper politicians still in the Ulster Unionist Party were also in broad unity. This group, led by Harry West, eventually called themselves Official Unionists.

On the other side, in support of the White Paper proposals, were Brian Faulkner and a minority of the Ulster Unionist Party still loyal to him, the SDLP, and the newly formed cross-religious Alliance Party – later referred to by the UDA leadership as the Catholic unionist party.

The British government's plan was to replace the demolished unionist institutions with a local government which would reflect the religious break-down of Northern Ireland – roughly 60 per cent Protestant and 40 per cent Catholic – in a 108-seat Assembly. If the proposed reforms had stopped there things might have worked. However, at a conference in the Civil Service College at Sunningdale in Berkshire in December 1973 the Faulkner unionists conceded the nationalist demand for an 'Irish dimension', structures that would effectively give the Irish government a say in the affairs of Northern Ireland. This was a bridge too far for the majority of Protestants.

The problem facing Tyrie and the UDA leadership, and the rag tag of dissident unionist politicians and community figures along with them, was how to properly mobilize, even motivate, the Protestant population against the new Assembly. The previous UDA-led strike, the killings and rioting showed that Protestants generally would have nothing to do with this destructive lawlessness in their own neighbourhoods.

Rioting on the Shankill in December 1973 had been particularly bad and, from the loyalists' point of view, unproductive. The army shot dead a young UDA man, Alexander Howell. In retaliation the UDA shot dead RUC Constable Michael Logue – by chance, a Catholic. While this incident made no major public impact at the time, it was highly significant because it was the second murder of an RUC member by the UDA. The RUC was being expanded rapidly. A new chief constable, Ken Newman, later to head the Metropolitan Police, was re-establishing the force's detective branch, improving its intelligence (informer-handling) base and beginning the fight-back against the terrorists. The UDA's murder of Constables Logue and Harron (in October 1972) set them as targets for the new, very tough 'A' Branch, whose job was to put terrorists in prison. This process started quickly in 1974 and, along with internment, it meant that many of the worst UDA killers were behind bars.

Things were still not under control in East Belfast. On the night of 17 February 1974 crowds gathered to celebrate the acquittal of the local UDA leader Ned McCreery and six other UDA men after the collapse of the James McCartan romper room murder case. The celebrations escalated quickly into rioting with stones being thrown at the army and RUC. This, predictably, led to shooting and a nineteen-year-old UDA man, Kirk Watters, was shot dead by soldiers during an exchange of fire. Another seventeen-year-old youth, Gary Reid, the cousin of East Belfast's most famous son, George Best, was also shot and died nine days later from his injuries. However, under the command of the new East Belfast brigadier, Sammy McCormick, discipline was re-established and by the spring of 1974 the East Belfast men were among the best organized and effective brigades in the UDA.

The random and brutal sectarianism that had characterized Herron's tenure in office had ended. From the start of 1974 until the end of May the number of UDA killings dropped markedly – only thirteen Catholics were killed. The Catholic staff of Abbey Meats, a meat-processing plant on the Shore Road on the northern outskirts of Belfast, was, however, an easy touch for the East Antrim UDA, which was at constant odds with the very tough Catholic enclave, Bawnmore on the Shore Road. On 11 February, as a small group of workers waited for a lift, two UDA men opened fire with a machine gun, killing seventeen-year-old Margaret McErlean and sixteen-year-old Thomas Donaghy.

Meanwhile, after the Sunningdale Agreement in December 1973, the new Executive was sworn in at the New Year and convened soon after. Brian Faulkner became prime minister, with Gerry Fitt as his deputy, and the division of ministries was finely balanced between the Faulkner unionists, the SDLP and the Alliance. The first meeting of the Assembly ended in uproar as the anti-Agreement unionists kept up a stream of abuse and had to be carried out of the debating chamber. The lack of Protestant support for the Assembly was evident in the snap general election called in February, in which eleven of the twelve Northern Ireland constituencies were won by anti-Agreement candidates who had banded into the United Ulster Unionist Council coalition led by the Fermanagh Unionist, Harry West. Despite this, the Assembly still sat and there was every chance that, if it was not brought down quickly, it would last the course as political opposition to it dwindled over time. Faulkner, Fitt and Oliver Napier of the Alliance Party had a sufficient, though narrow, majority over the combined UUUC opposition led by Harry West, Craig and Paisley.

Protestant labour had been organized since Belfast became a small centre for industry at the start of the nineteenth century. The organization of Protestant workers stemmed, in part, from the radicalism of the mainly Presbyterian United Irishmen who had come together under the banner of the Northern Whig Club in 1789. In Belfast trade unions became fiercely loyalist groups and every artisan trade and many employers had their own Orange Lodges from early in the nineteenth century. Two stonemasons who 'struck work' over pay in 1801 became the first trade unionists to take industrial action and ended up in the town gaol for three months. In the hierarchy of labour, skilled tradesmen (there were virtually no tradeswomen) defiantly protected their trades and jobs. The Catholics who flocked into the city from the 1850s onwards were despised and regarded as a threat – not simply because they were of an alien religion but because they represented a source of cheap labour that threatened to undercut Protestant labour. The Catholics were excluded from skilled jobs not because the bosses wanted it that way but because Protestant organized labour would have it no other way. In the shipyards Protestant workers literally looked down on Catholic navvies digging the dry docks beneath them.

This was how it remained. Catholics – described as the muscle and sinew of Belfast labour – were the brickies, joiners and chippies

who built a city where industry was dominated by the Orange
Order and governed after 1922 by the Ulster Unionist Party from
Stormont. When the Great Depression hit the city's shipbuilding,
engineering and textile industries it created a huge surge in unemployment (50,000 were out of work in 1932). Momentarily
Protestant and Catholic labour joined in common cause for better
public relief. Because of the need for manpower in the Second
World War boom more Catholics than ever before got skilled
work. But by the late 1960s, there were fewer jobs for everyone
and the heart of the traditional Protestant workforce in Belfast
was withering. Between 1961 and 1968 jobs in manufacturing
declined from 106,000 to 92,000. The arrival of the new synthetic
textile and light-engineering factories did little to alleviate the
employment gloom. They were also located out of town beside
the new housing estates to which the working-class – mainly
Protestant – worker elite decamped, leaving the Protestant heartlands in a state of decline and simmering anger. The last great
passenger liner, the *Canberra*, sailed out of the Harland and Wolff
yard in 1962, and employment in shipbuilding slipped below
10,000, severely affecting the Shankill and East Belfast. But
Protestant labour was still a powerful political resource.

As the republican violence grew and political power seeped
from unionist control loyalists began to look at the example being
set by their trade union brethren across the Irish Sea, where British
miners were engaged in a momentous struggle with the
Conservative government. The 1971 National Union of
Mineworkers' annual general conference had mandated its leadership to seek a 43 per cent pay increase from the government,
the miners' employer in the nationalized industry. The Tory government responded with an offer of 7–8 per cent. At the end of 1971
the union voted to strike. At first the miners picketed only their
mines but they soon started sending 'flying pickets' to close down
power stations, steel works, ports, coal depots and other major
industrial coal users. By 21 January the miners had halted almost
all coal movement in Britain. On 9 February the government
declared a state of national emergency and three days later intro-
duced the three-day working week to conserve electricity. It took

a further ten days of intense negotiations to unfreeze British indus-try. The miners won hands-down, becoming one of the best-paid workforces in Britain.

Within a year, due mainly to inflation, the value of the miners' wage increase was whittled down, and at the end of 1973 they voted to strike again. The Arab–Israeli war had created a world-wide oil shortage and the miners were in a good position to attack Britain's power supply. They came out on strike again on 9 February 1974. Edward Heath, the prime minister, who was trying to introduce a national pay freeze to fight inflation, again declared a state of emergency and a three-day week. An Industrial Relations Act to prevent flying pickets was put before the Commons. Heath called a general election for 28 February believing the rest of Britain would support his attempts to stem the power of the coal miners, but he was defeated. The new secretary of state for employ-ment, Michael Foot, quickly published a document showing that miners' pay had fallen since 1972 and the Labour government led by Harold Wilson struck a deal with the miners and also intro-duced a compensation scheme for sufferers of pneumoconiosis and a superannuation scheme for retired miners. They had won again. Britain's 'Winters of Discontent,' in which the industrial might of the unions probably reached its peak, had a salutary effect on the discontented loyalist workers of Ulster. The British coal miners had shown it was possible to bring a government to its knees, and this inspired the thinking for an industrial *coup d'état* that would bring the Ulster Executive crashing to the ground.

Muscle alone would not stop Northern Ireland. The IRA had been bombing the place for three years and almost everybody went about their life as before. Shops and businesses remained open; people still went to the cinema. The supply of oil and petrol was the key industrial means by which to bring about a shut-down. The only problem was that, even by 1974, when the loyal-ists had had two full years to organize since the British government removed their devolved government, there was no such thing as a loyalist industrial movement.

The coordination of industrial opposition was led by Harry Murray, a shipyard union convenor, who enlisted the assistance of

Hugh Petrie of Shorts and the key figures of Billy Kelly of the electricity power workers and Tommy Croft of the gas workers. From 1973 electricity was supplied by the Northern Ireland Electricity Service (NIES), a public utility with power stations in five locations – Coolkeeragh, Ballylumford, Kilroot, Belfast East and Belfast West. The workforces in all but Coolkeeragh were predominantly Protestant and predominantly loyalist. The NIES produced 720 megawatts of power, a third of which was used by industry and the rest by domestic, agricultural and public services. In theory Kelly's people would bring power supply down to 60 per cent, enough to maintain essential services but not to keep industry going.

Murray began organizing meetings under the banner of the Ulster Workers Council (UWC), which based its operations in Vanguard's headquarters in a house in Hawthornden Road, in the pleasant East Belfast suburbs. But he failed to attract any significant turn-outs across Northern Ireland. He toured the Belfast Harbour industrial estate, which included Harland and Wolff, Shorts, the oil refinery and the Belfast East power station, and was given a supportive reception by the predominantly Protestant workforces. Simultaneously, he arranged to meet the UDA and other loyalist paramilitaries under the pretext of joining forces with the Loyalist Association of Workers. But when Murray arrived for a meeting at the Shankill Road UDA headquarters he found that the LAW was in fact the two paramilitary organizations and not a loyalist trade unionist movement. To make matters even more complicated, the UDA and the UVF had also formed something called the Ulster Army Council which was to act as an umbrella for joint paramilitary operations for the duration of a strike. Murray was in bed with the devil but Andy Tyrie and Glen Barr, and Ken Gibson from the UVF, were able to convince him of their total support. He would coordinate the shop stewards and they would look after the rest.

Like the LAW the UWC existed only on paper. But Murray had elicited enough promises and put enough work in to ensure that if the strike got off the ground it stood a chance of success. In political and media terms he was a nonentity but he was decent, hard-working and a non-drinker, exactly the kind of person who would appeal to the Protestant sense of righteousness. The paramilitaries needed him and he needed them.

From the outset, it was intended that the paramilitaries, and the UDA in particular, would again provide the muscle – do the dirty work, as the UDA later put it. By the autumn of 1973 Tyrie and Glen Barr had begun preparing their men for the strike, drilling into the battalions that this could not fail; that there could be no repeat of the February 1973 fiasco. Tyrie had the job of marshalling the troops.

Bi-weekly UWC conferences were convened in Hawthornden Road with Glen Barr in the chair. Various dates were proposed for the start of the strike and reviewed. Tyrie, a shop steward himself, initially opposed the suggestion of Wednesday 15 May. He reasoned that a better day would be a Monday, when many workers would like the day off anyway. But the date was set to coincide with the end of the prolonged Assembly debate on power-sharing due on the evening of the 14th. As the House divided and the Assembly members began filing away from Stormont, Harry Murray approached political reporters, informing them that the strike was on from midnight. Few journalists and even fewer politicians paid much heed.

The following morning seemed to prove their scepticism right when a large section of the workforce ignored the strike call. There was, embarrassingly for the organizers, even a decent turnout at Harland and Wolff where Murray worked. Tyrie had anticipated this and had instructed his men to use 'intimidation but not violence'; in the paramilitary's mind there is a distinction between the two that might be lost on the ordinary citizen. When quizzed later about the widespread intimidation, he referred to it as 'discouragement' or 'persuasion'.

The UDA's response became more effective during the day. In Larne, the North's second most important port, UDA and UVF men sealed off the town and all shipping stopped. Billy Kelly's men delivered, and the electricity grid started shutting down. During the day factories and businesses in Protestant areas and town centres were visited by the UDA and many people began drifting home. At Harland and Wolff there was opposition to a shut-down until the remaining third or so of the workforce were told that they had better get their cars out of the car park if they didn't want them burned. The mainly Protestant workforce of the Sirocco engineering works in East Belfast almost all turned up for work but broke for home after a man in dark glasses walked into the factory shaking his fist. In most cases the threat of violence was all that was needed to intimidate people away from their jobs. Most of those with cars simply wanted to get them back safely to their houses rather than have them burned. There was no need for burning and battering, only the suggestion of it. Twelve buses were hijacked and services were immediately withdrawn in Belfast with the exception of the Falls Road where the service continued uninterrupted throughout the strike.

What Tyrie feared most was a large-scale security operation to break down the barricades set up in Protestant areas, but there was no army response at all. Soldiers stood by while barricades were erected along main avenues. Nor was there any significant response the next morning when the barricades and arrayed ranks of the UDA were sufficient to 'persuade' the vast majority of the workforce that it was in their best interests to stay at home. When the police and soldiers did begin removing barricades in mid-morning most people had already been turned back and had gone home. Hawthornden Road began issuing directives that only 'essential services' would be allowed through the barricades. From day two, industry was largely shut down. Farmers had to start destroying produce which could not be refrigerated. On the evening of the second day the order was issued to close all pubs and clubs. The strike leaders could not risk their men getting drunk and could not expect housewives to accept their men going out drinking while they sat at home in the dark.

The pub ban led to the murders of two Catholic brothers, Sean and Brendan Byrne, who owned the Wayside Bar outside Ballymena, County Antrim when UDA gunmen burst in and shot them dead. The body of a Catholic university student, Michael Mallon, was found at Shaw's Bridge on the southern outskirts of Belfast on 21 May. It is believed that he was waylaid by the Village

UDA, taken to a romper room and shot dead. And a young couple were killed in County Tyrone when their car struck a tree felled by strikers. The five deaths were enough to drive home the point that behind the strike was real terror. This was not a bloodless coup. In an interview with the *Belfast Telegraph* on the tenth anniversary of the strike Tyrie described the UDA's role in these terms:

We ran the strike and apart from one incident in Ballymena [the murders of the two Catholic brothers in their pub] it was carried out without injury, loss of life or undue force. On previous occasions where there had been demonstrations or strikes they had always ended in violence. We knew we had to stop being predictable and there had to be no violence this time. We had been assured by the workers' representatives that the Province would come to a standstill the day the strike was called. This, of course, was nonsense. People still went to their work the first day of the strike. We were asked why, if these people were loyalists, were they ignoring the call to down tools.

Communications were bad and we had to spread the word quickly that the strike was to be a total stoppage. Men were sent out to do this but there was little if any intimidation and when the workers realized what it was all about they stopped work and gave us support.

We organized the food supplies, the welfare and the means of keeping the peace ticking over. But the initial days of the strike were a big disappointment to us. The workers did not have the organization they said they had. The most effective workers were Billy Kelly and Tommy Croft who worked for the Gas Department. Other organizations offered support but let us down. I never saw a UVF man for the whole of the strike, for instance.

The UVF's actions during the strike were more lethal. Early on the morning of day three – a Friday – masked men hijacked a number of cars in North Belfast, the Shankill and Portadown. The matter of the 'Irish dimension' was about to be dealt with. The organization, which had decided to teach the Irish Republic a lesson in what it was like to suffer indiscriminate bombing like that perpetrated by the IRA on Belfast city centre, detonated three car bombs in Dublin and another in the border town of Monaghan. Thirty-three people were killed, making it the bloodiest day's bombing so far in the Troubles. The UVF had surpassed its previous record for fatalities from a single bomb – fifteen people killed at McGurk's bar in North Belfast in December 1971.

The Dublin and Monaghan bombings were specifically designed to force the Dublin government to withdraw from any attempt to implement a joint British–Irish Council for the governance of Northern Ireland. The attacks appalled and horrified most right-minded people, but loyalist Belfast, which had felt the brunt of the IRA bombing onslaught and was determined to fight and win the strike, responded with something approaching delight. There were open celebrations in loyalist areas. Although the UDA was not in any way connected with the bombing, it sent its members out on the Shankill Road with buckets to collect money from appreciative shoppers – showing that it wanted to cash in on the popularity of the cross-border attacks. Sammy Smyth told journalists: 'I am very happy about the bombings in Dublin. There is a war with the Free State and now we are laughing at them.'

The UVF admitted responsibility for the bombings only in 1993. It was also responsible for most of the loyalist bombings in the North, many of which were being claimed in the name of the UFF. It, too, used the expedient of a cover name to hide its activities. It didn't really mind the UDA taking credit for its operations as it diverted attention from its guilty members.

The Dublin and Monaghan bombings sent shockwaves through the Republic, which had been largely unaffected by the troubles in the North. However, it hardened the SDLP view that it must stand up for an Irish dimension against the threat of loyalist terrorism. The Executive was divided on the issue – unionists insisting that the Council of Ireland issue be put back for consideration at a later time because it was such a sticking point; the SDLP urging that it should be brought forward. Division on the issue almost brought down the Executive – even without the strike. The matter was partially resolved, but the Executive was far from saved.

With the exception of Craig, anti-Executive unionists were very wary of the strike organizers in the first days, but as it progressed and there was no sign of the uncontrolled street violence that had accompanied previous stoppages, they began to come around. Paisley, who had been absent for the first few days – he had been abroad at a friend's funeral – returned and appeared at Hawthornden.

Merlyn Rees, the new Labour secretary of state, refused point blank to meet the strikers. However, his deputy, Stanley Orme, eventually did and had a heated meeting with the political representatives of the UWC – Craig, Paisley and Ernest Baird of Vanguard. The paramilitaries, Tyrie and Tommy Lyttle of the UDA and Ken Gibson of the UVF, were eventually included in the meeting at which Orme unsuccessfully appealed for the strike to be called off unconditionally. By the 19th the strike had the total support of Harry West's unionists. There was now a full complement of political and Protestant paramilitary opposition to the Executive; Ulster loyalism was in full rebellion.

To Faulkner's dismay, Rees was utterly out of his depth. He saw the Executive slip away with every day of inaction. On army advice, Rees was reluctant to give the order for military intervention against the strikers. The military inaction gave rise to the criticism that the government was acting in the same manner as cavalry officers in the Curragh Command in 1913, when they refused to take action against Carson's UVF. Interestingly, one British army officer, writing anonymously in the Monday Club journal a year later, said:

The unwillingness of the Army to act to bring about the end of the strike (on the quite reasonable grounds that there was little or nothing it could do within the concept of minimum force) and the subsequent confrontation between the military and the politicians must be the most significant event in recent years. For the first time the Army decided it was right and the politicians had better toe the line. The consequences of this are yet to be fully appreciated.*

Four thousand troops were deployed to remove barricades on the second Wednesday but found the mission impossible, as where

*Quoted in Don Anderson's *14 May Days*, Dublin, Gill & MacMillan, 1994.

they were removed local people, including women and children, replaced them with pickets. The UDA had instructed its members not to form up in ranks against the soldiers and to avoid confrontation. The army moved only on the last Saturday night of the strike, rounding up twelve UDA men in Rathcoole, who were detained in Long Kesh. UDA spokesmen said that they had expected to be arrested throughout the strike and were confounded there had been so little action against them.

The blocking of roads was so widespread that Faulkner had to be airlifted to his offices. Stormont was blockaded. Rees had no option but to declare a state of emergency, adding to the propaganda that was being deliberately issued from the UWC headquarters to increase public tension and so put pressure on the Executive and the British government.

The Labour government's response to an open rebellion posing as a strike was increasingly feeble. It enlisted the services of the veteran TUC leader Len Murray, who went to Belfast to head a back-to-work rally to the Harbour estate. Fewer than 200 turned up and the marchers were jostled and pelted by loyalists and had to be protected by the RUC. A simultaneous back-to-work march in the Cregagh industrial estate in East Belfast attracted only seventeen people, who were also harangued.

Electricity, petrol and gas were in the control of the strikers and the UWC handed out directives on what could and could not move in Northern Ireland and what were and were not essential services. When it began issuing coupons for petrol, queues of cars formed up the Belmont Road, outside the UWC headquarters. People who wanted passes for essential work had to go to strike offices to seek them. The role of government was so usurped that it took to counterfeiting UWC passes, something that quickly came to the notice of the organizers, who simply changed the paper to another colour.

The fact that the UWC was able to react so quickly and effectively to the counter initiatives from Stormont led people to believe it had spies inside Stormont. It did – including a member of the Executive, Roy Bradford. When the Executive decided that the army should be used to distribute fuel from the oil refinery the strikers were ready and the workers were already on the way out of the gate before the soldiers arrived. The UWC was keeping 140 petrol stations open and supplied. The best the army could manage was twenty-one, and under emergency plans drawn up in the event of a Catholic uprising nearly all of these were in Protestant areas. It would also have been suicidal to station soldiers as sitting targets for IRA snipers in Catholic areas.

Small teams of engineers kept the electricity grid going on a wing and a prayer. They were allowed into the plants to ensure vital equipment was maintained, but at times the supply ran perilously low and Northern Ireland came very close to collapse during the middle of the second week. Nationalists claimed that the army could have taken over the power stations and run them, but the military had nothing near sufficient expertise. Also if the soldiers had been sent in the strikers could shut down the whole system, with the distinct possibility of damaging the grid irrevocably. Questions were asked at Stormont about why electricity was not being taken from the Republic's grid as an inter-connector had been built in the late 1960s. It was pointed out that the IRA had inadvertently helped the strikers in this regard by blowing up the cross-border power line in South Armagh. NIES spokesman Hugo Patterson's nightly broadcasts on the distribution of power, delivered in ponderous tones, added to the impression of doom at Stormont.

Laid-off workers, justifiably able to claim they were the victims of a lock-out rather than an illegal stoppage, were entitled to unemployment benefit and social welfare and dole officials were deemed essential workers. This was a vital element in soothing the Protestant working-class antagonism to the strike which would have emerged if children were going hungry and the family furniture had to be sold off to buy food.

The prime minister, Harold Wilson, could barely contain himself at the humiliation his regime was facing in Northern Ireland. No British prime minister since Anthony Eden had suffered such a calamity. He went on television to deliver a message to the entire nation in which he lambasted loyalists who he said were 'sponging' off the British taxpayer. The incredibly ill-judged speech was greeted with delight among the strike organizers and caused both indignation and hilarity among the Protestant population. The day after the speech strikers appeared wearing lapel badges in the shape of little slices of sponge.

The Executive's plans to try to break the petrol and fuel oil blockade had failed. The army was finally mobilized against the barricades, but with almost no petrol or diesel and very little electricity this was too little too late. The UWC continued turning the screw. The NIES warned that a single fault could create total blackout. Supplies of animal feed had been stopped by the middle of the first week and farmers who had already dumped an estimated £2.5 million worth of milk, and had had to slaughter vast numbers of animals, informed the Executive they might have to destroy the entire stock of pigs and chickens.

The UWC political leaders, Paisley and Craig, issued statements saying they would 'eat grass' rather than allow the Executive to survive and called for new elections to a non-power-sharing Assembly. On the morning of 28 May Faulkner's twelve back-benchers urged him to negotiate with the UWC and made it clear that if he did not, they would issue a statement calling for mediation. Thousands of farmers on tractors, carrying pro-strike placards, were gathering outside the gates of Stormont. Even before Faulkner announced his resignation and withdrawal from the Executive word spread to the UWC headquarters and was relayed to the loyalist heartlands. Celebrations started even before the announcement was officially made to journalists at Stormont and went on throughout the day. That night bonfires were lit across Protestant areas of Northern Ireland.

Not surprisingly, Paisley, Craig and West made a political meal out of the success of the strike, trying to steal the credit from the actual strikers. Paisley, who had been absent during the vital first days, when defeat seemed very possible, triumphantly addressed a rally of 5,000 around a bonfire in Rathcoole. Having defeated the British government, the strike leader, Ulster's Cincinnatus, Harry Murray, went home and back to work in the shipyard. Andy Tyrie received no public recognition for his marshalling of the UDA that forced a lock-out on a province with a population of 1.5 million people in defiance of what was still one of the world's superpowers. Instead, Tyrie and the UDA would be shunned by the unionist establishment.

Only on the tenth anniversary of the strike did Andy Tyrie speak out in an article for the *Belfast Telegraph* to set the record straight. The article is notable for the extraordinary change in tone – towards moderation with Catholics – combined with the idea, promulgated by people like himself and Glen Barr, of an independent Northern Ireland.

In the 1968–9 period when the great liberal Orange/Unionist point of view manifested itself (were they admitting fifty years of Unionist misrule?), some of the leaders worked themselves into a frenzy reminiscent of Women's Lib, and burned their (Orange) collarettes and bowler hats, instead of their bras. (This was due to their fear of being branded as Orange bigots because they rushed out and proclaimed to the world that they were 'free' of any bigotry, simply by cutting the umbilical-cord which tied them to the Orange Order. This was after they had used the Order to gain positions of power.)

When the Unionist Party disbanded the 'B' Specials, and the Orange Order was in disarray, the Ulster Defence Association was born as a means of front-line defence for the Ulster people. We were actively supported by many politicians who declared: 'We support you, lads, but we daren't say it openly or we would be ruined.'

These spineless jellyfish uttered catch-cries like 'liquidate the enemy', 'Protestant backlash' and shouted about 'Papish plots' and as a result our membership convinced themselves that they were soldiers and consequently that they were entitled to use every means suitable to put down the enemy (when a politician tells you that all Catholics are in the IRA, it makes you feel justified).

Nowadays these same politicians still boast about their experiences over a cocktail cabinet. The Ulster people have witnessed one of the greatest historical awakenings since 1921. Gone are the days when a 'John Bull' type would appear on our shores with a cultured accent and tell us that we should feel 'privileged' to have him serve us in Westminster. It is a sad reflection that we tolerated such imported representatives but this was mainly due to the people being informed that Ulster had no one suitable for this 'exalted' position.

This gave me the impression that the English were first-class citizens, the Ulster Protestants second-class and the Ulster Catholics third-class but during the past two years of political investigation conducted by the UDA I have recognized there is much common ground between both sections of the community in that both want to see Ulster – in the six-county sense – taking its rightful place in the world and not to be seen as a country with a death wish.

If this common-ground approach was given breathing space and we were permitted to concentrate on Ulster for the Ulster people – Catholic and Protestant – groups such as the Provisional IRA who are so twisted in their divisiveness and destruction, would be totally removed.

The people of Ulster have more in common with each other than their neighbours in Cork or Coventry and the political ghouls on both sides who have encouraged violence in order to stabilize their positions in the community would be social outcasts.

Lastly, whenever I ask a Unionist which choice he would make – Ulster or the Link? Alas he invariably replies: 'the Link'. It is my contention that Ulster is of supreme importance to the Ulsterman.

Tyrie was one of the most important figures in late twentieth-century Ireland and, in terms of achievement, arguably one of the most successful terrorist (he would say paramilitary) leaders to have emerged in Europe. The UWC strike was a lesson in the controlled use of violence: the one awful blow struck against Dublin and Monaghan by the UVF to check the Irish government's aspirations in Northern Ireland, and the absolute minimum amount of force (discouragement) against the workers needed to make the strike. By contrast, the IRA killed around 2,000 people in a thirty-year campaign for a united Ireland and eventually gave up in 1997 and opted for politics within the context of a Northern Ireland still united to Britain.

Loyalist terrorism worked in 1974 because the unskilled massed ranks of the UDA were able to combine with the much smaller UVF's more advanced terrorist capability. The terror groups and the UWC were helped by a dithering British administration at

Stormont and inaction by security chiefs who did not feel ready for the challenge of outright loyalist rebellion. The strike organizers had high-grade intelligence from sympathetic agents inside the Stormont administration, the RUC and the army. It had all the elements of a successful coup and Tyrie was the most important figure in its planning and operation. Ironically, probably the only other insurgent or terrorist leader to achieve such success before him was Michael Collins.

Tyrie's performance during the strike, with all its attendant publicity, irked Harding Smith, who was still a formidable character. He grew increasingly angry, looking for a way to get at Tyrie. He chose as his reason for attack Tyrie's decision to accept an invitation from the Libyan dictator, Colonel Gadafy, to send a delegation to Tripoli. Gadafy had already provided the IRA with guns and money but had a poor understanding of Irish politics. He was impressed by the reports of the successful UWC strike and sent Tyrie a message through an Irish businessman. Glen Barr, Tommy Lyttle and Harry Chicken, who was responsible for political development in the UDA, travelled to Libya on 14 November.

The thinking behind the trip was not that well worked out, but there was a tantalizing prospect that oil-rich Libya would provide massive funding to the UDA. Barr and others had proposed the idea of forming a provisional government at the end of the strike, and he and others in the leadership were strongly in favour of independence for Northern Ireland. But there would need to be massive funding to promote these big schemes. One idea floating around at the time was that Libyan money could be used to buy the ailing *Newsletter* newspaper to help promulgate UDA thinking. Tyrie saw the Libyan trip as a chance to garner funds, and maybe weapons, for the UDA, and to counter the relationship between Gadafy and the IRA.

When it became public, however, there was widespread unionist criticism of the UDA leadership and Paisley was particularly scathing. The army's 'dirty tricks' department circulated a leaflet purporting to come from the imaginary Ulster Citizen's Army, accusing the UDA men of consorting with communists and friends of the IRA.

Harding Smith, who was informed about the trip beforehand and said nothing, used the criticism as a pretext to start an argument with Tyrie and the other Inner Council members and stormed out of one of its meetings in December 1974. In January, he declared that the West Belfast brigade was splitting from the rest of the UDA. This was a direct threat to Tyrie, who was still living with his family in Glencairn, an area Harding Smith controlled. Harding Smith placed Tyrie and his family under house arrest with a UDA guard around the house, but they let Tyrie slip away and three car-loads of men were sent from East Belfast to collect his wife and children.

Two weeks after his unilateral declaration of independence, Harding Smith was in the UDA Shankill Road offices with Tommy Lyttle. Lyttle was not a particularly strong Harding Smith supporter, but with a house and family on the Shankill he had little option but to hang on. Unknown to him a sniper team had taken up position in a room over the optician's shop across the street. When Harding Smith presented himself as a target, the sniper fired two rounds, hitting Harding Smith in the chest. As it happened, they were armour-piercing bullets and passed through Harding Smith and right through the building. They left two neat holes in Harding Smith's chest but he would survive.

With Harding Smith out of the way, Tyrie called a meeting in a neutral city centre venue with the three company commanders on the Shankill: Tommy Lyttle, John McClatchey – Tyrie's successor in the Shankill estates – and Tommy Boyd from 'C' company in the Lower Shankill. They agreed that Tyrie and other Inner Council members would address the Woodvale UDA men. It was an extremely tense gathering but Tyrie was a Shankill man and there was near consensus that Harding Smith was not bigger than the UDA.

Harding Smith made a swift recovery and was released from hospital in two weeks and, to the surprise of the rest of the UDA, immediately announced he was again in control of the Shankill. But in a remarkably short time he had made himself an impressive array of dangerous enemies. During his time away, rumours had been spreading concerning evidence that had been used to intern two local men – information which some said could only have come from Harding Smith. It was the type of thing his own people had said about David Fogel two years earlier. He was also involved in a serious row with the UVF in West Belfast. He had approached its leaders, suggesting an amalgamation, and put his proposal in such a way that it was obvious he clearly thought he would be in total control. He left the meeting with the UVF pointing a gun at his head. Simultaneously, he was making thinly veiled threats against Glen Barr and Harry Chicken for their adventure in Libya, which resulted in friends of the two men issuing warnings that if they were harmed, Harding Smith would be held to account.

Shortly after leaving hospital, Harding Smith called a meeting of his local commanders in the UDA offices. Minutes into the discussion a gunman burst in and walked up to a surprised Harding Smith. In a scene straight out of a Hollywood movie, all the commanders dived under the table, while the gunman fired two shots from a handgun into Harding Smith's chest. As the commanders peered out from under the table they saw the gunman lean over the prone, but still alive, Harding Smith and point the gun at his head. He pulled the trigger. Nothing happened. After two more faulty rounds failed to fire he cursed, shook his head and left the room. From the floor Harding Smith looked at the men now coming out from under the table and asked: 'What do I have to do? Do I have to go?'

Harding Smith made another remarkable recovery but, not being the brightest of men, on his release from hospital a week later he went back to his house in north-west Belfast. During the early hours of the morning he had another unwanted visitor, Davy Payne, who was accompanied by one of the UDA's most notorious hitmen. At last Harding Smith seemed to get the message, and he was escorted from Belfast to the airport the following morning. Tyrie was the preferred and undisputed leader of the UDA.

4. Return to Bloodshed

For a while after the UWC strike the UDA was on everyone's invitation list. It sent delegations to Europe and America under the name of its new political wing, the Ulster Loyalist Democratic Party. Tyrie sent his more articulate lieutenants, Glen Barr, Tommy Lyttle, Harry Chicken and even Sammy Smyth, to raise awareness of the loyalist cause and to carry the begging bowl. The UDA also became the first loyalists to talk to the Dublin government. Within months the UDA issued an invitation to Catholic groups and a secret meeting was organized with the SDLP on 1 August 1974. At a time when Northern Ireland was highly polarized politically it was a brave move by both sides but it came to little.

Under the mantle of the Ulster Community Action Group fourteen UDA members took part in a cross-community conference in Holland organized by the European Council of Churches in March 1975. As well as holding discussions the delegates examined Dutch political and social structures. The UDA delegation included Hugh McVeigh who, two months later, disappeared and was murdered by the UVF.

The UDA, like all the other terror groups, needed money, but using stolen cash to finance election campaigns was a certain way of deterring respectable voters, and the organization was also losing too many men to arrest by the increasingly efficient RUC Special Branch.

Politically, however, it was downhill for the UDA after the strike, although there was worse in store for the Faulknerite unionists and the SDLP. In the October 1974 general elections United Ulster Unionist Council candidates again romped home. Harold Wilson and Merlyn Rees accepted that a Westminster-imposed political structure would not work and announced elections on 1 May 1975 to a Northern Ireland Constitutional Convention in which it was hoped the local politicians could work out their own solution. The UUUC took a majority of the seventy-eight Convention seats. The Convention, however, brought the strains in the coalition to the surface. In the realization that Westminster would not otherwise allow a return to majority rule, Craig, supported by the UDA and its sole Convention member, Glen Barr, favoured some form of power-sharing. Harry West and Ian Paisley held out for a return to the old straight unionist majority system, and the UUUC split acrimoniously.

The UDA–Vanguard alliance, calling itself the United Loyalist Central Co-ordinating Committee, said that it had plans for a provisional government in the event of a British withdrawal, including the formation of an Ulster army. Tyrie touted this as an army encompassing the UDA, UVF and other paramilitary groups. This was hardly likely as the UVF wanted nothing to do with it and the two organizations were fast moving into a bloody feud.

In September 1975 Tyrie used the opportunity of an interview in a Dublin newspaper to berate Paisley and West over their rejection of Craig and the UDA's proposals for a voluntary coalition government under the old UUUC banner. He said he would blame Paisley and West for all future killings in Northern Ireland. Paisley turned on the UDA, describing it as an organization 'guilty of the most diabolical crimes'. The Big Man went on: 'They have murdered Protestants as well as Roman Catholics in the most sadistic and inhuman ways and have sought to intimidate decent people who seek to carry on their business in a proper manner.' The Official Unionists had a number of acrimonious meetings with the UDA after which West pulled his people completely away from the men in the dark glasses and forage caps.

The euphoria of the UWC victory was quickly wearing off. Hopes fostered by the UDA leadership that it could build on its role in the strike by moving closer to the political leadership of unionism proved ill-founded. The mainstream did not want anything to do with the UDA and manoeuvred them out. And a reluctant UDA leadership was about to be dragged back into the sectarian conflict.

The IRA reacted to the success of the UWC strike by attacking civilian targets in England. The onslaught in Northern Ireland from 1971 to 1973 had made no real political impact in Britain, other than the revulsion caused by the deaths and injuries. And, worse, now in the middle of 1974 it was the loyalists who were crowing after their victory. The republicans' reasoning was as it had been since the first Fenian bombs in Manchester a century earlier, and again at the start of the Second World War when it set off bombs in London and Coventry – to 'bring the war to the enemy'.

The first fatal explosion on the mainland came in July 1974, when a 48-year-old librarian, Dorothy Household, was killed by a bomb that exploded in the basement museum of the Tower of London where she worked. Bombs placed at two public houses frequented by off-duty soldiers in Guildford killed five people and injured dozens of others. On 11 November the IRA responded to the Dublin and Monaghan bombs: twenty-one people were killed by bombs left in hold-alls in two crowded Birmingham pubs. After a year in which the sectarian killing had wound down, the war in Ulster was back on.

Two days before the Birmingham bombs the IRA attacked Jim Anderson's shop on the Crumlin Road and shot him several times. Billy Hull was shot in the same attack. Both survived. It was a highly provocative act as it was well known that neither was seriously involved in the 'military' side of the UDA. They were easy targets. Though the Dublin-based IRA leadership was in talks with the British government and considering calling a ceasefire, during the negotiations the IRA's Northern Command was simultaneously upping the ante, stirring up strife in Northern Ireland and launching bomb attacks in Britain.

The UDA's two-year campaign of sectarian assassination from 1971 to 1973 had petered out with the approach of the UWC strike. After Tyrie took control there was a significant decline in the number of UDA murders – there were only seven between June and October 1974. The South Belfast brigade had carried out a particularly brutal murder, in September 1974, of a young West Belfast man, Gerard Martin McWilliams, who had returned to the city after living for five years in London. He was a slight thin figure who was unaware of the risk he was taking in moving into a flat in the lower Lisburn Road area. His flamboyant hippy clothes drew the attention of the local UDA. They attacked him as he was walking back towards his house, dragged him into an alleyway and spent more than twenty minutes beating and stabbing him to death, cutting his throat and finally smashing his head with a concrete post. McWilliams had been in the Club Bar, a Catholic-owned pub close to Queen's University that was popular with students and the city's bohemian set. Bars in the city had become such frequent targets for attack that almost all now had security staff at the door. In many cases mesh cages with electrically controlled doors were being built around pub entrances to allow staff some control over who came in.

The pace of the UDA assassinations quickened in response to the IRA bloody bombing campaign in England. There were thirteen UDA killings in November and December. There was symmetry in the sectarian tit-for-tat murders in North and West Belfast. It was among the truly awful periods in the Troubles, when the daily drip-drip of murders became almost an accepted fact of life. Two months after killing McWilliams the UDA from Sandy Row shot dead Ivan Clayton, the popular 56-year-old doorman in the Club bar; the IRA had shot dead a Protestant doorman a few days earlier. On 22 November the UDA shot dead a young Catholic filling-station attendant, Geraldine Macklin, in West Belfast. So the following evening a young IRA man from Ardoyne walked into a Protestant-owned filling station on the Crumlin Road, ordered seventeen-year-old Heather Thompson and her 24-year-old workmate John McClean to kneel on the floor and then shot them both through the back of the head. Ardoyne and the Shankill were to exchange many other such acts of brutal retaliation as the Troubles wore on.

Catholics who worked in the evenings in the service and entertainment industries were very vulnerable. Michael Hanratty was shot dead at the doorway of the Hole in the Wall, a Catholic drinking club in Ardoyne, the day after the Birmingham bombings. The following night Mary Shephard, a Catholic woman working for the often targeted Arkle Taxi firm on Clifton Street, was shot dead in its offices. A Protestant customer, William Hutton, was also killed. Seven people died in sectarian killings in Belfast in the two days after the IRA bombed Birmingham.

UDA murders outside Belfast and East Antrim were rare at this time due to the fact that the organization had not taken in rural Protestant society – possibly a testament to the fact that it had a rakish and murderous reputation that the deeply conservative and mainly God-fearing country folk found hard to deal with. Another UDA killing outside Belfast in 1974 was in Derry in November when a 21-year-old Catholic, William Elliott, was shot dead in the Waterside district by gunmen in a passing car.

In Larne UDA members earned themselves a reputation for being particularly bloody and mindless. In February 1975 they kidnapped and shot dead Collette Brown, a 31-year-old Catholic single mother of four young children. Mrs Brown, who was separated from her Protestant husband, could not have been described as a republican by any stretch of the imagination. She was the sister of Jim Kelly, the first victim claimed in the name of the UFF in May 1973. They had grown up in Larne and were both part-time members of the Ulster Defence Regiment, the mainly Protestant replacement force for the old 'B' Specials.

The East Antrim UDA's campaign against Catholics was almost genocidal. Of the total estimated 80,000 people who were evicted from their homes during the Troubles, the single largest group were Catholics forced out of East Antrim, mostly by the UDA. One of its victims in 1975 was a retired Royal Navy man, shot at his home in Greenisland because he was a Catholic. The Catholic parishes of Whiteabbey (which included Rathcoole) and Monkstown (including Greenisland and Carrickfergus) were severely harassed and their numbers depleted due to the nightly terror of the UDA. Church records suggest that during the 1950s and 1960s more than 20,000 Catholics had moved into the parishes, seeking better housing and escape from the slums of the city just like most of their Protestant neighbours. However, by the end of the 1970s this Catholic outflow from the city had been entirely reversed. The UDA regularly set off crude bombs, or tried to burn Catholic churches and schools, in the South Antrim area.

Rathcoole's new Catholic secondary school, Star of the Sea, had to close as it was unsafe for its pupils to attend.

Probably the most famous of the Catholics intimidated out of East Antrim was the future IRA hunger striker Bobby Sands, who spent his childhood in Rathcoole until the family was forced out by the UDA. A Catholic neighbour recalled how her family had decided to leave a few days after the Sands when attackers in combat jackets had stoned their house and broken its windows. The woman, who had three children, went to the local UDA club and asked for reassurances that they would not be subjected to violence as her husband was of a nervous disposition. A senior UDA man called at the house a few hours later and assured her their home would not be touched. But, in darkness, about two hours later, a group of UDA men gathered outside the house and began stoning it again. The family realized it was time to go when the gang actually lifted a cooker, looted from another Catholic home, and dumped it into the front room. They packed up during the night and fled to safety, but much reduced circumstances, in a rented terraced house in the Catholic Newingtown area.

The UDA caused untold agony for innocent Catholic families like these. The ostensible reason for the pogrom was that Protestants forced out of Catholic areas of Belfast needed houses in an ethnically cleansed East Antrim. The average UDA man never stopped to consider that the effect of this ethnic cleansing was to make many ordinary Catholics turn to the IRA for 'protection'. Up to then Catholics in East Antrim and the previously religiously mixed parts of Belfast barely knew anything about the IRA, much less supported it. However, many young people forced from their homes and made to live in poorer circumstances in Catholic enclaves – people such as Bobby Sands – did find out about the IRA and helped boost its ranks.

The East Antrim and North Belfast UDA rounded 1975 off with the murders of four more Catholics and a Protestant man who was shot dead because he happened to be walking near the small Catholic enclave of Bawnmore.

The campaign against the Catholics in East Antrim reached its nadir in July 1976 when two gunmen entered the home of Mervyn and Rosaleen McDonald, a young Catholic couple living at Longlands near Rathcoole, and gunned them down in the presence of their two infant children. Neighbours said the gunmen had walked casually from the scene after the killings, while the eighteen-month-old little boy screamed in his playpen, looking at his murdered mother.

At the start of 1975 the South Belfast UDA carried out two sectarian attacks which resulted in the deaths of three Catholic teenagers. On 29 January a UDA gunman walked the short distance from Sandy Row to Great Victoria Street where a Catholic teenager just out of school and in his first job was working on a building site repairing bomb damage. The gunman singled out seventeen-year-old Robert McCullough and shot him twice in the head. On 9 February a Sandy Row UDA man entered the local Catholic church, St Bride's, during Sunday evening service and opened fire, killing two students, Gerard Kiely and Kevin Ballentine, both eighteen. The church, which served the mainly middle-class Malone area, was targeted on several occasions; it was a handy touch for loyalist vandals from the Lisburn Road and Sandy Row.

However, throughout 1975 and into the start of 1976 the focus of much of the media attention was County Armagh where the UVF and the IRA were involved in grotesque blood-letting. After a series of UVF assassinations including bomb and gun attacks on Catholic pubs the IRA upped the ante in September, shooting dead four men in the Tullyvallen Orange Hall – one aged eighty. The UVF struck back in similar style the following January, killing five members of the Reavey and O'Dowd families at the Reaveys' home in South Armagh. The families had no republican connections and were strong SDLP supporters. Two days later more than twenty members of the South Armagh IRA held up a minibus carrying Protestant mill workers from the village of Bessbrook, lined the ten men up against a ditch and shot them dead.

The IRA's reasoning was that the way to stop the loyalists was to out-murder them. The fact that the UVF assassination campaign in Armagh came to an end shortly after the Kingsmill Massacre, as it became known, was used as proof of its worth by hard-line

IRA figures. In fact, the UVF in Armagh stopped killing because the RUC's reorganized and highly motivated Murder Squad rounded its members up within the space of a few weeks and brought charges against most of them. None of the IRA men who slunk back into their border fastness was ever charged with Kingsmill.

The actions of the IRA in South Armagh inspired their Belfast counterparts to adopt the same reasoning – that the way to stop the UDA killing Catholics was to kill them and Protestant civilians. Northern Ireland may have hoped it had seen the worst of the slaughter in 1972, but the IRA and UDA turned 1976 into the second worst year of the Troubles, with the concentration of victims in the mean streets of North Belfast. The tit-for-tat killing had actually been sparked off the previous May when the UDA killed a nineteen-year-old Catholic in North Queen Street. The IRA struck back, shooting dead a man having a drink in the UDA club near the Ardoyne peace line. The following month the local UDA shot dead a Catholic mother of eight as she hung Christmas decorations in her front room in Mountainview Parade. Weeks later, on the evening of 15 January 1976 a UDA gang, which had been drinking throughout the day, burst into the home of a Catholic butcher at Wolfhill Road in Ligoniel demanding the takings from the family's business. The cash did not satisfy the Shankill Road men who then opened fire, killing Mary Veronica Sloan, her nineteen-year-old-daughter, Mary, and Doris McGrath, a middle-aged Protestant neighbour who happened to be in the house for a chat. Mrs Sloan's son was shot in the head but miraculously survived.

On 5 June the UDA shot dead a Sinn Féin member, Colm Mulgrew, at his house on the Limestone Road. A few hours later the IRA blew up the Times Bar in the heart of Protestant York Street, killing two patrons. In retaliation the UDA shot dead a Catholic man standing outside the Crumlin Star social club in Ardoyne. On 17 June a young UDA gunman boarded a bus heading down Oldpark Road, taking people to work in the city centre. He knew that at previous stops the bus would have picked up Catholics from Ardoyne. The gunman went upstairs and shot dead 21-year-old Gerard Stitt and 48-year-old Patrick Meehan.

Two days later the IRA shot dead a teenage UDA member at his home in the Westland estate – a vulnerable Protestant enclave lodged between Catholic Ardoyne and the New Lodge Road areas. The UDA struck back the next night stabbing a young Ardoyne man to death. Later that evening the IRA shot dead a Protestant man who was watching television in his house in Alexander Park Avenue. Five days later the IRA shot dead 64-year-old Thomas Passmore and tried to kill his wife at their home. The respectable Passmore family never had any terrorist connections, but the reason for this murder was apparently that the Passmore's son, Tommy, was the Grand Master of the Orange Order. A young Catholic couple, Joe and Jeannette Dempsey, and their eighteen-month-old daughter were burned to death when young UDA men firebombed their house in the New Lodge area in August. In September and October two teenage Catholic girls, Pauline Doherty and Ann Magee, and another Catholic shop worker, Annie Brennan, were shot dead by the UDA. After the killings of the women, the IRA drove into Tigers Bay and shot dead a woman who was standing in the parlour of her house. As it happened, the fifty-year-old victim, Georgina Strain, was a Catholic married to a Protestant. The UDA kidnapped and murdered Cornelius McCrory, whose teenage brother Patrick had been one of the UDA's first victims in 1972.

One of the UDA's key figures in North Belfast was a cat burglar. He struck on the idea of breaking into homes late at night and, instead of robbing people, assassinating them as they slept. On 22 January 1976 two UDA men broke into a house on a quiet leafy street off the middle-class Antrim Road and shot dead Niall O'Neill, a 26-year-old off-licence manager. The murder was a well-planned operation. Using the tricks of his trade the killer had brought grease and applied it to the bolt on the kitchen door. O'Neill's father and two of his brothers heard nothing when the gunman, using a silenced pistol, shot Niall six times as he lay sleeping, and then slipped away silently into the night. The young man was found the following morning after one of his brothers, a priest, checked his room when he failed to appear for breakfast. The murder was carried out so professionally that it caused speculation that it was the work of an undercover army team. Indeed, a melodramatic account of the incident appeared in a British adult 'adventure' magazine claiming that O'Neill was a senior IRA figure and the murder had been carried out by the army's Special Air Services. It was not, according to UDA sources.

The team responsible was displaying an eerie new sophistication in UDA killing. One UDA figure, a man with a dark sense of humour, nicknamed the team the 'window cleaners' after they had used stolen window cleaner's ladders to gain entry to a house through a bedroom window, another cat burglar's trick. Three UDA men went on each of these late-night jobs, one to drive the car and one to provide back-up if the main assassin was confronted inside the house. The street was reconnoitred beforehand, with one member of the gang sent specifically to identify the telephone pole nearest to the house. Another carried a hatchet or machete to cut the telephone lines down. The distraught family would discover the victim in bed the next morning, then find that the phone did not work. They would go to neighbouring houses to call for help, only to realize that those phones were also dead because each telephone pole usually fed up to six or eight houses.

Ten days after Niall O'Neill's murder the gang struck again a short distance away, at the home of Joe McAlinden, a forty-year-old publican who lived with his wife and four children on the upper Cavehill Road. This time, the UDA men disturbed their victim, who got out of bed and turned on the light as the assassin tried to open the bedroom window. His wife saw the barrel of a gun and then witnessed her husband being shot.

The gang's third victim was Peter Johnston, a 28-year-old accountant, who was shot dead as he slept in his home at Cooldarragh Park, just around the corner from the McAlinden house. His body was found in bed the following day by relatives. Again the phone lines had been cut. A month later, two teenage UDA members were arrested and confessed to their part in this killing. The court heard that they were acting under the influence of an older man who was not before the court – the cat burglar turned 'window cleaner' assassin.

The next victims of the gang, on the night of 6 October, were a 68-year-old widow, Catherine O'Connor, and her son-in-law Frank Nolan. These assassinations did not go as smoothly as the others. Mrs O'Connor was apparently awoken by the UDA men and met them on the landing, where one of them tried to cut her throat but failed and resorted to stabbing her in a frenzied attack – thirty-eight times in all. Her son-in-law and daughter ran from their bedroom and he was shot three times.

The 'window cleaners' operated in a tight neighbourhood of suburban houses where Catholics still lived happily alongside Protestants. Mrs O'Connor's house was in Victoria Gardens, just around the corner from the O'Neills' in Windermere Gardens and a few hundred yards from the Johnston and McAlinden homes. The late-night and early-morning killings – and another less subtle but equally effective version sometimes called the 'six o'clock knock,' in which a sledgehammer was used to batter down a door so the gunmen could run upstairs and shoot their victims still half asleep – had a major psychological impact on Catholics living in North and West Belfast. As it seemed almost anyone could be a target many began suffering nightmares and badly disturbed sleep. Only after the Troubles ended did people begin talking about what turned out to be a widespread phenomenon.

At this time there were also UDA killings outside Belfast. In January 1976 the UDA's Londonderry brigade killed three Catholics, one a man shot dead at the front door of his house in Greysteel, a village in a small rural Catholic enclave situated amid the strongly loyalist countryside between the Waterside of Derry and Limavady and Coleraine to the east. Seventeen years later the UDA would turn its attention to Greysteel again in one of the nastiest episodes of the Troubles.

As well as the renewed sectarian blood-letting through 1975 and 1976 bad blood between the UDA and UVF erupted into feuding. The feud had its origins in an incident during the UWC strike when two UDA men on patrol in Tigers Bay came across UVF men drinking in a bar that was supposed to be closed, as others were in the area. A fight ensued and Joe Shaw, a UVF man, was killed with a shotgun blast. The two organizations issued joint statements saying the killing was a result of a 'tragic' misunder-standing. But the UVF, which had a reputation for holding grudges for a long time, set up an investigation and identified the two UDA men responsible as Stephen Goatley and John Fulton.

Serious tension already existed between the two organizations. The UVF rank and file was resentful of the fact that the UDA had claimed responsibility for the Dublin and Monaghan bomb-ings. By and large the two groups stayed separate, drinking in their own pubs and clubs, but there were neutral venues where they occasionally rubbed up against each other and where fights broke out. On 21 February 1975 Robert Thompson, an East Belfast UDA man who had just been released from prison after serving a three-year sentence for arms possession, was unfortunate enough to become involved in a drunken row with UVF men, who beat and stabbed him to death. Antagonism grew between the two organizations. In March a row broke out in a North Belfast pub frequented by both the UDA and the UVF and Goatley and Fulton were involved in the fracas. A short time later two UVF gunmen walked into a bar and shot both men dead, precipitat-ing the bloody feud.

On 7 April the UVF kidnapped Hugh McVeigh, a 38-year-old furniture salesman on the Shankill Road who was a UDA colonel (and one of the delegation sent to Libya), and his assistant David Douglas, also a young UDA man. At first the UDA appeared unsure of what had happened to its two members. The IRA was blamed and a statement was issued in the name of the UFF saying it would kidnap twenty Catholics if they were not returned. The Revd William Arlow, a Protestant churchman, intervened. He was already engaged in trying to build a peace process between the warring republican and loyalist factions and organized a famous secret peace conference with the IRA at Feakle, in County Clare. Now he was trying to bring about peace between the UDA and the UVF.

McVeigh and Douglas had been grabbed by UVF men from the Shankill and taken out of Belfast to the British Legion Club in Carrickfergus, then controlled by the UVF. They were tied up and beaten. The local UVF men's job was to take the two along a lonely cliff path at the Gobbins in Islandmagee, to a picturesque spot overlooking the mouth of Belfast Lough, facing the Mull of Kintyre. There, in the dead of night, they were forced to dig their own grave before they were shot and quickly buried. For days the UDA mounted a search of Belfast streets and alleyways and of fields on the outskirts of the city. The two bodies were eventually discovered when a local UVF man, scared that he was about to meet the same fate, ran into the local RUC station. He made a full confession of his part in the McVeigh and Douglas murders and became Northern Ireland's first terrorist 'supergrass', sending almost the entire East Antrim UVF brigade to prison, several for life terms. Ironically, the UVF's murder of the two UDA men cost it what control it had in the area, and after the UVF's mass imprisonment the UDA consolidated its hold on East Antrim.

The feuding was at its worst in East Belfast where the UDA launched a series of gun and petrol-bomb attacks on the homes of more than twenty UVF men. Ken Gibson, spokesman for the UVF and a prominent figure in the UWC strike committee, was attacked and badly injured. The UVF struck back in kind, but also resolved to increase the stakes in a big way. It decided to blow up the UDA's headquarters on the Newtownards Road. A large bomb was assembled and placed in the boot of a hijacked car. However, because of the feuding, security had been stepped up in the east of the city by the police and the army and the car was stopped at a checkpoint before it could reach and obliterate the UDA's leadership.

The feud rumbled on for months. A UDA man was stabbed to death during another row with the UVF outside a pub in Tigers Bay in January 1976. The UVF also tried to attack the UDA's sometime spokesman, Sammy Smyth, at his home in North Belfast, but he managed to bar their entry and escaped with minor injuries. A couple of days later the UDA retaliated, attacking Alexander Frame, a UVF man from the Shore Road, and braining him with a concrete block. Another South Belfast UDA man, Dennis Berry, from Taughmonagh, was shot dead by the UVF as a result of a row on the night of 12 July. Another young UDA man, Charles

Moody, was shot dead by the Shankill UVF after a fierce row in a local drinking club. And in an outbreak of UVF–UDA fighting on the Shore Road in November, a fifty-year-old bystander, an ex-seaman enjoying a pint, was killed in crossfire.

The feud created an embarrassment for the UDA leadership which, in May and June 1976, was promoting the idea of a single Ulster army. This new group had, at its head, the eccentric figure of John McKeague, and its two other leading lights were UDA men, John Orchin and Jim Smith, but it failed to get off the ground. Tyrie's view was that if the Constitutional Convention collapsed then Ulster could be facing civil war and the UVF and the other loyalist splinter groups needed to be under one leadership. The UVF had different ideas and wouldn't even consider the initiative.

In 1977, amid growing loyalist anger at the British government's failure to reinstate local government, and with the IRA campaign still in full swing, Ian Paisley called for another strike. The United Unionist Action Council (UUAC) had been formed in 1976 after the Constitutional Convention's steering group of unionists fell apart. Now Paisley had decided it was time for the UUAC to take on the government with another strike. The UDA's most public and, from a unionist point of view, its only acceptable figure, Glen Barr, refused to support the strike.

The strike was scheduled for May. Paisley hoped it would again attract the support of the power workers and the general loyalist populace. On 3 May the UDA blocked roads and Paisley's people began picketing power stations. However, West's Official Unionists mounted counter-pickets to appeal to the electricity workers to stay in place. This time they listened to West's people and walked passed the UUAC pickets.

The new secretary of state, Roy Mason, was an entirely different character from the dithering Merlyn Rees, who had watched helplessly as the UWC brought Northern Ireland to a standstill. Mason, a tough former miner, issued clear orders for the RUC and army to clear the barricades. Under its confident new chief constable, Ken Newman, the RUC rose to the challenge. The police drove their new armoured Land Rovers straight through the barricades on the Newtownards and Shankill Roads, scattering the UDA men and their makeshift barricades.

After a week the strike descended into a violent shambles. The UDA in North Belfast shot dead a Protestant bus driver, Harry Bradshaw, as he picked up passengers on the Crumlin Road. The same day a UVF bomb exploded at a filling station, also on the Crumlin Road, killing an off-duty member of the Ulster Defence Regiment, who had driven into the station as the bomb went off. Two UDA men, William Hobbs and James McClurg, were killed while making petrol bombs in Rathcoole. Neighbours saw McClurg wandering up the street from the burning house, naked, with his skin smoking. The final indignity for Ian Paisley came at a rally in Ballymena, the heartland of his North Antrim constituency, when an RUC superintendent, Jack Hermon, later to become its chief constable, arrested him in front of his supporters and bundled him into the back of a Land Rover, which drove off leaving the loyalists leaderless and humiliated.

As the strike collapsed, Paisley turned on the UDA, accusing it of bringing the whole affair down by its violence. Tyrie was furious at having let Paisley lead him and his organization into a no-hope strike and being blamed for its failure. He decided never again to allow the loyalist blowhard to lead his organization into such a morass. The UDA would do its own political thinking from now on and have nothing more to do with Paisley or the Ulster Unionists.

5. Twin-track Approach: Politics and Terror

For the relatively few journalists who sought out the UDA on visits to Belfast in the late 1970s and early 1980s, the point of contact was the colourful Shankill Road man Sammy Duddy. With red hair and piercing eyes, Duddy balanced a background in extreme loyalist terrorism with a career as a semi-professional cabaret entertainer. He was a well-known and popular turn in loyalist clubs, where he performed a burlesque act in which he dressed up as a schoolboy or schoolgirl, or sometimes as a blonde sex-bomb, and told filthy jokes, using props that included dildos. Despite the occasional sneering jibes about his sexual preferences that his act attracted, it was not wise to confront Duddy with any slur on his masculinity. In his earlier days he had been a renowned street-fighter, and he had a formidable reputation in the UDA, having risen through the ranks largely due to his prowess as a terrorist.

Duddy was chosen as public relations officer by Andy Tyrie precisely because he was someone who was at ease in company and would not upset or frighten the press. He was approachable and rarely turned against journalists – the one exception being the New York-based reporter Jack Holland, who referred to him in an article as a 'transvestite', an accurate enough description of his drag act, but not a label a man could be expected to accept in the homophobic macho world of the UDA. Someone, and Duddy did not deny it was himself, let it be known that if he ever saw Holland again he would kill him.

Sammy Duddy became a fixture in the UDA's headquarters, which in the late 1970s moved across the Newtownards Road from a double-fronted building to distinctly less grand premises over a shop at the corner of Gawn Street. The move was necessary because the first HQ, formerly the home of an assurance company, was a sitting duck for attack. The UVF had attempted to blow it up in

1975, and it was almost impossible to defend against a concerted attack by even a relatively small armed force. The Gawn Street premises were set into a corner building and accessed through a series of electrically controlled steel-mesh gates at the front door and again at the bottom and top of the stairs. At the front of the first floor was the boardroom where the Inner Council met around a large oval wooden table. Off this room was Andy Tyrie's office, which led to a couple of rooms where the UDA's public relations and administrative departments were run by Duddy and the only woman who worked there regularly, Esther Dunne. Dunne, Duddy and Tyrie shared a sharp, typical Belfast sense of humour and were invariably engaged in running banter. The more serious-minded John McMichael, who became an increasingly common presence as he rose in prominence in the UDA, was sometimes left out of the badinage. Standing guard at the top of the stairs and making tea for visitors was the somewhat alarming figure of Bobby McKevitt, an inarticulate muscle-builder with tousled blond hair and a mad stare. He had suffered from poliomyelitis as a boy and as a result had wasted legs that overemphasized his massive, muscular torso.

When business was not being conducted – and things were often slack after the relentless early 1970s – there was often an air of indolence about Gawn Street. Tyrie tried to maintain discipline but bored commanders and staff often quit the offices for late breakfasts of heavy Ulster fries (bacon, sausage, egg, tomato with fried potato and soda bread) in some of the nearby cafés or pubs. Drinking was a serious problem – all-day sessions frequently took place, though Tyrie, McMichael and the permanent staff tended to avoid pubs. Work was usually finished by mid-afternoon when the Inner and Outer Council people left to spend the rest of the day in the social clubs where their local headquarters were situated.

Tyrie gave occasional interviews to visiting journalists, sometimes including other leading UDA men who would now and then give their point of view. The way things went in Gawn Street, there were many occasions when the approach to public relations was less than professional. Once when trying to impress a delegation of serious influential American journalists Tyrie found himself rebutting the argument that Catholics were out-breeding Protestants by pointing to one of his local commanders in the room who was the father of eight children. Raising his right forearm in a gesture known throughout the world, the man volunteered that he was 'keeping it up for Ulster'.

Increasingly, and with the help of some sympathetic loyalist intellectuals, Gawn Street began producing political and cultural tracts, on Ulster heritage. Documents outlining political ideas at variance with traditional conservative unionist thinking emerged. Pamphlets on independence and even power-sharing were issued under the auspices of the Ulster Political Research Group. Press statements were drawn up and sent out, and indignant letters were dispatched to the *Belfast Telegraph* and *Newsletter*.

The UDA produced two policy documents which were, at the time, taken seriously by political commentators and politicians outside Northern Ireland – 'Beyond the Religious Divide' and 'Common Sense'. 'Beyond the Religious Divide', published in 1979, was the Ulster Political Research Group's largest and most important report. It proposed negotiated independence for Northern Ireland with a new constitution and Bill of Rights. The UDA members involved in its production – mainly Barr, Tyrie, Tommy Lyttle and Harry Chicken – had help from a Californian lawyer and from local academics, including a young law lecturer from Queen's University and Vanguard activist, David Trimble. The report coincided with a period when the UDA was completely at odds with the constitutional unionist parties, as can be seen in these sentiments: 'Without the evolution of proper politics the people of Northern Ireland will continue to be manipulated by sectarian politicians who make no contribution to the social and economic well-being of the people or the country, but only continue to fan the flames of religious bigotry for self-gain and preservation.'

The UDA's political wing, later to develop into the Ulster Democratic Party, expressed its adherence to the 'Common Sense' document as a way forward for political change in Northern Ireland, and as a means of reducing violence. Subtitled: 'Northern Ireland – an agreed process', it proposed a written constitution as 'a foundation on which to build a new pluralist society'. This included a provision that the status of Northern Ireland could not be altered without the acceptance of a two-thirds majority in a referendum. In a foreword John McMichael, who would later become – simultaneously – the UDA's military and political leader, said it proposed a 'modern democratic political structure based on consensus government, proportional representation and shared responsibility'.

An important element of 'Common Sense' was a proposal for independence for Ulster, both as a response to the continuing violence, and as a means of emphasizing a sense of Ulster identity. Related to this, the UDA leadership – and most enthusiastically, John McMichael – supported Ian Adamson's ideas on the cultural and historical identity of Northern Irish Protestants. Adamson, a consultant gynaecologist at the Royal Victoria Hospital and later a Lord Mayor of Belfast, lived with his aged mother in the terraced house in Sandy Row where he was born. He was a remarkable figure who produced a series of books under his own imprint, Pretani Press, a body of work which includes titles such as: *The Identity of Ulster*, *Bangor: Light of the World*, *The Cruithin* and *The Ulster People*. Adamson emphasized the social and cultural integrity of Ulster, and held that a separate Ulster race existed in pre-Christian times from which the population of north-east Ireland is derived. The UDA's monthly magazine, produced from the late 1970s onwards, contained frequent articles and illustrations on the theme of Ulster nationalism, borrowing heavily from Adamson's work.

Tyrie's stated philosophy at this time was:

If there was no IRA there would be no UDA. We are here mainly to defend our country against attack. You cannot ignore the Catholic population. There must be some way in which we can work together. The problem is basically one of identity. Are we Irishmen, second-class Englishmen or first-class Ulstermen? No one really knows what we are. If the Catholics and Protestants had a common identity, say, Northern Ireland and be loyal to Northern Ireland we could work out our destiny from there. I am Northern Irish and certainly not a second-class

Englishman. Our country's biggest resource is its people. What other country in the world as small as we are could produce eleven presidents of the USA and a host of military men like Lord Alanbrooke, Montgomery, Alexander and so on? If the fighting stopped and we became a unit and had an identity of our own I think this is the only way we can be saved.

I want majority rule and if the majority of our election representatives wish to share power with the minority then that's OK. I think the loyalist politicians have learned a lot and if they formed a government they would make the changes the minority want. It would be wise of them to include some of them in government but only those loyal to the state of Northern Ireland. I would welcome power-sharing if the people we shared power with were loyal to Northern Ireland and not intent on destroying the state. I would like to see Catholics in government and realize that majority rule cannot be forced on them. But I say: give the loyalists a chance and they will make the changes they want, let some form of trust between them develop and let Northern Irishmen get on with the business of looking after Northern Irish affairs.

But other UDA figures had a different perspective. One said,

The UDA has stressed time and time again that it is not a political party. What we are doing is to act as a pressure group on various politicians to make sure that they do not take the wrong line on issues such as the ending of imprisonment without trial. We do not go on the big demonstrations any more. There is no need. The people know we are there. They know we are not bluffing. They know our strength.

The final break with mainstream unionism coincided with a period in which the UDA began to suffer heavily from increased arrests and weapons seizures by the RUC. From the mid-1970s internment was gradually phased out, and with Merlyn Rees's replacement by Roy Mason the security response to all Northern Ireland's terrorist groups was stepped up. The RUC was rebuilt and resources poured into its extremely active Special Branch and CID sections which went after the UDA, UVF and IRA with vigour.

Simultaneously, the UDA's operations in Scotland and England were also taking serious hits. Among the Scottish working-class Protestant districts there was strong sympathy for the loyalist cause and from early in the Troubles money and weapons came from Scotland. A Scottish UDA brigade was formed under the leadership of an Edinburgh bouncer, Roddy MacDonald. The self-styled Scottish UDA supremo was a common criminal, prone to making wild threats to his own men, and a dangerous liability. Within a relatively short period, the Scottish UDA was hopelessly infiltrated by the police.

Testimony given in a murder trial in June 1979 revealed MacDonald's style of management. He had warned there would be 'blood running off the walls' if Dumfries UDA did not come up with guns for their comrades in Ulster. At the time he was seeking safe addresses to which guns could be sent from Canada and he also made a deal with a young man who worked in a gun shop. The court heard that the Scottish UDA bought two boxes of guns from Ross Sutherland, an eighteen-year-old shop assistant for an Edinburgh gun dealer. Sutherland had been approached about guns by MacDonald, who worked at a pub in Edinburgh's West End. He stole a .22 pistol, which he sold to MacDonald. Then he hatched a plot to kill his employer. He walked into the shop with a handgun and shot him through the head. Foolishly he handed over the twelve rifles to MacDonald and his friends on a promise of later payment. Sutherland told his trial that the UDA men double-crossed him and he was never paid the £2,000 he was promised for the guns. He received a life sentence for murder. Nine UDA men were subsequently caught, tried, convicted and given heavy sentences by Glasgow High Court. MacDonald got eight years in June 1978, with the judge telling him: 'You, MacDonald, are obviously the ringleader and you have a deplorable criminal record. But for all your pomposity and bombast you are nothing other than a common criminal.'

The majority of the active UDA supporters were rounded up in early 1979 – forty of them in four days – and held under the Prevention of Terrorism Act. In all a total of ninety men and women – almost the entire Scottish UDA – were arrested, mainly in the loyalist strongholds of Paisley and Dumfries. Four of those detained were visitors from Rathcoole, outside Belfast. The Strathclyde Special Branch also arrested six Scots in Lancashire.

In January 1979 twenty-nine UDA men were sentenced. A short while afterwards the RUC raided the UDA headquarters on the Shankill just as a shipment of ten modern assault rifles and 1,000 rounds of ammunition arrived from Britain via Scotland. It was assumed that the arms deal was infiltrated in Scotland. However, eighteen months later the UDA on the Shankill shot dead one of its very well-known and longest-serving members, Artie Bettice, claiming he had supplied the information. At the time of his assassination Bettice was out on bail on a firearms charge with Jim Craig.

Six UDA men were given exceptionally heavy sentences in Perth High Court in July 1979, one receiving a sixteen-year sentence for conspiracy to support a terrorist organization by acquiring and making arms for use in terrorist crimes. By Northern Ireland standards, the offences – involving an amateurish attempt to manufacture bullets – were quite minor and the sentences exceptionally harsh. But the Scottish court took exception to the conduct of terrorism on Scottish soil. None of the Scottish prisoners benefited from the 50 per cent remission to which terrorist prisoners in Northern Ireland were entitled under the prison regime terms introduced in 1976 after the British government withdrew 'political status' for republicans and loyalists held in the Maze. The 50 per cent remission was an attempt to induce paramilitary prisoners to conform. If they didn't, they could lose their remission.

In an interesting postscript to the clearing-up of the UDA in Scotland, in 1980 the Irish National Caucus in Washington asked the FBI to investigate links between the UDA and the Ku Klux Klan. In 1978 the Klan leader, William Wilkinson, had been thrown out of Britain. He claimed to have met members of the UDA in Liverpool and Glasgow. Wilkinson almost certainly did meet some of the right-wing fanatics who had taken to supporting the UDA and who had set up an arms-smuggling route through Southampton for guns bought by supporters in Canada. Police investigations into the activities of the UDA in London and Liverpool, which has a sizeable Protestant population and a number of Orange Lodges, led them to three men who had been running the arms route of the UDA. Of the three, one – John Gadd – was found to have connections with the National Front. Another was a member of the right-wing Monday Club.

Following on from these links there were growing suspicions that the UDA was connected to right-wing and fascist groups. The UDA did meet fascists, including Dutch Nazis, but always with the purpose of obtaining either money or guns. Tyrie and the rest of the UDA leadership were implacably opposed to the political standpoint of the fascists. On one occasion when the National Front sent a delegation to Belfast, Tyrie detailed Louis Scott, a Shankill Road UDA man of mixed-race parentage to meet them.

The loyalist prisoner population had grown substantially with over 200 UDA men in the Maze by the end of the 1970s, a large proportion of them serving life terms for murder. Initially, UDA men had been content to serve their time under the command of the jailed UVF leader Gusty Spence, but as the antagonisms between the two organizations on the outside grew, the UDA prisoners broke away from Spence's command and the Shankill UDA figure Jim Craig became the UDA commander in the prison. Craig who had been one of the first UDA men to be interned, was a brutal boss, who imposed discipline through violence, sometimes with a lump hammer he kept for the purpose. The imposition of discipline went so far as to include murder. On St Stephen's Day 1973 George Hyde, a nineteen-year-old from Portadown, was killed in the UDA compound. He had been accused by the UDA of revealing information to the prison authorities about a planned breakout. He suffered extensive injuries inflicted, it is believed, by a heavy table smashed down on to his skull while he was held on the floor.

Unlike the republicans, who showed a remarkable determination and often incredible ability to escape, loyalists made only infrequent attempts to break out of jail. A tunnel was discovered from one of the UDA compounds in 1974 but UDA men were unsuccessful in escaping from Long Kesh or other high-security prisons in Northern Ireland. There was only one exception: Sammy Tweed, an East Belfast UDA man who absconded when his friends staged a fracas in Belfast Magistrates' Court and Tweed got out in the confusion. He disappeared and remained at large throughout the Troubles. He became a hero in East Belfast where graffiti about 'Super Tweed' quickly appeared. One UDA prisoner, Benny Redfern, from County Antrim died in a desperate attempt to get out of the Maze Prison in August 1984. He hid in a rubbish lorry and was crushed by its compactor; his body was discovered when it tumbled out on to the municipal dump in Lisburn.

Both police and army warned that the compound system in the Maze Prison (previously known as Long Kesh), where the paramilitary groups were able to maintain paramilitary structures, was a university for terrorism. If people were to be put in prison they should be under the control of the prison, not their own commanding officers. In March 1976 Northern Ireland Secretary Roy Mason, announced that 'political' or 'special' category status for prisoners was to end and introduced a policy of 'criminalization' of terrorists – their treatment as common criminals. The UDA prisoners resisted the attempts to move them into the new cellular 'H'-shaped blocks of the Maze, which would break down their command structure and even integrate their men with republicans. They fought prison officers as they were moved to new cells. Prison warders' homes were attacked and prison officers who lived in Protestant areas had their lives threatened. In May rioting, arson and hijacking broke out across Belfast.

The decision to remove the prisoners' political status provoked an ultimately more far-reaching reaction from the IRA. Its inmates smeared their cells with excrement and refused to wear prison clothes. An anti-H-blocks conference was held in Dungannon in 1976, and was attended by a broad coalition of Sinn Féin, the Irish Republican Socialist Party (the political wing of the Irish National Liberation Army, INLA), former civil rights people, and various Catholic political and community leaders. The SDLP sent an observer but declined to participate when it saw that the committee elected to move the campaign forward was heavily biased towards the republicans. A support and coordination group called the Relatives Action Committee was set up. The campaign was spearheaded for Sinn Féin by the veteran republican Maire Drumm.

Drumm was a hate figure for loyalists. She had been jailed for making seditious speeches in both Northern Ireland and the Republic. She had boasted that British soldiers would be sent home from Northern Ireland 'in their coffins' and was widely despised by loyalists and many Protestants. Drumm had correctly adduced that the prisoners' protest would become an issue of major importance and had driven the ideas behind the strategy which would lead the republican movement for nearly the next twenty years.

By chance Drumm had to receive hospital treatment for cataracts and was accepted as an in-patient at the Mater Hospital on the Crumlin Road in October 1976. On 28 October two gunmen, wearing white laboratory coats, walked into the hospital ward where she was lying in bed and shot her dead. She was the most prominent member of the Provisional republican movement to be killed.

Almost immediately, Jim Craig, recently released from the Maze, claimed responsibility for the assassination. His close associate Tommy 'Tucker' Lyttle told journalists the UDA had killed Drumm and, in the absence of any other admission, the Shankill UDA's claim was accepted at face value. In fact, and even though two UDA men were later charged in relation to the killing on the word of a UDA supergrass, the organization had nothing to do with it. The UVF killed Drumm. Letting the UDA take responsibility diverted attention away from its hit team and that suited the UVF. It was, at the time, actually encouraging this practice, issuing claims in the name of the UFF for its bomb and gun attacks, magnifying the UDA's profile as a terrorist organization while shifting suspicion away from its own people. It was the same trick that White and Payne had pulled with the invention of the UFF. This new arrangement where the UVF passed on blame for its work served to bolster the reputations of men such as Craig and Lyttle and two or three other UDA bosses whose military organization was actually shambolic.

Drunken sectarian assassinations of easy Catholic targets had no effect on the IRA, and the RUC was rounding up more and more UDA members and seizing more and more weapons. An example of how stupid parts of the organization had become emerged in a court case in the late 1970s. The RUC had found an arms cache in Rathcoole. A gun and ammunition were wrapped in a pair of jeans, in the back pocket of which the RUC found a letter containing a prize crossword cut out of the *Belfast Telegraph*. The UDA man's name and address were on the piece of paper.

Apart from Catholics living in the brutal streets of North Belfast, the border Protestants were probably the worst affected section of the civilian population during the Troubles. From the autumn of 1980 onwards the IRA unleashed a vicious attack against what it termed 'Crown Forces' in the border area running from South Armagh to West Fermanagh and northwards into South Derry. The fact that the 'Crown Forces' were all members of the rural Protestant community did not escape the notice of their co-religionists in Belfast. There were only about 100,000 Protestants living in these rural areas and by 1983 more than 150 men and women had been shot dead or blown up – very often at their homes and in front of their families. It was, by most definitions of terrorist activity, a genocidal campaign designed to drive Protestants out of the mainly Catholic rural areas to the south and west of the six counties of Northern Ireland.

It was a phenomenon largely ignored in the media and was almost completely written out of history by nationalist and pro-republican revisionists, but the suffering endured by the border Protestants had a tremendous effect in stimulating the vicious sectarian violence against Catholics unfortunate enough to live in predominantly Protestant areas in Belfast and the northern and eastern counties. The IRA's genocidal war of attrition against the border Protestants had a deep impact in the psyche of loyalist paramilitaries, particularly in the UDA. Every time a Protestant part-time member of the UDR or RUC was shot dead while feeding his stock or mowing hay in Fermanagh, Tyrone, Armagh or South Derry, the UDA had a motive for killing innocent Catholics in Belfast – revenge.

A particular feature of the IRA killings which gave support to the belief that they were engaged in a genocidal plan to force Protestants out of the rural areas to the west and south was that very many of their victims were 'only sons', men who were the sole inheritors of farms in areas where republicans sought to reclaim control. Unionist politicians such as Ken Maginnis and Harold McCusker, who represented the areas affected, could produce long lists of men who fitted the 'only son' category – men who were assassinated, leaving wives and young families with no hope of managing the family farm and left with only the option of selling up and moving out. The stoic Protestant farming community in many of these cases rallied together to help the widows and children through their ordeal but often the lands had to be sold. Where sales were caused by murders and enforced departures, the Protestant farmers tried to ensure that the land did not fall into the hands of unfriendly Catholics seeking to benefit from the killings.

The plight of the border Protestants was largely ignored in Westminster as well as at Stormont. It was brought to the attention of Secretary of State Jim Prior by a group of Protestant clergy and families of victims who went to see him at Stormont in May 1984. They had been spurred by the particularly callous murder two weeks earlier of Ivan Hillen, a 46-year-old part-timer in the UDR, who farmed his small holding and some rented fields near Aughnacloy, County Tyrone. Hillen lived with his wife and young son in a bungalow in the modest farm he had built up through his own toil and savings and was the archetype of the hard-working, unassuming Protestant who believed in law and order. He had joined the part-time security forces to stop what he saw as the assault on his and his fellow countrymen's liberty by the IRA – and to make a few extra pounds to pay the bills. Two members of the East Tyrone IRA crossed the nearby border to his piggery during the night and shot him dead as he went to feed his stock. *An Phoblacht* (*Republican News*), the republican weekly newspaper, edited and printed openly and legally in Dublin, marked his murder with the gloating headline 'Crown Forces Hit in IRA Ambushes' and said the IRA was engaged in an 'obvious and realistic approach to fighting to remove the occupier'. The term 'occupier' is telling, identifying Protestants such as Ivan Hillen with the Protestant 'planters' or 'occupiers' who had arrived in north-east Ireland in the seventeenth century and against whom republicans in the late twentieth century still harboured atavistic hatred.

The border Protestants could rely only on their own fortitude to see them through the IRA's remorseless campaign. With the exception of some in the Mid-Ulster area of South Derry and East Tyrone and some around Armagh city, almost all were simply too law-abiding to join in a loyalist terrorist campaign. The rural Protestants with their God-fearing ways were highly distrustful of the urban working-class Prods who made up the bulk of the UDA and whom they regarded as little more than corner boys. Their attempts at self-defence were pitiful and they continued to suffer heavy casualties into the mid-1980s, when the RUC Special Branch was finally able to make inroads into the East Tyrone, South Derry and Fermanagh IRA structures. The public in the Republic also eventually became aware of the border genocide and Taoiseach Garret FitzGerald denounced the barbarity of the IRA campaign.

The IRA was also stepping up its actions against indigenous, mainly Protestant, police and soldiers because it was becoming much harder to take on the British army. By the late 1970s and early 1980s, as the army became more adept at protecting its troops in urban warfare environments, the percentage of Protestant members of the security forces being killed was rising significantly. Of the forty-three victims of IRA attacks in 1980, twenty-seven were Protestants. In 1981 the IRA killed forty-four Protestants out of a total of sixty killings – 73 per cent of its victims. The percentage was even higher in 1982 when thirty-seven of the IRA's forty-three victims were Protestants. That year twelve were killed in County Tyrone and another twelve in South Armagh.

After the blood-letting of 1975–6 the UDA turned off its assassination campaign in Belfast. Only three Catholics were killed in 1977 and two in 1978. Remarkably Tyrie and McMichael were able to restrain the UDA during 1978 even when the IRA carried out a number of vicious murders, culminating in the blast incendiary bomb attack on the La Mon Hotel in East Belfast which killed twelve people attending a Collie Club dinner. It was designed to create instability and provoke a loyalist reaction but the UDA leadership held firm and called on the security forces to deal with the IRA.

However, by 1979 UDA military activity began to rise again. Some of its victims and intended victims were republicans who had been identified from security force intelligence documents leaked to the UDA. McMichael had ordered these documents to be collated into files of assassination targets by his new more professional breed of UDA assassins. The teams of young men even had a new name, the Ulster Defence Force (UDF), never used publicly to claim attacks but used internally to differentiate the teams of the UDA's political, social and cultural arm from those of the Ulster Freedom Fighters.

The newly reorganized commando units carried out four assassinations in 1979, three of which were specifically targeted against republicans. There were still, however, the old-fashioned straightforward sectarian murders. Two Catholics were shot dead outside a pub in the Short Strand in November and a twenty-year-old Catholic man was pummelled to death with cement blocks in January 1980.

At the end of 1979 McMichael turned his attention to the members of the Relatives Action Committee and the anti-H-blocks republicans, who he correctly adduced were being used as a front to promote the political wing of the IRA. He drew up a list of public figures on the committee for assassination; it was called the UDA's 'shopping list'.

The first victim was John Turnly, who came from a family of landed gentry in the Glens of Antrim. He was a member of the miniature Irish Independence Party and had joined the H-blocks committee. A UDA team from Larne shot him dead at his home on 4 June 1980. It was a relatively easy assassination as Turnly had little protection and had not suspected he would be a target.

Three weeks later McMichael's own hand-picked team arrived at the house of Jim and Miriam Daly in the heart of republican West Belfast. Miriam Daly was the representative of the Irish National Liberation Army (INLA) prisoners on the H-blocks committee. She was bundled into the living room and tied up while the team waited for her husband, a lecturer, whom they also intended to kill. They waited for almost three hours and then shot dead Mrs Daly before leaving West Belfast unseen in the evening traffic. In August the Larne UDA killed another INLA man, Rodney McCormick.

Then, on 15 October, McMichael's crews struck again, this time killing Ronnie Bunting, the INLA's founding figure and its Belfast commanding officer. Bunting was the son of Major Ronald Bunting, an extreme loyalist and occasional follower of Ian Paisley. He had sent his son to the prestigious Campbell College in East Belfast but later, at Queen's University, Ronnie junior rebelled against his father, rejected his unionist background, and joined a group of left-wing republicans. He gravitated towards the Irish Republican Socialist Party (IRSP) when it was formed in 1975 and became a leading figure in its military wing, the INLA, when it set itself up in Belfast. Bunting was more akin to a German or French left-wing terrorist than a traditional Irish paramilitary. He lived with his wife, Suzanne, and their two young children in Downfine Gardens in the Turf Lodge area. Shortly after five o'clock in the morning two gunmen sledgehammered down their front door and ran upstairs, where Bunting had just managed to get out of bed and make it to the landing. He was shot several times as was Suzanne. Downstairs in the living room the gunmen found Noel Lyttle, a 45-year-old IRSP and INLA man from Dublin who had been sleeping on the sofa, and shot him dead as well. There were immediate claims that the gunmen were either British soldiers or loyalists working in collusion with the army or RUC. In fact, McMichael's team, though using army intelligence documents, were operating in secret under his direct command.

On 14 January 1981 the McMichael team met again at a room over his public house in Lisburn where he had a carefully drawn map showing the network of small country roads leading to a run-down cottage near the shores of Lough Neagh outside Coalisland, County Tyrone. The road led to the home of Bernadette McAliskey, who as Bernadette Devlin had been one of the most famous radical Catholic politicians to have emerged in the North. Famous for her fiery and eloquent oratory, she was a hate figure for loyalists. After her career in politics had faltered in the early 1970s, she had largely disappeared from public view but had become highly active in the H-blocks movement. On 16 January, at around 6 a.m., two cars arrived at the roadside near her home and three men made their way on foot to the door of the cottage, two armed with guns, the other with a sledgehammer. They burst in and fired some eighteen shots into McAliskey and her husband, while the couple's three small children screamed in an adjoining bedroom.

As the gunmen ran out of the cottage they were surrounded by soldiers from the Parachute Regiment who had been hiding in rushes by the Lough Shore. The UDA men, led by one of McMichael's lieutenants, Ray Smallwoods, threw down their weapons and lay on the ground while the soldiers called on their radio for a medi-vac helicopter for the injured husband and wife. The swift evacuation to hospital saved the couple's lives. The army later stated in evidence that its men had been on a reconnaissance mission – they had been spying on the McAliskeys' house to see who was visiting the H-blocks spokeswoman.

The arrest of McMichael's team brought an end to his eradication of the figures on his 'shopping list', which was leaked to journalists by jealous UDA figures, including Tommy Lyttle. The next candidate for assassination was Michael Farrell, who along with Mrs McAliskey had been prominent during the civil rights agitation. He later moved south to Dublin.

In response to the UDA 'shopping list' assassinations, the IRA struck back, killing the 86-year-old former Stormont speaker, Sir Norman Stronge, and his son James at their home, Tynan Abbey, in South Armagh. The attack in January 1981 sent shockwaves through the rural Protestant community. It was carried out by an IRA commando of about twenty-four heavily armed men who confronted and fired several hundred bullets at an RUC car which arrived on the scene as they fled. Fortunately for the two officers the vehicle was bullet-proofed and they survived.

In a statement the IRA said it was an 'attack on the symbols of hated Unionism'. It continued: 'Our operations against these targets have been based on their involvement in the Crown Forces. But our decision to make reprisals for the activities of Loyalist paramilitaries is being taken on a political basis and the responsibility for reprisals rests full square on their shoulders.' It was a barely feasible attempt to justify the murder of an 86-year-old retired politician and farmer.

The IRA had clearly decided that, as it had believed the mass murder of ten Protestant workmen at Whitecross in South Armagh had stopped loyalist assassinations of Catholics in 1976, so the murders of such high-profile Protestants as the Stronges would convince the loyalists of the error of their ways. It was another instance of the 'you hit us big and we'll hit you bigger' way of reckoning in the Northern Ireland conflict.

The INLA retaliated for the murder of Ronnie Bunting and Miriam Daly by shooting a well-known UDA man, Sammy Millar, at his home in the lower Shankill. He survived but was paralysed. Millar was a popular local figure and not on the military side of the UDA. He was subsequently elected to Belfast City Hall and became the longest serving political representative of the Ulster Democratic Party (UDP). He was a hard-working local councillor, whose electoral support was personal and based on his record of community work.

Jim Craig, who styled himself Belfast military commander, was still a tin-pot sectarian gangster. In retaliation for the attack on Sammy Millar, he sent out two young UDA men – one later described in court as educationally subnormal – to kill a Catholic, 'any Catholic', in North Belfast. After they returned to the Shankill from shooting dead an innocent 26-year-old, Paul Blake, Craig told the youths they had done a good job. He gave one £2 and the other £7 and told them to buy themselves a drink.

The INLA struck again, this time shooting dead Billy 'Bucky' McCullough, a well-known UDA man, at his home in Denmark Street, a few doors away from Tommy Lyttle.

By and large, however, the UDA opted out of violence in 1981. The loyalists were enjoying the sight of IRA and INLA men dying on hunger strike. The Shankill held noisy celebrations every time an IRA hunger striker died. Loyalists opted for stirring it up for the republicans. A Shankill Road UDA man climbed over the 18-feet high 'peace line' barrier that had been erected by the army to separate the communities of the Falls and Shankill, and wrote: 'We will never forget you Jimmy Sands' on a gable wall looking on to the Falls Road.

The end of 1981, however, brought the IRA's assassination of 'another symbol of hated unionism', this time in the shape of the Revd Robert Bradford, Ulster Unionist MP for South Belfast, who was shot dead at his Saturday morning clinic in Dunmurry. Ian Paisley set off on a series of rallies called the Carson Trail at which he assembled groups of loyalists on hillsides in darkness. Reporters and photographers were brought to secret locations where the men raised pieces of paper said to be gun licences. A group called the Third Force evolved out of Paisley's rallies and he and his lieutenants took to parading through Protestant towns at night and holding mass meetings at which collections were made to fund Ulster's new defenders. While many UDA men participated, the leadership was not going to allow the organization to be misled by Paisley again. One member said: 'He was literally told to "fuck off".'

In 1982 Andy Tyrie wrote a clever and moving short play, *This Is It*, based on the experiences of a loyalist duped into joining one of Ian Paisley's excursions into 'Third Force' loyalism manoeuvres in the winter of 1981. The term 'Third Force' was used by Paisley and others on a number of occasions to refer to a loyalist militia in support of the police and army. The central figure in the play, an idealistic and genuine young working-class Protestant, finally retreats in cynical fatigue. It was good enough to be produced for radio by the BBC drama department.

In the early 1980s the attention of the UDA's leadership again turned to politics. A new Assembly was being established by Northern Ireland Secretary Jim Prior who set up a system of 'rolling devolution' designed to lead to elections in yet another attempt to replace Stormont. Like the previous efforts at constitutional reconciliation of unionists and nationalists it failed to elicit unionist support for power-sharing and was doomed to failure. But to the UDA and John McMichael it offered the prospect of a re-entry into politics and a possible escape from the ritual nihilism of terrorism.

In the first half of the 1980s the UDA examined with interest the IRA's development of its political wing, Sinn Féin, which won the Fermanagh–South Tyrone Westminster seat after the death of Maze hunger striker Bobby Sands in 1981. Most significantly, Sinn Féin had managed to hold on to the seat in the subsequent by-election after Sands's death. John McMichael – with less than enthusiastic support from other UDA leaders – felt it was time the UDA also developed a proper political wing and moved forward, as the republicans were doing, on an 'Armalite and ballot box' twin track.

The opportunity for his first foray into electoral politics was provided by Robert Bradford's murder. Paisley's DUP refused to allow another Ulster Unionist candidate to be returned uncontested and forced a by-election. The Revd Willy McCrea, who was a popular Gospel singer, was put forward by the DUP, and soon the SDLP, Alliance Party and a handful of independents entered the fray. When McMichael put his name forward there was initial panic in the Ulster Unionists that he would split their vote and let the DUP man in. They also had something of an unknown quantity in the candidacy of another Presbyterian minister, the Revd Martin Smyth, and there were justifiable worries that Bradford's huge margin would be severely depleted.

McMichael approached the by-election in a buoyant mood. At his opening press conference he said the Ulster Loyalist Democratic Party (ULPG) envisaged, in the long term, a negotiated independence for Northern Ireland. In the short term, it wanted an Ulster Grand Committee that would involve all shades of local political opinion and a governing Northern Ireland Office that would deal with 'bread and butter' issues such as unemployment and housing.

His manifesto also espoused the view that constitutional change would not take place without two-thirds consent – the power-sharing doctrine that had contributed to the demise of Brian Faulkner and his supporters in 1974 and which was a notion far from most unionist minds in the fraught climate surrounding Bradford's murder. McMichael argued that the British were intent on withdrawal anyway, oddly but accurately citing plans for a pipeline connecting the natural gas reserves on the south-west coast of the Republic with the supply network in Northern Ireland. He said a reliable source inside the Northern Ireland Office had told him the government's intention was to set up a local Assembly and then issue a proclamation that it was intending to withdraw from Northern Ireland.

The outcome of the election was that the huge Ulster Unionist majority was reduced but Martin Smyth came in with a respectable 17,123 votes – a majority of 5,397 over McCrea. For McMichael there was bitter disappointment. He was stunned by his miserable 576 votes – less than 1 per cent of the mainly Protestant electorate had voted for him.

McMichael was media-savvy, a good public performer and had worked hard on the hustings. What had happened? The massive political rejection of the UDA's political opportunism was simple enough to explain. For a start, it had no proper political or electoral machine. The 'Beyond the Religious Divide' document and its ideas on an independent Ulster simply frightened many unionist voters. South Belfast was a deeply conservative constituency whose middle-class Protestant voters baulked at the idea of voting for anyone associated with terrorism.

John McMichael's and the UDA's political ambitions virtually died on polling day, 4 March 1982. The UDA turned away from politics, though some of its old stagers – men such as Sammy Millar, who had backgrounds in trade unionism and community activism – were able to take local government seats in Belfast and some surrounding districts. However, its vote was never greater than negligible. It would take almost two decades and a ceasefire for the resurrection of its political dreams, when John McMichael's son, Gary, would make a respectable electoral impact.

6. Collusion

In 1982 the failure of politics and the mounting rate of arrests by the RUC were taking their toll on the UDA. Members saw that people were becoming bored with the war, but Gawn Street remained unconcerned, even after a series of internal security failures in the organization that was almost entirely of its own doing.

In December 1981 John McMichael and Sammy Doyle, then running on a UDP ticket for Belfast City Council elections, had produced military flight paths for Northern Ireland which they said had been 'found' in a derelict house conveniently located near the UDA headquarters in East Belfast. How, McMichael asked, could such sensitive maps fall into the hands of republicans?

The publicity stunt, apparently designed to get Doyle's picture in the papers, might have ended there, but Doyle made the strange claim that the maps had been found by a UDA 'policing unit' and called for a top-level security inquiry. The army said the maps were probably old and of no particular importance. In fact, the opposite was the truth. The army could only supply bases in South Armagh and some parts of Tyrone by using helicopters and such maps would be invaluable to the IRA, who had been for years trying to acquire ground-to-air missile systems. A high-level inquiry was launched into the missing charts and the RUC was prompted to take action and have a good look at the UDA.

Three months later UDA headquarters were raided. Documents were found containing addresses of judges, lawyers and policemen. They were arranged in an 'extremely well organized' index system, Belfast Magistrates' Court was told later. One hundred and fifty different fingerprints were taken off them. Andy Tyrie, John McMichael, Inner Council members, Sammy McCormick, the East Belfast brigadier, John McClatchey, Eddie Martin, and doorman Bobby McDevitt, were arrested and charged with conspiring to possess documents likely to be of use to terrorists. Sammy Duddy's house was raided and a blue index card containing the names, addresses and personal details of alleged IRA members was found in a jacket pocket, and he was arrested for possession of documents. Duddy said the material was for publication in the UDA's *Ulster* magazine.

The UDA leaders were held in prison on remand for between two and three months before receiving bail. Tyrie stood trial in a packed courtroom in April the following year. His defence counsel pointed out that the documents were found in an office which was used by dozens of people. The case against his client, he said, was 'coming home on a wing and a prayer'. Tyrie was acquitted when it could not be proved he had conspired to have possession of the documents or the weapons found at the headquarters. Charges against McMichael, McCormick, McClatchey, Martin and McDevitt were also dropped.

Despite the fact that the trial was based on the UDA's possession of what should have been tightly restricted intelligence documents, there was nothing particularly sensational about this at the time. There had also been no outcry when, in February 1981, the *Irish Times* reported that the UDA intelligence officer in Derry had defected by walking into a local army base and not reappearing. A senior UDA man told the paper there had been suspicions about the man for years 'but the quality of information he offered was so good that he was placed in charge of the Derry UDA's intelligence unit'.

The *Irish Times*'s Northern editor, David McKittrick, wrote that the UDA had showed him

a large selection of material which they say was obtained by the man. The information includes a number of British army-issue photographs of Republican suspects, and a photocopy of an aerial photograph of Letterkenny, County Donegal; this has marked on it a house said to be occupied by a number of Provisional Republicans. There is also a handwritten copy of what appears to be several pages from an army logbook, a detailed file on a Derry woman living in the United States, and a typewritten sheet giving details of alleged Provisional IRA activities in England and Wales. Dates on various documents range from 1972 to 1980.

The intelligence officer, who was English, had settled in Derry in the 1960s. In the UDA's view his function was to gather as much information as he could on their organization in Derry. They also claimed they had information that he was still in the British army on a major's salary.

With the charges out of the way things reverted to normal at Gawn Street. The pervading sense of complacency was not shaken even in 1983 when sixteen of its members were arrested on the word of the UDA 'supergrass' Stanley Millar Smith. At the same time the IRA, INLA and UVF were also being hit by the supergrass phenomenon and during the years 1982 to 1984 almost all serious terrorist activity in Belfast and Derry was brought to an end. There were some loyalist street protests against the supergrasses but nothing of the magnitude of previous UDA demonstrations. In one of the strange twists of the Troubles the supergrass system brought deadly enemies together to fight it. In 1982 there was even a joint attempt to smuggle strychnine into Crumlin Road Prison to poison seven supergrass witnesses held in the isolation wing. The plot failed when the poison curdled the men's custard and made it change colour. The supergrass system collapsed after the Northern Ireland Appeal Court ruled that mass trials using 'accomplice evidence' were contrary to the law.

At this time, it was an open secret that the UDA – and the UVF too – was obtaining intelligence documents and people's profiles from army and police bases. Already in September 1979 the Sinn Féin leader Gerry Adams had claimed that the UDA was using 'copies of RUC intelligence files'. There were thousands of these documents floating around army bases and police barracks and there were plenty of loyalists and sympathetic soldiers and police working in the same buildings. The UDA was receiving so much material that there was a permanent staff at Gawn Street and other venues collating the information and preparing it for assassination files. Indeed, just as the UDA officers appeared to be interested in politics and talking to the media in their headquarters,

Tyrie was also advancing the idea of a core terrorist organization that would operate away from the local brigade structures. On the top floor in Gawn Street, where journalists were not welcome, UDA people assembled assassination lists of suspected IRA members – almost entirely based on leaked intelligence documents. The UDA had a steady flow of information on suspected republicans from 1973 onwards. According to one senior figure in East Belfast, army officers used to deliver bundles of documents, sometimes hundreds of them, stuffed into plastic shopping bags, at a rendezvous in the Park Avenue Hotel or pubs on the outskirts of the city.

The army had suffered quite serious losses in Belfast to IRA sniper and bomb attacks throughout the early 1970s. The IRA, which lost nearly 100 of its own members in 'own goal' premature explosions at the start of the Troubles, was becoming more effective and more deadly. The army lost forty-four soldiers in 1971, the first year of IRA action against it, and the toll rose to 108 in 1972, most casualties being suffered in Belfast. By 1975, however, the army was defending itself better and military casualties fell to fifteen that year – a level at which it was to more or less remain for the rest of the 1970s (with the exception of 1979 when eighteen soldiers were killed in one IRA bomb attack at Warrenpoint and the year's total rose to thirty-two). In the 1980s, at the same time as loyalists became effective at targeting and assassinating republicans, the army suffered far fewer casualties in Belfast. In fact, over a four-year period between 1982 and 1986 it had no fatalities in the city.

Military sources insist that collusion with the loyalists was not official policy but concur that it went on and was quite widespread. One former soldier said non-commissioned officers, who had a commitment to ensure that the recruits they had nurtured and trained as soldiers got home safely, were mainly responsible. NCOs are the powerful middle-management of all western armies and much of what they get up to is often without official sanction. Officers often feel it is better to let the NCOs lead as long as it is in accordance with general army policy and is not mutinous. Much of the intelligence documentation on the IRA and other republican groups was handled by NCOs in intelligence. A practice started at the military bases in Belfast whereby at every four-month rotation the outgoing intelligence officer – usually a senior NCO – would take his successor round to a pub to introduce him to his UDA counterpart. When the relationship worked, documents were handed over.

Intelligence officers, however, also wanted to know what was going on inside the UDA, and from early in its operations in Northern Ireland the army began recruiting agents in the UDA, using the supply of documents as a way of working its way into the organization. The primary intention, in soldiers' minds, however, was to get information to loyalists on the IRA people who were trying to kill soldiers. It was, after all, war.

The UDA in most areas had a fairly tightly knit structure – members knew each other, often since childhood. It was a difficult organization to infiltrate. When a former Scottish soldier turned up at the Shankill Road UDA headquarters in 1976 seeking to join, he was taken away to a romper room, beaten and shot dead on suspicion that he was an army spy. In fact, the man had been discharged from the army as unfit and it seems he might have been an adventurer who had genuinely wanted to join the UDA to fight the IRA. Belfast attracted strange people like that. By the mid-1980s, however, with the UDA virtually on ceasefire, its internal security defences were dropped and it became easy to infiltrate agents. The RUC Special Branch used the simple expedient of doing deals with men caught with firearms or for other serious offences, and dropping the charges in return for them becoming, in Belfast parlance, 'touts'. The army used its own independent system whereby men from Protestant areas, usually former soldiers who had also been in the UDA in the early days, were re-hired into the army and told to join the UDA to work as spies.

The level of rank-and-file support within the security forces ensured that the flow of intelligence documents into Gawn Street continued. Each UDA brigade had an intelligence officer who had access to these documents and identified the names of IRA suspects in their general area. This man worked to his local commander, who also had control of the 'commando' or Ulster

Freedom Fighter unit and of the quartermaster who stored and prepared guns. The UDA was extraordinarily open in the way it handled some of these documents – and it was this habit that would eventually lead it into trouble. In July 1976 the UDA had told journalists it proposed to publish an 'A to Z' list of IRA suspects it had compiled on the basis of intelligence documents from security sources. The threat to publish the IRA men's names was made after a local business magazine published the names of Northern Ireland's top businessmen at a time when the IRA was assassinating members of the business community. UDA bosses occasionally showed off or even gave photocopied lists of IRA suspects to trusted journalists. The lists were usually of individuals in places like South Armagh or Tyrone which were out of the UDA's range. The intention, presumably, was that the journalists would write about the suspects and frighten them. However, the effect of the UDA's improved targeting, based on these documents, was that many IRA people in Belfast had to keep on the move or to live in houses turned into fortresses.

In 1981 Andy Tyrie more or less confirmed that soldiers or police were colluding with the UDA when he told an American journalist that there was a 'small offensive unit' called the Ulster Freedom Fighters which was illegal but had good intelligence. 'They go through a careful process with many documents and good intelligence before they do anything.' It was just after the attempt to murder Bernadette McAliskey and he commented: 'Political assassination carried out against active republicans is not wrong. I defend them. I don't know anything about it and I can't say any more.'

Persistent republican assaults on unionism and the British connection over the ensuing three years included shocking and provocative attacks such as the INLA's massacre of Protestant evangelists at Darkley in South Armagh in November 1983; the murder of prominent unionist Edgar Graham; the bombing of Harrods in London the following month; and the IRA attack on the leadership of the Conservative Party in October 1984.

In April 1984 the UDA and the UVF simultaneously attempted to murder the president of Sinn Féin, Gerry Adams. This was the loyalists' response to the IRA's murders of the Revd Bradford and Edgar Graham. Adams was scheduled to appear in Belfast Magistrates' Court on a charge of disorderly behaviour arising from an election rally in North Belfast the previous year in which a tricolour had been flown on the Antrim Road. A three-man team from East Antrim was waiting for Adams and his four minders as they drove from the court towards West Belfast. The UDA men pulled up alongside the Sinn Féin men's car as it drove past the back of the City Hall and fired two sustained bursts of gunfire into the Cortina, hitting Adams and three others in the vehicle. Adams was hit four times in the upper body. His driver, who was also shot, was able to accelerate away from the scene to the Royal Victoria's accident and emergency department, where they received immediate treatment and survived.

The UDA team was caught on the spot almost immediately in a military operation that clearly suggested the security forces had prior knowledge of the plan. The UDA men's car was pursued and rammed. It was then approached by two British soldiers who forced John Gregg, the head of the Rathcoole's UDA commando, out on to the pavement along with one of his fellow gunmen. The third UDA man was bleeding profusely as one of the bullets fired had hit the vehicle's interior and ricocheted into his body. All three were arrested.

The official version of the arrest was that the soldiers had happened to be in the location by accident. The unofficial version was that the security forces knew that an attack was likely but that was all. The Rathcoole UDA had kept the mission as secret as they could but there was an awareness at senior level in the UDA that an attack would be mounted. The RUC's two top informants in the UDA did not have its precise details but may well have known it was being planned.

There was another telling, unreported detail. A well-placed UDA informant had tipped off the RUC's Special Branch about the arms dump from which the guns to shoot Adams were to be taken. According to police sources, they were able to replace the ammunition with similar-looking but much lower velocity bullets. This was done on a regular basis by the police. If they had simply seized the guns, suspicion would have fallen on their informant in the UDA. By replacing the live rounds with less dangerous ammunition the police had inadvertently saved Adams's life.

Although the issue of security force collusion with loyalists has been the source of frequent – and sometimes manufactured – controversy, it should be remembered that the relationship between the military and the UDA was barely an issue in the 1970s and 1980s. There was no need for Westminster security bosses to dream up a scheme of collusion because loyalists had been doing it all by themselves from the outset of the Troubles. In the early years senior British military figures actually felt there was no conflict of interest in dual membership between the military and the UDA. John Todd, a serving UDR soldier, was shot dead by members of the Parachute Regiment during rioting on the Shankill Road on 17 October 1972. Todd was given a paramilitary funeral, with shots fired over his coffin by the UDA. The UDR's commanding officer, Brigadier Ormerod, said he saw no reason why he should take action if one of his soldiers was also a member of the UDA.

There was long-standing and concerted infiltration of the Ulster Defence Regiment by loyalists. UDA men were instructed to join in order to receive military training, get their hands on intelligence documents and work out ways that arms could be stolen. The UDA raided the UDR base in Magherafelt in 1975, although the weapons they captured were lost when they were hidden in pig slurry and rusted by the corrosive acids of the pit. A security review by the army found that vetting procedures were not sufficient to detect the entry of loyalist paramilitaries into the UDR. Tyrie, interviewed on RTE (Radio Telefis Eireann, the Irish state broadcasting corporation), frankly admitted that many of the UDA's men joined the UDR for military training.

In January 1976 a full-time soldier in the UDR who was also a member of a UDA unit in South Derry kidnapped and murdered an elderly Protestant man who had been preparing to give evidence against another UDA man in an arms trial. A UDA team abducted 71-year-old Sam Millar from his home, beat him to death with an iron bar and slung his weighted body into a lake. The UDR/UDA man later confessed to RUC detectives and was sentenced to life imprisonment.

While serving his life sentence in England for the murder of the Catholic barman Philip May, the former soldier and East Belfast romper room killer Albert Baker sent letters to politicians and journalists stating that he had worked secretly for the army which was aware of his activities. His claims led to his being questioned by English detectives but little developed from there. Baker wrote a letter to the *Irish News* in Belfast saying he had absolute proof of collusion but feared the 'terrible truth' he wanted to reveal would result in a cover-up. Baker also claimed that the second-in-command of his UDA unit had been a member of the RUC. He wrote: 'Half the assassinations in the early 1970s wouldn't have been committed if there hadn't been RUC backing. Half the people who died in those assassinations, or more, would have been living today if the RUC hadn't supported the assassination teams.' Baker, who was a deserter from the Royal Irish Rangers, was a highly unreliable and unstable figure, and though his claims were given plenty of press in the early 1990s and were even raised by Ken Livingstone in Parliament, they were never verified.

Other, more plausible figures, such as the former British army civilian press officer Colin Wallace and a former army major, Fred Holroyd, have built careers out of the collusion issue. In the 1970s Wallace and his colleagues in the army's press office in Lisburn did a good job of stoking the conspiracy theory about collusion, 'dirty war' and secret shenanigans. In the early 1970s the press office ran a scheme called 'psy-ops'. Psy-ops are part of all modern low-intensity military peace-keeping operations – even those of the United Nations – where armies have to ingratiate themselves as much as possible with an unfriendly native population.

Wallace and his associates were responsible for issuing a regular stream of half-truths and outright lies aimed at promoting the army's cause and somehow confusing and enfeebling its enemies. At times it would have been even entertaining, if it hadn't been for the backdrop of real suffering. For instance, after several young IRA female bombers were killed, the army press office was responsible for issuing a story saying that static electricity in women's knickers was causing premature explosions. There were also 'Red Plot' scare stories claiming that Soviet spies had been smuggled into Ulster by submarine. The UDA was the target of the Lisburn psy-ops people, who created a fictitious loyalist group called the Ulster Citizens Army (UCA) that was said to be a Marxist or communist group intent on infiltrating the loyalist cause. Stories about the UCA, which seemed to take on a life of their own, were planted and appeared in reputable newspapers. Deaths of UDA men such as that of Ernie Elliott were mysteriously linked to this secretive left-wing conspiracy group. The UDA leadership was mystified about the UCA claims and only later learned it was a figment of someone's overactive imagination at army head-quarters in Lisburn. In some thirty years since the mysterious UCA emerged, no loyalist has come forward to claim to have any information about it. There was, inevitably, a great deal of mystery surrounding the necessarily secretive operations against terrorist groups in Northern Ireland. It was a world of smoke and mirrors. But the fact that no one has come forward to claim this organ-ization in all this time suggests only one thing: it never existed.

One simple truth was that ordinary soldiers and police, under constant attack, operating under the rule of law, felt unable to take the war to the IRA. Many who had friends blown up or shot took the law into their own hands and handed over docu-ments to the UDA. As a result, though it may have been in a state of internal disrepair, by the 1980s the UDA had a remarkably up-to-date picture of the membership of the IRA and INLA in Northern Ireland. It was fortunate for many on the lists that the *laissez-faire* attitude of the leadership permitted infiltration by the RUC and the army. They were able to stop the vast majority of UDA operations and to save many lives.

7. Spies and Spooks

Despite the upsurge of support during the Maze Prison hunger strikes in 1981 and its high-profile terror attacks – 'spectaculars' – the IRA was getting nowhere in its aim to break up the union of Northern Ireland and Britain. Then, in October 1984, it carried out its most spectacular bomb attack so far, almost succeeding in killing Margaret Thatcher and wiping out her cabinet as they attended the Conservative Party conference at Brighton. The political after-shock from the bombing hit Ulster in the following months when Thatcher began talks with the Irish prime minister, Garret FitzGerald, that would lead to a fundamental change to the governance of Northern Ireland.

Thatcher was determined there would be some political movement in Northern Ireland. Despite having insisted in parliament that there would be no Irish dimension in the government of the Province, she then did one of the most striking U-turns of her career and signed the Anglo-Irish Agreement in October 1985 – effectively giving Dublin a say in the running of Northern Ireland. The Agreement set up an Anglo-Irish Secretariat, with Dublin civil servants sitting in Belfast, and included a commitment to hold regular meetings with the Irish government to discuss the affairs of Northern Ireland. This was the very thing that the loyalists had risen against in 1974. Now, with no Stormont in place, unionists would have no say in governing their Province but Dublin would. It was a stunning blow.

As the Agreement was signed 100,000 protesters marched to Belfast city centre in a rally larger than any of Craig's Vanguard gatherings and the largest since the anti-Home Rule rallies at the start of the century. There was a great deal of unionist huffing and puffing: unionist MPs resigned their seats in Parliament; Paisley took off to the hills again, raising yet another 'Third Force'. But there was no sign of any major revolt that would make Thatcher back down. Irish political leaders began to appear in Stormont for summits with the British government on an increasingly regular basis.

This was not 1974. There was no weak power-sharing Assembly to be brought down. The army and RUC were at the peak of their capabilities, and there were no mass ranks of UDA men to blockade the power stations and fuel depots. The UDA was in disarray and still bitter about the way it had been snubbed by the unionist establishment. Tyrie had no intention of being used by unionist politicians who would then turn on him and stand back as his men were sent to prison. Although the UDA despised the Agreement, this time it was up to the politicians to get themselves out of the mess. When Paisley made tentative approaches to the UDA to see if it was ready to support another strike, again he was told, literally, to 'fuck off'.

Paisley's new 'Third Force', this time called Ulster Resistance, was scorned by both the UDA and the UVF, which had been hit badly by the RUC supergrass system. So Paisley was left to organize his own marches and rallies at which he posed wearing a red beret like that worn by members of the British army's crack Parachute Regiment. Alongside him stood his most unmilitary-like deputy, Peter Robinson. With these men leading the amateurs of Ulster Resistance there was no hope of defeating one of the most powerful British prime ministers of modern times.

However, anger at the British betrayal ran deep in the heart of loyalism and Tyrie and McMichael, under pressure from the Inner Council, accepted that the war would have to start again. The intelligence files were pulled out and the victims lined up. The UDA decided to hit Dublin. John McMichael, put in charge of a campaign to firebomb shops and businesses in the Republic, organized his teams out of the UDA social club at Taughmonagh in Dunmurry. The rallying cry was that Dublin should be a sea of flames. To set an example for his men, McMichael, the UDA's military commander, travelled to Dublin to mount a peaceful protest outside the Irish parliament. At the same time he was eyeing up potential targets for the crude but effective incendiary bombs his men were making back in Belfast.

McMichael was also considering plans to assassinate members of the Irish government. A UDA man in the East Belfast brigade had a plan to shoot down the RAF helicopter carrying the Irish premier or his deputy to Stormont Castle for one of their regular intergovernmental conferences. The helicopter had to follow a narrow flight path that brought it on to the front lawn of Stormont Castle and it would be within easy reach of heavy machine-gun fire from a number of vantage points in loyalist East Belfast. Inquiries were made about the type of weapon that would be needed. A medium machine-gun might do the trick. There were even suggestions that a ground-to-air missile could be stolen from the Shorts plant in East Belfast. The plan was finally turned down by a nervous UDA leadership, ostensibly because it involved killing the RAF crew and the RUC Special Branch minders on board. Plans for the FitzGerald assassination were leaked to the Special Branch, and flight plans were redrawn and security stepped up around the Irish government leadership in case a second plot was hatched.

Instead the UDA embarked on a morale-boosting, but ineffectual, incendiary bombing campaign in the South. They had done this before. In fact, in 1977 one of its Shankill Road members, Freddie Parkinson, was arrested after a firebomb went off in his pocket at Boyer's department store in North Earl Street. He was subsequently sentenced to eight years' imprisonment. Parkinson was later joined in prison in Dublin by two UDA men from Rathcoole who were caught by the gardaí on a mission to shoot dead Francis McGirl, the County Leitrim IRA man who had planted the bomb that had killed Lord Mountbatten in his boat in August 1979. The two UDA men had spent four days searching for McGirl but were caught when a major security operation was mounted in the area after an IRA bomb exploded just across the border in County Fermanagh and the gardaí tried to catch the escaping IRA team. The two Northerners raised the suspicions of the gardaí, who found their guns and a picture of McGirl they were carrying.

But McMichael was determined to show that his new UDF group had the skills to hit the South where it hurt, and on

7 February 1987 they simultaneously firebombed shops in Dublin and Donegal causing damage estimated at £2 million – the greatest success the UDA ever had in bombing any targets. The UDA leaders realized that even small bombs in Dublin grabbed headlines in the South and had a dampening effect on the Dublin government's enthusiasm for Northern Ireland. Regular, small-scale incendiary attacks followed, until they petered out in the mid-1990s. Gardaí and Irish army ordnance people described most of the devices as crude and unstable, the sort of thing that a moderately clever secondary-school student could assemble. The only casualty was an Irish army bomb disposal officer who lost a thumb when a parcel bomb sent to the Sinn Féin headquarters in Parnell Square exploded.

But not all of the UDA was as measured or organized or blood-less as McMichael wanted it. In North Belfast it was back to basics – sectarian murder. As the political campaign against the Agreement faded, the UDA in North Belfast returned to its old habits: abducting a Catholic man, taking him to the drinking club in the Tynedale estate in North Belfast and beating him to death. John O'Neill's body was dumped in the stream running down from the Cavehill through countryside above North Belfast.

In March 1987 members of the UDA's drinking club at the end of the same small housing estate beat to death an unfortu-nate young local woman, a single mother of two, during a late-night orgy of drink and violence. Lorraine McCausland's half-naked, shattered body was dumped where O'Neill's had been. It is believed that she became involved in a row involving other women at the club, that the men joined in and this led to her brutal death. In April 1987 the same group was involved in another fight which resulted in the death of one of its own members, Hugh McFarlane, a dogsbody who was regularly picked on by the gang. He was killed by having concrete blocks smashed on his head as he lay prone outside a local pub.

Another North Belfast UDA man, Tommy Dickson, was shot dead after an unrelated local internal row two months later. In July two Ballysillan UDA men forced a Catholic taxi-driver they had hailed in the city centre to drive out to the countryside at

Ligoniel, where they shot him dead. The following night the IRA in North Belfast retaliated by walking into a pool hall in the upper Crumlin Road and shooting dead a local UDA man, William Reynolds, who was not connected with the previous murders. A few weeks later a young Catholic who was engaged to a Protestant girl in Ballysillan was shot dead while he sat chatting to his fiancée outside her house.

On the evening of 9 August William Cockburn, a 35-year-old Scottish Protestant who happened to be walking near the Shankill/ Falls interface was murdered. Cockburn, a member of the Apprentice Boys, was on his way home from the Shankill when he was waylaid by a gang of young UDA men who had been drinking after the band's parade. Under the drunken misapprehension that he was a 'Taig' (pejorative slang word for Catholic), as one later admitted to police, they attacked him and used the familiar method of dropping a concrete block on his head to finish off the job. The spectre of the 'window cleaner' killings was raised in May 1976 when UDA men from Ballysillan broke into a house in the upper Cavehill area and shot dead Margaret Caulfield, a Protestant married to a Catholic. The gunmen quizzed the couple about their religion before opening fire on Mrs Caulfield and her Catholic husband, who survived.

One of the least active UDA units until then had been Tommy Lyttle's West Belfast brigade. But there was an influx of very aggressive young members, and Lyttle had to find them something to do. They wanted to kill. Lyttle turned to his intelligence officer, a quiet sheepish man called Brian Nelson, to draw up an assassination list. One of the names Nelson came up with was that of a West Belfast man who was down on RUC and army documents in Nelson's possession as the head of the IRA's internal security squad – the group that sought out and murdered suspected informants. This man had been living in the South for some time but was now reported to be back in West Belfast. Another figure on Nelson's list was a relative of the Sinn Féin leader Gerry Adams, a man thought to be the commanding officer of the West Belfast IRA.

A team was equipped and readied on the Shankill. However,

late into the planning to hit these targets, Nelson announced that he had come across an even more important one: 66-year-old Francisco Notorantonio, a man who he claimed was a top figure in the IRA. And so a UDA unit was dispatched to West Belfast late one evening in October 1987, burst into the Notorantonio home in the poor Ballymurphy housing estate and shot dead the ageing, frail taxi-driver, as he sat in an armchair. There was no security on the house and the gunmen were surprised at how little resistance they met.

When Gerry Adams turned out at the funeral to carry Notorantonio's coffin it seemed to be some proof of republican connections, but the truth was that Notorantonio had only the slightest link with the IRA or Sinn Féin, and that had been years before. He was, however, a well-known and well-liked man in his neighbourhood, and it was natural that Gerry Adams, who had grown up in West Belfast and had his electoral base there, would attend Notorantonio's funeral, if the family permitted.

The Notorantonio killing had been preceded by furious activity at the very top of the British army's secret intelligence operations in Northern Ireland. Nelson's original plan would have been a disaster for British intelligence. At the centre of the furore, and at the top of Britain's intelligence machine in Northern Ireland, which involved the most senior figures in army intelligence, the RUC Special Branch and MI5, were two of their top agents in Northern Ireland. The one on the loyalist side was the shy, quiet UDA man – Brian Nelson. The other, on the republican side, was one of the IRA men he had been setting up for assassination in West Belfast.

Nelson was born in Belfast in 1948 and, after what appears to have been an uneventful childhood, like many Northern Ireland youths he eventually joined the British army. Around 1971 he was granted a medical discharge from the Black Watch (Royal Highland Regiment), and in 1972 became a member of the UDA, where he was a relatively minor figure in the early days. In 1974 he received a seven-year prison sentence for the kidnapping of a Roman Catholic man but was released in 1977, and seems to have immediately rejoined the UDA.

He took up a role in intelligence gathering, mainly collating the leaked security documents on republicans. By the early 1980s he was also working for army intelligence. When he came under suspicion by other UDA men of tipping police off about an operation on the Shankill Road, he left Northern Ireland for Germany. He appears to have settled well there but also retained his contacts with the British army. Shortly after the Anglo-Irish Agreement, and amid fears of a loyalist uprising, he was brought back to Northern Ireland. Tommy Lyttle recruited him as head of the UDA intelligence section in West Belfast.

Nelson had reported the intention to kill the two IRA figures to his handlers, two soldiers who were part of the agent-handling undercover unit known at that time as the Force Research Unit (FRU). They in turn passed the information up the line where it was assessed by the top security officials – figures with access to the names and details of agents working on both sides of the terrorist fence in Northern Ireland. Alarm bells started ringing. Nelson was helping to plan the murder of one of the British army's top agents inside the IRA and this had to be stopped at any cost.

His unfortunate choice was the British agent known by the code name Stakeknife. It was, according to very well-placed sources, a coincidence. The IRA man, later identified as Freddie Scappaticci, had as important a role within the IRA as Nelson had with the UDA. The spooks had to protect Stakeknife at all costs – including murder – but Nelson was equally as important and also had to be protected. Some alternative to murdering Stakeknife, while protecting Nelson had to be found; they needed a scapegoat. Nelson was ordered to divert the attack away from the two IRA men. Whether or not Nelson's handlers suggested Francisco Notorantonio may be disputed but it seems likely. It appears that the unfortunate man was chosen simply because he, like the army's agent inside the IRA who had been initially targeted by Nelson, happened to be of Italian extraction and lived in a republican stronghold. Such was the harsh, dirty reality of under-cover operations and spy-handling in Northern Ireland.

There had been only minor puzzlement among the UDA when

the plan for the senior IRA man's murder was scrapped. Nelson was trusted by his boss, Lyttle. He had a prodigious number of files, some even on computer, about IRA people. He was an industrious 'quiet wee man' who supplied the UDA with what they believed to be top-grade intelligence documents on the IRA from some unknown but highly placed source in the security forces. So when he said Notorantonio was big in the IRA there was no reason to disbelieve him.

Nelson's 'contacts' were his handlers, and rather than there being a one-way stream of high-grade intelligence (some was, some wasn't), the flow of information was greater in the other direction. Nelson was informing them of UDA thinking at its highest levels. He had almost singled-handedly kept the UDA's military wing under tabs for two years. In the period after the Anglo-Irish Agreement when Britain feared another UDA uprising, Nelson had become one of its most important agents in Northern Ireland. He was perfectly placed to tip off the army of any attempts at a re-run of the UWC strike of 1974, and to undermine any attempts at another popular uprising – or at least give his masters adequate warning of any such plan.

For his services Nelson was receiving £200 per week spending money and had been given the promise of a new life and new identity if things became too dangerous. If his associates in the UDA learned he was an agent he would be tortured and killed, but he seemed to relish his secret life, and from the intelligence services' point of view he was a national treasure.

The role of army and RUC spies of this time would, more than a decade later, attract an extraordinarily high level of interest. But the facts of life in Northern Ireland then determined that murders such as Francis Notorantonio's were passed off by the security establishment as part of the daily butcher's bill of infiltrating loyalist and republican organizations. Security chiefs would allow the murders even of soldiers and policemen and women to protect the identity of their highly placed spies in the IRA.

Brian Nelson was one of the most effective loyalist informants ever operated by the security forces in Northern Ireland. The real importance of his role was that he provided information that went to the top of the intelligence community and from there to the top of Whitehall. The government did not want a rerun of 1974. Brian Nelson was planted in the UDA at the start of the Anglo-Irish process and served to ensure that the British army, the intelligence services and their political masters were informed of loyalist intentions at every turn.

Nelson overcame a rough interrogation in a Shankill Road club in 1988 after he was released from RUC custody, having been caught with incriminating intelligence documents, hidden in a false spirit level. Some UDA members believed that he should have been charged, but he managed to convince his UDA interrogators and escaped with his life. However, a number of units in West Belfast began to refuse to carry out operations in which he was in any way involved.

In a unique gesture, the head of the FRU, which had handled Nelson, testified before the court, seeking leniency for his former agent. The officer, identified in court only as Colonel J (he was named later and is currently the subject of possible prosecution by the still ongoing Stevens inquiry into collusion) admitted:

We wished to infiltrate him into the loyalist paramilitaries, to gain inside knowledge of their workings and to prevent or at the very least limit their murderous activity. Our aim was to get inside knowledge, but we didn't want him to get involved with murder gangs. We had to decide where he should be infiltrated, where he could get information for us which we would pass on to the RUC.

The officer told the court that Nelson had passed some 730 reports to his army handlers, including information on plots to kill a total of 217 republicans that the security forces were able to thwart.

In later evidence, it was explicitly acknowledged that Nelson was a British army agent: 'We would run the agent – he was always our agent – and we would be responsible for passing on the information to the RUC, which we did in all cases.' Referring to his return to Northern Ireland, the officer stated that Nelson was given the £200-per-week salary to recompense for the disruption of his family life.

Nelson's career ended on 12 January 1990 when he was arrested by members of a British police team investigating collusion between the Northern Ireland security forces and the UDA. He was charged with aiding and abetting the murder of two men in 1988, conspiracy to murder four others, and twenty-six counts of possessing information useful to terrorists. By this stage he had more than fulfilled his role. It was probably with relief that he left West Belfast and was taken into custody. The day Nelson appeared before Belfast Magistrates' Court two days after his arrest on the aiding and abetting charges, his wife, children and all their family possessions were moved from their home in North Belfast under police protection.

Nelson had been withdrawn from Belfast just in the nick of time as there were growing suspicions among UDA members, if not the leadership, that he was a 'tout'. One West Belfast UDA man said:

I knew Brian Nelson very well. He was a friend of mine and I believe Brian had never really left the army. When something falls into your hands as good as that you have to grab it and that's the way it was. In hindsight it was definitely an own goal. His intelligence was becoming very, very good. You might think we were a bit naïve but we knew he was getting good information, and that carried risks.

Another, commenting on the detail and quality of Nelson's intelligence, said: 'He could tell you the colour of [a target's] eyes.'

In February 1992 Nelson was sentenced to ten years' imprisonment on five charges of conspiracy to murder, receiving also a six-year concurrent sentence for possession of a machine gun, a four-year concurrent sentence on three charges of collecting information useful to terrorists, and a further concurrent three years on eleven counts of possessing documents useful to terrorists. Nelson was never heard of again until he died of a heart attack in 2003 in the south of England, where he had been living under an assumed identity. He had done more than possibly any other person to help destroy the UDA as an important force in Northern Ireland.

Following the signing of the Anglo-Irish Agreement in November 1985, the Shankill UDA swelled with eager young loyalists seeking to fight it, and to take on the IRA. The young men were 'blooded' with a number of assassinations, some on targets and some involving innocent victims. The West Belfast units were on the move and determined.

In a brief call to the BBC newsroom on the morning of 13 February 1989, an anonymous voice said: 'We have shot Pat Finucane the Provisional IRA officer, not Pat Finucane the solicitor. While the Provisional IRA threaten and shoot loyalist construction workers, removal men, and those who simply share their lunch-boxes, the inevitable retaliation will take place.'

Had the UDA shot anyone else, in the ordinary run of loyalist assassinations in Belfast, there would have been little more said or heard about this murder until a suspect was arrested or charged. But the victim and the UDA people who killed him were anything but ordinary. For a start, at least two members of the unit involved in his assassination were working for the RUC and army intelligence. Brian Nelson was one. Another, William Stobie, had prepared and supplied the gun that killed Finucane. Stobie was the RUC Special Branch's key agent inside the West Belfast UDA. Like Nelson, he had been in the UDA in the early 1970s, left and joined the army and then returned to Belfast and rejoined the UDA as an armourer. And, like Nelson, he was quiet and did his job satisfactorily and efficiently, unlike many of the others who were incompetent drunks. In addition, Tommy Lyttle, the UDA commander in West Belfast, was also almost certainly compromised by the RUC and may have been a Special Branch agent. Given the amount of infiltration, there are clear grounds for suspecting at least dangerous complacency, if not complicity, on the part of some members of the security forces in Finucane's murder.

Pat Finucane came from a well-known republican family; a brother was shot dead while on an IRA operation in 1972. In

1981 Pat Finucane was chosen by the republican leadership to represent the seven IRA hunger strikers in the Maze Prison. But there were persistent suspicions among police and loyalists that there was more to Finucane than a clever lawyer. The whispers about him and one or two other lawyers reached the House of Commons in the month before his death when junior Home Office minister Douglas Hogg said that some solicitors in Northern Ireland were 'unduly sympathetic' to terrorists. It was known that Finucane was detested by some RUC detectives who privately accused him of being – on a secret, confidential basis – the IRA's legal adviser, and this rumour was later repeated by a former IRA Southern commander. Both republicans and Finucane's associates deny this. Whether the whispering campaign contributed to Finucane's murder and whether there was a guiding hand behind the UDA gunmen who shot him dead are questions which have since haunted the case.

Many people found the timing of the UDA's assassination of Finucane strange. A few years earlier, at the time he was representing the IRA hunger strikers and still building up his practice, he had lived in a terraced house off the Cavehill Road directly across from the loyalist Westland housing estate. His home was only a few yards from a pub which was frequented by the UDA. If there had been suspicions about Finucane earlier he would have been the simplest target to kill. He represented republican prisoners as much then as he did at the time of his death.

Initially Finucane's murder did not raise the spectre of collusion between members of the security forces and loyalist terrorists. The legal profession was deeply shocked at the assault on one of its most high-profile members but that was as far as it went. However, the question of collusion emerged in public a couple of months later during the first of a series of court cases against members of the security forces caught passing documents to loyalists. A Scottish soldier working in the intelligence section of Girdwood Barracks in North Belfast, and a woman soldier in the Ulster Defence Regiment, appeared in court charged with giving files to the UVF and UDA. Statement evidence in the case concurred fairly precisely with the accounts of collusion from UDA figures in Belfast at the time. It included this:

She said that the Royal Scots were about to end their tour in Northern Ireland and that Cammy [an NCO in intelligence] and some of the others were talking about leaving information for the UVF in Tigers Bay or the UDA headquarters on the Shankill Road.

She said that one night she was at the NAAFI at Girdwood and Cammy called her outside. He said that some of the others had handed stuff to the UDA headquarters and he gave her a bit of white paper with photographs on it and another bit of paper with typing on it. She said that [name of well-known UVF man] had, on one occasion, asked her to try and get hold of photographs, names and addresses of republicans. The last time he asked her this was three or four months ago. She said she would try to do this and [UVF man] told her to pass on anything she got to him. She told us the next thing that happened was that Cammy told her that he had got some photographs, names and addresses to give to the loyalists and asked her could she pass them on. She told Cammy she could.

In her confession she said she knew the loyalists she supplied were going to 'set up' the IRA men and she was worried that an innocent man had been shot dead. She was also worried that she had broken the Official Secrets Act. She said 'Cammy' had warned her that some of the addresses in the files were wrong and the court heard that one of the names on the files was a North Belfast republican whose brother was shot dead by the UDA as a result of an incorrect address.

Still the controversy did not break fully – not until August the same year, after the murder of another man whose name appeared on the files supplied to the UDA. The 'files uproar', as it was termed in the media, began after Tommy Lyttle was prompted to reveal to a number of journalists that the UDA had good reason – in its eyes – to kill a man called Loughlin Maginn at his home in Rathfriland, County Down six months after the murder of Pat Finucane. The murder had received scant attention when it happened on 25 August. Maginn had been watching television at home with his wife and four children when two gunmen smashed in the front window, threw a carpet over the broken glass and climbed in. They shot him a number of times, but he tried to escape, running up the stairs. They pursued him and shot him dead on the landing.

There was no indication that Maginn had any terrorist connections and in the following weeks this became a big issue. Lyttle decided to act to counter the claims of Maginn's innocence. He called a local television reporter and produced an army document of a collage of IRA suspects with Maginn's picture, name and details on it. There was an immediate nationalist uproar, with the SDLP calling on the new chief constable, Hugh Annesley, to carry out an investigation. The Irish government joined in the demand for an inquiry. As there were criminal allegations that could involve members of his force, Annesley was entitled to bring in a senior officer from another police force to conduct it. He sought and received the services of the deputy chief constable of the Cambridgeshire Constabulary, John Stevens. Stevens, who would later rise to the highest position in British policing – chief constable of the London Metropolitan police – was beginning the longest investigation in the history of British police. At the time of writing, his investigation into loyalist collusion, which started in September 1989, continues.

Lyttle was arrested a month after the Stevens inquiry was set up, and was subsequently sentenced for possessing material likely to be of use to terrorists. By the time Stevens's team had finished its first three-year tour of investigations in Northern Ireland, it had rounded up and charged forty people including UDA and UDR members.

From the start the finger of accusation about collusive activity was pointed at the UDR, which, as the almost exclusively local and Protestant wing of the British army, was the most likely source of army documents. The case against the UDR was strong. In August two former UDR soldiers had been sentenced to nine years for their part in the UDA-inspired operation which led to the theft of 140 rifles and thirty handguns from the UDR base at Laurel Hill outside Coleraine. In January 1987 another Royal

Irish Rangers member had been sentenced to four years in jail for storing a gun for the UDA in a separate incident in 1976. He told detectives he had been in the UDA since he was sixteen and in the UDR since he was eighteen. In February 1987 the UDA was able to remove 144 rifles, twenty-eight handguns and a large amount of ammunition from the Laurel Hill UDR base in Coleraine. Three cars carrying the firearms back to Belfast were stopped at Templepatrick and Davy Payne, who was driving the lead vehicle, was arrested. Payne, who had had no weapons on board, escaped prosecution but the four others, including two UDR members from Coleraine, were convicted and received heavy sentences.

The UDR was quick to try to counter the allegations against its members. The commanding officer, Brigadier Michael Bray, said six-monthly intelligence checks on all his soldiers to make sure they had no paramilitary connections had been instituted the previous year after guns were stolen from Palace Barracks in Holywood. 'As a result of doing this for the first time last autumn I was satisfied that we do not have a problem of association with paramilitary organizations.' Out of 6,500 members he decided only one should be dismissed – because he had taken part in a UDA parade. 'Nowhere did we find a reasonable cause for concern,' he added. A short while later it was reported that yet another photo-montage of nine IRA suspects had gone missing from a UDR base in Ballykinlar, County Down. There was no way to stop soldiers and police passing information to loyalists.

Amid all the intrigue and failure, the end of the 1980s brought the rank and file of the UDA something they had needed for more than a decade – a hero.

Michael Stone had been a member of the UDA in East Belfast since he was recruited at the age of sixteen by Tommy Herron. When Herron was killed, Stone wisely stepped back from the UDA fearing he would also be killed by the people who had assassinated Herron and his brother-in-law, Michael Wilson. He tried a career in the army in 1979 but was discharged after only a few months. Very few people in the UDA knew about Stone when he re-entered the organization and, acting largely without the knowledge of members of the UDA's Inner Council, began a one-man war against the IRA in the mid-1980s. In fact, he was working under John McMichael. Stone killed a Sinn Féin member, Patrick Brady, in West Belfast in November 1984, and later claimed he was responsible for another assassination, this time of a Catholic joiner working on a building site in Lisburn, County Antrim. Kevin McPolin had no connections with the IRA and may have been the innocent victim of an internal loyalist dispute over the collection of protection money from building sites. Stone also claimed to have travelled to Omagh in May 1987 and shot dead Dermot Hackett, a bread-van driver who lived with his wife and son. However, in his autobiography Stone said he made these claims to divert blame from other UDA men after he had been arrested and was facing life imprisonment anyway.

Quietly working and keeping himself to himself around his home in the Braniel estate, Stone was an enthusiastic if not yet very successful assassin. He had made several attempts to infiltrate republican rallies and even the funeral service of an IRA man to try to get close to Gerry Adams or Martin McGuinness in order to assassinate them but had failed. His big moment was to come on the afternoon of 16 March 1988 when he set out to have another go at the Sinn Féin leadership as they attended the funerals of three IRA bombers shot dead by the SAS in Gibraltar. Like everybody else, Stone had watched the dramatic events unfold in Gibraltar over the previous few days and was prepared for something approaching a suicide mission when the bodies were returned home and the funeral set out for the republican plot in the Milltown Cemetery in West Belfast.

Stone made his way on to the Falls Road and into the cemetery. Having established that his best route of escape was down the Bog Meadow below the cemetery and across the M1 motorway into the relative safety of the loyalist Village area, he mingled with the huge crowd of republican mourners that had turned out for the three funerals. His plan, though brave, was flawed. He had organized a getaway car to pick him up on the M1 motorway, at the point beneath the cemetery, but this fell through when an

RUC surveillance van drew up and his getaway team decided not to wait. Stone launched his gun and grenade attack as the coffins were being lowered into their graves, and tried to make his escape. He was pursued by dozens of enraged young republicans who caught up with him on the motorway. Out of ammunition and grenades, Stone was pounced on and given a savage beating. He was bundled into a hijacked car and saved only by a heavily armed RUC patrol which stopped the vehicle and pulled him into a Land Rover.

Although he had come nowhere near to assassinating the republican leadership – only one of the three men he killed was actually in the IRA – Stone became an instant loyalist icon. While he was on remand in Crumlin Road Prison, bands formed up outside the perimeter walls and played tunes to cheer him up. Inspired by Stone's zeal, McMichael's southern brigade was reactivated and killed four Catholic men. One of them, Jack Kielty, was an innocent businessman who had fallen foul of Jim Craig's racketeering activities. (His son, Patrick, later became a famous comedian and television personality.)

To the UDA leadership, Stone was a major liability as his attack on the republican leadership was bound to bring retaliation. And he had also compromised very lucrative extortion business in the building industry which worked on both sides of the sectarian divide – as long as boats were not rocked. To the fury of ordinary UDA members, Tommy Lyttle issued a statement saying Stone was acting alone, was not a UDA member and was mad. However, to a new generation of young UDA men Stone was an inspiration to 'take the war to the IRA'.

8. Collapse and a New Beginning

Three days before Christmas 1987 John McMichael set out from his home in Lisburn for a last-minute trip to a local off-licence. As his car began to reverse slowly from the short driveway outside his front door it activated a movement-sensitive switch in the detonating mechanism of an IRA booby-trap bomb. The switch, attached by a magnet to the chassis under the driver's seat, formed the circuit between a battery and an electric detonator placed in a slice of Semtex plastic explosive. The explosion ripped through the car, tearing off both McMichael's legs and causing severe internal injuries. A physically strong man, he held on to life for about two hours, drifting in and out of consciousness, occasionally muttering words which suggested he was still thinking of his wife, Shirley, and their son, Saul, who was two years old. He died of haemorrhage and shock.

Those who knew McMichael had noticed that he had become a less buoyant figure in the four or five years before his death. His political ambitions had been crushed in the 1982 Assembly elections. Despite his relatively high media profile and an expensive electoral campaign he returned less than 600 votes in the South Belfast constituency – probably the most conservative and middle class of the North's electoral divisions. His hopes to become a player on the political stage had waned, and the UDA had turned its back on its political aspirations.

He had led some of the most striking attacks on republicans in the history of the UDA but this, too, had begun to feed into his sense of fatalism. He and others in the UDA had watched as Sinn Féin built on the electoral foundations laid in the 1981 Fermanagh–South Tyrone by-election victory by hunger striker Bobby Sands to take five Assembly seats in 1982. While their enemies were establishing a viable political wing the UDA was reverting to form as a purely paramilitary organization, shunned by the unionist voters.

In an interview with the *Irish Press* on 26 March 1984 McMichael later summed it up:

The shooting of Ulster Protestants, whether they are named as part-time members of the UDR or anything else, does have an effect in that the Ulster Protestant community more and more believe that this is nothing less than a war of genocide. Edgar Graham [the Ulster Unionist Assembly member and law lecturer assassinated by the IRA at Queen's University] wasn't a member of the British war machine. He was a politician, just as Gerry Adams calls himself a politician. Now you have actually got what is supposed to be a political wing of the IRA publicly talking about it. Real faces, on real people, giving justification for the 'armed struggle', standing over the Harrods bombing, the murder of Edgar Graham, young Jim Montgomery, a 23-year-old in Moira. While this may be nicely slotted in for people abroad as members of the 'British occupation forces' these people, to Ulster Protestants, are Ulster Protestants.

And Ulster Protestants believe they are on their own, nobody has any interest in them and their backs are to the wall. And it looks that some time in the future they are going to have to fight. It was always mooted before. I think it is accepted now. It is consciously accepted there is not going to be a political solution. British security forces are buying time, they are only the referee.

To some, McMichael's death was a signal that the UDA was in terminal decline. It had been stung by a remarkable series of apparent setbacks – deaths of prominent figures, internal scandals and bitter infighting among the old leadership – culminating with the Stevens inquiry into allegations of collusion. It is of some significance that the decline of the UDA in this period was associated both with increasing racketeering and extensive penetration of the organization by security force agents. By the mid-1980s the UDA's West Belfast intelligence officer, Brian Nelson, and possibly one or more of its six Inner Council members were working as agents for either British army intelligence or the RUC's Special Branch. A Belfast Special Branch officer responsible for 'turning' loyalists at the time has confirmed to the authors that at about this stage the RUC had twenty-six informants inside the UDA. As one senior RUC officer put it, the security forces did not need another UDA informer as they had too many already. By the early 1990s, the UDA leadership also began facing the fact that senior UDA members were implicated in criminal activities that involved associating with republican paramilitaries and may have led to collaboration in the assassination of other loyalists.

Then, a series of seemingly unconnected events between 1987 and 1990 resulted in the re-emergence of the UDA as a renewed and effective terrorist organization.

The first of these was a British television investigation into UDA racketeering. In March 1987 Central Television's *Cook Report* programme set up a meeting with the UDA's western brigadier, Eddie Sayers, through one of its 'front' security companies, Borderline Security, in Omagh, County Tyrone. Sayers was secretly filmed as he attempted to extort money from the reporter Roger Cook who was posing as a businessman seeking to open a factory in Northern Ireland. At one stage in the meeting the blundering Sayers, who had fallen for the sting despite being warned by other UDA men that he might be walking into a trap, struggled over simple arithmetic as he worked out the amount of his extortion demand.

The programme appeared in the late summer of 1987, and caused immense embarrassment to the UDA leadership, especially John McMichael. He was appalled by its effect on the organization's image which was now truly in the gutter. Others in the Inner Council were amazed that Sayers should have fallen for so obvious a trick.

The Central Television programme also exposed the activities of Jim Craig who was, at one stage, self-proclaimed 'military commander' in the UDA, but whose real job was controlling rackets in Belfast. Craig was an archetypal gangster, fond of expensive clothes and jewellery and of holidaying in the Costa del Sol and Florida. If it were not for the Troubles in Northern Ireland, Jim Craig would have been a career criminal. His RUC record went back to 1971, when he was sentenced to seven years for the armed robbery of Simon Seith, a warehouse manager. Craig and two other men burst into Seith's house, viciously assaulted him, beating him about the head, and stole £50. Craig also pleaded guilty to assault with intent to rob, and received a concurrent three-year term. In passing sentence, the judge made reference to Craig's record which included previous cases of assault.

The first public acknowledgement of Craig's senior role in the UDA occurred in September 1974, when he was described as UDA commander in the Maze Prison and was involved in protests over conditions following disturbances at the jail. He subsequently acted as liaison between prisoners and the authorities. In 1981 Craig appeared in court jointly accused with Arthur Bettice of having guns under suspicious circumstances and of membership in the UFF. These charges arose out of a press conference allegedly addressed by Craig where seven hooded men displayed weapons. Craig was eventually acquitted, as he was on several further occasions between 1981 and 1986 when he appeared in court on charges related to para-military activities. Few business people were prepared to risk their lives and the lives of their families to give evidence against him.

By the late 1980s Craig's gangster activities had begun to overwhelm McMichael's attempts to improve the UDA's image. In spite of this, even as Craig slid into deep involvement in racketeering, much of which was clearly for personal gain and involved collaboration with republican paramilitaries, he managed to remain in favour with the Inner Council – by making sure his Inner Council friends got their cut.

Craig was responsible for extortion on a previously unknown scale in loyalist paramilitary circles and, during extensive public sector development in Belfast involving massive public housing and civil engineering projects, he was raking in large amounts of money from building contractors pressing to win tenders and obtain these public contracts. The extent of extortion at the time was well known to the authorities in Northern Ireland. In fact, some in public authority were of the view that without Craig's 'protection' many large housing and other contracts in Protestant areas would not have been completed.

Craig's profits ensured that any reservations among the UDA leadership about his free-spending activities, which included taking a party of more than twenty friends and relatives on holiday to Spain, were tempered by his ability to effectively bankroll the entire organization. It has even been reported that his corrupting influence extended to making a 'loan' of several thousand pounds to McMichael, whose sole income was from a rented public house in Lisburn, County Antrim and who had recently divorced and remarried. It is no exaggeration to say that by the mid-1980s the UDA's military organization existed virtually only as the prop to support its racketeering. Craig and other UDA figures involved with him were persuading the business community to pay protection money largely because of the organization's well-deserved reputation for violence.

While Craig was raking in the money, McMichael was trying to create a new 'clean' army through his and Tyrie's Ulster Defence Force initiative. Figures who emerged at this period and were to rise in prominence in the organization say it was the UDF project that allowed those members committed to the organization and its aims – rather than to Craig's racketeering and ill-gained lucre – to exchange views and express concerns about the activities of the old leadership. As one put it:

The one big plus was that it brought all the various geographical areas together. I'm talking about north, south, east and west Belfast, south-east Antrim, north Antrim, Londonderry. Whereas lads had social contact with each other in Belfast it drew the country people in. It set up the network where views were exchanged that maybe didn't reflect the views of the leadership. It gave the organization a broad pool to draw from while they were doing the training in various camps.

It was the first time we ever crossed the [brigade] boundaries. They used to call it Andy's Army. Certain brigades [Payne's in North Belfast and Lyttle's in West Belfast] told men from their own areas, they weren't to join us because if they failed obviously they couldn't hold rank. But people joined it anyway.

Some of the existing brigadiers were unhappy with the development, and actively took steps to discourage membership. The UDA
man continued:

Brigadiers were frightened of it because it was the first time that people
knew what was going on in different areas. I think what scared the
higher ones at that time was seeing the quality of the leadership, the
quality of personnel that was coming through. They were showing very
distinct leadership skills and a good leader should always ensure there
is someone to replace him no matter what comes or goes. If he fails
to do that there are two things wrong – either he hasn't the ability to
be a leader himself or he's shit scared of the lads taking over. I think
that he [Tyrie] said it must go on, it must continue. And I think his
council round him were starting to get a bit afraid of it. Because Andy
had no brigade behind him at that time, he was sort of isolated and
then, all of a sudden, there was this crowd coming up that he took a
personal interest in.

The concerns of this broad group included the apparently osten-
tatious life being led by Craig and his coterie, and suspicions that
a pact had been agreed upon between the UDA leaders and some
leaders of republican paramilitaries – the IRA, the Irish National
Liberation Army and the Official IRA – to protect each other
from assassination. By 1987 the dissent within the ranks was
growing, reaching levels of near mutiny in the North Belfast
brigade area, particularly annoyed at the imposition of David Payne
as its brigadier by the Inner Council.

While the public view was that McMichael's investigation
was directed at the *Cook Report* allegations, a further immediate interest within the UDA itself appears to have been centred
on the move against Payne in North Belfast. Payne was hated
by his men, several of whom had received vicious beatings,
torture – including the use of a blow torch and electrocution
with an infamous 'black box' – and humiliation. The popular
myth in Northern Ireland that loyalists used electric drills on
victims' knees – instead of a handgun which was usually used
in kneecappings – stems from Payne, who is alleged to have

threatened this against other UDA members. It was, however, never carried out.

Payne was seen as a highly unsuitable local leader by the membership and had previously been the target of an attempted assassination by the UDA in North Belfast. The North Belfast brigade had been put in charge of robbing a County Armagh bank in summer 1987 to raise funds for buying arms. When a part of the money from the proceeds of the robbery went missing and Payne went on holiday to Florida, the local members acted and sent a delegate to the Inner Council to complain.

The disquiet over Payne, the developing relationship among the second-tier leadership and the public disclosures of the *Cook Report* precipitated a leadership crisis in the UDA. In response, the Inner Council announced that an investigation into the racketeering allegations would be carried out by John McMichael, This was undoubtedly as much a public relations exercise as a serious attempt to explore the allegations, and was designed to address both internal as well as external criticism. However, as it progressed, the investigation does seem to have gained a momentum of its own.

The most significant pressure for some form of inquiry came from the second-tier leadership, a group officially referred to as the 'Outer Council'. It had around thirty members, about five from each of the UDA's six brigade areas. Several members of the Outer Council came together through participation in the UDF. As a result of sharing experiences outside their own brigade, members at this level began to realize they had little knowledge of why decisions were being made, and increasingly began to distrust the Inner Council leadership. One Outer Council member who later rose with the ousting of the old leadership said: 'We were kept like mushrooms.'

By the closing months of 1987 John McMichael was indicating that he had prepared a report on allegations of racketeering and misappropriation of funds. It gave precise details of Craig's associations with republicans and blamed him for setting up several loyalists, including some leading UVF men, for assassination by the IRA. However, before McMichael could announce his findings, he was killed. The day after his death someone broke into his office at the UDA headquarters and rifled through his desk and cabinets. Somebody in the UDA definitely didn't want the report to get out.

The bomb that killed McMichael was of a type made only by the IRA and the IRA subsequently claimed responsibility for the killing. Only days after the murder the RUC hinted that McMichael's death might have been a result of collaboration between certain members of the UDA and republican paramilitaries which fuelled the mounting suspicions of those in the UDA who suspected treachery.

McMichael's killing coincided with the arrival in Northern Ireland in January 1988 of a major arms shipment for loyalist paramilitary groups organized through Ulster Resistance via a Lebanese arms dealer. The shipment was partly paid for with £150,000 from the loyalist bank robbery led by the UDA in County Armagh in July 1987 (some of which Davy Payne was suspected of pocketing). The arms shipment consisted of 200 Czech-manufactured assault rifles, 90 Browning pistols, 10 RPG7 rocket systems and 150 warheads, 450 fragmentation grenades, and ammunition for the rifles and handguns.

The arms were brought to a farm between Armagh city and Portadown where they were to be equally divided between the UVF and the UDA. As leader of the brigade that had played a role in raising the funds for the weapons Payne saw an opportunity to raise his profile further in the UDA by personally overseeing their reshipment to Belfast. He hired two Ford Granada saloon cars for the job from a hire company in Belfast. The vehicles were driven by two trusted and experienced UDA men, Jimmy McCullough and Thomas Aiken, from Larne. Payne drove a third car, a small Metro.

The operation was compromised by one of the RUC informants inside the UDA leadership. On the night that Davy Payne drove to the farm outside Portadown to collect the weapons a checkpoint manned by members of the RUC's elite E4A squad

was waiting at a blind junction off the stretch of motorway
bringing the convoy back to Belfast. All three were arrested and
most of the UDA's portion of the shipment was seized. (The UVF
successfully smuggled its share out of Armagh and stashed the
weapons in different hides in Belfast.) The UVF subsequently
allowed the UDA access to this stockpile of arms.

The new generation of UDA leaders believed that Payne precipitated this disaster for the UDA because he was aware of the
declining standards in the organization, and of the opportunities
this presented him with to boost his personal profile. He had
ambitions to replace Andy Tyrie as overall leader. But he had taken
a foolish gamble and ignored the advice of other UDA figures.
One recalled: 'He was told not to physically go because of his
high profile. Organize it but under no circumstances go yourself.'
The mission was in tatters, and, already approaching middle age,
Payne was finished in the UDA. He was sentenced to nineteen
years' imprisonment in October 1988.

In a way, however, the worst was still to come for the UDA.
The information which led to the capture of the arms could have
come from a number of informants within the organization, but
the prime candidate was (and remains) the head of intelligence
of its West Belfast brigade, Brian Nelson.

The old UDA had collapsed almost totally as a result of this
succession of blows, but far from disappearing, the fall of the old
guard laid the ground for the emergence of a new UDA leadership – drawn from the ranks of the second-tier leadership that
McMichael had put in place before his death. His disciples, the
men who had met and trained under his UDF initiative, were
poised to take over.

Andy Tyrie, the chairman of the Inner Council of the UDA
since 1973, was forced to resign in March 1988. He was blamed
for the organization's woes by other, more culpable Inner Council
members. He was unpopular with the West and North Belfast
rank and file for appointing Davy Payne as North Belfast brigadier
against the wishes of local members, and for then refusing to
acknowledge complaints that Payne was stealing UDA funds. Tyrie
was also regarded as Craig's 'protector' in the organization against

elements in West Belfast who wished to see him 'put off the [Shankill] Road'.

It wasn't just the Inner Council that blamed Tyrie for what had gone on. A few days after he resigned a booby-trap bomb was placed under his car by the UVF at his East Belfast home. The UVF, which holds grudges obsessively, blamed Tyrie for allowing Jim Craig to set up some of its members for assassination by the IRA and INLA. Without the protection of his high rank in the organization, Tyrie became a target for the UVF, although at the time it was assumed enemies in the UDA had attacked him.

With Tyrie gone, Craig's time was also quickly running out. He was assassinated in an East Belfast public house in October 1988. Two UVF gunmen shot him repeatedly as he stood at the bar with a pint in his hand. A 68-year-old customer, who apparently tried to shield Craig, also died. Although it was not involved in the killing, the UDA issued a statement claiming the UFF was responsible and saying that Craig was 'executed for treason and other activities which resulted in death of innocent people, including John McMichael' (see Appendix for the UDA's damning indictment of Craig). The UDA in East Belfast colluded in Craig's murder – reputedly he was lured to the pub by a call from local UDA men seeking to fence a large amount of stolen jewellery – but it left it up to the UVF to carry out the assassination. The gun used to kill Craig was a UVF weapon and subsequently it was used in an attack on a Sinn Féin social event in Dublin in 1994 in which an IRA man acting as doorman was shot dead.

By the early 1990s changes had taken place in all four Belfast brigades of the UDA. In the West Tommy Lyttle was arrested, along with Nelson, by the Stevens team in July 1991. The new leaders emerging on the Shankill Road sent word into Crumlin Road jail, where Lyttle was being held on remand, that no one in the UDA was to associate with their former boss. He was isolated for his own safety and sent to the wing of the prison where, among others, sex offenders and child molesters were usually locked up. Or as one of his young usurpers, Jim Spence, put it: 'Tucker's on the wing with the bull roots.' Lyttle was given a seven-year jail sentence for possession of documents likely to be of use to terrorists. The judge at his trial referred to his 'evil' plotting to kill witnesses in the trial of UDA men charged with racketeering.

In South Belfast the appointment of John McDonald as McMichael's successor had much the same effect as Payne's had had in North Belfast. McDonald was distrusted and lasted less than a year before being deposed after being arrested, and later imprisoned for ten years, on extortion charges in January 1990. (His predecessor was subsequently ousted and Jackie McDonald returned to his old post on release from prison.)

In East Belfast, William Elliott, who had become brigadier in the 1980s, was arrested and detained for a while during the Stevens operation. At the time of his release significant arms finds occurred and the new leaders became suspicious of Elliott who, according to one senior figure, was 'frozen out'. Elliott, fearing he was going to meet the same end as Craig, skipped out of East Belfast and it was reported that he had found religion. He survived but never made it back into the organization. Like several of the new leaders, the new East Belfast brigadier was barely out of his twenties, but his tenure of office was short-lived after he was arrested for arms offences within months of his appointment. While he was in prison he was replaced by Jim Gray, who was to establish a firm grip in East Belfast.

Joe English, who had been a staunch opponent of Payne's, succeeded in East Antrim. But neither English nor the man who temporarily assumed control in North Belfast were sufficiently strong-armed to prevent younger, more violent types, allied to the increasingly powerful Shankill leadership, from taking over. Members of this new group now controlled the UDA in East, West and South Belfast, as well as Londonderry, where Billy McFarlane took over the reins and has stayed in power since.

This was a new UDA. The strongest supporters of the internal power struggle that deposed the Tyrie leadership were the North, West and South Belfast Outer Councils, groups based in the urban cockpits of sectarian conflict. The North Belfast UDA in particular was consistently at the centre of the bloodiest sectarian violence in Northern Ireland. The inner northern suburbs of

Belfast, a jigsaw puzzle of already segregated or segregating areas, were fertile ground where a strongman could rise in the UDA. One in every five deaths in the conflict took place in North Belfast which, in its 40:60 per cent Catholic–Protestant mix, is a microcosm of the Province itself. In the early 1990s there were similar and growing tensions in South Belfast.

In fuelling the pressure for change within the UDA, these front-line UDA brigades were possibly more concerned that the old Inner Council was leading the organization towards becoming a political pressure group rather than a paramilitary army, than they were about the alleged pilfering and colluding by some of the then leadership.

In the early 1990s loyalists and even moderate unionists, including some in the Alliance Party, began warning of yet worse violence to come from both the UDA and the UVF. For the first time in almost two decades the catchphrase 'loyalist backlash' reappeared in the media and in political circles. Indeed, in an interview in the *Belfast Newsletter* on 18 February 1992, the Church of Ireland Primate said the threat from 'so called loyalist sources is one of the most sinister, ruthless and best organized ingredients of our tragic situation'. The Democratic Unionist Party deputy leader, Peter Robinson, the Alliance Party leader, Dr John Alderdice, and the former UWC leader, Glen Barr, expressed similar sentiments.

At the heart of this new loyalist militancy was a group of largely unknown figures who had salvaged the near-moribund remains of the monolithic UDA of the early 1970s and were turning them into a smaller, more effective terrorist group. In addition, with the outing of Brian Nelson by the Stevens inquiry, the organization was now free of the most highly placed agent in its upper ranks, along with his sponsor, Tommy Lyttle.

One of the first acts of the new Inner Council after Tyrie was deposed was the symbolic removal of a large oval table which the old Inner Council had sat around in the boardroom at the UDA headquarters. A smaller, round table was installed in its place. This change in arrangements recognized a more substantial change in the structure of the UDA leadership – there was now no longer an official chairman of the UDA. Instead it gained the services of an official adviser, Ray Smallwoods, who, despite his claims to have no official function, was a key figure in the new regime and a major influence on the direction of the new organization.

Smallwoods had served a lengthy jail term after he was arrested following the shooting of Bernadette McAliskey at her home in 1981. He was one of John McMichael's chosen elite and had spent his time in the Maze contemplating the state of the UDA from the outside and quietly making plans for changes along with others of a like mind who felt badly let down by the organization. Smallwoods was a personable, retiring figure who was badly affected by his time away from his family. Other inmates remember him as being somewhat reclusive, a man who listened to BBC Radio Four and the World Service in his cell at night rather than the pop stations that most others preferred.

A new rule came into effect that media interviews on an individual basis were banned and that all interviews would from then on be done as a group with all or as many Inner Council members as possible present – emphasizing the collective nature of the new leadership, and perhaps also suggesting a certain nervousness that stemmed from their predecessors' tendency to float stories about each other in the newspapers. Interviews with the press, which were the principal form of outside communication the leadership used, were now held by the full Inner Council. Journalists who were thought to have been too close to the old UDA leadership were no longer given interviews.

The first interviews granted were with one of the authors and Professor Max Taylor, head of the Applied Psychology Department in University College Cork and an international expert on the psychology and dynamics of terrorism. At the end of one of a series of interviews held over a period of months a brash and not particularly articulate young member from the Shankill joined the Inner Council members without apparent invitation but with no sense of self-consciousness. 'This is Johnny. He's always barging in where he's not wanted,' one of the Inner Council joked, raising laughs all round.

This was Johnny Adair. At later Inner Council press briefings he became a regular figure and no one seemed to question the fact that he was not, on paper anyway, entitled to be there. Subsequently, Adair was greatly taken by the *Guardian*'s Maggie O'Kane during an interview and offered her a lift back into Belfast city centre from the Alpha club in Rathcoole where the briefing had taken place. The journalist reported that Adair had asked if she was a Catholic – something that would have been obvious from her name and Southern Irish accent. After she said she was, he joked that she was the first Catholic to be in his car – well, the first live one. When she was preparing her article, O'Kane asked one of this book's authors for his impressions of the young UDA man. She was told of a Scottish academic's comment that Adair appeared to have the political brain of a Rottweiler. The subsequent article was the first to coin the phrase 'Mad Dog' to describe Johnny Adair – another legend was born.

The purging of figures associated with the old leadership continued in 1992–3, with assassinations and attempted assassinations of suspect members of the old guard. For example, the long-standing East Belfast figure, Edward 'Ned' McCreery, who was implicated in the 1973 romper room killings trial, was shot dead outside his home. He was described in a later UFF statement as 'an enemy of Ulster' and was one of the first of a line of UDA figures to be implicated in drug-dealing. There were active efforts to identify informers within the organization. Some, in fact, emerged as a result of an 'amnesty', and were assassinated by the UDA or fled.

The new leadership made decisions as a group on both political and military matters. It agreed to reorganize the political wing, the Ulster Democratic Party, under the leadership of Gary McMichael, the young and able son of John McMichael. Subsequently, a few UDA members were elected to and successfully held council seats in some of the twenty-six local government constituencies, but none of these made any significant political impact. Some councillors associated with the UDA also stood as independent loyalists, and were elected largely on personal votes.

On the military side, the new UDA tried its hand at bombing in an effort to increase its terrorist capacity, but with little success.

In 1992 it attempted to detonate two van-bombs in Catholic housing areas in West Belfast and Downpatrick, County Down using butane gas as the explosive. The gas bomb was viable in theory: a gas canister was opened and the van allowed to fill up with explosive gas which would then be detonated by a timed fuse. However, the gas leaked out and, as one senior RUC technical officer later put it, such bombs could be rendered ineffective by simply opening the van door. Both the devices were incapable of detonating, and revealed the UDA's continued lack of bomb-making skills.

These bombs were to have been the UDA's response to the huge IRA bombs, up to four tons in weight, which damaged some 1,800 houses, mainly in Protestant areas, in 1992. This republican campaign, largely unreported outside Northern Ireland, deeply aggravated the Protestant population and was undoubtedly one of the contributory causes of the retributive assassinations of Catholics.

In March 1993, attacks occurred in which new types of bombs – again crude but serviceable and dangerous – emerged. A British army bomb disposal officer and a Catholic construction worker both suffered severe hand and arm injuries while handling a new type of anti-personnel device. A customer at a Catholic-owned public house in West Belfast suffered severe injuries to the hand and face when another UDA bomb exploded in the entrance to the bar. Home-made grenades were thrown into the homes of two Sinn Féin members in North Belfast.

Once the security forces found two fingers close to the scene of a small explosion in North Belfast. With no innocent victim in hospital to claim the fingers it was presumed they had been lost by a UDA man handling a badly made bomb. Efforts were made to rectify the UDA's embarrassing lack of bombing skill: 'One day we will get it right, it is coming,' Smallwoods said privately in 1992. But, it never did happen.

The UDA arsenal of assault rifles and sub-machine guns provided it with sufficient resources to pose a small but serious threat in terms of taking life. However, one of the widely believed stories about its weapons sources was completely untrue. In 1989 three Ulster Resistance members walked into a well-laid trap – ironically laid by the same British intelligence services which nationalists were blaming for arming the loyalists in the first place – and were arrested in Paris during an attempt to sell trade secrets about the Shorts-manufactured Starstreak missile to the South African government, in return for weapons and explosives. This led to media speculation that there was a conspiracy between loyalists, South African arms dealers and, because Brian Nelson had visited South Africa, British intelligence. It is an attractive plot for an espionage thriller but it was not true: the UVF would never have trusted the UDA to be involved at the source stage of any arms deal. When it had arranged the 1987 deal with a trusted Lebanese arms dealer, the UDA's role had been simply to stump up money for its half of the weapons.

Aside from the increased supply of weapons available to the loyalists from arms shipments, they had shown they could manufacture their own. During the 1970s, using locally available machine tools and patterns 'borrowed' from the British arms industry, loyalists were able to make a working replica of the Sterling submachine gun. Hundreds were manufactured and used, and the discovery of these weapons in or around UDA premises was a regular occurrence. In September 1988 the RUC raided a small engineering facility in a farm at Ballynahinch, County Down. They found the largest illicit weapons factory ever uncovered in Northern Ireland, and possibly in western Europe. In the plant, the loyalists were close to completing almost 800 sub-machine guns, based on the Israeli Uzi. Thirty were finished, and when tested were shown to be highly serviceable weapons.

The new regime claimed that overt corruption in the UDA had been wiped out and announced a determination to clean up its act 'making the organization acceptable to the people'. A phrase often used was 'returning to the basic principles of the organization'. Raymond Smallwoods was optimistic for the future of the UDA. In a conversation with one of the authors in mid-1992, he said, 'For what my opinion's worth, I believe these guys mean it. The UDA was always the last line of defence between us and an enforced United Ireland. We can't trust the British government and we can't trust anyone else. Without us being here, it would be so much easier for our country, and our way of life to be taken from us.' From this perspective, he said, 'Stevens was a blessing in disguise.'

His comments captured the spirit of the reinvigorated UDA, heralding a new phase in the balance of paramilitary activity in Northern Ireland. In 1985, the year of the signing of the Anglo-Irish Agreement, there was a noticeable rise in loyalist killings. However, from a plateau at sixteen to nineteen deaths per year between 1986 and 1990, there was a striking increase in murders in 1991. The UDA was on the rise again.

9. Mad Dogs off the Leash

They *Sieg Heil*ed all the way from one of Belfast's famous Victorian institutions to another. Disgorging from buses that had transported them from the Shankill Road, Oldpark, upper Ardoyne and other loyalist redoubts in the north of the city, they formed up into military style ranks across the entire width of Donegall Square East. And then they marched, right arms outstretched, while chanting: 'The National Front is a white man's front, join the National Front.'

The uniform mass of shaven heads surged past the memorial garden to Irish soldiers – Protestant and Catholic, unionist and nationalist – who had died fighting for Britain in the blood-stained conflicts of the twentieth century. As they passed by the marble cenotaph some of them shouted 'Hitler was right'; others wore Nazi symbols on the lapels of red and black Harrington jackets or had swastikas stencilled on to bleach-stained jeans. They seemed oblivious to the irony of bellowing fascist slogans at a monument dedicated to servicemen and women who gave their lives in two world wars against Germany, including the crusade to defeat Nazism. As they crossed Bedford Street their pace quickened until they reached the foot of Windsor House, then Belfast's only skyscraper. Then the throng of several hundred Protestant Skinheads charged.

Spearheading the assault was a number of teenage Skins from the lower Shankill and Oldpark districts. Within a decade they were to become the household names of loyalist terrorism. They included Sam 'Skelly' McCrory and Big Donald Hodgen from the Shankill, and their friend from the Oldpark, Johnny Adair. These young men, reared on a diet of violence and sectarianism, whose early lives were dominated by the carnage of the Northern Ireland Troubles, were to form the nucleus of a future paramilitary force – 'C' company of the Ulster Defence Association.

Their quarry on that cold night of 14 January 1981 was a line of anti-fascist – mainly Catholic – Skins, Rude Boys, Mods, Punks and assorted Ska enthusiasts queuing outside the Ulster Hall. The NF Skins had also come to see two of Ska music's leading bands – The Specials and the Beat – even though both groups' message was racial harmony and opposition to neo-fascists. But, more than for the music, the Skins had come to fight.

The other concertgoers (including one of the authors) were hopelessly outnumbered and implored the bouncers at the giant doors to the hall to allow them inside first. Fighting had already broken out along the lines as knots of the Shankill Skins attacked their targets. A few fought back bravely, including one Specials' fan who used a hammer he had hidden in his coat pocket in anticipation of a major assault. All around were blood, screams, insults and the thump and thud of boots and fists.

Having lost control in the street, the door staff ushered scores of anti-Nazi Skins into the Ulster Hall, guiding them towards the stairs and the top tier seating above the dance floor. They then barred the staircases and locked the doors to the upper level, preventing a massacre prior to the gig. Relieved to have escaped from the vengeful loyalist band, the anti-fascist Ska fans settled in their seats and cheered wildly when The Specials came on to the stage. As the first bars of 'Concrete Jungle' blasted out from the stage the 'refugees' in the upper tier danced with delight, and when Terry Hall sang the line in the chorus about 'animals' being after him, they pointed to the NF Skins below. There was a constant exchange of threats, taunts and spittle. One Catholic Skinhead from North Belfast leaned over the balcony and urinated on to a group of Shankill Skins.

After the gig there was only one escape route for the small number of Catholic Skins and anti-Nazis: through the backstage, into Linenhall Street and onwards to the nearby nationalist Markets area. *En route* they ran into the bands' dressing room, greeting a perplexed Jerry Dammers and Terry Hall with handshakes and pats on the back.

Though a brief and relatively bloodless encounter, the 'battle of the Ulster Hall' established the NF Skins' reputation for causing trouble and provoking sectarian violence in the city centre. Strangely, the disturbances were hardly reported in the local media. The *Ulster Newsletter* simply noted – under the headline: 'The Specials bring message of peace' – that £4,000 from the proceeds of the concert were given to the Corrymeela reconciliation centre on the North Antrim coast and the Crescent Youth Centre in South Belfast.

Many who formed up to attack Catholics, socialists, anarchists, anti-racists and anyone else who got in their way, on that infamous night in the Ulster Hall, would eventually graduate from the street-fighting thuggery of the NF to the bigger battalions of the Ulster Defence Association and the Ulster Volunteer Force. In the early 1980s, however, the NF Skins, mostly Shankill Road teenagers, roamed the city centre picking fights with rival Catholic Skinhead gangs (who could be equally vicious and sectarian).

These youngsters became the praetorian guard of the National Front when it staged a number of rallies in central Belfast. During one notorious NF march the Shankill Skins formed the core of the 200 neo-fascist marchers parading into Belfast city centre on a Saturday afternoon in August 1983. Astonishingly, the Royal Ulster Constabulary had granted the Front permission to goose-step through the busy shopping area, despite the fact that it clashed with a demonstration by the Campaign for Nuclear Disarmament. The RUC just about managed to keep apart the NF and CND protesters, who included dozens of left-wing activists.

The march was Johnny Adair's second public outing in central Belfast. With the exception of Adair, all the other Shankill Skins were sniffing glue from plastic bags while marching behind rows of Union Jacks. *An Phoblacht*, the official organ of the Provisional IRA, printed a picture of the marchers with the headline 'Sniffing for Britain'.

The Shankill/NF Skins' activities were not limited to attacking concertgoers or getting high at fascist rallies. Earlier in 1983 three Shankill Skinheads, who referred to themselves as 'NF Skinz', killed a Catholic man, Patrick Barkey, in North Belfast. William Madine, Clifford Bickerstaff and Albert Martin had lured Barkey

to a flat on the promise of a drinking session. When they discovered he was a Catholic, they beat him about the head with a
concrete block. The killers had picked on the softest of targets:
before the murder Patrick Barkey, who had alcohol problems, lived
in a hostel for homeless people. He was found semi-conscious in
the derelict flat. They took his life in the same manner loyalist
gangs had done when they captured Catholics during the 1970s.
The prosecution dropped charges of murder against Madine and
Bickerstaff after they pleaded guilty to the lesser charge of
manslaughter. 'Character' references were provided by 'respectable'
unionist politicians on the Shankill and they were sent to a Young
Offenders' Centre rather than jail. Albert Martin was given a
twelve-month suspended prison sentence after admitting to
causing grievous bodily harm.

As well as attending demonstrations and street-fighting the
Shankill/NF Skins followed a band of their own. Offensive Weapon
was formed in 1983 and modelled itself on Skrewdriver and the
other Oi Skinhead bands that emerged as an offshoot from the
more pacific and progressive Punk movement in the previous
decade. The new group hero-worshipped Ian Stuart, Skrewdriver's
lead singer and a Hitler-loving lunatic (the Jewish Board of
Deputies once described him as 'the most anti-Semitic man in
Britain'). Johnny Adair and Sam 'Skelly' McCrory were two of
Offensive Weapon's founders; Adair played the bass guitar while
McCrory sang. Offensive Weapon wore Skrewdriver T-shirts and
copied their heroes' buzzsaw guitar music and Stuart's overtly
fascist lyrics.

In an interview with the community newspaper *The Shankill
Bulletin* in April 1984 Adair (then twenty) and nineteen-year-old
McCrory denied that their songs were nothing more than Hitlerite
rants. 'We've nothing to do with Nazis, Hitler fought the British,
we're against him,' McCrory said. Given Ian Stuart's love for the
Nazis perhaps McCrory, who later had 'White Power' tattooed on
his arm, was protesting too much. According to *The Shankill
Bulletin*, Offensive Weapon's lyrics were 'full of protest against the
establishment, the government, the police, republicans and blacks'.

Adair, Skelly and their fellow band members, Ken Roy and

Brian Watson, described themselves as the voice of 'Protestant White Youth'. The foursome clearly enjoyed their notoriety through the mid-1980s. When The Specials released 'Free Nelson Mandela' to highlight the plight of the jailed ANC leader, Offensive Weapon responded by holding a 'Hang Nelson Mandela' concert at a loyalist drinking club in the Shankill. Some of their fans turned up wearing T-shirts echoing that demand.

Not every young person on the Shankill was seduced by the hate-filled lyrics of Skrewdriver copy-bands like Offensive Weapon. The author of the *Shankill Bulletin* piece claimed that Offensive Weapon was the only rock band to emerge from the Greater Shankill area in twenty years. In fact another group of Shankill-born teenagers had risen from the Punk/New Wave movement in the late 1970s. Ruefrex, whose drummer Paul Burgess described himself as a lifelong socialist, was performing on Channel 4's pioneering pop programme *The Tube* while Offensive Weapon was still playing to small audiences in dingy loyalist pubs and social clubs.

The importance of the Shankill/NF Skins' emergence is that they were a ready-made street army, ripe for recruitment into the loyalist paramilitary organizations. UDA leaders such as John McMichael, who wanted to raise the tempo of loyalist terrorism in response to the Anglo-Irish Agreement, realized this. For these terrorist chiefs the Skins were the 1980s version of the Tartan gangs, the teenage Protestant thugs at the start of the Troubles who became the first generation of loyalist 'infantry soldiers'. On the Shankill, UDA commanders, including the Special Branch agent and West Belfast brigadier Tommy 'Tucker' Lyttle, started to entice these shaven-headed street fighters into the UDA fold.

After the fall-out from the Stevens Report, when most of the entire top echelon of the old UDA command structure had been removed and was either in custody like Tommy Lyttle, in purdah like Andy Tyrie or dead like Jim Craig, the resulting vacuum allowed younger more militant men to seize control of the organization, end the policy of restraint imposed by Craig and Lyttle, and go on the offensive.

Johnny Adair, Sam McCrory and a large number of their friends in the Lower Shankill estate had been recruited into the Ulster Young Militants (UYM), the UDA's youth wing, sometime in 1987. Some were brought into the UYM after being accused of 'anti-social activities' – Northern Ireland-speak for burglaries, car theft, shoplifting and other petty crime. They were faced with a stark choice: be kneecapped or else join the UYM; most chose the latter option. They included Adair who received three separate beatings for house-breakings in the lower Shankill and lower Oldpark. Following his third hammering Adair agreed to sign up with the UYM.

Looking back on his early assocation with the UDA, Adair admitted that he and his gang regarded the leadership as a 'bunch of oul' Jinnies' who had sat on their behinds and refused to take the 'war' to republicans. However, within a year of joining, Adair and his chums finally found someone to look up to inside the parent organization. They were among the hundreds – possibly thousands – of young working-class loyalists inspired by Michael Stone's near suicidal attack on the funerals of the three IRA members killed at Gibraltar. His exploits in Milltown Cemetery were celebrated on gable walls all over Protestant Belfast. 'Stone loves a Trio,' read one legend in the Village area of South Belfast. 'Three birds dead with one Stone' read another on the Shankill itself.

For Adair, here at last was a UDA 'doer', someone prepared to enter the republican heartland and kill and maim without a concern for his own safety. 'I remember watching it on TV and thinking, "That guy has balls",' he told one of the authors a decade later. 'When you mentioned the UDA before to young loyalists like me on the Shankill, you thought of fat bastards driving big cars who never went out of the office or the bar. Then this man Stone comes along and starts killing republicans on television. We all wanted to be like him and do what he did.'

Stone was the UDA's home-grown superstar and the organization cleverly exploited his status as a loyalist folk hero. Under its then editor, former cross-dressing cabaret singer Sammy Duddy, *Ulster* magazine reported Stone's trial with salacious glee. In the March 1989 edition its correspondent 'Barry Black' (probably

Duddy himself) wrote a résumé of Stone's two-week court appearance on the Crumlin Road. Under the headline 'Loyalist salute as "Rambo" Stone goes down', the writer paid tribute to a 'brave lad . . . who stood bravely in the middle of rebel scum and let them have it'. Black went on to claim that 'In every corner of Loyalist Ulster, in Scotland, Wales and further afield, loyalists are toasting 'Flint Stone' (or Rambo, as he has been dubbed). His name is universally known. He typifies the endurance, bravery and no surrender attitude of Ulster loyalists in the face of adversity.'

Ulster's 'court correspondent' then launched a barbed aside at the old UDA leadership which was still in place at the time of the Stone trial. 'Sadly, Ulster is short of similar heroes. Our penchant for 'jaw-jaw' instead of 'war-war' is being passed on to our children . . . As Michael Stone begins his thirty-year sentence, let us not forget that he gave everything for us. Let us remember with pride, a man among men who refused to pussy-foot in the face of provocation.' That was a sentiment shared by many of Stone's young admirers such as Johnny Adair.

The June 1989 edition printed Stone's message from the Maze to his loyalist brothers and sisters, particularly those in Britain.

I and my fellow loyalist associates value and take great pride in the knowledge that we have your love and support in our struggle. Historically, in blood and kinship, our Scottish bonds are second to none in the world. I, as an Ulster loyalist, salute you, the true loyalists of Scotland, England and Ulster. Long live Ulster. Yours in the cause, Michael Stone.

At the end of the year *Ulster* published a photograph of Stone who, with his long permed hair and moustache, looked like a flashy football player. The picture ran alongside an advertisement for T-shirts signed by the Milltown killer and priced at £4.99. There were UDA polo-shirts, sweaters and tracksuits, some with the Michael Stone logo imprinted on them. The Michael Stone industry was one of the most thriving enterprises of the Ulster Defence Association at the beginning of the 1990s.

Ray Smallwoods was playing an equally decisive role in the

intensification of the loyalist 'war' against republicans and the wider nationalist community in the late 1980s. When he left prison at the beginning of 1990 he was co-opted on to the Inner Council as a political adviser and was asked to play a prominent role in the UDA's political wing, the Ulster Democratic Party. The first time his name appeared in public since his high-profile trial nine years earlier was as the UDP's spokesman. This prompted Bernadette McAliskey to ring one of the authors to ask for a description of the 'Ray Smallwoods' quoted in the *Irish News*. That was how the former civil rights campaigner and MP found out that one of her would-be killers was not only at large but a rising political voice within loyalism.

Today Smallwoods is portrayed as a restraining influence on the UDA's young guns, someone who was intent on pushing the movement towards a ceasefire back in the early blood-stained 1990s. In fact Smallwoods was one of the organization's back-room politico-military strategists. Like his murdered mentor, John McMichael, he believed in targeting the public faces of violent republicanism. And that target area had expanded considerably because by 1990 Sinn Féin had forty-three representatives on district councils ranging from Belfast in the east up to Limavady in the North-West. The party had built up a Province-wide network of advice centres in every nationalist city, town and sometimes village. It had an army of full-time workers in communities through the North to run these centres.

During one of his first interviews with the authors Smallwoods asserted – astutely and prophetically – that there had been a major shift of influence within the republican movement. He zeroed in on Martin McGuinness's 1987 statement that the IRA had now become the 'cutting edge' of a republican struggle based not only on paramilitary violence but on street protest and political activism. The ex-loyalist prisoner recognized the changing role of the Provos' armed wing: 'The army is now subordinated to the party inside republicanism,' Smallwoods said. 'Sinn Féin's leadership is where the power lies now. The IRA just does Sinn Féin's bidding when it needs it.' Ironically, his analysis echoed Gerry Adams's description of the IRA's campaign as 'armed propaganda'. In essence the IRA's terrorism constituted spectacular acts of adver-tising – especially its bombing campaign in London – which trans-mitted the Sinn Féin message to the British.

However, Smallwoods concluded that while the IRA was the cutting edge, a growing Sinn Féin was the republican movement's vulnerable underbelly. A number of UDA members active during the upsurge in loyalist violence have confirmed that while Smallwoods was in favour of loyalists seizing the political initia-tive, of offering a ceasefire and end to violence in the right condi-tions, the former UDA assassin was one of the key strategists behind the ruthless assassination campaign against Sinn Féin coun-cillors and party workers. As one UDA veteran put it: 'Thanks to their electoral successes more and more republicans were coming out of the shadows, were becoming visible.'

At first Johnny Adair and his associates mistrusted Smallwoods because of his emphasis on the politics of loyalism – they simply wanted to kill republicans and Catholics. Davy Adams, a young loyal-ist community worker who lived beside the Maze Prison, joined the UDP because of Smallwoods's influence. Adams remembered that when Adair learned that the man at the edge of the Inner Council meetings expounding about politics, was the same one who had almost killed Bernadette Devlin, his attitude suddenly changed. 'Once Johnny knew that Ray had at one time been a military man he stood up and started to listen to him,' Adams recalled.

The way the UDA went about its business was changed in the early 1990s. Fewer meetings were held at its old 'national' head-quarters in Gawn Street. More interviews with journalists were conducted in the top attic of offices above Frizzels fish shop on the Shankill Road. Inner Council members now meeting on the Shankill talked openly and with considerable contempt about security lapses in Gawn Street. They also cited the scandal over John McDevitt, a 'security guard' at Gawn Street, who was convicted of assaulting underage girls in the East Belfast office, as an example of the old lax ways. Influence was flowing back to the Shankill just as its units became the most active in loyalist terrorism.

*

Stone's one-man gun and grenade attack at Milltown, the decap-
itation of the old UDA leadership, the recruitment of the street
fighters from the Shankill, and the release of Smallwoods coincided
with a new political and security crisis in Northern Ireland. For
loyalists the intensification of the Provisional IRA's campaign and
the first moves to bring together the forces of Irish nationalism
in the North posed the greatest threat to the Northern Ireland
state since Stormont was prorogued in 1972. Loyalism entered the
1990s nervous and paranoid about the future of the union with
Britain.

Since February 1988 the SDLP leader, John Hume, had been
talking in secret to both the IRA and Sinn Féin with a view to
securing an end to republican violence. Although the talks failed
to bear fruit, with Hume accusing the Provisionals of being guilty
of 'undiluted fascism' at the SDLP annual conference in the same
year, behind the scenes he continued to pursue dialogue with
republicans. Facilitated by the Catholic clergy at Clonard
Monastery in West Belfast and St Clements retreat house in the
north of the city, Hume met Gerry Adams throughout 1993.
Mainstream unionist politicians as well as loyalist paramilitary
groups raised the spectre of a Pan Nationalist Front comprising
the Irish government, the SDLP and now Sinn Féin. (The PNF
phrase was not a unionist invention: Gerry Adams had been the
first to use it as far back as 1984 when he called for the formation of a 'pan-nationalist' electoral pact.) Throughout the various
phases of the Hume–Adams talks (or the Adams–Hume talks as
Sinn Féin liked to remind its voters on the walls of the Falls
Road) the SDLP leader had dangled the prospect of an all-Ireland
peace conference if the IRA called off its violence. To unionists
this strategy was merely a tactical ploy to create a nationalist pincer
movement that would encircle Ulster Protestants while forcing
the British to become the 'persuaders' for a United Ireland.
Revelations in the *Observer* in 1993 that the British government
had in fact been holding clandestine discussions with Martin
McGuinness in Derry merely exacerbated unionism's siege
mentality. In the collective unionist imagination not only were
the forces of moderate nationalism allying themselves with the

IRA's political wing and ganging up against them, but they were also being 'stabbed in the back' by their own government.

Although there were several attempts to kick-start all-party talks (excluding Sinn Féin) after the demise of Margaret Thatcher in 1990, aimed at forming a new devolved government in Northern Ireland, Hume–Adams cast a long – and unionists argued, withering – shadow over every political initiative. The unionists suspected that the success of talks involving the UUP, DUP and SDLP were secondary in John Hume's mind to his on-going dialogue with Sinn Féin. Their suspicion was compounded by the increase in IRA violence in the late 1980s and early 1990s. Even while Adams held out the hand of friendship publicly to his SDLP opponents and latterly the unionists themselves, the IRA had been ratcheting up its 'armed struggle' since around 1987 when the Provisionals started using the large caches of weaponry smuggled in from Colonel Gadafy's dictatorship in Libya. For loyalist 'thinkers' such as Ray Smallwoods, and a number of mainstream unionist politicians, as well as legal figures advising the UDA's Inner Council, this new wave of violence represented not just the 'cutting edge' of Sinn Féin but rather the entire Pan Nationalist Front.

The 1972 crisis had transformed the UDA from a federation of local defence committees into a mass underground loyalist army; this new crisis created a different kind of violent reaction in loyalism. The UDA and the UVF had watched the IRA refining their armed campaign by using smaller tight-knit units to carry out assassinations and sabotage. The loyalists, who were still organized along the lines of the regular British army with companies, battalions and brigades, also now honed their killing machines, slimming them down to groups of four or five men per team. In the lower Shankill, for instance, 'C' company subdivided into sections of up to a half dozen activists in each one – C1, C2, C3, C4 and so on. Loyalism's resistance to any constitutional change would no longer be to put thousands on the streets and the picket lines, as they had done in 1974. Instead they would send out a series of armed gangs to spread terror and mayhem within the general Catholic population of Northern Ireland and, ultimately, they intended, the citizens of the Irish Republic.

In 1989 the UDA had killed five people, including Pat Finucane, but within two years its murder rate had more than trebled with nineteen nationalists alongside a handful of suspected informers shot dead. The leap in the killing rate was largely down to the activities of two brigades, South and West Belfast. Back in 1989 it could be argued that all the five victims had either past, present or family connections to the republican movement. By 1991, however, the UDA's target range had broadened once again to the general Catholic population: out of the nine nationalists murdered at the UDA's hands in 1990, five were politically un-involved Catholics. The following year the number of murders of Catholics with no connection to republican groups more than doubled: twelve out of the nineteen UDA victims were ordinary nationalists.

The breakdown of which areas were responsible for the various murders also indicates the growing importance of West Belfast, and in particular 'C' company in the lower Shankill. In 1989 the West Belfast brigade, specifically members of 'A' company from the Highfield district, had been responsible for one death, albeit a high-profile one – Pat Finucane's. A year later 'C' company activists carried out three of the five UDA murders. In 1991 the same unit was behind a further six murders in West and North Belfast.

By 1990 the UDA's redoubts on the Shankill were awash with new guns, rocket launchers, grenades and ammunition. A tranche of the weaponry smuggled by three loyalist organizations from Lebanon in 1987 had significantly boosted the UDA's arsenal, enabling it for the first time to carry out rocket attacks on repub-lican targets. But the UDA's first attempt to 'test fire' the Rocket Propelled Grenades (RPGs) that had once belonged to the IRA's Middle Eastern allies, the PLO, almost ended in carnage on the Protestant side of the peace line separating the Shankill from the Falls. (For some reason Sinn Féin, Relatives for Justice and other nationalist pressure groups still insist that these weapons origi-nated in South Africa. One can only guess that this persistence is due to propaganda rather than reaching out for the truth. The fact remains that the haul came from Lebanon; the only South

African connection was the arms dealer Douglas Bernhart who set the deal up between the loyalists and the Lebanese business-man Joe Fawzi.)

The UDA's new recruits on the lower Shankill were eager to learn how to fire the RPG in preparation for a series of attacks on Sinn Féin advice centres and offices around Belfast. Early in January 1990 a team was selected from the area to test the weapon. It included Johnny Adair's old friend Gary 'Smickers' Smyth and a man who was to become within a matter of months his second-in-command in 'C' company. A former British soldier had been chosen to train them in how to arm, handle, aim and fire the RPG. Following a brief 'GL' (Belfast-speak for gun lecture) in a house on the left-hand side of the lower Shankill Road, the rocket team took the weapon outside. They positioned the RPG in Dover Street, from where marauding loyalist gangs had come to attack Catholic homes in the Falls Road in August 1969. A 20-foot peace line now cut off Dover Street from the Falls and the 'C' company rocket team planned to fire the warhead over the concrete barrier and into waste ground on the nationalist side. But the rookie RPG squad made a near fatal mistake – assuming that the warhead travelled through the pipe and out via the round bottom of the weapon. The unit was firing the weapon the wrong way round. When Adair's future second-in-command pressed the firing mech-anism the warhead shot off behind and the men were knocked off their feet by the blowback from the RPG. Instead of hurtling over the peace line and into no-man's land the rocket struck the wall of an old people's residence in Dover Street, narrowly missing a window leading to one of the pensioner's bedrooms. A few inches either way could have spelt disaster for the residents.

Former members of 'C' company admit that there were 'so many weapons now available we didn't know what to do with them'. But since it was open season on nationalists, whether involved with the IRA or INLA or not, these young sectarians were going to get the chance to use them.

The IRA rather than loyalists drew first blood as the new decade opened. On the morning of 2 January 1990 a booby-trap bomb exploded under Harry Dickey's car outside his house in the Sydenham area of East Belfast. Dickey died at the scene of the blast, just 200 yards from his home. He had been taking his sixteen-year-old daughter to school and she sustained minor injuries in the explosion. Although Dickey was a member of the Ulster Democratic Party he had no active role inside the UDA. At the time of the murder though, his brother-in-law was the East Belfast brigadier and for a short period spoke on behalf of the UDA's flag of convenience, the Ulster Freedom Fighters.

Eighteen days later Brian Nelson finally appeared at Crumlin Road court house, faced in the public gallery by at least two members of the Inner Council, along with his sister, Brigid Drumgoole. A week after Nelson's initial appearance in the dock he was isolated from other prisoners after it emerged that the UDA's intelligence officer had been an army agent. But Nelson's revelations did nothing to deter his West Belfast comrades from going on the offensive.

On 11 March one of 'C' company's teams, led by Stephen McKeag, crossed the peace line via Lanark Way, a main arterial route linking the Shankill to the nationalist Springfield Road, *en route* to a bar close to where an IRA commemoration was being held. Eamon Quinn was cleaning his car outside his home on the Kashmir Road in the Clonard district when the gunmen pulled up in the street. McKeag opened fire with a handgun at point-blank range, killing the 32-year-old Catholic father of one almost instantly. Thus began a new campaign of sectarian murder that was to strike terror into the hearts of Belfast's Catholics.

10. A Temporary Peace

The fear on the streets of working-class North and South Belfast was replicated in the landings, stairwells, mess halls and exercise yards of Crumlin Road Prison. Inside the Victorian jail loyalists and their republican enemies were living cheek by jowl. The Northern Ireland Office (NIO) had imposed a regime of integration on paramilitary inmates who were on remand waiting to be sentenced for various terrorist offences ranging from murder and bombing to extortion and blackmail. Unlike in the Maze, where individual H-blocks were under the control of the various terror groups and rival factions rarely interacted, in 'the Crum' IRA, INLA, UVF and UDA suspects met each other every day. Inevitably there were violent clashes between remand prisoners, which eventually led to the deaths of two loyalists. Both Sinn Féin and the UDA argued, with logic on their side, that it was absurd to forcibly integrate sworn enemies who on the outside lived behind Berlin wall-style barriers that kept their respective communities apart. Contrary to the opinion of the then NIO security minister John Cope, there was no collusion between republicans and loyalists to end the integrated regime at the jail.

For the average UDA man on remand it was the first time he had ever encountered his republican foes in the flesh. Joe English, then serving as an adviser on the Inner Council, recalled confronting the former Sinn Féin publicity director, Danny Morrison, on a landing one afternoon. Morrison was on remand, having been arrested in connection with the abduction of IRA informer Sandy Lynch in 1990; English had been arrested on charges relating to the Stevens inquiry into collusion (he was later freed). 'Morrison passed me on the stairs and I just looked at him and thought: is that what we are meant to be afraid of?'

Other prisoners under paramilitary control were more inclined to engage in violent clashes with their enemies. Inmates threw

hot tea and boiling water over each other; there were fistfights,
attempted stabbings and constant death threats. One UDA remand
prisoner said the pressure of living beside men they were determined to kill beyond the Crum's walls became unbearable.
'Something had to give because it was obvious prisoners were
going to be killed in there. Something had to be done.'

That 'something' was a series of mini-riots, with loyalists smashing up their cells and attacking prison officers, on 16 April 1990.
Republicans joined in separately and by lunchtime up to 100 prisoners from both sides were running amok in 'C' wing of the jail.
To quell the trouble the anti-riot unit known to the prisoners as
the Ninjas was sent in. Dressed head to toe in black uniforms,
only their eyes showing from black masks, and armed with riot
shields and batons, the unit had a reputation among inmates for
heavy-handed tactics. Several loyalists sustained minor injuries as
they were beaten off the landings and back into their cells.

The violence inside the Crum threatened to spill out to the
streets when on the same evening the UDA (again using the UFF
cover name) issued a chilling warning to prison officers. The terror
group's leadership said prison staff – almost all of whom lived
either in or on the edge of loyalist areas – would be killed if there
was further 'persecution' of loyalist prisoners. The death threats
were another example of the UDA going for the soft underbelly.
As the Prison Officers' Association pointed out three days later,
their members had no power over NIO policy and attacks on
staff would not change the position.

The assaults on prison officers inside the jail continued the
following month. On 13 May eight were injured during clashes
with UDA inmates who eventually got on to the roof of the
Crum to protest about integration. Eleven days later there were
more disturbances, cells were wrecked and staff beaten up. Outside,
in Lisburn, several homes belonging to prison officers were petrol-
bombed.

For two months the UDA concentrated its energy in greater
Belfast on the Crumlin Road prison dispute. But once the loyalist marching season began it embarked on a summer–autumn
offensive against nationalists, with 'C' company to the fore of the

campaign. On 15 July the UDA's Lisburn unit shot dead 34-year-old Catholic, Martin Hughes, outside his home in Huguenot Drive, Lisburn; a 21-year-old man was also injured in the shooting. Both victims had just returned from an evening out in the Ancient Order of Hibernians local hall. Hughes's mother heard the shots that killed her son while she sat watching television and cradled Martin in her arms as he lay dying.

In a statement the UDA (again through its UFF cover name) alleged that Martin Hughes was a member of the IRA – a claim totally disputed by his family. Their parish priest, Father Denis Newberry – a staunch critic of violence who knew plenty of active republicans from his time working in the lower Ormeau/Markets area of Belfast – rejected any suggestion that Martin Hughes was even a member of a political party, let alone the IRA. The truth was that he was an easy Catholic target living in a predominantly Protestant area. Although the UDA denied that the Hughes killing had anything to do with the murder of a Protestant twenty-four hours earlier, loyalist sources in Lisburn now admit that it was a simple tit-for-tat operation and that the Catholic victim had no IRA connections.

On 31 July the UDA struck again, this time across the peace line between the Shankill and Springfield Roads. John Judge, a 34-year-old married man with three children, had been drinking outside his Valleyside Close home off the Springfield Road around 11 p.m. It had been a happy day for the Judge household where one of the children had just celebrated a fifth birthday. He was sharing a beer with his brother-in-law and two friends when a UDA unit appeared at the gate. As the men ran for safety two masked gunmen fired their handguns. After the shooting they fled the scene in a hijacked Ford Orion taxi, which had been stolen from a family in Heather Street off the Shankill Road just fifteen minutes earlier. John Judge was hit five times in the body and died at the scene.

His killers, who included the UDA's Top Gun, Stephen McKeag, and his team from 'C' company, did not have far to go for sanctuary. As with the Eamon Quinn murder, they drove the short distance through the Lanark Way route to the Shankill and back to a safe house where they were able to dispose of their weapons, masks, gloves and clothes they were wearing and then take a shower to destroy any forensic evidence. Given that there had already been several attempted murders by 'C' company using Lanark Way to get to and from nationalist West Belfast, the spiritual leader of Belfast's Catholics, Bishop Cahal Daly, led calls for it to be sealed off.

To justify this random murder the UDA claimed that John Judge was an IRA bomber – again a charge dismissed not only by his family and the Catholic clergy, but also by the RUC.

The UDA's revamped terror campaign switched to South Belfast on 7 September, when a unit commanded by Joe Bratty killed 34-year-old Emmanuel 'Senior' Shields, shooting him five times as he slept with his pregnant girlfriend in their Deramore Street home off the Ormeau Road. Although the victim had a criminal record (he was jailed for a year in the 1970s for possessing a firearm and in 1979 was given a nine-year sentence for an armed robbery at an off-licence), he did not belong to any republican faction at the time of his murder. When they were finished, at 3 a.m., Bratty's two-man gang was able to make off on foot towards Haywood Avenue and on to Annadale Flats, at one time a UDA stronghold in the upper Ormeau. The Shields family later revealed that Emmanuel had been the repeated target of murder attempts and savage beatings at the hands of Joe Bratty's team. A few years earlier, when Emmanuel Shields was living with his mother in Burmah Street, the UDA had fired several shots into the house but he had escaped uninjured.

In the upper Ormeau/Ballynafeigh the tensions between local Catholics and the small pocket of loyalists holed up in Annadale Flats were personal. Unlike in other areas of Belfast, the UDA killers and their Catholic victims knew each other, grew up together – in many cases in the same streets – and even played as young boys, in the same soccer teams. Since childhood men such as Emmanuel Shields had been tormented by Joe Bratty, his closest associate, Raymond Elder, and Thomas 'Tucker' Annett. Given the close proximity of victim and perpetrator, in many of the murders and attempted murders in this part of South Belfast, naked sectarian hatred was compounded by long-standing vendettas and personal grudges nurtured from boyhood.

'C' company struck again on 16 October when one of Stephen McKeag's teams gunned down 41-year-old father of three Dermot McGuinness as he walked home along Rosapenna Street in North Belfast after buying a bottle from the off-licence on the Oldpark Road where his wife worked. The 'C' company team tried to force their victim into a car, but when he resisted they shot him six times at point-blank range. Again the UDA tried to blacken its victim's reputation by claiming he was an activist in the republican splinter group the Irish People's Liberation Organization (IPLO). Jimmy Brown, one of the IPLO's founders (who was to die in a feud two years later), contacted one of the authors that night to say that McGuinness had never had any connection with his organization. Dermot McGuinness was shot dead just minutes after a former policeman, Stephen Craig, was murdered less than half a mile away, outside the Chester Park Hotel on the Antrim Road. Craig had been lured by IRA spies from a pub in Belfast city centre and brought to the Chester Park, where he was killed while waiting outside for a taxi.

Between late September and late October 1990 the UDA also shot dead three former members it initially – and it turned out incorrectly – accused of being informants for the RUC Special Branch. The South Belfast brigade's Lisburn unit killed William Allister when it mistook him for a man who was a close associate of the murdered racketeer Jim Craig. Two gunmen had burst into the County Arms pub on the Hilhall Road, singled out two men drinking at a table and shot them several times at close range. The UDA later admitted to killing the wrong man. The victim's friend, Geordie Friars, died of his wounds on 7 October. Though Allister was not the intended target of the assassination, Geordie Friars was one of those the Lisburn UDA believed was working for the security forces. The gunmen's real target was Clifford McKeown, the loyalist supergrass from Mid-Ulster. They set out to kill him because the UDA believed he was passing on information about it and the UVF to his RUC contacts. They believed he would be in the County Arms when their unit burst in.

(McKeown is currently serving a life sentence for the 1996 murder of Catholic taxi-driver Michael McGoldrick. It now seems likely that he was being run as an agent in the early 1990s – certainly the UDA were so sure of it that they were prepared to hunt him down and kill him – so there is a question to be answered as to whether his handlers knew he had rejoined the ranks of loyalist paramilitaries and was about to kill a Catholic in the midst of the 1996 Drumcree crisis in Portadown.)

A fortnight later the South Belfast brigade admitted they killed 28-year-old Robert Skey – just forty-eight hours after he had been released from police custody, having been questioned about the kidnapping and beating of a Catholic man in North Belfast. On his return to Suffolk estate, the last Protestant stronghold in the Upper Falls ward of West Belfast, he was abducted from his house in Donegore Gardens. On 25 October Skey was found with gunshot wounds to the head on the Taughmonagh estate, a loyalist working–class area on the southern edge of Belfast. The UDA alleged that the murdered man had been working for the Special Branch. The murder put enormous pressure on the Skey family especially since the victim's brother Robert was on remand as a UDA prisoner in Crumlin Road jail. (He was later killed in an IRA rocket attack on the prison.)

The only member of the republican movement the UDA murdered in 1990 was the 57-year-old father of eleven children Tommy Casey. The Sinn Féin member was shot as he went to check an empty house in Moveagh Road, Cookstown for its owner, a friend who was on holiday. It was clear that the killers had accurate information on Casey's movements, although the UDA in South Belfast (which carried out the assassination) later admitted it was actually hoping to target the brother of an IRA man killed at the 1987 SAS ambush in Loughgall in which eight top IRA activists from East Tyrone had been shot dead. A fortnight after the shooting, the UDA took over the empty house where the killing had taken place. They waited an hour for the brother of the IRA 'martyr' to arrive. When no one appeared they set fire to the house.

It might appear strange that the South Belfast brigade was

providing the personnel to conduct 'operations' in Mid-Ulster and beyond, but the South Belfast remit did not end in the Lagan Valley running from Sandy Row in central Belfast to the edges of Lisburn. It was and remains the largest UDA brigade area in Northern Ireland and is responsible for units from as far away as the Fermanagh border, Tyrone, Lurgan, Cookstown and South Down. At its core were two killing machines – Lisburn and the Sandy Row/Village teams – which carried out most of the murders in the region under their control. After West Belfast, and particularly 'C' company, South Belfast was the most ruthless and feared UDA brigade in Northern Ireland.

The UDA had almost doubled its killing rate in a year, but in 1991 its violence was to reach new and frightening levels. Indeed, in autumn 1990 it had threatened to intensify its violence, issuing a statement that it would now consider all Catholics working in Protestant areas as 'legitimate targets' – the phrase the IRA had used in its September warning against contractors working for the security forces. And in all this time the UDA was still a legal organization operating under the Ulster Freedom Fighters *nom de guerre*. As its murders rose steadily so did the demands that it be proscribed.

On 27 January 1991 'C' company again attacked the Rosapenna area of the Oldpark, this time Rosapenna Court, just yards away from where Dermot McGuinness was slain. A 'C' company team travelled the short distance from the lower Shankill, up along the Oldpark Road and into the nationalist area. They broke through the door of Sean Rafferty's house and fired at their target several times. As Rafferty lay on the floor the killers pumped more bullets into his body. A teenager was later given a four-year sentence for hiding the guns used in the shooting. In court he confessed that a day later he had brought them up to the UDA's headquarters above Frizzels fish shop. Two days after Sean Rafferty's murder – another case of 'any Catholic will do' – Rhonda Paisley, daughter of DUP leader Ian Paisley, called for the UDA to be banned.

More killings followed in March and April including, on St Patrick's Day, Stephen Audley, a 23-year-old UDA man. Audley and two members of the Ulster Young Militants had been given a gun to shoot a man accused of robbing an elderly woman. At first Audley and his UYM companions could not find their target. Later they went to a party where they got into a row. One of the UYM members, inexperienced at handling guns, started waving about the weapon threatening partygoers. Audley grabbed for the gun and it went off. He died from his injuries. Four years later a UYM mural dedicated to Stephen Audley's memory was painted on a wall off Roden Street. In the same year his name appeared on a roll of honour on a large mural headed 'UDA's A battalion Sandy Row'.

Another of the victims was Sam Bell, a Protestant who had converted to Catholicism. He was found in his burnt-out taxi at Thompson's Lane off the Glencairn Road. He had been shot in the head and then his car set alight.

Although the UDA's 'A' company in Highfield had been responsible for the shooting, the weapon used to murder Sam Bell, a .45 revolver, belonged to the UVF. On the surface this may seem puzzling given the historic enmities between the UDA and UVF on the Shankill and the bouts of feuding between the two factions. The picture on the Shankill, however, was complex. Personal relations between the UVF in the upper Shankill and the UDA's 'A' company, based in the Highfield and Springmartin estates, were relatively warm, and on a number of occasions the two forces had swapped weapons, ammunition and intelligence. In Springmartin, a small Protestant estate on high ground overlooking the republican Springhill and Ballymurphy, the UDA and UVF shared the keys to a flat. They used the apartment to spy into the heart of the republican areas and it was from there that they carried out a surveillance operation against a senior member of the IRA's Belfast brigade in 1987, only to have army agent Brian Nelson divert them away from the IRA operative and on to Francisco Notorantonio.

Sam Bell's murder marked the start of an escalating campaign against Catholic taxi-drivers in greater Belfast. On 17 April John O'Hara, a 41-year-old driver for a taxi firm in the Markets area, was shot dead after answering a bogus telephone call to pick up a fare in Dunluce Avenue off the Lisburn Road. The address

O'Hara had been given turned out to be a derelict house out of which stepped four masked men from the UDA's Sandy Row/Donegall Road/Village unit. A number of them directed fire into O'Hara's car and then made off across a footbridge at Fane Street. A nurse who appeared at the scene at first thought she had encountered a drunk driver because John O'Hara was still conscious at the wheel driving along Dunluce Avenue, smashing into a number of parked cars before finally hitting a wall. Given the close proximity of Belfast City Hospital to the shooting it can perhaps be speculated that the victim was trying to get to its accident and emergency department. In a ghoulish twist the UDA men who made the bogus call to the Markets depot called back and started laughing and joking about the murder.

John O'Hara had no connections with republican paramilitary groups; he had simply been another available target in the UDA's new campaign to intimidate and terrorize the Catholic population of the city. For the murdered man's widow it was the second tragedy of the Troubles. Sixteen years earlier her first husband, Hugh Duffy, had been shot. On that occasion too, the UDA had claimed that its target had republican connections – in this case to the Official IRA. Both the coroner, and later the Officials themselves, denied Hugh Duffy had any links to the organization.

Just a few hours after John O'Hara's death the UDA, along with the UVF and its satellite organization the Red Hand Commando, declared a temporary ceasefire. The cessations were announced twelve days before the start of talks between the parties (except Sinn Féin) convened by Northern Ireland Secretary Peter Brooke. The suspension of violence – at least in Northern Ireland – for the duration of the talks was to give the parties breathing space and demonstrate that loyalists wanted a peaceful, just solution to the deadlock in Ulster.

The ceasefire was the product of months of discussions between the rival loyalist factions brought together under the umbrella of the Combined Loyalist Military Command (CLMC), which included senior military and political figures from both wings of loyalism. The UDA was represented by political and military liaison officers (LOs): Ray Smallwoods was the political LO and Alex Kerr the organization's military representative. Kerr, from South Belfast but with antecedents across the border in County Donegal, worked closely with the UVF's LO, its second-in-command for the whole of Northern Ireland, who later opened up a secret dialogue with the Irish government. Kerr was an articulate, capable and ruthless UDA leader who, unlike many in the ranks, possessed keen political instincts. At the time South Belfast brigadier and a member of the Inner Council, he was sceptical about the reaction of the IRA to the CLMC's unilateral gesture and suspicious about the entire nationalist camp, which he regarded as having wrung concessions from the British on the back of IRA terrorism. While his influence was critical in securing support for the ceasefire on the ruling body, Kerr insisted to the UVF that the UDA's suspension extended only as far as the frontier with the Irish Republic.

Just three days before the loyalist guns fell silent the UDA tried to murder a 23-year-old Catholic joiner in South Belfast. Barry Tracey was blasted in the back with a shotgun while carrying out repairs to a house off the Ravenhill Road. The UDA, as always using its UFF cover name, said the shooting was in retaliation for the IRA's attacks on Protestants working on security force installations and bases. Barry Tracey underwent emergency surgery in the Royal Victoria Hospital and was very seriously ill, but pulled through.

Throughout the CLMC cessation, which lasted from 29 April until 4 July, the IRA actually intensified its bombings and shootings. The Provos killed thirteen people, including three policemen, a retired RUC officer, four UDR soldiers, two regular British army soldiers and two civilians, including a member of the Ulster Democratic Party. They also bombed Protestant villages and towns and caused widespread devastation. Loyalists inside and outside the CLMC suspected that the carnage and destruction were designed to provoke them.

Alex Kerr felt vindicated by the intensified IRA campaign. In an interview with one of the authors in the summer of 1991 he said the events of May and June proved the IRA was not ready for peace. 'A lot of the guys on the ground taking the war to republicans said to us, "Look where did it get us, this ceasefire." They saw Protestant homes destroyed, Protestants slaughtered on their streets and they wanted to hit back.'

11. The Gravedigger's Tale

The UDA hit back against the republicans even before the CLMC officially announced the end of its short-term cessation of violence. On 25 May 1991 a special UDA unit comprised of members from Lisburn and Belfast broke into a house belonging to 56-year-old Sinn Féin councillor Eddie Fullerton in County Donegal. The four-man murder squad was taken to Fullerton's home at Cockhill Cottages in Buncrana in the back of a trailer that belonged to a local Protestant farmer who, like many of his co-religionists in the county, loathed Sinn Féin and the IRA. Local Protestants had offered help and information through the UDA's North-west brigade, some of whose members in Derry had family ties across the border in East Donegal. Among the team lying in hay bales *en route* to the Sinn Féin councillor's home was one of the most senior UDA members in Northern Ireland, accompanied by another Lisburn UDA man, known as 'Gravedigger'. The UDA commander directed the killers, including the 'Gravedigger', into Fullerton's house with a series of hand signals. Once inside, the Lisburn UDA men ran up the stairs and into Fullerton's bedroom, where he was gunned down in front of his English wife. The unit then fled the scene in a hijacked car that was waiting for them nearby. Within fifteen minutes they were back in the relative safety of Northern Ireland.

Between 1989 and 1991 the South Belfast brigade was responsible for a dozen murders and it is estimated by his former comrades that ten of these were the work of the 'Gravedigger' from Lisburn. Those who knew him inside the UDA remark on his 'professionalism' as a top UDA hitman. 'He never left any patterns to his jobs,' one UDA associate recalled several years after the murder,

He would go out very early in the morning, be picked up walking in a rural area somewhere by the car used for the hit rather than have it come to his house. On returning from hits he would be dropped off somewhere remote, say near a bus stop, and he would take a rural bus journey far away from where the job was done. He was always efficient, cool and very ruthless.

The UDA claimed they selected Councillor Fullerton for assassination because he allegedly passed on a missing garda file to the IRA. The result, the UDA alleged, was the death of Ian Sproule, a 23-year-old Protestant shot at his parents' house in Castlederg, County Tyrone, close to the Donegal border. Justifying the Sproule murder, the IRA leaked a photograph allegedly handed over to them by the 'Free State Police', along with information that he was a loyalist suspect. The picture bore a resemblance to Ian Sproule although there were no other personal details about him on the leaked document. The May edition of *Ulster* seized upon the Provos' claims and, while dismissing wholesale collusion between the IRA and members of the Republic's security forces, said it was 'highly probable that collusion definitely exists'.

Eddie Fullerton's family have since proposed an alternative theory about why he was sought out by the UDA. They allege that he had upset powerful vested interests both in business and the police in County Donegal and was about to expose a major corruption ring in the county. The Fullertons claim that it was these powerful interests that set up the Sinn Féin councillor, using local Protestants on the Donegal side of the border to help carry out the hit, although the shooting was the work solely of the UDA unit. While the UDA has dismissed these allegations, pointing out that loyalists would never be foolish enough to trust 'Free State citizens' offering intelligence for fear that they were in turn being set up, there remains one mysterious and controversial aspect to the Fullerton murder. The killers chosen for the operation came not just from nearby in the UDA's Derry brigade, but also from South Belfast and Lisburn. And although he was not himself on the team in Buncrana that night, one of the UDA's most senior members in Lisburn was aware that Eddie Fullerton was about to die. This same man, Ned Greer, was an agent for both the RUC Special Branch and the Force Research Unit.

Greer was a disciple of John McMichael and had joined the UDA in the early 1980s. Following McMichael's assassination in 1987 he worked his way through the ranks until he became second-in-command of the UDA in Lisburn. He impressed his comrades because he was able to provide them with leaked security files that originated not only from RUC sources but also from the British army's Northern Ireland headquarters at Thiepval barracks on the edge of Lisburn.

Greer's sources provided him with high-grade intelligence on IRA suspects, including Padraig Ó Seanacháin, a 33-year-old Sinn Féin activist from Castlederg, County Tyrone. Ó Seanacháin had been a thorn in the British army's side for several years, and had been behind a series of IRA under-car booby-trap bombs that killed several members of the Ulster Defence Regiment along the border over a four-year period. On 12 August 1991 Ó Seanacháin was travelling to work on a road at Killen outside Castlederg when a UDA sniper opened fire on his car and killed him. The murdered man's family maintained that he was just a political activist in Sinn Féin with no connections to the IRA, but the UDA insisted otherwise – safe in the knowledge that British army intelligence files pinpointed Ó Seanacháin as the booby-trap bomb expert. (In 2002 the IRA acknowledged Ó Seanacháin as one of its own in a tribute-book to dead 'volunteers' of the Troubles.)

Greer's career as an informant for Special Branch and FRU outlasted Brian Nelson's by three years. He managed to inflict some damage on the Lisburn UDA with operations foiled, men arrested and weapons recovered by the police. Yet his tenure as second-in-command of Lisburn coincided with a hike in UDA activity with more than a dozen people killed and scores injured. One senior figure in the South Belfast brigade back then subsequently described Greer as having been as important as Brian Nelson. 'Ned did as much damage to us as Nelson, in fact he may have done more. Ned has as many secrets in his head as Nelson took to his grave. When he disappeared there were a lot of worried people in Lisburn.'

By late 1992 Greer's handlers had realized from other sources inside the UDA that the organization had grown suspicious of him, and his time as an agent was effectively over when one of his comrades spotted Greer's car being driven into Thiepval barracks one afternoon shortly before Christmas. In January 1993, when a murder bid on a suspected informer had to be aborted, due to a heavy security presence in the bar in Lisburn town centre, the UDA's fears were confirmed. But before its internal security department had a chance to 'arrest and interrogate' (a euphemism for torture) Greer his handlers set in motion the plan to move their agent and his family out of Ulster for good. Removal vans took everything from the Greers' Lisburn home to a secret location across the Irish Sea and Ned Greer was spirited out of Northern Ireland early one morning in March 1993.

The Greer case apparently confirms the conventional theory of collusion between the loyalists and the security forces, that the UDA, UVF, and so on are merely inventions of British intelligence, the military or Special Branch; that these organizations are British-controlled 'pseudo gangs' with no autonomy of their own, directed by some 'big brain' outside the loyalist rank and file. However, the truth about collusion is that it was, and probably still is, multi-faceted, complex and unstructured. All the evidence suggests that in many areas of Northern Ireland the UDA's intelligence on republicans was patchy, outdated and at times hopelessly inaccurate.

The events in the Markets on a winter's afternoon in 1990 bear this out. A month earlier, on 2 January, an IRA unit left a bomb under the car of UDP member Harry Dickey. His brother-in-law, the UDA's brigadier in East Belfast, learned that the Provo team responsible for Dickey's death included a number of Provisionals from the Markets, the working-class republican area contiguous to Belfast city centre. He was hell-bent on revenge. Around lunchtime three UDA men, one of them a talented Irish League footballer, Thomas Elliot – Harry Dickey's nephew, drove in a hijacked taxi past the Lagan Social Club in Friendly Street. At the door of the premises one member of the unit opened fire with a sub-machine gun. No one was injured although one bullet passed through a parked car, there were strike marks on the club's walls and pillars and bullets punched holes in security railings around the Lagan. One man narrowly escaped death and his identity reveals that the UDA in East Belfast had no idea which republican faction it was attacking. Its would-be victims included a DJ from the lower Falls, as well as Paddy Lynn, the Workers Party's South Belfast representative.

The assassination squad fled from the Markets towards the Albert Bridge, an arterial route over the River Lagan and a gateway to loyalist East Belfast. Unfortunately, at least for Elliot and his two comrades, Samuel Dunwoody and Paul McCrory, they drove straight into an army roadblock. The soldiers on duty, all members of the locally recruited UDR, had heard on their radios that a shooting had taken place at the Lagan Social Club. The patrol trained their SLR rifles on the car and forced it to halt. The UDA team was dragged from the vehicle and forced on to the ground while the sub-machine gun was taken away. Assuming that the Lagan attack was part of another bout of intra-republican feuding between the Provos and the Official IRA and that these three were on their way into the nationalist enclave across the river, the Short Strand, a number of UDR soldiers started kicking their captives and shouting: 'Dirty Provie bastards'. Elliot and his comrades had to plead with them to 'Stop kickin' us, we're loyalists!'

Elliot, Dunwoody and McCrory had clearly been intent on mass murder: they had another sub-machine gun in the car as well as several magazines full of ammunition. McCrory later told police officers who charged him that they wanted to shoot Catholics. Asked why they had targeted the Lagan, he replied that they believed it was a 'Provie' club. In fact the 'Provie' club in the Markets had closed in the mid-1980s and the nearest one was situated a quarter of a mile away, on the other side of Cromac Street. No 'Provie' would have been permitted, or been willing to go, into the Lagan, a club controlled by their long-standing rivals in the Workers Party/Official IRA movement. Whoever briefed Elliot and his comrades on the geo-politics of the Markets clearly had no grasp of the allegiances or personalities in the area.

It is obvious that there was no overall 'command and control' of loyalist terror groups by the security forces. While leaking of security information was frequent and the files were voluminous (leading one UVF commander to say that intelligence documents were 'more common than beer mats'), there appears to have been no structure or direction to the collusion.

None the less, there were plenty of individual instances of collusion between loyalists and the forces of law and order in the early 1990s, although in the initial stages of this controversy one wing of the security services appeared exonerated from the charge of aiding terrorists. When John Stevens published his first report into collusion following an eight-month inquiry, he concluded that the leaking of information was 'restricted to a small number of the security forces and is neither widespread or institutionalized'. His findings were extremely critical of the UDR, but had little or nothing to say about the RUC. Stevens recommended that the director of public prosecutions in Northern Ireland look at the cases of fifty-eight people. Among that number were ten UDR soldiers, twenty-six UDA men and six UVF 'volunteers'. Crucially not a single member of the RUC, full or part-time, was arrested or charged as a result of Stevens's early endeavours. Yet even a cursory glance at court appearances relating to collusion cases in early 1990 shows that the leaks were not just the work of disgruntled UDR or regular British army soldiers.

Robert Alexander Allen was a 32-year-old UDA activist from Sperrin Drive on the mainly Protestant Waterside of Derry and press officer for the Ulster Democratic Party in the city. He was arrested in March 1990 after police raided his home and found sheets containing photos and names and addresses of IRA suspects in Derry. Allen was furious that the Stevens inquiry had concentrated on the UDR as the alleged source of leaks and had not looked at the RUC. He held a press conference during which he claimed that the leaked montages of IRA members had originated in RUC bases rather than UDR army camps, and was later able to prove in Belfast High Court that the documents had come from three RUC stations, one in Limavady, the other two on the Strand Road and Shantallow. Moreover, Allen had indicated before the court case that he wanted to be interviewed by the Stevens team but eight months after the inquiry started they had still not spoken to him.

In Belfast too the UDA sought to embarrass the RUC. In February 1990 the UDA in West Belfast embarked on a poster-ing campaign, pasting up hundreds of copies of security files. Painted beside the documents on a wall in the Forthriver Park area was a message from the UDA's flag of convenience: 'Targets set up by the RUC for UFF'. Another message daubed on a wall at Forthriver Road read: 'UFF – Stevens we have plenty more of these!'

In the same month Tommy Lyttle appeared at Crumlin Road court house in connection with the discovery of leaked security force documents. He was also accused of sending threatening letters to Crown witnesses, including Brian Nelson's sister. He was alleged to have left a bag of bullets on her doorstep in a bid to intimidate the former UDA intelligence officer into retracting his evidence. The absurdity of the trial was that Lyttle himself was an agent for another wing of the security forces, the RUC Special Branch. He had been stymieing UDA operations for several years and had betrayed a number of its members to Special Branch. Yet he, like Brian Nelson, was also receiving high-grade intelligence on IRA suspects from his handlers.

Security force collusion with the UDA appeared to work on two different levels. On the one hand, there were numerous cases of individuals serving in the RUC and British army offering their services to the terror group. On the other hand, these men were usually part-time soldiers or policemen living in loyalist working-class areas and often drinking in UDA- and UVF-controlled pubs and social clubs. Although in many instances these rogue troops and police officers claimed they were forced under duress to leak intelligence files to loyalists, the vast majority were in fact willing participants in the conspiracy. In December 1990, for example, a former Royal Navy radio operator appeared in court charged with keeping guns for the UDA at his home on the Ballybeen estate in Dundonald. Edward Stewart, a 33-year-old UDR soldier, claimed he had been forced to hide the weapons because he had been in a fight with a local UDA man and feared retribution. In the trial it emerged that the solider was actually fixing UDA guns, including an automatic pistol owned by the local Ballybeen unit that constantly jammed when they tried to use it. The judge, Lord Justice MacDermott, refused to accept Stewart's excuse and jailed him for ten years.

Many UDR soldiers, and even some members of the RUC Reserve, sympathized with the loyalist cause and believed that the security forces had their hands tied behind their backs when dealing with republican paramilitaries. Some of these soldiers and police officers had seen colleagues killed, and in a number of instances knew through intelligence reports in their stations and bases exactly who the culprits were. As a consequence, a smaller number was prepared to aid the loyalist killers and help 'set up' republican targets. Certain army bases and RUC stations leaked like sieves in the late 1980s and early 1990s.

Derry in particular was a hot-bed of collusion between the UDA and the police and troops. Following Robert Allen's arrest in the city those RUC officers given the job of investigating loyalist collusion, who were themselves untainted by its corrosive touch, uncovered further evidence of links between the Derry UDA and the security forces. In William Logan's home they found documents on over 500 people in the city, some of them prominent in the IRA, Sinn Féin and the dissident Republican Sinn Féin. These were British army files and they contained photographs, personal details, car registration numbers and even information such as the times some of them collected their children from school. Among those documented in this way were the murdered Sinn Féin councillor John Joe Davey and party activist Gerard Casey – both killed by the UDA. Alongside their names was one word: '*Dead!*'

Although William Logan protested that he was keeping the intelligence merely in the event of a doomsday civil war scenario, the judge took a different view, noting that Armageddon must have already happened given that Davey and Casey were now dead.

But while the UDA in Derry possessed detailed intelligence about republican suspects in the city, they did little or nothing with this information in the autumn of 1991. This period saw a major upsurge in UDA murders, shootings and bombings, almost all of which were located outside Derry and carried out by other brigade areas. Indeed the Derry UDA suffered two major blows in the summer of 1991 when the IRA took revenge for Eddie Fullerton's death – first killing Cecil McKnight on 29 June and then gunning down Gary Lynch outside Foyle Meats plant on 9 August.

A unit from the South Belfast UDA was dispatched to County Derry three days later to avenge Lynch's death. Thomas Donaghy, a Sinn Féin election worker and former IRA prisoner, was shot dead on his way to work at the Portna Eel fishery on the banks of the River Bann near Kilrea. As he drove into the car park gunmen wearing balaclavas and army jackets came towards him and shot him several times in the head. A relative of the murdered republican later claimed that police officers had told Thomas Donaghy he would be dead by Christmas. He was the thirteenth member of Sinn Féin to die at the hands of loyalists. He would not be the last.

12. Offensive Weapons

In North Belfast 'C' company reapplied the pressure on the beleaguered nationalist community. On 31 August 1991 they selected the softest of soft targets. In the early hours of the morning 57-year-old Francis Crawford, a fast-food delivery driver for a Chinese takeaway on the Antrim Road, was lured to a house in nearby Vicinage Place. When he got there Crawford knocked on the door and out stepped a number of masked UDA gunmen. This defenceless father of five, who had just recovered from a heart by-pass operation, was shot at point-blank range, around 18 inches from his killers. The team which carried out the murder had taken over the house and used a woman in the Lower Shankill estate to ring the Chinese and give the address. They included the second-in-command of 'C' company, who was one of the actual killers, a man who later fell out with his boss, Johnny Adair, when he became disillusioned and sickened with the carnage Adair and his comrades were causing.

Over the next three months the UDA's murder rate surged and by the end of the year the terror group had killed eleven more victims than they had in the months before and after the temporary loyalist ceasefire. Just four days after Francis Crawford's slaying 'C' company switched its attention to West Belfast. Seamus Sullivan was shot dead in a council depot at Springfield Avenue, off the Springfield Road. Stephen 'Top Gun' McKeag had again crossed the peace line though Lanark Way in search of a nationalist victim. McKeag shot Sullivan through the window of the bin lorry in which he was travelling, hitting the lower Falls man once in the head. Seamus Sullivan's father, Jim, was a former city councillor and leading light in the Workers Party. At the beginning of the Troubles he was also the commanding officer of the Official IRA's Lower Falls battalion. Sullivan, or 'Solo' as he was known locally, had broken with republican violence. 'I have been totally opposed to murder and violence from whatever source. I will not change my mind, even at this point,' he said in a statement just hours after the shooting. 'The killing must be stopped. I would not wish any other family to have to suffer the grief that my family are suffering tonight.' At his son's funeral he appealed for an end to terror.

The former Official IRA commander's appeal fell on deaf ears on both sides of the peace lines of West and North Belfast. 'C' company continued to target as many nationalists as they could. In many cases their would-be victims were spared death only because of faulty weapons and ammunition. Indeed, the UDA in Belfast had a major problem with bullets. The ammunition it smuggled into Northern Ireland in the Lebanese arms consignment was of Chinese origin and of poor quality. On numerous occasions lives were saved because guns jammed due to the faulty rounds. In 2000 one loyalist involved in terrorism during the early 1990s said: 'There are an awful lot of people walking about the streets of Belfast today who don't know how lucky they are to be alive.'

One of those would-be victims who survived was a white South African-born Queen's University lecturer, Dr Adrian Guelke. The 44-year-old academic was shot in the back after UDA gunmen burst into his South Belfast home in Fitzwilliam Street at around 4.30 a.m. on 4 September, while Dr Guelke lay asleep.

At first the murder bid bewildered the RUC. Although he had written about Northern Ireland affairs, Dr Guelke's main interest was in his native South Africa. A year later in parliament Labour MP Kevin McNamara, the shadow Northern Ireland secretary, claimed there had been collusion between the UDA and elements of South African military intelligence who had set the academic up to be killed. He alleged that the South Africans had provided information to the UDA through contacts first established in 1989 when three loyalists attempted to steal Starstreak missiles from Shorts in East Belfast and sell them to the apartheid regime.

It was indeed the case that Dr Guelke was the victim of a plot hatched back in his native country. The lecturer was an outspoken critic of the apartheid dictatorship and many years later he discovered that the South African Defence Force (SADF) intelligence branch had doctored details from a leaked RUC Special Branch file to make him a target for loyalists. The file, originally about an English-born lecturer working in Northern Ireland who was a secret link between the IRA and the African National Congress (ANC), was revised by a South African agent, Leon Flores, in such a way as to suggest that Guelke was the IRA–ANC link. Flores flew to Belfast via London in the autumn of 1991, contacted the UDA and provided its South Belfast brigade with the revised intelligence report. He even took a UDA unit to Guelke's home in Fitzwilliam Street in the university area. The UDA fell for his story and duly targeted the unfortunate academic a few days later. (The real target of the RUC intelligence operation had also helped the IRA obtain an arms cache from the PLO in the Middle East and had worked closely in the early 1980s at Queen's University with Eamon Collins, the IRA activist who later betrayed his former comrades and turned his back on republican violence.) Some rogue element within the RUC sent copies of the original file to MI5 and to Israel's intelligence service, Mossad, which is now believed to have forwarded the file to South African intelligence. (The same information was sent to the UVF on the Shankill Road but the organization's intelligence officer at the time was suspicious from the outset about the source and the UVF did nothing to act on what it received.)

Ironically, Guelke was also an opponent of republican violence in Northern Ireland and in his academic pursuits had established a working rapport with the old UDA leadership of John McMichael and Andy Tyrie. 'I used to go to dinner with Andy Tyrie and spoke to McMichael regularly,' Guelke said twelve years later. 'I got on extremely well with both UDA leaders. Obviously the UDA men who Flores sent out to kill me never knew this.'

Flores continued to dabble in the murky world of loyalist terrorism after Adrian Guelke was shot. In London he linked up with a UDA unit and urged it to kill a South African dissident in exchange for weapons. Flores worked out of the South African embassy in London and collaborated with Pamela du Randt, the SADF agent who was involved in trying to procure stolen Shorts

Starstreak missile systems from the loyalists of Ulster Resistance in 1989. British intelligence learned about Flores's collusion with the London UDA, led by James Portinari, and he was deported from the UK in April 1992. (He received an amnesty from the post-apartheid Truth and Reconciliation Commission and has since moved into the Kwazulu tribal area of South Africa where he lives a quiet life.)

The UDA now acknowledges that it was being used by the South African authorities to take out a political opponent, and that Dr Guelke was innocent of the charge of aiding the IRA. 'The joke is that if we had got our hands on the original cop file and found out who the real IRA link was, the other lecturer, we would have used that and put him down a hole instead,' said one UDA commander more than ten years after the Guelke débâcle.

The same commander, who has since come to regret the organization's role as a patsy in the SADF's dirty war games in Belfast and London, also admitted that the organization had a tendency to take information and source material from anyone willing to provide it and it did not look for hidden agendas. 'Very few times did we sit back and ask ourselves if we were being set up or used. No one asked questions, we just took the stuff and did the business.'

Johnny Adair was one of those who rarely asked questions about who was providing him with intelligence from inside the security forces. He readily accepted files, reports, names, addresses and the merest hint that someone in the nationalist community was an active republican.

In the summer and autumn of 1991 the UDA attacked an eclectic list of targets – anti-apartheid academics, taxi-drivers, soccer supporters, sportsmen and women, and, ultimately, the entire population of the Irish Republic. On the last weekend of July 1991 the organization launched its first serious bombing blitz across the border in years. Fifty crude incendiary devices were placed at locations in Dublin, Dundalk, Drogheda, Dun Laoghaire, Sligo, Bundoran, Ballyshannon and Donegal town. The bombs consisted of a watch-timer, a battery and a cassette box filled with flammable material. Although the devices were unsophisticated compared to the huge bombs the IRA was using to devastate

Belfast and parts of the City of London, the UDA caused major disruption to the lives of shoppers and business people across the Republic. In this respect they were merely copying the IRA's tactic of disruptive sabotage and economic warfare.

The main tactician behind this copycat campaign was Ray Smallwoods, who had argued for some time that the most effective way to counter what loyalists viewed as the 'Pan Nationalist Front' was to 'bring the war' into the Irish Republic. Others around him on the Inner Council and beyond saw greater benefit from spreading terror among the nationalists of the North and in particular among the swelling ranks of Sinn Féin. On 16 September a UDA unit, including men from Lisburn, shot Sinn Féin councillor Bernard O'Hagan outside Magherafelt College of Further Education several times at point-blank range in front of horrified students. He was the fourth member of the party to be killed since May.

'C' company on the lower Shankill, and particularly Stephen McKeag's team, were even less discriminating about their targets. On 28 September Top Gun used the same .38 magnum special revolver that had killed Seamus Sullivan to murder another Catholic in the city, Lawrence Murchan. Murchan was burning rubbish near his shop in the St James's Road area of West Belfast when Top Gun and his team stepped out of a white Vauxhall Astra and fired five shots into his body. Their explanation was that the shopkeeper stocked *An Phoblacht*, a claim denied by the murdered man's wife. According to police statistics McKeag's unit had claimed the 2,000th death of Ulster's Troubles – a grim achievement for the killers of 'C' company.

Following the Murchan murder the UDA opened up a new front against Northern Ireland's nationalists: it targeted the Gaelic Athletic Association (GAA). On 8 October the UDA, via its UFF cover, declared that members of the GAA were now considered to be 'legitimate targets', claiming that the association in the North had close ties to the 'republican war machine'. To back up the threat the UDA set fire to a GAA hall in Kircubbin, a small, mainly Catholic, village on the Ards Peninsula. Ironically, the clubhouse in Kircubbin was used by all sections of the community in this relatively harmonious village. Moreover, one of the club's members was a part-time policeman who played Gaelic sports despite the GAA's official ban on members of the British security forces taking part in its games.

Although the UDA later qualified its initial statement, claiming that in fact it would target only those GAA players, officials and fans allegedly involved in republicanism, the association's membership in the North knew different. Since the Troubles began, loyalist terrorists regarded GAA members, supporters and their social clubs as convenient and soft targets for murder and arson. In fact the Kircubbin GAA hall had been attacked five times since the early 1970s, and was burned down by loyalists in 1974. The UDA's decision to incorporate the GAA into the so-called Pan Nationalist Front meant that the association's 40,000 members and 400 clubs were now under threat.

It seemed that every month the target range was broadening at an exponential rate. Between the October warning to the GAA and Christmas the UDA's murder teams shot dead three more Catholic taxi-drivers – Harry Conlon, ex-internee Brian McCabe and James McCaffrey. The latter was delivering a Chinese meal to a house in Candahar Street off the Ormeau Road on 25 November when he was confronted by two masked men with pistols who fired up to five times into his blue Ford Sierra car. It was the second time the 48-year-old delivery driver had been shot at while out working in South Belfast. In August McCaffrey had escaped death after a pillion passenger on a motorcycle pointed a gun at him while he was travelling along Kimberly Street near the Annadale Embankment. For the McCaffrey family it was a second Troubles tragedy in thirteen years: the murdered man's mother, Mary, had been killed by an IRA bomb in 1978.

In the autumn and winter of 1991 Belfast was a frightening place, particularly at night. Communal tensions were compounded by a new tactic of the republican splinter group the Irish People's Liberation Organisation. Born out of a 1987 internal INLA feud, and led by the Marxist Jimmy Brown, the IPLO was far more indiscriminate in its attacks than the IRA. In response to escalating loyalist violence between 1990 and 1991 the IPLO launched a counter-campaign of terror on Protestant working-class areas. Its military commander, known as 'Geek', made it clear that every time a Catholic was killed the IPLO would hit back, even if it meant shooting up loyalists in pubs and clubs. In 1990 its only victims had been the former UVF prisoner Stephen McCrea and a politically uninvolved South Belfast man, William Sloss, but in the following year the IPLO went on the rampage, answering UDA and UVF attacks on Belfast nationalists with shootings and bombings at Protestant-owned bars.

Far from saving Catholic lives the IPLO's activities merely made things worse. On 10 October it raked the interior of the Diamond Jubilee Bar on the lower Shankill with a machine gun, killing a Loyalist Prisoners' Aid member, Harry Ward. Within hours of the attack Johnny Adair sent out a 'C' company team to hit back. Its victim was Hugh Magee, who was gunned down in nearby Ardoyne.

Adair and his cohorts nursed a deep hatred for 'Geek', Jimmy Brown and the IPLO's main assassin, Martin 'Rook' O'Prey. One dank autumn day in October 1991, before a routine interview in the office above Frizzels, Adair confronted one of the authors. 'You know Jimmy Brown?' he asked, but it was more a statement than a question. 'Tell him that if we get the chance we're going to kill him.'

IPLO's series of wildcat attacks against loyalist drinking dens did little to deter Adair's unit. It killed two Catholics – timber-yard worker John McGuigan and Brian McCabe – between 15 and 16 October. And on 5 November the UDA nearly caused a massacre at Windsor Park during a local derby between Belfast sides Linfield and Cliftonville. Two young UDA men threw a Soviet hand grenade on to the Spion Kop, the end of the ground where, traditionally, Cliftonville's mainly Catholic supporters massed. In a statement the UDA said it intended to kill 'republican scum' in retaliation for an IRA bomb attack against troops in nearby Musgrave Park Hospital three days earlier, a blast that killed two soldiers. No lives were lost when the grenade exploded at Windsor Park simply because the Spion Kop was half-empty on the night of the Gold Cup clash.

Although the IRA had nothing but contempt for the IPLO the Provos concluded that they too had to be seen to do something against the loyalists and their autumn offensive. Eight days after the grenade attack on Cliftonville fans the IRA launched a series of attempted murders of known loyalist targets across Belfast. On 13 November the IRA shot dead four Protestants, only one of whom, Billy Kingsberry, was a confirmed member of the UDA. He was killed along with his stepson Samuel Mehaffey at their home in Lecale Street off the Donegall Road. Fourteen shots were fired into the house from an AK47 assault rifle and a .9mm pistol. Three bullets struck Billy Kingsberry's five-week-old granddaughter who survived after seven and a half hours of extensive surgery. The IRA went on the rampage in South and West Belfast that night seeking out top loyalists to assassinate. Among the dead were brothers Stephen and Kenneth Lynn, coal merchants on the Shankill Road, who were working on a house belonging to a senior UVF man when the IRA struck. They almost killed Joe Bratty in an apartment at Annadale Flats. The Provos also fired on Johnny Adair's house and booby-trapped the car of one of his associates, Gerry Drumgoole (who was Brian Nelson's brother-in-law). Although Adair's man escaped death he lost a leg in the explosion in Hazelfield Street.

The IRA failed to decapitate the UDA's military command across Belfast, and far from stemming loyalist violence succeeded only in prompting the UDA and UVF to shoot and kill more Catholics. In the week up to Christmas the UDA targeted William Johnston, a Catholic living with his Protestant girlfriend off the Donegall Road. Two UDA gunmen burst into the couple's home in Fortuna Street just four days before Christmas, ran upstairs and found Johnston in one of the bedrooms. He started to plead for his life by pretending to be a Protestant. His girlfriend recalled that the UDA men kept shouting: 'You are a liar. You are Liam Johnston.' One of the gunmen shot him once in the side of the head, then shoved a pistol into the victim's mouth and fired again. As they ran out of the house the other masked gunman told the woman: 'You better go up there. Your boyfriend is dead.' Liam Johnston had moved into the Donegall Road area only a couple of weeks earlier. Because he was known as 'Liam' locals had worked out that he was a Catholic and someone somewhere in the Village had conveyed that fatal piece of information to the UDA.

Twenty-four hours later 'C' company was on the move into the heart of republican West Belfast. Their destination was the Devenish Arms off Finaghy Road North where customers were enjoying lunchtime drinks. At least two 'C' company gunmen burst into the bar and opened fire on the people inside. At first the punters thought someone had let off Christmas crackers and no one dived for cover. Aidan Wallace, a 22-year-old Catholic civil servant, was shot twice in the back from a range of just 9 inches. A lone gunman – some sources say Stephen McKeag himself – then walked calmly around the bar pointing his .9mm pistol around various tables to work out who he would shoot. His quarry included an eight-year-old boy – presumably because he was wearing a Glasgow Celtic shirt. The child was shot in the head and lost an eye. Groups of terrified men, women and children huddled together at the far end of the bar, some praying for their lives, as the UDA men stalked the premises. The other loyalist fired several more shots before crying: 'Out, out, out' to his companion. At the subsequent inquest into Aidan Wallace's murder the coroner said the attack on the Devenish Arms 'must rank among the worst incidents of the Troubles. That more people did not die can only be described as a miracle.' The reason why more people did not die was prosaic rather than miraculous: the hitmen were using the faulty Chinese ammunition from the Lebanese arms haul. Their guns kept jamming.

By the end of 1991 the UDA had killed fifteen people while the UVF was responsible for nineteen murders, and on the Shankill Road the young guns of 'C' company were becoming living legends. They significantly increased the UDA's murder rate and were attracting hundreds of teenage loyalists who wanted to emulate the new killers terrorizing nationalists. The UDA murder squads never stopped targeting, tracking and in some cases killing their victims, mainly in greater Belfast. Even over Christmas there was no let-up despite a three-day seasonal ceasefire by the Provisionals.

Back in 1984 *The Shankill Bulletin* had tried to be kind to two aspiring young rock stars, Johnny Adair and Sam McCrory. 'As for Offensive Weapon, well they are a good band, with a big following,' the *Bulletin*'s reporter wrote. 'They are dedicated to working hard at their music and to success. For this Belfast band almost certainly has to go to London and there as here, their NF connections will almost certainly guarantee that they won't go too far.' He couldn't bring himself to admit that Adair and McCrory's band would never be famous. However, he was wrong about 'C' company's future leaders. Adair, McCrory and their followers were already on their way to achieving lasting fame – but through murder not music.

13. Here's Johnny

Almost a decade on from the official end of Northern Ireland's Troubles a new revisionism is taking hold in the media regarding loyalism. The present UDA leadership has downplayed Johnny Adair's role in cranking up and then directing the loyalist terror offensive of the 1990s until the ceasefires of 1994, and the UDA command is attempting to airbrush Adair out of history. However, those who lived and worked in Belfast during this dangerous period, when Ulster was pushed to the edge of civil war, know how critical Adair was to the UDA murder machine. He effectively ran its military campaign and travelled the length and breadth of Northern Ireland encouraging dormant units to carry out hits. He provoked the IRA into a sectarian shooting war at the time when the Provos were trying to tailor their violence towards more strategic political targets, especially in London. He created a climate of fear that, regardless of its absolute immorality and inhumanity, played a major role in forcing the republican movement to find a way out of the 'armed struggle' cul-de-sac by the mid-1990s.

Herbert Asbury's description of a typical member of the gangs which ran New York's Five Points at the end of the nineteenth and early twentieth century could as easily be written of men like Adair, Stephen McKeag or any of 'C' company's other luminaries, who sought to run Belfast's Shankill Road at the end of the twentieth and into the twenty-first century:

Political corruption and all its attendant evils fostered his growth. He generally began as a member of a juvenile gang, and lack of proper direction and supervision naturally graduated him into the ranks of the older gangsters. Thus he grew to manhood without the slightest conception of right and wrong, with an aversion to honest labor, that amounted to actual loathing and with a keen admiration for the man who was able to get much for nothing. Moreover, his only escape from the misery of his surroundings lay in excitement, and he could imagine no outlets for his turbulent spirit save sex and fighting. And many a boy became a gangster solely because of an overwhelming desire to emulate the exploits of some spectacular figure of the underworld, or because of a yearning for fame and glory which he was unable to satisfy except by acquiring a reputation as a tough guy and a hard mug.

(*The Gangs of New York*, 1927)

The popular image of Johnny Adair is the shaven-headed, earring-wearing, designer-clad, tattooed muscle man. But in his early incarnation as a UDA leader Adair was slight and soft-spoken. Female reporters from across the globe whom the authors brought to meet Adair and the UDA Inner Council in the early 1990s remarked on his attractiveness. One Dutch journalist described him as 'cute' following an interview above Frizzells fish shop in early 1992. He certainly had a knack for charming women and, although married to Gina Crossan, who also came from the lower Oldpark and had been dating Adair since he was thirteen, he played the field and was regarded as quite a catch for the legions of UDA groupies who followed paramilitary commanders like pop and sports stars. He had a string of mistresses whom he met in UDA-controlled bars, social clubs and shebeens during the time he was military commander of the UFF.

One of his lovers was a young Shankill Road woman called Cathy Spruce. Spruce – who was blonde and tattooed and of medium height – had met Adair shortly after she was released from the Whiteabbey Training School for Girls in Newtownabbey. But Spruce had a dangerous secret: since 1990 she had also been sleeping with IPLO military leader Martin 'Rook' O'Prey, whom she had met in the Washington Bar in central Belfast, a favourite haunt of republican dissidents in the late 1980s and early 1990s.

For months Spruce managed to keep her secret until one evening in bed, fed up with Adair teasing her and putting her down, she decided to play a joke on the 'C' company boss. Spruce used to tie up Adair during sex and while he was still bound and helpless she confessed to her affair with 'Rook' O'Prey and told him about their rendezvous in the Washington Bar. Then she threatened to make the short journey across the peace line from the lower Shankill to O'Prey's home in the lower Falls to fetch 'Rook' and bring him back to claim the greatest scalp for any republican. She got Adair rattled according to a former friend of hers: 'He was pleading for his life and she was only having a laugh.' But she never had any intention of carrying out her threat and she was laughing as she left the bedroom with Adair still tied up.

This bizarre episode reveals that no matter how much rivalry and hatred there was between them, Belfast's terrorist community was very closely knit. For this reason the editor of the *New Ulster Defender* magazine probably wasn't being ironic when, in April 1992, he warned loyalists about republican Mata Haris operating in Belfast city centre bars. Highlighting the case of Rosena Brown, the actress who had a liaison with a prison officer from the Maze, used him to set up members of the prison service for the IRA and was convicted, along with her prison officer lover, of offences including the attempted murder of members of the prison service in Northern Ireland, the editor wrote:

It would appear she is one of a number of very evil women who play an integral part in the republican war machine. And recent information would suggest that these evil persons are frequenting drinking establishments in loyalist towns and along the Golden Mile in Belfast, to try and tempt off-duty Security Force members and loyalist paramilitaries back to their lair to receive a *coup de grâce*. So loyalists beware when you are drinking in town or you could end up on your backs for all the wrong reasons.

Adair was on safer ground with another of his secret lovers, Jackie Robinson. They met in the Taughmonagh Social Club in South Belfast in 1992. After a failed marriage in Birmingham, Robinson had come back to Belfast and settled in Taughmonagh, a working-class loyalist housing estate situated at the edge of the prosperous and, by this stage largely Catholic, Upper Malone area. The blonde mother-of-two had slimmed down to 10 stone, was working out in the gym and sported a new sexy wardrobe. When she walked into the Taughmonagh Social Club one evening in January Adair took an instant fancy to her.

'I went to the club because there were never fights. It was hassle-free. Everyone knew everyone else and it was great fun,' Robinson remembers. 'He was standing at the bar but I didn't have a clue who Johnny Adair was. He was getting a name for himself but not one that I was aware of. I was with a crowd of girlfriends. I barely looked at him but a friend said he was staring at me.'

The following Sunday Adair turned up at the club again – and again he sought her out.

I had on a short pink dress and I had my hair put up. I sat down with my friends at the table and the national anthem was about to be played. But this figure came from nowhere and grabbed my friend and said, 'What's her name? Tell her I want her. Tell her I want her.'

It was Johnny Adair. Someone tapped him on the shoulder and said to him, 'The national anthem is playing here, do you mind standing still, mate?' And he did. I sort of looked at him but I was quite taken aback. He kept trying to draw my attention but I was embarrassed.

A fortnight later Adair made his move. As she left for home that evening he blocked her in the car park of the Taughmonagh club.

He started banging on the window, shouting, 'Where are you going? Where are you going? Can I come too?'

That is what finally did it for me because I hadn't looked at him properly before. As I turned round I saw his blue woollen waistcoat and his cap on back-to-front and his face was peering through the window. And that was it. I just looked at his face and saw a different person. My heart literally skipped a beat.

Surprising as it might seem, during their eight-year affair Robinson saw a tender side to the man who became known as 'Mad Dog': 'I never had to worry that he would be rough because there was always gentleness in him and that's how he treated me. There was safety and there were loving feelings.'

Robinson regarded the young UDA commander as often child-like in his behaviour, even when in precarious situations. Six months into their affair RUC officers smashed their way into her home and arrested her, hoping to use her to build a case against Adair. She was taken to Castlereagh Holding Centre in East Belfast where terrorist suspects were interrogated during the Troubles. She was ordered to strip off, and given a white boiler suit to wear. She was told she was in big trouble.

It was October 27. The detective said, 'Did you know it was your boyfriend's birthday yesterday?' The police doctor came to examine me to make sure I was OK to be interviewed by the detectives. Then one, a woman, asked me if I knew Johnny Adair and I said, 'No.' Then she told me, 'You've been fucking him for nine months,' and she threw down a file on the table that was almost a foot high.

She refused to talk and kept silent over the next day – until Adair himself was brought handcuffed into the same police station. 'I heard him coming into the holding cells shouting, "Yoho, fuck the IRA, put me in a cell with Jackie." I couldn't believe he'd been so daft. After spending twenty-four hours denying that I knew him, he came into the cells with loads of his cronies shouting my name.'

In total Robinson spent five days under severe questioning but refused to sign any statements that would implicate her lover. She claims that police officers switched from stick to carrot in their approach – first threatening to have her children taken off her by social services, then offering her a million pounds to make statements. Incredibly, this young mother, who had little or no knowledge of terrorism prior to meeting Adair, refused to cooperate. Such was the loyalty he instilled in his women; such was the magnetic power of his personality within large sections of the loyalist working class.

Like many other working-class Protestants in the greater Shankill, Adair had shown very little interest in formal education and was barely literate. Yet despite this handicap he was street-smart, extremely cunning and had an instinctive and acute sense of danger. He also had a highly manipulative streak, matched only by his devotion to the UDA cause. 'When Johnny was going it was twenty-four hours a day, seven days a week,' says one 'C' company veteran. 'You never got a moment's peace with Johnny. He was urging us on all the time, motivating teams to do hits, to go out and shoot this Provie or that Taig. He had bags of energy and never seemed to stop.'

Unlike their republican counterparts loyalist paramilitaries have always had a penchant for the flamboyant lifestyle: Jim Craig was as notable for his gold chains and garish jewellery as his extortion and racketeering activities. Ken Gibson, the UVF's former commander on the Shankill, used to go into bars on the 'Road' for a pint wearing the full military regalia of a British army colonel, complete with the correct pips and insignia on the lapels of his shirt. By contrast, republicans kept a low profile, led frugal lives (apart from in South Armagh where many were millionaires) and blended in with their communities – one of the reasons for a deeper reservoir of support for the IRA in republican strongholds than for loyalists on their home ground.

Johnny Adair upheld that flashy loyalist tradition, but integrated it with the new uniform of the working-class streets. In his early phase he wore shell suits, sported baseball caps and constantly dyed his hair. The colour changes were not just to make a fashion statement, but also to avoid being recognized when he travelled through nationalist areas reconnoitring the houses of republicans that 'C' company was planning to shoot up. Although a fanatical Glasgow Rangers supporter, Adair kept a wardrobe of Glasgow Celtic kits in his house. When scouting areas such as the New Lodge, Falls Road or Newington he would walk the streets dressed in the green and white hoops of Celtic in order to convince residents he was just another Catholic.

He looked after his murder teams in the lower Shankill, rewarding them with cash, drugs or both. In England commentators noticed that the rise of the Acid House/Rave dance culture, combined with the introduction of the drug Ecstasy, dubbed the 'love drug' because it engendered feelings of love towards fellow ravers, had contributed to a sharp drop in soccer violence; many

1. During 1972 the UDA organized massive displays of strength in Belfast and working–class Protestants flocked out to support – and to join – the new organization.

2. Tommy Herron, the UDA's East Belfast brigadier and its most influential figure until he was killed in September 1973. Herron's criminal activities were a sign of things to come. His murder was never solved but it is widely accepted that it was an officially sanctioned UDA hit.

3. Harry Murray, the Belfast shipyard shop steward who led the Ulster Workers Council strike in May 1974. He was not a UDA member.

4. Andy Tyrie, the UDA's Supreme Commander between 1973 and 1988 and the mastermind behind the 1974 Ulster Workers Council strike. He was never convicted of any paramilitary activity. Tyrie came out of 'retirement' to convince loyalist sceptics to support the Good Friday Agreement in 1998, and he joined Johnny Adair and John White in their attempts to end the Holy Cross School crisis in 2002.

5. Tommy 'Tucker' Lyttle, a leading UDA man since its early days, was the West Belfast brigadier through the 1980s. He recruited the double-agent Brian Nelson to head his intelligence section and was himself suspected of being an RUC special branch agent. As a result of the Stevens Inquiry into collusion he was jailed for six years and was ousted from the UDA elite. He died of natural causes in 1995.

6. A UDA march in the mid-1970s.

7. John McMichael (*left*), seen here with Tommy Lyttle in January 1987, was the UDA's political and military leader from the late 1970s until his murder by the IRA in December 1987. However, it was alleged that another leading member of the organization, Jim Craig, colluded with the republicans to set up the assassination.

8. Jim Craig, a leading UDA member and a notorious racketeer, was known to have colluded with republicans against fellow loyalists and, directly and indirectly, was involved in several murders. In October 1988 he was shot dead by the rival UVF, which blamed him for setting up its members for assassination by the IRA.

9. Seen here at a 'C' Company UFF commemoration ceremony in November 1999 are (*left to right*) William 'Winky' Dodds, William 'Mo' Courtney and Stephen 'Top Gun' McKeag. All three were once close to Johnny 'Mad Dog' Adair, the man who was the UDA's most charismatic and dynamic figure through the 1990s. McKeag, 'C' Company's leading assassin, died of a drug overdose in September 2000. Dodds fell out with Adair in November 2002 and Courtney deserted his old ally in February 2003.

10. John White was a co-founder of the Ulster Freedom Fighters, the flag of convenience under which the UDA murdered Catholics, and he served a life sentence for the 1973 murder of Senator Paddy Wilson. In the 1990s he became a prominent ally of Johnny Adair's and an advocate for the peace process. Expelled, with Adair, from the UDA in October 2002, the following February he fled Northern Ireland after Adair's faction was finally routed.

12. Johnny Adair and his children; Jonathan ('Mad Pup'), Chloe and Natalie. In March 2004 Jonathan, at the rear, was sentenced to five years in a young offenders' institution for heroin-dealing in Bolton.

11. Johnny Adair, seen here with Jackie 'Legs' Robinson, his main mistress in the 1990s. There were many others.

13. Johnny Adair pictured in Maghaberry Prison with one of his closest allies, 'Fat Jackie' Thompson. Thompson fled the lower Shankill in February 2003.

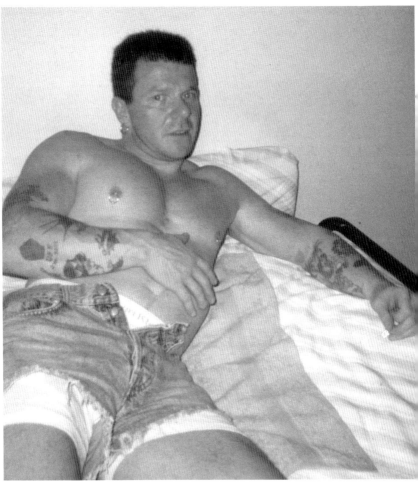

14. After making war with the rival loyalist paramilitaries, the UVF, and then within the UDA itself, Johnny Adair returned to prison in January 2003. He has two options when he is released in January 2005: leave Northern Ireland for good or fight a battle to stay alive.

of the hardened hooligans had mellowed. But such was the Alice-in-Wonderland nature of life in Northern Ireland that often 'C' company units sent out to hunt down and kill were given Ecstasy before rather than after they carried out their hit, and the 'love drug' helped fund and facilitate the war.

On 6 February 1991 Kevin Sheehy, head of the RUC Drug Squad, issued a statement alleging that the UDA, the UVF and the IPLO were involved in major drug-dealing. The UDA's initial reaction was one of self-righteous indignation and it released a full-page rebuttal on the front of the February edition of *Ulster*. 'We, the Inner Council, being the governing body of the organization, wish to make it clear yet again that the Ulster Defence Association is totally and unequivocally opposed to any dealings in, or abuse of, illicit drugs.'

Older UDA men either on the Inner Council or on its fringes regarded drugs with disdain. They were from a different, socially conservative generation which regarded drug use as a hippie trait and preferred the pleasures of alcohol. Joe English, who acted as an adviser and media liaison officer for the Inner Council, loathed drugs so much that when individual brigadiers and team commanders started to deal in them, the Rathcoole man briefed journalists privately about the illicit business. Inner Council members such as Ray Smallwoods and Billy McFarland from Derry also despised drugs and did their best to keep their members from either using or dealing in narcotics. Their problem was that by early 1991 the drug genie was already long out of the bottle. The massive availability of drugs, particularly Ecstasy, was too much of a temptation for younger UDA men, most of whom became dealers and, in some instances, heavy users.

In the early 1990s two areas became infamous for the importation and distribution of 'E' – the Lower Shankill and Rathcoole estates. In the Lower Shankill members of 'C' company started using empty flats in the estate as 'drug houses'. In Shankill Parade they would deal the drugs from a flat they controlled, hiding their stashes up the drainpipe adjacent to the premises. In 1992, with the UDA's murder campaign at full throttle, young drug users and ravers would travel from every part of Belfast to buy their 'gear' from the 'C' company drugs flat. Many of the customers were Catholics from republican districts who, if they couldn't get 'gear' from the IPLO, crossed the peace line into the lower Shankill.

INLA used camper vans and supporters posing as tourists to smuggle arms via the French ports of Le Havre and Roscoff into Southern Ireland. After the organization split in 1987 the newly formed IPLO maintained the same route but smuggled in bottles of Ecstasy tablets as well.

Those elements of the UDA dabbling in the drugs trade had a shorter route. They bought drugs from criminal gangs in Scotland, London and north-west England, usually employing UDA sympathizers in Britain to set up the deals. Consorting with ordinary criminals exposed these UDA units to the security services, which had legions of informants in the underworld across the Irish Sea. The drugs and guns trades intersected and the criminals behind both had no allegiance to anyone, least of all the warring factions of Northern Ireland. The London UDA in particular had links to organized crime in south-east England and a number of the brigade's members, men such as James Portinari, were convicted of possessing not only weapons but also Ecstasy.

'C' company, one of the supply bases for Ecstasy in greater Belfast, became rich from the trade, and team commanders in the lower Shankill could afford to pay their members for carrying out murders, attempted murders, sabotage or intimidation. This is not to suggest that those waging the UDA's terror campaign either in Belfast or beyond were mere mercenaries. The overwhelming majority of those at the sharp end of the sectarian war believed that they were soldiers in an army fighting a deadly and extremely effective enemy. None the less, the lifestyles of those in the inner sanctum of the 'struggle' contrasted glaringly with the grim frugality of life in places such as the lower Shankill.

Johnny Adair's family homes, first in Hazelfield Street and later at Boundary Way, contained all mod-cons: top-of-the range leather sofas, pine wooden floors, the latest stereo hi-fi, television, video equipment and even a large tropical fish tank in the living room. Adair's fashion sense had evolved from the Fred Perry jumpers and Skrewdriver T-shirts of his youth to the shell suit and baseball cap and then to the designer label black polo-neck jumpers, sweat-shirts, dress shirts, trousers and footwear.

Given Adair's centrality to the violent loyalist upsurge, he was Belfast republicans' number one target and his houses became mini-fortresses. A number of leading loyalists, including the UVF's overall leader, John 'Bunter' Graham, had been seriously wounded when the IRA and INLA directed volleys of shots through their front windows. Drop bars, inch-thick iron blocks, were put in place to strengthen steel-enforced doors, while elaborate alarm systems were deployed around the front of Adair's houses and steel shutters were pulled down on the front and back windows at night. Adair had also got his hands on CCTV cameras and they were erected at strategic entry points to his house, beaming pictures around-the-clock to television monitors in the hallway and kitchen. Apart from not having a police guard in the garden, Adair enjoyed almost the same protection from republicans as a high court judge. The taxpayer even footed part of his security bill: the CCTV equipment around his house in Boundary Way had been stolen from an RUC depot at Seapark, County Antrim.

Despite all the security measures one young nationalist was able to breach Fortress Adair. Peter McBride was well known to the RUC in North Belfast as a petty criminal from the New Lodge Road who had, according to the RUC's intelligence, burgled a number of houses in the lower Shankill in early 1992. They later discovered that the Catholic teenager's associates in the New Lodge had thrown down the greatest challenge of his 'career' – to break into Johnny Adair's house – and that he had managed to do so while Adair and his family were out one evening in the spring of that year.

One officer, who was later to play a leading role in the operation to put Adair behind bars, recalls McBride's exploits with a certain amount of admiration. 'There was all this sophisticated equipment around the house but young McBride still managed to break in and steal Johnny's VCR. And he knew whose house it was, that must have amused him. It was the biggest dare of his life and if they [Adair and his cronies] had found him there he would have been skinned alive.'

Adair reported the break-in to the RUC's main station in the Shankill area, Tennent Street. The CID in Tennent Street already had Peter McBride under suspicion for several of the burglaries in the lower Shankill and finally linked him to the raid on Adair's house thanks to a bottle of milk. 'The lad must have been thirsty and he took some milk from Johnny's fridge during the break-in and drank it. He then left the milk bottle on the kitchen top. He had also left his prints which we matched to Peter McBride.'

The RUC never got the chance to arrest Peter McBride over the theft of Adair's video. On 4 September 1992 the eighteen-year-old was shot dead in Upper Meadow Street as he ran away from two British soldiers in nearby Spamount Street. Witnesses reported that one of the soldiers shouted, 'Shoot the bastard' as McBride fled from the scene. Two shots were fired into his back.

The officer who had investigated the burglary at Adair's house said he was 'gutted' when news broke about Peter McBride's murder: 'Most of the cops regarded Peter as a 'likeable rogue'. A number of us felt very bitter about the shooting. There was, to be honest, a certain admiration for him for breaking into Adair's house. And in my personal opinion what happened to him was pure and simple murder, nothing less.'

Mark Wright and James Fisher, two Scots Guards, were convicted of McBride's murder in February 1995. They served six years in prison and were readmitted to the British army on release.

14. War on the PNF

The UDA presaged the slaughter of 1992 by spurning pleas from Protestant clergymen and politicians to match the IRA's Christmas 1991 ceasefire. The new hard-line militant and active leadership headed by Adair said the IRA cessation would not affect its plans. 'Loyalists are carefully watching the situation and will strike against IRA targets when the opportunity arises. We are not restricted by IRA ceasefire announcements. There is no ceasefire, whatever the Provos say,' a UFF source warned.

In Lisburn the organization was becoming extremely active again and in 1991–2 had embarked on a mass recruitment campaign of Protestant teenagers. In early 1992 it emerged that the Lisburn UDA were using schoolchildren to deliver threats of kneecappings to so-called 'anti-social elements'. The teenagers distributed hundreds of copies of *The Loyalist* through the letterboxes of three estates, warning 'thugs' that 'retribution will be swift and stern'. Meanwhile, their elders in the UDA itself were preparing to murder.

On 9 January they shot dead Phillip Campbell, a Catholic caterer, inside his fast-food trailer near the Moira roundabout close to the M1 motorway. An unmasked gunman, none other than the 'Gravedigger', fired a number of shots at Campbell through an open door and he died less than an hour later in Lagan Valley Hospital. Yet again the victim was singled out because he was an easy and available Catholic target and the UDA made no allegations that the dead man had been involved in republican activity. (At the time of his murder Phillip Campbell's mother, Anne, was a prominent peace campaigner with the group Women Together. In an incredible act of forgiveness, six years later she welcomed the presence of UDP spokesman David Adams at a remembrance ceremony for terrorist victims in nearby Hillsborough Castle. Adams, one of the moderate voices advising the UDA even in the darkest days, praised her as 'a shining example to us all'.)

At the end of January the UDA's Lisburn unit drew blood again when a lone masked gunman shot dead 33-year-old Paul Moran as he walked out of a newsagents in the County Antrim town. He was just another convenient Catholic target for the UDA which was seeking revenge for the IRA's sectarian slaughter of eight Protestant workers at Teebane crossroads on 17 January. At Moran's inquest an RUC detective inspector described the UDA's claim that its victim was a member of the IRA in Lurgan as 'absolute nonsense'. The officer added that Paul Moran was such a law-abiding citizen that he had never come to the RUC's attention in his life.

Two days later, on 2 February, 'C' company claimed its first victim of the New Year. As Paddy Clarke, 54-year-old taxi-driver, tried to bar the UDA gunman from getting into his home off the Cavehill Road in North Belfast, the assassin, Johnny Adair's second-in-command, fired four times and killed him. The UDA had targeted Clarke because of his links with the Falls Taxi Association; he was the seventh FTA employee to be killed by loyalists. Using its UFF cover name, it described Paddy Clarke as a staunch republican and said it regarded the FTA as part of the so-called 'republican war machine'.

In fact, Clarke was an Irish-language activist and a prominent member of the Gaelic League who had suffered ill-health after donating a kidney to keep his brother alive. The murder merely illustrated the fact that the UDA's definition of 'republican' had become as wide and all-encompassing as the IRA's 'legitimate target' tag which, post-Teebane, included Protestant builders who happened to work on security force bases.

The UDA's thirst for revenge after Teebane had hardly even been slaked by the Moran and Clarke killings. The Inner Council sanctioned something more spectacular, more callous and even more indiscriminate than observers of loyalism had imagined hitherto. On 5 February two gunmen entered Sean Graham's betting shop on the lower Ormeau Road in South Belfast. Using an AK47 rifle and the .9mm pistol that had killed Aidan Wallace in the Devenish Arms attack the previous December, they sprayed the premises with bullets. One of the authors was at the time undergoing a medical examination in the Ormeau Health Centre just across the road and heard the sustained burst of gunfire. In total forty-four shots were fired at the fifteen customers and staff. As the gunmen left Sean Graham's they shouted: 'Remember Teebane.'

The scene inside the betting shop was akin to a channel house. There were bodies lying everywhere, men groaning and screaming, blood splattered on the walls and the air filled with the sour reek of cordite. And while some of the victims lay dying, the horse race they had been watching at the time of the shooting was coming to a finish on the television, the cries of the victims competing to be heard above the frenzied voice-over from the race meeting.

Four of the victims, eighteen-year-old Peter Magee, 51-year-old Christy Doherty, 54-year-old Willie McManus and 66-year-old Jack Duffin died at the scene. The fifth victim, fifteen-year-old James Kennedy, originally from the Markets area, died on arrival at hospital. His last words to a friend in the ambulance were: 'Tell my mummy that I love her.' Following her son's murder Kathleen Kennedy refused to leave the family home and lost a dangerous amount of weight. Just two years later she died from an unexplained illness. She was fifty years old. In an interview a month after his wife's death, James Kennedy senior spoke poignantly about the impact of terrorist murder on families. 'The bullets that killed James didn't just travel in distance, they travelled in time. Some of those bullets never stopped travelling.'

Apart from the five men killed, there were ten other people in the betting shop that day, of whom only three escaped injury. The massacre left the lower Ormeau, a small Catholic enclave wedged between the main bridge over the River Lagan and the railway line bridge close to Ulster Television's headquarters, in a state of collective shock and trauma. However, the suffering of families in this small Catholic area of the city had no impact on the consciences of those who had sent out the killers that day. In a defiant statement, the UDA claimed the lower Ormeau was 'one of the IRA's most active areas' and it repeated the last words the five victims at the betting shop had heard: 'Remember Teebane.'

Of course the UDA never consulted the relatives of those who died in the Teebane bomb to ask them what response, if any, there should be to the IRA's mass murder. Those families were more concerned about the victims of the Sean Graham's slaughter than the perpetrators. Betty Gilchrist, the widow of one of the workers killed at Teebane, sent a letter which was read out at Jack Duffin's funeral. She said her heart had gone out to the families of those killed in the lower Ormeau.

About a month after the betting shop murders the Inner Council sought to 'explain' the reasons for the attack. Pushing aside the rather obvious point that such killings only garnered support for the IRA in beleaguered Catholic enclaves like the lower Ormeau, the UDA leadership adopted a stone-cold, hard-nosed attitude to the carnage. They told the authors that if there were further Teebanes there would be further mass killings like that in Sean Graham's bookies. Alex Kerr was explicitly unapologetic: 'The IRA was extremely active in the lower Ormeau and the nationalist population there shielded them. They paid the price for Teebane.'

Joe Bratty, rather than Kerr, the South Belfast brigadier, was singled out by nationalists in the area as the man behind the Sean Graham's murders. The post-massacre mythology had Bratty, and his sidekick Raymond Elder, at the scene. In truth, the unit Bratty sent out that afternoon was picked from the UDA in East Belfast and included one man who was subsequently charged with providing the weapons for the attack. No one was ever convicted for the murders.

(It is a measure of the lack of 'military' coordination between the UDA and UVF that on the day of the Sean Graham's slaughter a UVF unit had been about to carry out an assassination in the lower Ormeau. The East Belfast UVF men who were to kill a senior Sinn Féin official living in the area had just picked up the guns in a hide inside Ormeau Park, across the River Lagan, when the shots rang out from the bookmaker's. The gunfire persuaded them to call off the murder bid.)

Not content with inflicting mass murder on the lower Ormeau, the UDA and their fellow travellers in South Belfast compounded the community's pain by gloating over the massacre. Six months after the shooting the Orange Order marched along the lower Ormeau Road. As the procession from the Ballynafeigh Orange Lodge swaggered past Sean Graham's betting shop some of the marchers taunted the local residents who had come to protest against the parade. A number of loyalists, including Orangemen in their sashes and dark suits, held up five fingers in the faces of the lower Ormeau people – a reminder of the number the UDA had gunned down. The scenes were a PR disaster for the Orange Order from which, arguably, the loyalist marching institution has never recovered. It inspired the local community to come out in greater numbers (albeit with the help of a travelling road-show of republican protesters from across Belfast) to block future Orange and Apprentice Boys' marches through the enclave.

Inside the Maze the UDA 'celebrated' the achievements of their comrades on the outside in South Belfast by painting a portrait of Sean Graham's bookies out of which strolled, on its hind legs, a giant muscle-bound British bulldog wearing a Union Jack T-shirt and clutching a Kalashnikov rifle. The photographs taken of the mural (still displayed at the UDA's headquarters in Tigers Bay) show the dog looking very pleased with itself.

As the IPLO continued its attacks on what it perceived as loyalist targets in North Belfast, so the loyalists responded in kind. On 16 February IPLO gunmen, including Conor Maguire from Ligoneil, riddled with bullets a video shop on the Crumlin Road. Their sole victim was a born-again Christian youth worker, seventeen-year-old Andrew Johnston, who was working behind the counter when they burst in. Two months later the UVF killed Conor Maguire. 'C' company answered the Johnston murder by targeting 32-year-old Liam McCartan at his home on Alliance Avenue, the arterial route separating nationalist Ardoyne from the loyalist Glenbryn estate. McCartan was branded an IPLO activist but, again, he was just an available Catholic. The following month the UDA killed a further four victims: a Sinn Féin councillor, a former IRA prisoner, a Catholic woman and one of its own former activists.

The Inner Council's twin-track strategy of targeting Sinn Féin representatives and ordinary nationalists living along the interfaces between Belfast's Catholic and Protestant communities continued on 2 April. Up to five UDA men from the South Belfast brigade were involved in the murder of Danny Cassidy, a Sinn Féin election worker, who was shot dead in his car at Kilrea. The UDA was able to pinpoint its victim from leaked security montages, which originated in a police station in County Antrim. Although Danny Cassidy had worked as an election agent for Pauline Davey, whose husband John had been killed by the UVF in the same area, the IRA initially denied that the Sinn Féin activist was a volunteer. It wasn't until ten years later, when his name and photograph appeared in *Tírghrá*, a book in homage to dead IRA volunteers, that the Provos finally admitted that Danny Cassidy was an IRA man.

The UDA's second victim that month, Ned McCreery, had a violent and brutal past. He had been a UDA assassin from the early 1970s and had taken part in murders, attempted murders, bombings and intimidation against Catholics in East Belfast. The 46-year-old loyalist's brothers and cousins were renowned soccer players (a cousin, David, played for Manchester United under Tommy Docherty), and the family was well known in East Belfast. McCreery had been part of Albert 'Ginger' Baker's gang which, along with John White's team in North Belfast, pioneered the use of torture killings in the early 1970s. McCreery, a one-time member of the UDA's Inner Council, had also been involved in a grenade attack on Catholic workers travelling in a minibus near Dundonald, and his pedigree as an active loyalist was unchallenged. But by the end of the 1980s he had grown corrupt and venal, like his old boss Jim Craig.

In the course of investigating Craig's bizarre links to republicans – he had even been seen drinking with a member of the IRA from the Unity Flats district of Belfast – and his willingness to pass on intelligence about his loyalist rivals to the IRA and INLA, the UDA's Special Assignments Section (its version of the IRA's internal security unit, the 'Head-hunters') uncovered evidence of McCreery's double life. They found out that the East Belfast UDA man was a police agent and had, like Craig, passed on intelligence to republicans. Moreover, McCreery's association with both Craig and Tucker Lyttle compounded his isolation and, in the eyes of the new leadership, confirmed him as untrustworthy. On 15 April McCreery was shot dead outside his home in Grahams Bridge Road, Dundonald.

The age of potential victims did not deter 'C' company assassins, nor did their sex. For some time the UDA had been determined to hunt down and kill a number of women working for the IRA's Belfast brigade, particularly a woman from the Andersonstown Road who played a leading part in the IRA's firebombing campaign in Belfast's commercial centre. Several blast incendiary devices were placed outside her semi-detached home in a lower-middle-class enclave of Andersonstown. One of the firebombs was hidden in a tin of chocolates, mimicking the IRA's attempt to kill British soldiers at a checkpoint in County Tyrone when a female member of the Provisionals had driven up to troops and handed them chocolates – for doing such a good job, she said. Fortunately, their vigilant commanding officer prevented the young soldiers from opening the box.

The UDA also claimed to have high-grade intelligence on a number of IRA Mata Haris who scoured the pubs and clubs of downtown Belfast searching for British soldiers, off-duty policemen and loyalists to lure into honey-traps. On 28 April Johnny Adair sent Stephen McKeag's team off across the peace line to shoot one such alleged Mata Hari. Top Gun travelled on to the Springfield Road on a stolen motorbike, parked outside a chemist shop, casually walked in and singled out 26-year-old Philomena Hanna. After shooting the shop assistant dead McKeag and his driver sped back to the Shankill through Lanark Way, singing their favourite tune 'Follow the Yellow Brick Road'. The UDA alleged that Hanna was the sister of Sinn Féin's chief press officer, Richard McAuley, a claim that was totally untrue. Their follow-up allegation in the *New Ulster Defender* (the revamped *Ulster* magazine) that Philomena Hanna was part of the female intelligence-gathering wing the IRA used in Belfast was entirely false. But that hardly mattered to Top Gun and the rest of 'C' company: in their minds once again they had struck into the heart of republican West Belfast.

The winter–spring of 1992 saw a major upsurge in UDA violence across the North, principally in Belfast. But the organization also set its sights on the Irish Republic and, once again, the GAA. On 16 February undercover SAS troops shot dead four IRA men in the car park of St Patrick's Church in Coalisland. Among the dead was Kevin Barry O'Donnell, a 21-year-old student who had convinced large sections of the British liberal left and media that he was innocent of involvement in an earlier IRA bombing campaign in England. On this occasion O'Donnell was part of an IRA unit which launched a gun attack on a joint RUC–army base in the County Tyrone town.

After the IRA team was killed several GAA clubs in Tyrone placed sympathy notices in the nationalist *Irish News* paper. Only one of the four IRA men played Gaelic football but, through family and friends, all were connected to various Tyrone clubs. At first a UDA source said all Tyrone GAA clubs were now 'legitimate targets', although the Inner Council later toned down the threat to include only those with 'strong republican links'. None the less, the warning once again pointed to the UDA's Pan Nationalist Front offensive, its extending of its target range to include not only members of the republican movement but constitutional nationalists and all of Catholic civic society in Northern Ireland.

For the UDA militants, attacking the PNF also meant setting their sights on Dublin. On 29 March UDA units, which included at least one woman, placed an incendiary device in a fabric store in Talbot Street near Connolly station. The device – about the shape and size of a cassette tape box – contained gunpowder ground out of a shotgun cartridge, a small plastic container of lighter fuel and match-heads. The gunpowder was detonated by a camera flashcube, which in turn was set off by an improvised timer, in this case a travel alarm clock. The store was badly damaged, and the blaze could have spread to other shops but for the vigilance of a Garda officer on the beat along Talbot Street who noticed the fire shortly after it broke out and called the Dublin fire brigade. To sow confusion, on the morning of the blast the UDA issued a communiqué warning that further devices had been left on the Dublin to Belfast rail line, usually a preferred target for the Provisional IRA.

While the type of device used was antiquated, and first seen back in the early 1970s, it demonstrated that the UDA was prepared to go into what it regarded as 'enemy territory'. Although the disruption and economic sabotage caused by the incendiary bombs was not on the scale the IRA was inflicting in the City of London, they sent a message to the Republic that it would pay the price for Dublin government interference. As one member of the Inner Council put it at the time: 'The bombs were more important as a wake-up call to the people of the Irish Republic, to remind them that there would be a price to pay if their government continued to interfere in Northern Ireland.'

The man behind the crude, but often effective, firebombs was a gay North Belfast hairdresser who began his terrorist career in the Red Hand Commando, a satellite group under the UVF's control. He became, effectively, a freelance bomb-maker, offering his services to the UDA and other smaller loyalist groups. (After the UDA ceasefire this maverick crossed over to the dissident loyalists.)

From January until the end of April 1992 the UDA was responsible for thirteen murders and scores of murder bids, firebombs and incidents of sectarian intimidation. By now their military commander, the head of the Ulster Freedom Fighters, was Johnny Adair, whose force of personality and total dedication to the loyalist cause drove the young killers on. Yet, a number of groups in Protestant civic society believed there was still a chance to reach out to the UDA and, through dialogue, persuade it to abandon its campaign. On St Valentine's Day three Presbyterian clergymen and the six men on the Inner Council sat down to pray inside the Park Avenue Hotel in East Belfast. The trio from the Presbyterian Church included two former moderators, Dr Godfrey Browne and Dr Jack Weir. Having held peace talks with the IRA at Feakle, County Clare in 1974, Dr Weir already had experience of sitting down with paramilitaries. The meeting was facilitated by a third Presbyterian minister and former Vanguard member, the Revd Roy Magee. Dr Magee had won the respect of the UDA through his fierce opposition to the Anglo-Irish Agreement (he had shared a platform at Belfast City Hall with Ian Paisley and Jim Molyneaux at the huge Ulster Says No rally). He came into contact with the UDA and their supporters both as a minister in Dundonald and also in loyalist West Belfast, where he was chairman of the Farset Community Development Group.

After a two-hour discussion during which the ministers outlined their opposition to loyalist violence, the meeting broke up. There were further secret talks over the following month but nothing came of the dialogue. On 3 March the Inner Council gave its definitive answer to the ministers' plea for an end to violence – they respected their views but the 'war' would go on.

'It was a frank exchange of views and we would not turn our back on people from our own Church,' the Inner Council told one of the authors shortly after the talks ended, 'but the bottom line is: the Provisional IRA and the rest of the republican paramilitary elements [must] cease their campaign of genocide against the Protestant loyalist unionist community. We don't see an end result while their activities would be carried on.'

The official reason for the UDA's decision to break off the dialogue was the revelation that some of the churchmen, specifically Jack Weir and Godfrey Browne, had been involved in parallel discussions with Sinn Féin. Those on the Inner Council who had been behind the talks, such as Ray Smallwoods, feared that their meetings would be misconstrued as proxy negotiations with the Provos.

However, Roy Magee did not give up. He detected a willingness on the part of some of the Inner Council to listen to the argument that not only was violence morally wrong but it was also counter-productive. In particular Dr Magee focused on Smallwoods, the most politically astute UDA figure and adviser to the Inner Council. The East Belfast minister believed that if he could get to Smallwoods he, in turn, would influence the harder men on the ruling body. Because they respected his unionist credentials, the UDA maintained contact with Dr Magee. 'There are plenty of people alive today thanks to the efforts of Roy

Magee,' says one former UDA commander. 'He understood our fears about the pan-nationalist front and the IRA's campaign. But he never stopped telling us that violence was a cul-de-sac and we needed to get out of it. In terms of the peace process Roy Magee was our Father Alec Reid.'

The reference to Gerry Adams's confessor, the Redemptorist priest from Clonard Monastery who engaged in secret communications between the IRA and the British government, is telling. Around the same time as the talks with the Presbyterian clergy opened up, Ray Smallwoods embarked on what for many loyalists was an unthinkable initiative: he entered into talks with the Clonard priests as well. Through Protestant ministers and community workers from either side of the sectarian divide Smallwoods was able to hold discussions with Father Reid and his colleague Father Gerry Reynolds.

These two priests, courageous men with a deep commitment to peace, had already established connections across the peace line from the Falls to the Shankill. Father Reid had even become a confidant of the Shankill Butcher, William 'Basher' Bates. While serving a life sentence in the Maze for the torture and murder of Catholic victims – often with knives, hammers, screwdrivers, batons and other implements – the UVF mass murderer had converted to Christianity and become involved in an ecumenical group that included the Clonard priests. For Reynolds and Reid therefore there was nothing unusual, objectionable or outlandish about parleying with leading loyalists engaged in a murderous campaign against their flock.

As with the Magee dialogue, nothing tangible in terms of a future ceasefire emerged from the talks between Smallwoods and Father Reid and later Father Reynolds. However, they did point to a desire on every side of the three-cornered conflict between republicans, the loyalists and the British government in 1992 to break the deadlock somehow and achieve a multi-lateral end to the violence.

15. The Shankill Versus Ardoyne

The breakdown in the semi-clandestine talks between Protestant clergymen and the UDA, combined with its rising tally of murders and attempted murders, increased demands for the organization's farcical legal status to be removed. For two decades it had operated without being proscribed, even though it was responsible for murder, extortion, blackmail, firebombs, sectarian intimidation and, now, drug-dealing. The British government maintained the organization's legal status on the spurious premise that banning it would drive it further underground and inhibit the chances of more 'progressive' pacific elements wresting control. The fact that the government kept up this fiction became all the more embarrassing as details emerged of the links between the UDA and elements of the security forces.

At the end of April 1992 it was revealed that Brian Nelson had been involved in ten murders, all carried out with the full knowledge of his army handlers. Nelson had also selected a further sixteen men who had either been killed or narrowly escaped death. In all these instances, Sir John Stevens's team found, the FRU agents had failed to pass on details of these planned attacks to the RUC's CID unit. Coupled with the discovery that rogue police officers were leaking intelligence files from RUC stations, as well as passing on tip-offs and titbits of information, a web of collusion was being exposed.

Much of the Nelson scandal centred on the role of Colonel Gordon Kerr, the then head of FRU operations in Belfast (more recently British military attaché in Beijing). Kerr had made a spirited defence of Nelson and his activities during the double agent's trial at Belfast's Crumlin Road court house in September 1990. He even revealed that Nelson had helped foil a plot to kill Gerry Adams when the UDA planned to attach a Soviet-made limpet mine to the Sinn Féin president's car. While republicans have made great capital out of the collusion controversy, it is worth noting that the FRU went out of its way to ensure Adams escaped assassination. Like the IRA man in West Belfast who avoided death only because Nelson diverted a UDA hit team to the unfortunate Victor Notorantonio's door, Adams was regarded as an out-of-bounds target given his importance in pushing the Provos down the political path.

However, Gordon Kerr was not the only senior military intelligence officer to fall under suspicion for leaking classified military documents to loyalist terrorists. Retired RUC Special Branch officers have revealed that in the early 1990s a high-ranking officer struck up a 'working relationship' with Johnny Adair and other loyalists. The officer effectively headed up the FRU in Belfast and was even more senior than Kerr had been at the time of his involvement with Brian Nelson, reaching brigadier rank inside the FRU long before Kerr. According to these disgruntled former RUC men, he oversaw the relationship between the secretive army unit and both Adair's 'C' company and Billy Wright's UVF unit in Portadown, and even boasted to Special Branch officers that he had had dinner with Adair during the height of the loyalist terror campaign. The Stevens inquiry team has since found Adair's fingerprints on at least twelve top-secret military intelligence dossiers. One retired Special Branch officer told the authors: 'He [the Brigadier] knows that the documents could lead Stevens or a future inquiry into what he was up to in the 1990s. Everybody thinks the collusion went allegedly as far as Kerr. It went much higher than that inside the army.'

If these ex-policemen, who were at the sharp end of counter-terrorist operations in the early to mid-1990s are right, then could Adair have been an agent like Brian Nelson? The new UDA leadership, in its desire to denigrate Adair's role in the resurgent loyalist terror campaign, likes to think so. It has briefed journalists that Adair was merely an FRU servant. The reality though is much more complex, and to appreciate it requires an understanding of Adair's personality.

Johnny Adair met his downfall because he believed that he and his comrades were effectively on the same side as the security forces. He was willing to accept intelligence files from British serving and former soldiers, many of them with family ties on the Shankill, because he felt they were one in the same. As far as Adair was concerned 'C' company and other active UDA murder teams were doing the security forces' job, dispatching republicans whom the police, being constrained by the law, were unable to put behind bars. The UDA's young commander put far too much trust in rogue policemen and soldiers who came to him with information. He even confided in ordinary policemen and women on the beat along the Shankill how he was targeting known IRA activists and terrorizing the republican support base. Adair was not the classic type of agent who is recruited to infiltrate a terrorist organization and ordered to disrupt its operations, or even, as in the case of Brian Nelson, to improve and hone them. Rather, Adair was used by elements within military intelligence to pile pressure on the republican movement.

The editor of the *New Ulster Defender* recognized this strategy of remote control as far back as 1992. In the magazine's April edition an anonymous writer pondered on the future of the intelligence services after the Brian Nelson débâcle. 'Who in their right minds would consider working for the British war machine given their record?' the author asked, and then concluded that 'the main theme of all of the cases surrounding the Nelson affair was to attempt to get targets the intelligence community perceived to be a threat eliminated from the theatre. At the same time, as loyalists are constantly seeking to eliminate IRA terrorists, what better than to do their task? Bring on Mr Nelson!' Here was a blunt admission in the UDA's own journal that the organization had become an unwitting (if at certain times, willing) tool of British military strategy in Northern Ireland.

And yet the collusion picture is more complex and murky still. Take one of Johnny Adair's principal obsessions, Brian Gillen. Named in parliament by David Trimble as the commanding officer of the Provos' Belfast brigade, Gillen was a hate figure for unionists. He was accused of masterminding the bombing campaigns in the city that, during the early 1990s, caused maximum disruption and damage costing millions of pounds. Gillen was regarded as an extremely calculating and tough IRA figure and, apart from one terse reply to a question as to what he did for a living – 'I make car parks' (a brazen reference to his role in directing the IRA's Belfast bomb blitz) – it was known that he had not uttered a word during numerous interrogations at Castlereagh Holding Centre.

Adair regarded Gillen as loyalist enemy number one and often vowed to UDA colleagues that he wanted to kill the IRA commander himself. He organized four attempted bids on Gillen's life between 1992 and 1994. On at least two occasions, however, when Adair and his team were close to shooting Gillen, the security forces arrived on the scene and thwarted the UDA hit. Once Adair himself, along with Sam McCrory and another young UDA man from the Suffolk area, took over a Catholic home in the Riverdale area of republican West Belfast. With their loyalist tattoos concealed by long-sleeved shirts and jackets, Adair and his gang told the householders they were from the IRA and were about to attack a joint British army/RUC patrol in the area. In fact Adair had been given intelligence from a British soldier that Gillen, along with two other senior Belfast brigade Provos (one of whom was the woman they had targeted in the chocolate box firebomb attack), was due in the street that afternoon for a meeting at a safe house.

Adair and McCrory cocked their AK47s when Gillen and his comrades appeared in the street. But just then a British army patrol in a Jeep pulled up beside the three IRA activists and stopped and searched them. Helicopters clattered overhead and more troops, and then police, swamped the street. Their presence forced Adair to abort the planned attack on Gillen and his colleagues and the team had to wait until the security forces pulled out of Riverdale before escaping.

The incident puts a question mark over whether or not there was structured collusion and centralized direction of loyalist murder squads. Clearly Adair and 'C' company had accurate information about the movements of important IRA players, but in this instance they were unable to do anything with it. Having ventured into a republican heartland Adair had to abandon what would have been one of the most prestigious loyalist hits of the Troubles. If there was centralized security forces collusion with the UDA the puzzle is why army Land Rovers, police patrols and helicopters were not removed from the area just prior to Gillen's appearance in the street. Surely the assassination of one of the most active IRA officers in Belfast would have benefited overall British military strategy? The obvious conclusion is that collusion was neither formally structured nor centrally coordinated: one wing of the security forces did not know what the other wing was up to. (Two years later Adair and 'C' company would again try to kill Gillen – an attempt that would cost Mad Dog's closest ally, Sam McCrory, his freedom. This time the security forces captured the would-be 'C' company assassins.)

On 10 August 1992 Northern Ireland Secretary Sir Patrick Mayhew bowed to the inevitable and announced that the UDA would be banned. The organization responded with predictable machismo, warning that the ban would do nothing to halt its campaign. In September's *New Ulster Defender* the UDA described the ruling as a 'sop to the SDLP and the Dublin government' that would never break the movement.

Bizarrely for a terrorist group up to its knees in Catholic blood, the UDA also repeated its belief in a fair power-sharing government between nationalists and unionists based on its 1987 document, 'Common Sense'. And in the midst of its onslaught against nationalists, the UDA's political leaders, notably Ray Smallwoods, reached out to Catholics with a political manifesto that, when it was published, won the praise of even the late Catholic Cardinal Tomás Ó Fiaich. 'There is no section of this divided Ulster community which is totally innocent or totally guilty, totally right or totally wrong,' its statement said. 'We all share the responsibility for creating the situation, either by deed or acquiescence. Therefore we must share the responsibility for finding a settlement and then share the responsibility for maintaining good government.'

The UDA leadership was right on one count: the ban had no practical effect whatsoever on its 'military' campaign. A fortnight after the British army killed Peter McBride in the New Lodge, the UDA committed a second murder in the area. On 27 September UDA gunmen travelling on foot from nearby Tigers Bay, burst into the home of eighteen-year-old Gerard O'Hara in North Queen Street and shot the teenager dead. His mother, Bridget O'Hara, pleaded with the two masked UDA men to shoot her instead of Gerard. It was the UDA's first murder since July, when it had gunned down a Catholic teacher, Cyril Murray, at his East Belfast home, because it claimed he had set up Protestants for the IRA. In fact the UDA's intelligence was hopelessly wrong. There was a Catholic civil servant living and working in East Belfast who supplied information on police officers, judges, UDR soldiers and loyalists. The UDA had simply got the wrong man. At the time he was murdered the 51-year-old was looking forward to retiring from his job at Holy Cross Primary School in North Belfast.

The O'Hara murder marked an autumn escalation in the UDA's murderous activities in Belfast. On 14 September 'C' company had tried to emulate the South Belfast brigade's February slaughter at Sean Graham's by spraying the Dockers Club in central Belfast with gunfire. John McCrystal had just been presented with a golf bag for his achievements on the greens at Fortwilliam Golf Club when masked gunmen burst through the door. He was seriously wounded and two friends, Johnny Denver and Gerry Cunningham, were also shot in the attack. Carnage was prevented only because one of the doormen at the event managed to close the door before the gunmen were able to get fully inside the club. The three injured men survived.

Two months later 'C' company would try its hand at mass murder again when UDA killers entered another bookmaker's in a Catholic enclave, this time on the Oldpark Road in North Belfast. On 14 November Stephen McKeag and Adair's second-in-command in the lower Shankill entered another branch of Sean Graham's bookies, close to the peace line between Protestant lower Oldpark and Catholic upper Oldpark. On the Saturday afternoon the premises were packed with punters, many of whom came from the Protestant end of the road. Three Catholic men – one in his fifties, the others pensioners – were killed when McKeag opened fire and the 'C' company second-in-command hurled a Soviet-made fragmentation grenade into the betting shop. One of the pensioners, 72-year-old John Lovett, was a Second World War veteran who had survived torture in a Japanese camp as an RAF prisoner of war. Several other customers were injured in the indiscriminate attack, including a number of Protestants, one of whom almost died due to his injuries.

The UDA on the Shankill justified the killings by pointing to the devastating IRA car bomb that tore through the commercial heart of Coleraine the same weekend. In its eyes, the nationalist population would have to pay the price for renewed IRA bombings of mainly Protestant towns across Northern Ireland. Indeed, just eight days before the Oldpark murders, the UDA had warned that it would extend its campaign to 'the entire republican community' following IRA bombings in Protestant housing estates.

The South Belfast brigade had also been busy terrorizing not only Catholics who either lived in or came from the Ballynafeigh area (men such as Michael Gilbride, a Catholic taxi-driver from the upper Ormeau area who had settled in the lower Ormeau, and was shot dead by Joe Bratty's unit on 4 November) but also Protestants who happened to transgress against them. Three days after the Gilbride killing the UDA carried out its own form of 'community justice' on a thirty-year-old mother of three young girls, Donna Wilson, who had moved into the Annadale Flats six months earlier. She was a divorcee with a drink problem whose three daughters had been taken into care by social services. She had originally lived on the loyalist Tullycarnet estate in East Belfast but had been forced to move out after neighbours complained about her all-night parties and drinking sessions. On Friday night 4 November Mrs Wilson was drinking with three men in her flat and playing loud music on her stereo. A number of neighbours on her balcony, including a sixty-year-old man, went to the local UDA commander and demanded that he do something about the noise from Mrs Wilson's flat. The UDA leader assembled ten men, all of whom were armed with baseball bats and pickaxe handles, and within the hour they had marched on Mrs Wilson's home. The UDA's very own self-appointed 'noise abatement society' burst through the door, held Donna Wilson on the ground and battered her to death. Her three companions were also beaten and much of the flat was destroyed. Only one person was ever charged after the killing – the elderly man who had first called for the UDA's assistance. Mrs Wilson's fate is a warning to the Northern Ireland vocal lobby – including many who, oddly, proclaim themselves to be defenders of human rights – which argues that paramilitaries play a part in policing their areas.

Throughout the autumn and winter of 1992 the UDA sent more firebomb teams across the border. At the end of August it had placed bombs at Clery's department store and the Exclusively Irish shop on Dublin's O'Connell Street and at Dunne's Stores in the Irish capital's North Earl Street. On 10 December it returned to the Republic and left seven incendiary devices in Dublin and Dundalk. The complete destruction of Dunne's Stores in Dundalk was its most successful bomb attack to date. Asked later why it had continually targeted Dunne's Stores, one of the Inner Council said it was because of the link to a political scandal in the Republic. During the summer it had emerged that Ben Dunne had made secret payments to the former Taoiseach Charles Haughey. Given his unapologetic republicanism and the taint that followed him after the 1970 arms trial, when he was accused, and acquitted, of importing arms for the IRA, Haughey was a hate figure for unionists. (That the chain's founder, Ben Dunne senior, had been a Catholic from Rostrevor in County Down was probably just a happy coincidence of which they were unaware.)

   The UDA was buoyed up by the success of its cross-border attack and in its Christmas message promised more of the same in the New Year. 'Sheer luck prevented our operatives from bringing you a fiery Christmas. You will not be lucky in 1993. We will bring 1993 in with a bang,' the terror group boasted shortly after the Dublin and Dundalk bombings. The UDA's final victim of 1992 was another Sinn Féin member, 36-year-old Malachy Carey, who was shot on 13 December while walking through the centre of Ballymoney, a mainly loyalist town in North Antrim. The UDA had found out that Carey had spent three years in jail for IRA membership and handling explosives; in its mind that was more than enough to single him out for assassination.

For the first time since 1975 the UDA and the UVF were coming close to matching republican terrorists in terms of body count. At the close of 1992 the UDA had killed twenty-two people while the UVF was responsible for sixteen deaths. The combined killing total of the IRA, INLA and IPLO (now defunct) was forty-nine. The UDA's Christmas message was hardly full of good tidings. In a relatively short communiqué the Inner Council said it was about to intensify its campaign to 'a ferocity never imagined'. On this bellicose promise at least the UDA was true to its word: the following year was to see the worst escalation in loyalist violence since the 1970s.

Two days after issuing its New Year warning the UDA officially declared war on the Pan Nationalist Front, which included not only Sinn Féin and the IRA, but also the SDLP, the GAA and the Irish government. Nationalists living in a collective state of fear could be forgiven for wondering when there had not been such a war. *The New Ulster Defender* reflected the UDA's resurgent militancy and, mimicking the Sinn Féin/IRA publication *An Phoblacht*, started to publish a chronology of attacks by its military wing. Under the title 'War Commentary' the UDA's official organ detailed not only the murders but also the bombings and shootings for 1993 directed at the Pan Nationalist Front.

The first killing was of a well-known South Belfast drug dealer and former INLA man, Tony Butler who was found shot dead in his flat at Agra Street in the university area. That murder was the starting point for a major escalation in UDA violence across greater Belfast and East Antrim. During February and March the UDA launched ten attacks on nationalists and republicans. The death toll in March alone was six, including two people with strong Sinn Féin connections. Fifty-six-year-old Robert Shaw, a builder from Larne, was gunned down by killers from the East Antrim brigade on 16 March at Newtownabbey on the outskirts of North Belfast, simply because his son was a Sinn Féin election worker. On 24 March a UDA gunman from the Village cycled on a purple mountain-bike across the West Link, the main arterial route through the heart of Belfast. Around 8 a.m. he singled out 44-year-old Peter Gallagher who was opening the Westlink Enterprise Centre on the Catholic side of the motorway. The Sinn Féin election worker was shot ten times with a .9mm Browning pistol. He was the twelfth Sinn Féin member killed by loyalists since the UDA and UVF campaigns took off at the end of the 1980s.

A new militant UDA unit had been formed from young loyalists in Derry's Protestant Waterside area, and in Coleraine, Limavady and New Buildings. They were spurred on by Johnny Adair who, according to detectives, travelled across Northern Ireland urging these new units to carry out their own operations and take the pressure off the Belfast UDA. One police officer closely monitoring Adair from Belfast's Tennent Street station said Adair was particularly influential in the north-west, 'and held as much sway over them as their own brigadier'.

On 25 March came another dark day, as the UDA struck again in two different locations. In Castlerock, a picturesque town on the Derry coast with a view across Lough Foyle to the Irish Republic, four Catholic workmen were ambushed as they arrived that morning for work. They had just pulled up in their van on the Gortree Place estate when another van drove up beside them. Two gunmen got out, one of them Torrens McKnight, and sprayed the workers' vehicle with bullets, killing James McKenna, Noel Kane, Gerry Dalrymple and James Kelly. Although the UDA claimed all four were republicans the terror group was particularly jubilant about James Kelly's death. The UDA had obtained a classified security document with Kelly's photograph on it a few months before which they had leaked to a local paper. It later emerged that he had been commanding officer of the IRA in South Derry and in that capacity had been responsible for the Teebane massacre the previous year, as well as the bombing of Coleraine.

Back in West Belfast 'C' company killers struck once more, this time at a youth training scheme at a shopping centre near Twinbrook. Two armed men entered the Dairy Farm shopping centre in the heart of the republican constituency. They sought out a man who worked there and shot him several times in the legs using both an automatic weapon and a pistol. One of the UDA men aimed the automatic at the intended victim's head but it jammed; once again, the defective Chinese ammunition saved a life. Witnessing this horror was seventeen-year-old Damian Walsh who would usually not have been in the premises at the time but had swapped his shift in order to take his girlfriend to the cinema that evening. The teenager was shot several times with the pistol and died later in hospital.

Rather than reflect on the pain they had inflicted on five families that day the UDA leadership issued a defiant statement: 'We have the arms, we have the information and more than enough volunteers and the dedication is almost certainly there as well. It is a terrible thing that anyone should lose their lives, but if you are talking in terms of success rate, yes, this week has been a success and it's still only Thursday.'

The late winter–early spring offensive of 1993 saw a new tactic: attacks on the leading figures of the SDLP in Belfast. On 1 February incendiary bombs were left outside the homes of two SDLP councillors, Alasdair McDonnell and Dorita Field. Despite both politicians' long-standing opposition to republican violence and their dedication to the democratic process, the UDA still accused them of being part of the Pan Nationalist Front. Several on the Inner Council were known to be uneasy about attacks on SDLP members but they were overruled by Adair and his militants who argued that they never intended to kill the councillors but merely intimidate them.

These crude scare tactics were designed to de-couple the SDLP from Sinn Féin, to underline to the constitutional nationalist party the price of building an alliance with republicans. In fact the terror campaign against the SDLP, later directed at other democrats such as Dr Joe Hendron, had the reverse effect. For some time there had been unspoken but widespread unease within the party about John Hume's dialogue with Gerry Adams. A number of SDLP figures who, to this day, out of deference to Hume, will not go public on the matter, privately expressed disquiet in 1992–3. They felt that the SDLP was being used by Sinn Féin to gain credibility in the eyes of not only nationalist Ireland but the wider world beyond, especially Washington. Hume countered that his talks would deliver the main prize, an IRA cessation and an end to republican terrorism. One senior SDLP member, looking back now at that period when the party was coming under savage pressure from the UDA, said the loyalists' tactic had been entirely counter-productive. 'If their aim was to break up the talks between the SDLP and Sinn Féin they did the opposite. The intimidation made even those who were sceptical about talking with Adams determined to support John Hume come what may.'

Sinn Féin paid the main physical price of the UDA's upsurge in this period. In March 'C' company launched two separate grenade attacks on the homes of Sinn Féin representatives Gerard McGuigan and Joe Austin. On the night Joe Austin's house was bombed the UDA left a further two incendiary devices at the homes of two SDLP councillors in Banbridge. Between 31 March and 29 April 'C' company almost killed eight nationalists in North and South Belfast; faulty ammunition saved most of them. On 29 April the Tigers Bay UDA tried to emulate Joe Bratty's team by spraying with gunfire a betting shop on North Queen Street. Five customers were injured; again, more injuries were prevented and lives were saved because the attackers' weapons jammed.

Adair and 'C' company had a specific obsession: to kill Alex Maskey who, in 1983, had been Sinn Féin's first councillor elected to City Hall. There were repeated attacks on his home between 1993 and 1994 and he was wounded several times in three different murder bids. Curiously, he was spared thanks to a change of heart by one of Adair's trusted lieutenants. Rather than assassinate Maskey at home, Adair dispatched the second-in-command of 'C' company, the man responsible for killing Francis Crawford and Paddy Clarke, to shoot Sinn Féin's City Hall leader during a republican rally in the Oldpark. Maskey's would-be assassin, unknown to republicans in North Belfast, arrived on the road and mingled with the crowd, pretending to be an IRA supporter. Nearby was a hijacked motorbike, which the gunman was to use to make his escape to the lower Shankill less than half a mile away. When the moment arrived and 'C' company's second-in-command was within inches of Maskey, he failed to draw his gun. Instead he allowed him to pass by and take the podium as guest speaker. The seasoned UDA killer sauntered off, mounted the motorbike and drove back into the lower Shankill. He later admitted to friends that, seeing Maskey so close, in the flesh, he could not bring himself to shoot him. Although he told Adair he aborted the shooting for fear of being cornered by republicans, he was banished into purdah. Adair never forgave him for, as he saw it, 'bottling it', and eventually the young loyalist who had grown up with Mad Dog fled to England fearing his commander's wrath. In 2002 Alex Maskey became Belfast's first Sinn Féin Lord Mayor.

Alan Lundy, one of Maskey's closest friends, was not so lucky when it came to surviving UDA bullets. On 1 May the 39-year-old Sinn Féin member and IRA activist was murdered while carrying out work designed to provide additional security at Maskey's home in Gartree Place. The gunmen shot him in front of Alex Maskey's children and then ran upstairs looking for their father, but he remained undetected in the bathroom where he was hiding.

Finally, on 8 June, the UDA went after the biggest fish of all: Gerry Adams. Around midnight a team from 'C' company lobbed a Soviet-made grenade at a bedroom window of Adams's house in Norfolk Road, West Belfast. It bounced off the reinforced glass and exploded on the front porch. No one was injured in the blast.

Friends and colleagues of Sinn Féin councillors were not the only ones to find themselves in the UDA's crosshairs, even their children became targets. On 8 August 21-year-old student Sean Lavery was shot three times during an attack on his father's home on Belfast's Antrim Road. Stephen McKeag fired at least twenty-five times into the house with the aim of killing Sean's father, Bobby, a Sinn Féin councillor from the New Lodge Road. The assassins didn't care that they had killed the councillor's son – any alternative Catholic would do if they failed to get to their Sinn Féin quarry. The murder was one of three unsuccessful attempts to kill Councillor Lavery and prompted Sinn Féin to demand that party officials be allowed legal personal protection firearms, a demand the Northern Ireland Office refused.

The Inner Council believed that not only was the UDA taking the 'war' to the republican movement, but that increasing numbers of Protestants supported the campaign. They pointed to a report in the *Ulster Newsletter* on 1 April that 42 per cent of Protestants not just agreed with, but fully supported, loyalist paramilitary violence. With escalating IRA atrocities, coupled with dire warnings from mainstream unionist politicians that a secret deal was being done between John Hume, the Provos, the Irish government and a supine British government, it was hardly surprising that grassroots loyalists feared they were being pushed out of the UK. What is still astonishing is the ambivalence of more than 40 per cent of the unionist population to the carnage being committed in its name by both the UVF and the UDA.

From the end of the summer until mid-October the UDA killed a further five Catholics, none of whom had IRA connections. They included Marie Teresa Dowds de Mogollon, a Catholic mother of four, murdered at her home in Fortwilliam Park, not far from Pat Finucane's house. In a statement the UDA said it had intended to kill her Peruvian husband. Before the murder, he had been warned by the RUC that his life was in danger from loyalists. Stephen McKeag and his crew drew blood again on 7 September with the murder of hairdresser Sean Hughes. And the following day McKeag's unit shot dead shopkeeper Michael Edwards at his home in Finaghy Park Central. Three weeks earlier 'C' company spies had entered Edwards's shop on the Glen Road and asked if they could buy *An Phoblacht*. Even though the shop didn't stock the republican weekly, that did not deter them from killing Edwards a few weeks later.

The UDA attempted another massacre on 5 October when a unit from the South Belfast brigade armed with two pistols and a shotgun burst into the Derby House, a popular bar in the upper Andersonstown area. They opened fire on a number of men playing pool and killed Jason McFarlane, a caterer at Belfast's Royal Victoria Hospital. There would have undoubtedly been further fatalities but for the fact that the shotgun failed to fire. Ten days later Paddy McMahon was killed in front of his girlfriend and young son in Newington Avenue by a gunman who entered the area from nearby Tigers Bay. As bullets ricocheted all over the woman's house she dived on her child and shielded him from the firing. The lone killer escaped by climbing down a drainpipe and then running along an alley towards Tigers Bay. In this period there were a further eight murder attempts on nationalists in North and West Belfast, as well as more firebombings of the homes of SDLP councillors, including the MP for West Belfast, Joe Hendron.

Given the close proximity of the engine room of the UDA's violence, the Shankill Road, to nationalist West Belfast and Catholic enclaves in the north of the city, it was inevitable that the 'war' between the loyalists and the IRA evolved into a personal feud. Ardoyne in the 1970s and 1980s was one of the killing fields of North Belfast. UDA and UVF units shot up clubs and pubs. Catholic residents were the targets of loyalist murder bids. The area also produced some of the IRA's most viscerally sectarian activists, who were responsible for bombings on the Shankill Road that claimed scores of civilian lives.

With his reputation and notoriety growing by the day on either side of the peace line, Adair was the IRA's most wanted loyalist. Less than a mile away, in Ardoyne, an equally ruthless and, in paramilitary terms, equally formidable foe, Eddie 'Bubbles' Copeland, was determined to get him. Like Adair, Copeland was a child of the Troubles. His father, John, had been shot dead by the British army in 1971 and he grew up in an area dominated by the Provisional IRA. Martin Meehan, for instance, who engaged in gun battles with the British army along the border, and was eventually arrested for holding a suspected informer captive during an IRA interrogation, was a local republican legend. There was a feud between Ardoyne and the Shankill long before Adair and Copeland came on to the scene, but their emergence as paramilitary commanders (Copeland was named in parliament as the IRA's commanding officer in Ardoyne) at the start of the 1990s exacerbated it.

'We knew of instances where Copeland and Adair's cars were halted at traffic lights and they would be taunting each other from just a few feet away,' a Tennent Street CID officer recalled in

January 2003. 'It's strange, but there was a kind of duel going on in North and West Belfast between Copeland and Adair, they hated the sight of each other but they maintained an obsession about each other as well.' Copeland dispatched several IRA teams from Ardoyne to shoot Adair. On one occasion Mad Dog's car was fired on in the middle of the Shankill Road. Police officers involved in monitoring the two men lost count of the number of times they tried to kill each other.

The climax of the Adair–Copeland feud occurred on the afternoon of Saturday 23 October along the Shankill Road. And the impact of this very personal dispute would have near-disastrous implications for Northern Ireland, pushing the Province to the brink of all-out civil war.

The office above Frizzels fish shop, the UDA's Shankill headquarters, had become well known as a favourite meeting place, not only among Protestants but also within the media. Most journalists who talked to the Inner Council were briefed in the pokey attic room at the apex of the building. The atmosphere during these encounters was oddly cordial and casual. During lengthy lunchtime interviews reporters were plied with tea in mugs decorated with little figures of armed and masked UDA figures; sandwiches, and fish, chips and burgers from a takeaway up the road.

It was known that the Inner Council and/or the West Belfast brigade met above Frizzels regularly on Saturdays. For several months the IRA had the premises under heavy surveillance. On the morning of 23 October Eddie Copeland had sent several IRA scouts into the Shankill to keep watch on the building. When one of them reported that he had seen Johnny Adair enter the office just before lunch, presumably for a meeting, a haphazard plan to carry out a bomb attack was put together. The idea was to send out a two-man team to enter Frizzels, order the customers out at gunpoint, and set a bomb timed to detonate once the shop was evacuated. The likely outcome, the Provos concluded, would be to bring the building down and with it the six-man Inner Council. But due to poor intelligence, incompetence and a fatal technical glitch the plan was doomed from the outset.

The two men selected for the operation were Ardoyne

'volunteers': Sean Kelly and the bomber, 23-year-old Thomas 'Bootsy' Begley, who had already been blooded when he was part of a Provo unit which shot dead an off-duty Royal Irish Regiment soldier, Stephen Waller, at his home on the Westland estate in December 1992. Barely literate and with a low IQ, Begley was an ideal recruit for the potentially suicidal mission. Kelly ran into the fish shop and held up the customers while Begley placed the shoe-box containing the bomb on the counter. The timer was faulty and the second Begley primed it, the device exploded. He was killed instantly.

Nine Protestant civilians were killed by the bomb, including two pensioners – the shop owner, John Frizzel, and George Williamson. Two children – seven-year-old Michelle Baird and 13-year-old Leanne Murray – also died. Amid chaotic scenes shoppers, drinkers from nearby bars and residents of the surrounding streets searched the rubble with their bare hands for survivors. Among the severely injured they rescued was the other bomber, Sean Kelly.

It was immediately obvious that the Ardoyne IRA had not decapitated the UDA leadership but had slaughtered nine innocent Protestants. In a hastily concocted statement the IRA leadership in Belfast confirmed that one of its members had been blown up in the bomb attack and another was missing, at that stage presumed dead. Responding to the mounting death toll that afternoon the Provos said, 'There is a thin line between disaster and success in any military operation.' The sophisticated Sinn Féin spin machine then went into overdrive. Gerry Adams was reported that night to be 'incandescent with rage' over the massacre; republicans had never meant to target ordinary Protestants.

Over the next twenty-four hours rumours spread that Johnny Adair had been in the building at the time of the explosion but had somehow, miraculously, walked away uninjured and unscathed. In fact, no UDA member was in Frizzels when Begley and Kelly arrived on the Shankill. Unknown to the IRA spotters, Adair and other UDA commanders had left the building by a back entrance. Moreover, Adair and 'C' company had stopped using the office above Frizzels for important meetings because they had received a tip-off from inside Tennent Street RUC station that their Shankill HQ was under both human and electronic surveillance.

Even with the final death toll not counted, under its UFF banner the UDA issued a chilling warning to the entire Catholic population of Northern Ireland:

This afternoon the loyalist people of West Belfast were at the receiving end of a blatantly indiscriminate bomb attack supposedly aimed at the leadership of the UFF. The number of women and children killed is still unclear, but shows that this was a false claim. As and from 6 p.m. all brigade active service units of the UFF across Ulster will be mobilized.

John Hume, Gerry Adams and the nationalist electorate will pay a heavy, heavy price for today's atrocity, which was signed, sealed and delivered by the cutting edge of the Pan-Nationalist Front. To the perpetrators of the atrocity we say 'You will have no hiding place. Time is on our side.'

And we ask John Hume: 'Is this part of your peace?'

The feud between Copeland and the Ardoyne IRA and Adair and his 'C' company had reached an appalling apogee. Despite hints of ceasefires, the Hume–Adams talks, and the growing co-operation between the Taoiseach, Albert Reynolds, in Dublin and the prime minister, John Major, in London, Northern Ireland was closer to outright civil war than at any time since the mid-1970s.

16. Peace by Day, War by Night

A Bible-thick pile of Sunday newspapers thudded on to the table in front of Johnny Adair. On the morning of 31 October 1993 every headline screamed out the same message: 'Slaughter at Greysteel'. The young RUC inspector who had dropped the bundle in front of Adair hoped to unnerve the cocky young commander.

I tried to get him talking about Greysteel. I pointed to the headlines and the photographs of the victims and said, 'What the hell do you think about that?' I remember he just sat there, staring at the papers, and then he smiled and replied: 'Whoever organized that must have been some operator. He's some boy whoever he is.' I was furious because I knew he was playing games with me. He was trying to tell me something without implicating himself.

For three days police officers had been questioning Adair about the UDA's ferocious response to the Shankill bomb on 23 October but Adair had said nothing that would have implicated himself in the UDA's on-going murder campaign. The previous night, the Saturday of the Hallowe'en weekend, that campaign had climaxed with mass murder in Greysteel, a quiet village on the shores of Lough Foyle. Five men and two women, aged between nineteen and sixty, had been gunned down by Adair's UFF assassins. Masked men in boiler suits had burst into the Rising Sun bar and fired on the customers with an AK47 rifle and a Browning pistol. As the killers entered the bar they shouted 'Trick or Treat' before opening fire.

The location of the UDA's main revenge mission for the Shankill bomb was deliberate: the Rising Sun bar was a soft target just inside John Hume's Foyle constituency. Just before the loyalist ceasefire of 1994 one UDA commander told the authors that this was calculated. 'John Hume was the figurehead of the Pan Nationalist Front so we decided to bring the war into his own backyard.'

As mourner after mourner spoke to him at the victims' funerals Hume looked a broken man, but he was encouraged by the exhortations of family members of the Greysteel dead to carry on his talks with Gerry Adams. If anything, the massacre only deepened his determination to press ahead, a determination strengthened by the belief that eventually he could deliver an IRA ceasefire.

The Greysteel massacre brought the death toll for one single week to twenty-three dead and hundreds injured and plunged Northern Ireland further into the abyss. Gloom descended on the Province. Catholic-owned bars and clubs were deserted. City and town centres reported a sharp downturn in business in what should have been the busiest shopping time of the year. Life was becoming unbearable and infected with paranoia. For a few bleak weeks in the run-up to Christmas it seemed as if the Province was finally about to degenerate into civil war.

The policeman given the job of catching the Rising Sun killers was Eric Anderson, an RUC superintendent with more than twenty years' experience in the force. (He would later lead the investigation into the Real IRA's 1998 Omagh bomb.) From the start Anderson knew that the planning for the retaliation at Greysteel had come from the top. 'The man whom we suspected decided [on targeting] Greysteel was not got,' he said later. He might have been referring to the UDA's North-west brigadier, Billy 'The Mexican' McFarland, or to Johnny Adair.

Even before Greysteel both the UDA and UVF had been on the rampage throughout greater Belfast. On 26 October 'C' company sent out a team which shot dead two Catholic street cleaners – 54-year-old James Cameron and Mark Rodgers, who was twenty-eight – at their workplace, the Belfast City Council depot on Kennedy Way in West Belfast. In an ironic twist it turned out that Mr Cameron's wife worked at the Royal Victoria Hospital and had tended the victims of the Shankill bomb just three days earlier. Following these killings detectives at Tennent Street and Antrim Road RUC stations were ordered to take Johnny Adair off the streets, although at this stage there was little hope of building a case to put him behind bars.

On the morning after Greysteel the inspector who showed Adair the newspapers hoped he would crack. He had been known to boast about his own exploits and speak carelessly to police officers in the streets of the lower Shankill. However, although Adair had a tendency to talk about his power and prowess within the UDA, he was smart enough not to fall into any traps. His preferred ruse in these sparring sessions with his interrogators was to switch from the first to the third person – hence the response that whoever organized the massacre must have been 'some operator'.

The RUC had intelligence that prior to the Greysteel shootings Adair had been in the north-west goading on individual unit commanders to strike back, to seize the initiative. 'He moved around the Province, holding meetings all over the place, mainly with young UDA men who looked up to him and held him in awe,' his interrogator said. 'Adair once boasted that the ball was at his feet when it came to loyalist violence; there was a certain amount of truth in that boast.' Adair was reported to have denigrated the UDA's Derry leadership, labelling it, as he once had Tyrie and Lyttle, a 'bunch of oul' Jinnies'.

On his release Adair went back to what he did best – directing the UDA's killing machine and its war on the Northern Irish Catholic population. Between Hallowe'en and Christmas the UDA killed four more Catholics: Sean Hagan was shot dead outside a car components factory in East Belfast on 30 November; fifteen-year-old schoolboy Brian Duffy died alongside taxi-driver John Todd when their car was raked with gunfire outside a taxi depot in Ligoneil on 5 December; and two days later Robert McClay was shot dead on his doorstep in the middle-class East Belfast suburb of Ballyhackamore.

But 'C' company's final victim of 1993 was a 26-year-old Protestant man with a mental age of eleven. Big Noel Cardwell was a part-time glass collector in a local bar and hung around with 'C' company cadres for whom the 6ft 4" giant was a figure of fun. One night in early December Cardwell sat down at a table in the Diamond Jubilee bar. The men he was drinking with decided it would be entertaining to spike his drink with Ecstasy. When he later complained of being unwell he was rushed to the nearby Mater Hospital on the Crumlin Road, where police officers asked him whom he was drinking with when he started to feel sick. He named the two, both 'C' company luminaries, and they were subsequently arrested and questioned but later released without charge.

In the same week the RUC had raided a flat in the lower Shankill and seized a number of 'C' company weapons. For reasons unknown Johnny Adair concluded that Cardwell had betrayed the weapons hide, and ordered that 'C' company 'arrest' him. On his release from hospital on 13 December Cardwell went to the Royal Antediluvian Order of Buffaloes club on the Shankill Road to play snooker. On his way home to his sister's house he was abducted and taken to a flat in the lower Shankill. He was repeatedly kicked and punched and urged to admit that he was a police informer (which was somewhat ironic given that the RUC and FRU between them had twenty-seven informers working inside the West Belfast/Shankill UDA). His fate was sealed when Adair arrived on the scene and asked if he had admitted that he was working for the police. When Cardwell's interrogators said no, Adair left the room. He returned wearing paramilitary garb – black bomber jacket, trousers, shoes and gloves – and carrying a Magnum 10 pistol equipped with a silencer. Adair yelled at his underlings to 'get him on his knees'. When the terrified captive sank to the ground Adair put the gun to his hooded head and fired. The bullet went straight through Cardwell's skull and exited on the other side.

Cardwell was dumped in waste ground in the lower Shankill. After the UDA's 'Special Assignments Section' informed the media that they had killed him, police rushed to the scene. They found him lying in a large pool of blood, but still alive. He had probably not yet bled to death because the freezing temperatures may have prevented his blood flowing at its normal rate. He lived until the next morning.

The Cardwell murder had demonstrated Adair's callousness and, to the men who witnessed it, his determination to keep an iron grip on the UDA. To the police officers monitoring Adair and his cohorts it merely underlined the necessity to get him off the streets permanently.

In the New Year the UDA intensified its campaign against Sinn Féin, starting with another gun attack on Alex Maskey's house on 2 January. But its target range extended beyond Sinn Féin to encompass the SDLP and the Irish Republic. On 24 January incendiary bombs were found in a Dundalk school and in Dublin's main sorting office. Three days later a gunman killed 51-year-old Desmond Doherty at his lodgings in Candahar Street off the Ormeau Road. The South Belfast brigade claimed Doherty was an IRA member; his family and the coroner investigating the murder denied this.

'C' company went on the offensive again in February launching two brazen attacks on Connolly House, Sinn Féin's main office in West Belfast. First Adair dispatched Gary McMaster (his fellow suspect in the Noel Cardwell murder) and Gary Smyth to fire an RPG rocket at the building. The rocket team travelled into the heart of Gerry Adams's constituency on the morning of 12 February. McMaster casually got out of the car, aimed the warhead at the front window of Connolly House, and fired. The blast caused extensive damage but no one was injured. Six days later Stephen McKeag led a 'C' company team back up the Andersonstown Road, picked the same position as McMaster and, using an AK47 rifle and a sub-machine gun, opened fire on the workmen repairing the Sinn Féin building. Incredibly, no one was killed although there were some minor injuries.

The previous day 'C' company had left a bomb in a St Valentine's Day chocolate box outside the home of one of the IRA's senior female members from West Belfast, but the device was not picked up by the target or any member of her family. Ex-members of 'C' company later confessed that FRU contacts had given them British army files with the woman's name, photograph and home address.

At the end of March 'C' company, now effectively under McKeag's command, picked on another Sinn Féin office – the party's press centre at 55 Falls Road, a building known for the mural of Bobby Sands on its side and as the place where republican spokesmen such as Danny Morrison briefed the international media. Again the rocket attack caused only material damage.

Although 'C' company had not killed anyone in the RPG assaults (arguably because they lacked training in firing the weapon) the loyalist terror unit was adept at talking up its exploits. A new mural appeared on the Shankill Road, depicting a masked man in a black uniform crouched down and holding an RPG on his shoulder. The legend beneath read: 'UFF rocket team on tour 1994'. While the UVF had been the first loyalist group to use the RPG against republican targets it was the UDA that exploited the weapon best for propaganda purposes. Many young loyalists saw that it was the UDA, and 'C' company in particular, that was taking the 'war' into the republican heartlands. Recruitment to the organization, especially to its junior wing, the Ulster Young Militants, soared.

The two units that had been most active in greater Belfast prior to 1994 – 'C' company and the South Belfast brigade – maintained their reputations for ruthlessness in the months running up to the ceasefires. Around 11.30 p.m. on 14 April Joe Bratty, accompanied by Thomas 'Tucker' Annett, drove a stolen car into Balfour Avenue off the Ormeau Road. An accomplice travelling with Bratty and Annett broke the window of a house with a concrete block and Annett sprayed bullets through the hole, hitting 33-year-old Teresa Clinton up to sixteen times. Bratty's unit later claimed the intended target was Mrs Clinton's husband Jim, a Sinn Féin election candidate in the area (the man the UVF had planned to shoot on the day of the Sean Graham's massacre). But as Ronnie Flanagan, the RUC's assistant chief constable for Belfast, pointed out, it was clear that the gunman did not care whom he killed given the indiscriminate way the shots were directed into the Clintons' living room. Jim Clinton, who had been upstairs at the time of the shooting, said that the UDA killers would have been able to see a woman's profile in the window before they smashed the glass. (One of the assassins, Thomas Annett, died on the night of 12 July 1996 when, following an internal dispute, two UDA comrades kicked him to death outside an Ormeau Road bar.)

Twelve days after the Clinton murder 'C' company killed its first victim of the year when it shot ex-republican internee Joseph McCloskey, at his home in the New Lodge Road area of North Belfast.

The stepping up of UDA attacks in the city drew a response from a rejuvenated INLA, who killed UDA member Gerry Evans at his angling shop in the Northcott centre at Glengormley on 27 April. A few hours after the Evans murder, the UDA in Highfield sent two gunmen over a peace wall separating the Catholic Springfield Park from the loyalist Springmartin estate. One of the men jumped out of nowhere and aimed at a car which drove into the area, hitting the front-seat passenger, Paul 'Topper' Thompson, in the chest. He died instantly. The gunmen then climbed back into the Springmartin estate through a hole in the peace wall. (Because of incidents like this, for years Springfield Park residents demanded that the barrier be made higher and stronger. Eventually a wall containing one million bricks was built.)

On 12 May 'C' company killed 23-year-old Martin Bradley as he played with his one-year-old nephew outside his aunt's house on Belfast's Crumlin Road. His killers fired even though he was lifting the child in his arms at the time and the little boy was covered with his uncle's blood. In two statements the UDA named someone else as their victim that night; Martin Bradley was the wrong man.

Even while it seemed that the terrorists were locked into vicious murder campaigns, behind the scenes there was significant political movement. At the end of 1993 the stakes were incredibly high. John Major and Albert Reynolds's Downing Street Declaration on 15 December held out the prospect of Sinn Féin entering into talks on Northern Ireland's future if, and only if, the IRA declared a ceasefire. While secret dialogue continued on two fronts with republicans – Hume's talks with Adams and MI5's clandestine discussion with Martin McGuinness in Derry – a parallel process was underway with loyalists. The UDA's rivals in the UVF had opened a direct channel to the Dublin government through the Irish peace activist and trade unionist Chris Hudson, and had even established a secret communications code using terms such as the 'cricket team' to describe the UVF and the 'full cricket team' to mean the Combined Loyalist Military Command – the organization representing all loyalist groups in the run-up to the 1991 cessation. The UVF–Irish channel had produced some results for loyalists because they were able to play a part in diluting some of the more grandiose proposals Albert Reynolds had wanted included in the Downing Street Declaration. And crucially, the Declaration said any agreement about Northern Ireland's future would have to gain the consent of a majority within the Province.

The UDA leadership had no such back channel to the Irish, or for that matter the British, governments. Instead they communicated via Roy Magee and perhaps more crucially through the Church of Ireland Primate, Robin Eames. Magee had threatened to walk away from the UDA following the Greysteel massacre but was implored to stay in communication by Ray Smallwoods. To this day the Presbyterian envoy insists that Smallwoods, despite his militancy and strategy of targeting Sinn Féin, was central to the UDA's painfully slow creep towards ceasefire and the peace process: 'There would never have been a loyalist ceasefire and peace process without Ray Smallwoods. He was one of the key people who saw the necessity to end it all.'

Robin Eames also played a critical role in his talks with the CLMC and his advice had an impact on the Inner Council, particularly on advisers such as Smallwoods and veterans such as Joe English. Like Magee, the Church of Ireland Primate decided not to break off contact with the UDA after Greysteel. Eames's message to the UDA and UVF, following the archbishop's talks with John Major in Downing Street, provided comfort for sceptics on the CLMC. He said he was convinced that the British government had not done a secret deal with the IRA. Somehow, in the darkest days, a chink of light remained visible on the political horizon, even though the loyalists, like the IRA, were still not ready to call off their violence for good.

Another important, if shadowy, figure behind moves to bring the UDA towards a cessation was John White. On three days' Christmas parole in 1990 White, who was part of a UDA gang which committed torture killings against random Catholic targets in the early 1970s, had been treated by the young UDA guns like a returning war hero. In the office above Frizzels, 'C' company militants elbowed each other out of the way to shake White's hand and his young admirers bombarded him with bottles of vodka and Bacardi. (Since White is a teetotaller the gifts went unopened.)

White was serving a life sentence for the slaughter of SDLP Senator Paddy Wilson and his girlfriend Irene Andrews. As a young officer Eric Anderson, the Greysteel investigator, had had White put behind bars for the double murder. He estimated that there were more than 100 stab wounds on both bodies. The ferocity of the attacks, which matched any of the excesses of the Shankill Butchers, a gang of UVF members who tortured and slaughtered Catholics in the 1970s, was undoubtedly psychopathic. But as one of White's fellow killers, Davy Payne, who had participated in several torture killings in the early 1970s and was close to White both inside and out of prison, said twenty years later, there was also a basic political purpose to such brutality. While in Crumlin Road jail during the 1990s Payne, who had cut his ties with the UDA, became friendly with a republican prisoner who was isolated from fellow IRA inmates, the informer Sean O'Callaghan. The Provos' former Southern commander asked Payne why he, White and others had embarked on such a callous and vicious campaign against Catholic civilians.

Payne quite coldly told me that they just didn't pick up ordinary Catholics for the fun of it. The UDA's military wing believed that by inflicting unbearable cruelty on the Catholic population they could weaken support for the IRA in nationalist areas. They wanted to make the price of IRA violence too high for the Catholics of Northern Ireland to bear. Back then Payne told me he and White and others genuinely believed this strategy would work.

White was impressed by Official IRA members he encountered in the old Long Kesh compounds, particularly by their path away from violence towards democratic politics. In time he claimed that he too had seen the error of his ways. While in jail he studied for a degree and received a diploma in criminology. But at times White could still reveal a ruthless side, even with fellow UDA inmates. One former UDA prisoner recalls a ribbing White received about the reason he was inside.

We were jibing him about how many times he stabbed Paddy Wilson and Irene Andrews. One friend of mine said he only stabbed them about a dozen times and White got very angry. He stared into my mate's face and corrected him – he said, 'You're wrong, it was forty-seven times.' That freaked my friend out completely, the way John looked into his eyes. We never slagged him again.

On his release on licence in early 1992 White said that he wanted to put his past behind him and work for peace. As Johnny Adair kept emphasizing long after the ceasefire, White had credibility in the UDA: like Smallwoods, he had the cachet of being an ex-prisoner, someone who had been prepared to kill for the loyalist cause. When he said the time was right to stop, the new generation would listen. Nationalists might view the convicted double killer with disdain, but it is undeniable that he played a part in persuading the UDA's young militants to halt their murderous activities.

With the possibility of an end to violence, the British government wanted to remove anything or anyone that could undermine moves towards peace. Loyalism's unknown variable was undoubtedly Johnny Adair. For several months RUC Chief Constable Sir Hugh Annesley had been planning a move against Adair. Together with the head of Special Branch, Ronnie Flanagan, and Superintendent Derek Martindale, Annesley put together a team to focus solely on Adair. It would use a new tool at the security forces' disposal – the 1991 charge of Directing Acts of Terrorism. (This had been used just once before, in 1993, to help put an IRA commander from the Provos' East Tyrone brigade into prison.)

The team included Superintendent Brian McArthur, Inspector

Tim Gorrod, several uniformed officers and Detective Sergeant Johnston Brown, known, even to the killers of 'C' company, as Janty. For some time senior officers in the force suspected that one, or possibly two, policemen had been leaking information from the station to Adair and his cohorts, so members of the special unit were ordered not to discuss what they were planning – even with other colleagues. The fear was that if Adair got an inkling of it, he would change his behaviour, including his habit of chatting to uniformed officers on the beat in the Shankill. It was also kept secret from British military intelligence for fear that elements in the FRU who had links to UDA informants would compromise the operation.

Up to 500 detectives had been involved in investigations into the loyalist upsurge between 1991 and 1994. Not only were they hampered by the fact that other branches of the security services were leaking information to the loyalist murder gangs, but they were up against an extremely streetwise and cunning figure who was the driving force behind UDA killings in greater Belfast and beyond. Adair had developed a system aimed at countering any attempts to thwart attacks on nationalists and republicans – the 'five-minute warning'. Hit squads from 'C' company would be called to safe houses in the lower Shankill, where guns would be distributed, masks and gloves donned, and only five minutes before the teams were sent out of the door Adair would give them details of the target. This was his way of preventing any potential informant finding the nearest phone box and ringing his police handler to alert him about an imminent hit.

The only chink in Adair's armour was his bombastic nature, his inability to shut up about his position at the top of loyalist terrorism, and Flanagan's team was encouraged by this tendency to boast, hint and sometimes admit to uniform officers that he was a player. Annesley and Flanagan believed that their men could build a case that would result in Adair being jailed for fifteen years. Towards the end of 1993 and at the beginning of 1994 uniform policemen who might encounter Adair on a daily basis wore hidden microphones. (In one infamous conversation outside his old Hazelfield Street home in February 1994, the

UDA's military commander dismissed suggestions from two officers that there was a chance for peace. 'If you make peace,' he
said, 'I'll start something else.' And when the policemen asked if
he didn't want peace, he uttered the immortal words, 'Shove
your doves.')

Police chiefs also decided that when he was arrested everything
Adair said would be recorded and kept – even if he did not admit
to specific acts of terrorism. In January 1994, two days after a gun
attack on Councillor Alex Maskey's home, Adair was brought in
for questioning. During informal conversations, not under caution,
Adair boasted that he had sent the gunmen out to kill Maskey
and displayed remarkable knowledge about the shooting. He told
the interviewing officers that the gunmen's car had broken down
on the way back to the Shankill. 'The boys had to walk back
home, even with their guns,' he said. Adair also mentioned that a
new gun had been used in the shooting. When officers found the
car the UDA team had used in the attack on Alex Maskey's home,
they saw that it had indeed broken down. And when they tested
the bullet casings found outside the house, it was clear that they
had come from a new weapon.

The secret case against Adair was slowly building up. Detective
Sergeant Janty Brown was critical to its success, ingratiating himself
with Adair and his cohorts, even sipping tea in their homes. It all
seemed very cosy and Adair clearly did not think that the RUC
would have the audacity to charge him with a serious terrorist
offence. He even taunted young uniform officers in the street:
'You know who I am and what I do and you can't do anything
about it.'

But they could do something about it, and in May 1994
Inspector Tim Gorrod led a team of detectives into Hazelfield
Street to arrest Adair. As he read out the charges the UDA
commander was stunned.

Adair was sitting in his armchair and he just looked at me and said,
'You're not serious, are you?' When I said I was he replied again that I
was having him on. Finally when we put it to him again that he was
about to be charged his attitude changed. He was crestfallen and couldn't

even get up out of his chair. I had to help him up before we could take him into custody.

It was Adair's third and final arrest and the end of his domination of the UDA – at least temporarily.

17. From the Edge of the Abyss

In the first six months of 1994 the UDA invoked the spectre of the Pan Nationalist Front in all its statements. To justify its attacks on SDLP members and their homes, the organization accused the moderate nationalist party of 'exercising a veto over political development and democratic progress'. It insisted – publicly at least – that it had intended to kill the likes of MP Dr Joe Hendron, and activists such as Donovan McClelland and Cassie McDermott. Privately, some members of the Inner Council have confessed that their attacks were designed merely to strike terror throughout the nationalist community, even in those politicians who opposed republican violence, but they were not really intended to kill.

In this same period elements both inside and on the fringes of the Inner Council were toying with a doomsday plan in the event of Northern Ireland falling under any form of joint authority between London and Dublin. Many unionists and loyalists believed any IRA ceasefire would be predicated on some sort of sell-out to the Provisionals and Pan Nationalism. And while the Downing Street Declaration explicitly stated that there would be no change in Northern Ireland's constitutional status without the consent of a majority in the North, a number of unionist politicians continued to stoke fears about secret deals between republicans and the British government.

On 16 January the UDA came up with its alternative plan for the future of Northern Ireland should Britain seek to disengage, whether overtly or covertly. The leadership published a document that effectively proposed ethnically cleansing Catholics from large parts of the province and re-partitioning it. Essentially the areas east of the River Bann would be turned into a Protestant-only zone, with thousands of Catholics outside Belfast being transferred to the western side of the river, which could then become Republic of Ireland territory. A land corridor would be established linking

West Belfast with the new Catholic zone. In other words, Catholics living in other parts of Belfast would either have to be resettled in the new region or else moved into an overcrowded and encircled West Belfast ghetto. Meanwhile, the new exclusively Protestant zone would have autonomy within the UK, be linked with the EU, have its land borders sealed and all points of access except for the West Belfast corridor defended by military installations.

The plan was copied from a paper written by Southern-born economic historian and Queen's University lecturer Liam Kennedy. Dr Kennedy, a peace campaigner and strong opponent of IRA violence, had explored the viability of re-zoning the North into Protestant and Catholic cantons. He was horrified to learn that the UDA had stolen his study and turned it into a blueprint.

The UDA doomsday plan even included a breakdown of 'men in military useful trades' whom the organization could call upon in the event of civil war and who would be useful in building the economy of a new state. As with everything in Northern Ireland, the skilled workers, scientific technicians, metal work operatives as well as full- and part-time soldiers broke down into the P and C categories – Protestant and Catholic. In almost every trade and profession, according to the UDA analysis, Protestants outnumbered Catholics.

Most chilling of all was the plan for those Catholics left behind in a re-partitioned Northern Ireland. There were three options: 'expulsion, nullification, internment'. Given that the UDA was already in the business of sectarian slaughter, the middle option seemed preferable to the document's authors. The blueprint looked and sounded like something straight from the wars in the former Yugoslavia, where hundreds of thousands of Bosnians, Croats and Serbs had been driven from their historic homelands. Indeed the plan referred to the objective of establishing an 'ethnic Protestant homeland'.

Although seen as a last resort by a majority on the Inner Council, the re-partition plan had support throughout the organization, especially among those such as Alex Kerr who saw no long-term prospect of historic compromise between unionism and nationalism. (Re-partition was not just the fantasy of a few loyalist extremists. Back in the early 1980s the Upper Bann MP, the late Harold McCusker, had spoken openly about unionists seeking re-partition if Catholics became the majority community in Northern Ireland, and in her memoirs Margaret Thatcher admitted that the Conservative cabinet had considered re-partition as an alternative solution to the Ulster crisis.) One former member of the Inner Council conceded to the authors shortly after the ceasefires that the UDA plan would have led to thousands of people losing their homes, and hundreds, if not thousands, being killed. 'The plan reflected the desperate circumstances many loyalists felt themselves to be in during the mid-1990s. We really believed the Brits were going to pull out if the Provos declared a ceasefire. We felt surrounded by Pan Nationalism and this was the final solution, the one way of securing a British Ulster.'

Given that the organization had always been involved in informal ethnic cleansing – driving Catholics out of mainly Protestant areas – re-partition appealed to the UDA. Plagiarizing Liam Kennedy's paper merely formalized that policy and it was a precursor to the kind of anti-Catholic activities the UDA in areas such as East Antrim engaged in even after the ceasefires were called. Although it sounded outlandish and dangerous, even back in the bloody days of early 1994, the concept of 'land grab' and of ethnic cleansing remained as a last resort for many inside and outside the UDA. But the paradox in the spring and summer of 1994 was that, while the UDA contemplated ethnic cleansing and a unilateral declaration of independence, there was growing awareness throughout loyalism that a ceasefire was inevitable, particularly since it was only a question of when rather than if the IRA was going to declare its cessation.

One thing was certain: Johnny Adair would play no more part, at least on the outside, in either the 'war' or the push for peace. After his arrest Adair appeared in the dock at Belfast Magistrates' Court on 20 May. It was a bizarre occasion. The leading figures of 'C' company turned up in the cramped court house and wedged themselves in beside more than a dozen reporters. When

Adair was brought up from the cells, flanked by two police officers, there were waves and smiles from many of his comrades and
female admirers. He seemed amused by all the attention. Throughout
the brief hearing, during which he was charged formally with
directing acts of terrorism, Adair sniggered and smiled, nodding over
to journalists he knew as well as to his small army of supporters
in the public gallery.

While the scene inside the Magistrates' Court resembled nothing
more serious than a headmaster chiding an errant schoolboy, in
Adair's lower Shankill lair the atmosphere quickly turned nasty.
Buses and cars were hijacked close to the Shankill estate and
parked across the road leading into the loyalist stronghold. Police
officers and troops were attacked by around seventy young loyalists and the violence lasted for several hours. (It was a measure of
the contempt in which the UVF held Adair and his followers that
there was nothing but disgust with the rioters inside the group's
Shankill HQ on the day of the hearing. One of the authors was
there to interview a senior commander and rank-and-file UVF
men wandered to and fro reporting the scenes at the bottom of
their road, every one of them furious that 'C' company's actions
were wreaking havoc in the very area they purported to defend.)

Northern Ireland's most infamous remand prisoner entered
Crumlin Road jail at a critical junction in prison history: his UDA
comrades were about to wreck the NIO's policy of forced integration with republicans. They chose the bright summer's morning
of 16 July to stage a rooftop protest.

Eddie McClean (who had the dubious notoriety of being the
very last prisoner married in the Victorian jail) recalled in June
2003 how the UDA wrecked 'the Crum':

We were allowed out for exercise in the yard and the lads basically
didn't want to go back inside because it was a lovely day. They mingled
in small groups and then fanned out across the yard. Then they started
pulling corrugated iron and other debris including broken up furniture
from the cells, walls and a shed in the yard. They built this rampart that
eventually allowed a few prisoners to climb up to the roof. From there
they started pulling up the tiles and flinging them on to the road below.

It was very spontaneous but the UDA prisoners showed great courage. When the prison authorities sent in the Ninjas [inmates' term for riot squad] the UDA prisoners used anything they could find to fight them back. Loads of our guys were beaten and injured but more and more of them fought back against the Ninjas until there were dozens of comrades on the roof.

Another of the former prisoners claimed in June 2003 that the protest's planners had been influenced by a television drama they had seen in prison showing Roman soldiers breaking a long siege by building a ramp to the top of their enemies' fortress.

It was not long before UDA supporters from the nearby lower Shankill and Oldpark turned up outside the prison. Nor was it long before the UDA on the outside informed the media about the protest. Within an hour of reaching the roof the prisoners were on prime-time television. The atmosphere below on the Crumlin Road was akin to a party, with the wives and girlfriends of UDA inmates bringing deck-chairs to the scene, a few training binoculars on the roof-top protesters. One woman brought along a CD-player with powerful speakers and prisoners above danced to the music.

Their ingenuity and derring-do eventually led to every inmate being transferred from the Crumlin Road to the Maze and thus into a totally segregated, paramilitary-controlled prison environment. Crucially, it allowed Johnny Adair to mix with sentenced prisoners – including his hero, Michael Stone – on the H-blocks in the run-up to the October ceasefire when they would be called upon to back it.

Adair's absence from the Shankill gave the Inner Council leadership breathing space and time to convince units across the Province of the necessity for a ceasefire. But others had plans to prevent the UDA and UVF from going along that road. Loyalists on either side of the Combined Loyalist Military Command were convinced that the IRA's strategy was to instigate a 'summer of provocation' designed to kill any chance of a joint UDA/UVF ceasefire. David Ervine, an ex-UVF prisoner and a key figure on the CLMC, put its view succinctly in January 2003: 'The Provos wanted to swan around the world portraying themselves as peacemakers, while the bonehead loyalists kept killing Catholics.' In other words, the IRA's two-month-long concentrated fire on loyalists was an example of 'armed propaganda'. But there was undoubtedly an element of visceral revenge for the Provos, a settling of scores before the IRA suspended military operations.

One of the IRA's prime targets in the run-up to its ceasefire was Ray Smallwoods, whom the Provos believed, correctly, was the brains behind the UDA's campaign of assassinating Sinn Féin members. On the night of 11 July an IRA unit took over a pensioner's house in Donard Drive, Lisburn, which was directly across from Smallwoods's home. The following morning as he went to his car two masked men emerged from the house and blasted him with two shotguns. Coincidentally, David Ervine was in the estate at the time of the shooting and rushed to where Smallwoods lay dying, comforted by his wife. 'We tried to give him assistance, but it was to no avail. To stand and watch someone die: these are sights and memories, which I would never forget.'

Smallwoods's death was a devastating blow to the UDA, not only in the short term but in the long run. The Inner Council was robbed of its most able thinker, an individual who was ruthless in directing terrorism but someone who was also prepared to sit down with his republican enemies and talk peace. Among those who attended his funeral on 14 July were the Clonard priests Gerry Reynolds and Alec Reid, the men who played a central role in bringing together Gerry Adams and John Hume. Several unionist politicians – the same politicians who said they would never talk to terrorists – attended the service as well, including the DUP MP Peter Robinson, Belfast's former Lord Mayor Sammy Wilson, and North Belfast Ulster Unionist councillor Fred Cobain. In contrast to the reaction when nationalist politicians were seen to have anything to do with IRA or INLA activists, there was little or no outcry over why politicians who argued that democrats should have no truck with terrorists chose to honour a man who was unapologetic about his involvement in terrorism.

By just four votes Smallwoods had missed being elected to

Lisburn Borough Council the previous year; it would have been only a matter of time before he took a seat. Davy Adams, the UDP man who was elected in Smallwoods's ward, was shaken to the core over the loss of his mentor. Adams, an articulate, well-spoken, grammar school-educated loyalist from the Maze area, later accepted that Smallwoods's death in the summer of 1994 had far-reaching consequences for the UDA. 'Ray's sound advice was sadly missed. I often wonder if he had been around would the movement have ended up in the mess it found itself in.'

Undoubtedly, the murder of two senior UDA members on 31 July, exactly one month before the Provisionals' ceasefire, was another case of the IRA getting its revenge in before laying down its arms. The peace of a Sunday lunchtime was punctured by machine-gun fire echoing across the Ballynafeigh area of South Belfast. Minutes earlier Joe Bratty and Raymond Elder had been enjoying a drink at a loyalist band hall off the upper Ormeau Road. An IRA unit was hidden in a white van outside. The second Bratty and Elder appeared outside the hall two men wearing black balaclava masks and white boiler suits sprang from the back of the vehicle and fired repeatedly at Bratty and Elder. As the duo lay on the ground the gunmen continued to fire into them at close range until they were sure they were dead. The gunmen raced back into the van which was then driven towards the nationalist lower Ormeau. When the RUC from nearby Ballynafeigh police station eventually pursued the van, they were met by a hostile crowd which hampered the search for the killers.

In the days following the double murder Bratty and Elder's relatives alleged that an unmarked police car had been in the area and initially failed to chase the white van into the lower Ormeau. And UDA members opposed to a ceasefire later claimed that elements on the CLMC had somehow set Bratty and Elder up for assassination. They argued that because Bratty in particular would have been opposed to a loyalist cessation he had to be removed.

The truth about the murders is far more prosaic. Bratty and Elder broke the golden rule of men who live by the gun: they failed to vary their movements. They were known to have a drink in the local loyalist club every Sunday morning. All the IRA had to do was monitor their movements and build up a pattern.

The assassination of Bratty and Elder was enormously popular in the South Belfast Catholic community, even among those opposed to the Provos. In the paramilitary underworld, where enemies live near each other, personal vengeance and long-standing vendettas play a key role. The two men had terrorized nationalists in both ends of the Ormeau Road for two decades, first as teenage street-fighters and later as the UDA's hitmen in the area. Even though he had grown up with young Catholics in the religiously mixed Ballynafeigh area, Joe Bratty nursed a dark hatred for Catholics and nationalists – as well as black people and the police. Known to local Catholics as 'Chinky Bratty', in the 1970s he and his gang had defaced a Workers Party anti-sectarian slogan, 'Sectarianism Kills Workers', daubed on the wall of Ulster Television's headquarters along the Ormeau Road, by changing the last word and thus transforming the socialist message to 'Sectarianism Kills Taigs'. Reflecting his admiration for the Ku Klux Klan, Bratty added the letters KKK, the initials of the American white supremacist group, which he also had tattooed on one of his hands.

IRA coat-tailers celebrated the killings on the walls of the lower Ormeau and the Markets with admiration for 'The IRA's Black and White Minstrels' (a reference to the assassins' garb). Another slogan in the Markets read:'Daniel O'Donnell sings for his mammy, Joe and Ray cried for theirs.'The death of the UDA duo in South Belfast was seen as revenge for the Sean Graham's betting shop massacre and the murder of Teresa Clinton.

Inevitably it was ordinary Catholics who paid the price for the Bratty and Elder killings. On 10 August a unit from the South Belfast brigade shot dead a security man, Harry O'Neill, outside Stewarts supermarket in Orby Link. On the same day, the Lisburn UDA sent a unit to Lurgan to attack a printing firm with supposed republican connections. Michael L'Estrange, a Catholic printer from the County Armagh town, was shot dead inside the Ronan Press. Following his murder, the UDA issued a statement claiming the Ronan Press published the IRA newspaper *An Phoblacht*.

In fact it did not publish the republican paper but rather a series of community newspapers across Northern Ireland – including the *Shankill People*.

Four days later there was a murder which showed how bigotry and sectarian hatred cut across all generations. A young Catholic, Sean Monaghan, was abducted near the peace line in West Belfast. Initially he was taken to a house in the Woodvale area for interrogation by a local UDA unit. He managed to escape but was terrified and uncertain about how to get out of the Shankill. He made his way to an elderly woman's door, but instead of telephoning for the police to come and rescue him the woman contacted the UDA. He was taken away and shot four times in the head.

When the RUC later interviewed the pensioner, acting on intelligence from a UDA informant, she sat in Castlereagh Holding Centre, her hand on a copy of the Bible, swearing that Sean Monaghan had never even been in her house. Although the subsequent murder trial found that she had lied, she escaped a prison sentence. And before the man who fired the fatal shots went to jail he managed to inflict further hurt and pain on the Monaghan family. He screamed at the judge and then the public gallery where Sean's parents were sitting: 'I shot your son – four in the back of the head. I shot him – I'm proud of it.'

With incidents like these taking place it was hard to imagine that the UDA was inching ever closer to a ceasefire. Its path to a cessation was made all the more difficult by continuing IRA attacks in the run-up to its ceasefire on 31 August. Three days after Sean Monaghan's murder the IRA bombed a bar on the York Road owned by Tom Reid, a former Inner Council member and one-time North Belfast brigadier. On the same day the army defused another bomb, outside the Diamond Jubilee in the lower Shankill.

Perhaps, however, the greatest deterrent to a UDA ceasefire was the perception within the general Protestant community that the IRA would have declared a 'total cessation of military operations' only as a result of a secret deal between the hated Pan Nationalist Front and the British government. Indeed forty-eight hours after the IRA's historic announcement a *Belfast Telegraph* opinion poll found that 56 per cent of people in the North believed the cease-fire had come about due to a clandestine pact between the IRA and the British.

A number of stabilizing forces though helped the Inner Council guide the organization towards the loyalist ceasefire of 13 October 1994. A loyalist cessation had been a distinct possibility since the Downing Street Declaration, particularly because of its promise that constitutional change could come about only with the consent of the Northern Ireland people. One of those who had gained that assurance from John Major was Archbishop Robin Eames who, during the summer of 1994, continued to hold talks with the CLMC representatives. The highly regarded Roy Magee also played a pivotal role, encouraged initially by the CLMC's temporary ceasefire in 1991, which had lasted twenty days in the face of undoubted IRA provocation. Convinced that the leading lights in the CLMC were prepared for peace, he acted as an envoy between the British government and both wings of loyalism, although he had more contact with the UDA. 'My sole aim is to move the paramilitaries from violence to a more political agenda,' he said at the time of the loyalists' cessation of violence. 'I have no political mandate but, rather, I do it because of my position as a minister of the gospel. I was in the business of nudging, putting my elbow into people to change direction. That applied to both governments as well as the loyalist paramilitaries. I think, because of the trust we have built up over the years, they allowed me to do that.'

Internally, all six UDA brigadiers were prepared to test the water and give the ceasefire a chance. One Inner Council member would even have been prepared to open up a secret back channel to Dublin. A few months after the loyalist ceasefire Chris Hudson, the Dublin trade unionist who was acting as envoy between Albert Reynolds's government and the UVF, had a chance meeting in Wynnes Hotel in Dublin's Abbey Street with Joe English, the UDA's representative in Rathcoole. His role as a go-between had become public knowledge when English approached him. 'Joe asked me why I had never approached the UDA and offered to act as go-between with the Irish government as well. Frankly, I was stunned. I had never thought of it before. Certainly if they [the UDA] had asked me before the ceasefires I would have gone to the Irish government and done the same.'

One of the main hurdles the UDA leadership had to vault before signing up to any joint cessation with the UVF was the opposition led by prisoners locked inside the H-blocks. The Inner Council was dealt a temporary setback on 1 September 1994 when the UDA inmates, led by Adrian Bird, the commanding officer in the blocks, voted narrowly against a ceasefire. If they wanted to, the UDA prisoners could exercise a veto over a cessation, and for a short time everything seemed lost. The situation was made more difficult by instability on the streets. Rioting broke out and shots were directed at RUC Land Rovers on 13 September at the start of Johnny Adair's trial in Crumlin Road court house. Even female members of his lower Shankill fan club took part in the violence and a number of young women wielded baseball bats and clubs at cameramen and journalists on the road outside the court.

The moves towards ceasefire, however tentative, did not stop the UDA from killing Catholics. Less than twenty-four hours after the IRA ceasefire a gunman from Tigers Bay, firing from a moving car, shot and killed 32-year-old John O'Hanlon as he changed a car wheel in Skegoneil Avenue, North Belfast. He was to be the last UDA murder victim for almost two years.

Paradoxically, Adair's court case, and his transfer from Crumlin Road to the Maze, played a key part in winning internal support for a ceasefire. On 10 October the NIO took the unprecedented step of allowing a joint delegation of loyalist political leaders into the Maze. Their aim was to overturn the previous vote and ensure that the prisoners publicly backed a cessation. Two men became central players in the unfolding drama: John White and John Adair. On the orders of the Inner Council, Adair replaced Adie Bird as UDA commanding officer in the prison. Adair was heavily influenced by White, who was one of the strongest advocates for ceasefire.

'Although John White wasn't on the Inner Council – he wasn't even a brigadier – Johnny thought more of him than all the other

six brigadiers put together,' said one of Adair's former confidants
in April 2003.

In Johnny's mind John White was the founder of the UFF, he was the
one that had terrified the Catholic community in the 1970s and had
done a long prison stretch for his activities. White for Johnny had proven
himself. So if John White said it was time for peace then Adair was
prepared to listen. Whatever people think of John White and what he
did or what he later became involved with, there might not have been
a UDA ceasefire without him.

When the vote against a ceasefire was reversed in the H-blocks,
White, Gary McMichael and the other UDP members of the
CLMC delegation were jubilant. They were so overjoyed that
they wanted to declare the ceasefire there and then. One of them
even wanted to announce the CLMC cessation to the media
while standing in the Maze car park. However, the UVF and its
political wing, the Progressive Unionist Party (PUP), resisted and
managed to persuade the UDA that the CLMC should seize the
agenda and exploit the propaganda value of a ceasefire at a carefully staged press conference.

Three days after the meeting in the Maze the CLMC announced
its ceasefire in front of the world's media. The venue was a poignant
one – Fernhill House in the Glencairn district of loyalist West
Belfast, which had been a training ground for Lord Carson's original UVF in the struggle against Home Rule prior to the First
World War. (The house is now a museum and among its historic
artefacts is the table on which Carson launched the Ulster
Covenant, swearing opposition to Home Rule, in 1912.)

The announcement was meticulously choreographed to reflect
the two wings of Ulster loyalism. Six men were seated at the top
of a table above which was a legend – 'A Progressive Democratic
Process' – which united the names of the paramilitary-linked
parties, the UDP and the PUP. Davy Adams, Gary McMichael
and John White were from UDA backgrounds. The PUP trio were
Gusty Spence, the modern UVF's founder, along with Jim
McDonald and William 'Plum' Smyth. The job of reading out the

ground-breaking ceasefire statement from the CLMC was given to Spence who, like John White, had spent a considerable part of his life in jail serving a sentence for murder, studied to university degree level and had also been impressed by the Official IRA's willingness to turn from 'armed struggle' towards compromise with unionism.

Spence's statement, unlike the IRA's, touched on the issue of victims. 'In all sincerity, we offer to the loved ones of all innocent people over the past twenty-five years, abject and true remorse. No words of ours will compensate for the intolerable suffering they have undergone during this conflict.' The overt apology to victims was seized upon by the international press corps in Fernhill House. For once, the loyalists were stealing a march on the IRA's well-oiled propaganda machine.

In the days after the ceasefire announcement both wings of loyalism were rewarded with a pioneering tour of the United States. Three UDP men – Joe English, Davy Adams and Gary McMichael – accompanied Spence, David Ervine and Billy Hutchinson on a visit to Boston, New York and Washington DC. They were guests of the National Committee on Foreign Policy, the same think-tank that had invited Gerry Adams to the USA in early 1993. For the first time since Andy Tyrie attended peace talks in Boston back in the 1970s alongside republican figures such as the Irish Republican Socialist Party founder Seamus Costello, the political voices of the UDA and UVF were putting Ulster loyalism's case to the American public.

It was during this period that the UDP started to cultivate links with academics and writers who, the party believed, could help it shape a more coherent programme and thus challenge the electoral hegemony of the Ulster Unionists and Paisley's DUP. One of those academics, who became close to the UDP, particularly Gary McMichael, was Dr Kirsten Schultz, an American lecturer from the London School of Economics. Dr Schultz, who has expertise in conflicts such as those in the Middle East, travelled with UDP delegations to the United States throughout the mid-1990s. Indeed her presence on one trip almost caused a bust-up between the UDP and PUP delegations. Just prior to meeting

Bill Clinton in the Oval Office, the PUP and a representative from the UVF objected to Dr Schultz attending private talks with the US president. McMichael and John White at first insisted on her being present but eventually reneged under PUP pressure.

These were halcyon days for loyalism, with Ervine and McMichael fêted around the world as peacemakers and statesmen. McMichael's speech in late October 1994 to the National Committee on Foreign Policy in New York was laced with moderation and compromise. McMichael accepted, as his father had, that there had been structural discrimination against Catholics in the old Stormont regime. Loyalists would support power-sharing with Catholics in Northern Ireland as well as good neighbourly relations with the Irish Republic, he told his audience. He even went further. He said unionists should be prepared to sit down with Sinn Féin if the IRA's war was over for good.

18. Demon Pastors, New Divisions

Back in Northern Ireland the UDA set about solidifying support for the ceasefire and the new-found interest in politics. In an interview in the December 1994 edition of the *New Ulster Defender* Michael Stone threw his weight behind the cessation and attacked those unionists opposed to the peace process. He dismissed DUP charges that the union was far from safe and that the process was a sell-out:

The Grand Old Duke of York types are seen by us as nothing more than yesterday's men. Sabre-rattling from afar is a thing of the past, as we, the men who put our lives on the line, all know too well. Our faith is with those with constructive ideas, leaving behind the negative rhetoric of times best forgotten. Those of the Ulster Democratic Party and Progressive Unionist Party recognize that dialogue to find a way forward is imperative for a peaceful future.

Stone's reflections on the ceasefires summed up the central paradox of Ulster loyalism: on the one hand, both the UDA and UVF were responsible for sectarian slaughter; on the other, their political ideas were more forward-thinking, realistic and moderate than those of 'respectable' unionist politicians. The next battle ahead for the UDA, and thus the UDP, would be to see if their progressive approach would be rewarded at the ballot box.

When the British and Irish governments published the Frameworks Document at the end of January 1995 loyalism and unionism in general faced a crisis. It was meant to be a blueprint for political progress and a means of enticing Sinn Féin permanently into constitutional politics. The sticking point for all unionists was its discussion of cross-border cooperation. The authors of the document proposed island-wide harmonizing of more than seventy aspects of society and economy. To many ordinary unionists Frameworks represented a stepping-stone towards Irish unity. A number of leading loyalists, including Alex Kerr, South Belfast brigadier, lost faith in the political process. Along with Billy 'King Rat' Wright, leader of the UVF in Portadown, Kerr regarded Frameworks as a United Ireland by stealth.

Throughout the spring and summer of 1995 Kerr became disillusioned with the UDP's stance on the Frameworks document and secretly plotted to undermine the UDA leadership. His friendship with Wright crystallized into an alliance that would eventually challenge the entire CLMC. Kerr started his campaign by linking the UDP to the drugs trade, persuading two young UDA members from the Village area of Belfast to paint 'Ulster Drugs Party' on the walls off the Donegall Road. He also held briefings with journalists, arguing for a change in UDA policy and outright opposition, with violence if necessary, against Frameworks. The Kerr–Wright axis was boosted on 2 June when nine UDA prisoners, including the Greysteel killers Torrens Knight and Stephen Irwin, were expelled from the organization's wing at the Maze for objecting to a mural depicting a dove of peace inside the UDA-controlled H-block. Eventually they were relocated to a wing controlled by a new loyalist terror group, which would become the Loyalist Volunteer Force, officially founded by Wright and Kerr the following year.

It was Adair, still on remand, who ordered that the dissenters be forcibly moved out of the wing. He was still in awe of John White and, to a lesser extent, Gary McMichael, so he continued to support the peace process. On 6 September he was finally sentenced to fifteen years for directing acts of terrorism. Like many other prisoners, both republican and loyalist, he held on to the hope that an eventual peace settlement would lead to some form of amnesty.

Through 1995 the UDA and UVF kept their ceasefires: there were no loyalist murders for over twelve months. All of the dozen paramilitary-linked deaths of 1995 were carried out by the IRA under the cover name Direct Action Against Drugs and every one of its victims was a drug dealer operating within the Catholic community.

Even before the ceasefires were declared drugs had been flood-ing into Northern Ireland via the Irish Republic and Britain. Several working-class loyalist areas were blighted by drug culture, especially the Lower Shankill and Rathcoole estates. The irony was that, while the UDP canvassed for support, set up advice centres, volunteered for community work and argued for economic investment in deprived Protestant areas, leading cadres in the UDA were growing rich on the back of drug-dealing. In Rathcoole drugs were smuggled in and sold to teenagers under the command of John 'Grugg' Gregg, while Adair and his 'C' company comrades sold Ecstasy, cannabis and cocaine from what became known as the 'drugs flat' in the lower Shankill.

The drug-dealing culture was to become a millstone around the neck of the UDP and would play a large part in the party's failure to make an electoral breakthrough. Older UDA veterans were extremely uncomfortable about the dealing, but they kept their counsel because those in control of drugs, men such as Gregg, Adair and Stephen McKeag, were feared paramilitary command-ers with awesome reputations for violence. Joe English in parti-cular was vocal about his opposition to drug-dealing, but only to the media. He gave off-the-record briefings to journalists about the UDA drug dealers, including Gregg, and this proved to be his downfall. Gregg and his allies found out about English's exposés of their dealing and forced him out of the UDA. English and Ray Smallwoods had been instrumental in pressing the Inner Council for a ceasefire. He was one of the public faces of the UDP at its meeting with Bill Clinton on 17 March 1995. During the St Patrick's Day festivities, which loyalists and unionists shared with republicans and nationalists, including the faces of what had only recently been dubbed the Pan Nationalist Front, Gerry Adams and John Hume, English became emotional when one of the other guests sang 'Danny Boy' ('The Londonderry Air'). But within a year English was gone, simply because he detested drug-dealing. It was a warning of things to come.

While the UDA did not kill anyone in 1995, grassroots sectari-anism continued unabated. One Catholic family living on the

Blacks Road close to the only Protestant housing estate left in the upper Falls, Suffolk, was subjected to repeated intimidation by the local UDA. During the 1990s its home was attacked fifty-six times by young UDA members determined to drive the family out of Suffolk. The campaign climaxed in the summer of 1995 as the dispute over Orange Order marches spread from flashpoints such as Drumcree and the lower Ormeau across Northern Ireland. While the UDA and UVF told their rank and file to stay out of protests against the rerouting of loyalist parades, many individual members got involved in acts of sectarian harassment, driving Catholic families from their homes in Larne, Carrickfergus and Antrim.

The provocation caused by the republican movement's manipulation of local sensitivities over the marching issue was nothing in comparison with what was about to happen next. Angered over John Major's insistence that there had to be a quarantine period before Sinn Féin entered all-party talks, the IRA struck at the heart of the City of London, exploding a huge bomb on 9 February 1996 at Canary Wharf. The IRA leadership had been planning the bombing even during Bill Clinton's historic visit to Belfast just before Christmas. Over the ensuing eighteen months it would launch further strikes in England, bombing cities such as Manchester, as well as firing mortars at a British army base in Osnabruck, Germany.

Throughout this period the CLMC held firm and resisted the temptation to go on the counter-offensive. However, the UDA ceasefire came extremely close to breaking point in September when the IRA left a bomb inside Thiepval barracks in Lisburn – the British army's headquarters in Northern Ireland. A soldier from England, James Bradwell, was critically injured and died four days later. In the hours after the blast the UDA contemplated ending its cessation and targeting republicans. One senior loyalist on the CLMC explained in December 1997 how members held back the organization:

Initially we thought no one had been killed in the explosion. Jim Bradwell lived on for a few days in hospital. To be honest the fact that he did gave us time and space to convince the UDA that striking back was counter-productive. Had anyone been killed instantly in the blast, especially Protestant civilians working at Thiepval, that would have been a different story.

Paradoxically, the IRA's return to 'war' was a boost to the Kerr–Wright alliance. The duo was convinced that the British government would buckle under IRA bombs in Britain. When the authorities banned the annual Drumcree parade from passing down the Portadown's nationalist Garvaghy Road in early July this merely confirmed their view that the government was intent on appeasing armed republicanism.

The Drumcree crisis of 1996 would produce the greatest challenge to the CLMC's authority since the ceasefire was declared. One loyalist killer in Portadown saw his chance to ingratiate himself with Billy Wright once the troops and police descended on Drumcree on 1 July and an effective stand-off ensued with thousands of Orangemen on the hill beside the parish church. Knowing that most of its drivers were Catholic, Clifford McKeown, a former UVF supergrass, called a local taxi firm in Lurgan and asked to be picked up near the town's leisure centre. He asked the driver, Michael McGoldrick, who had just graduated from Queen's University Belfast, to drive to the rural outskirts of the County Armagh town and then shot him in the back of the head. McKeown later told loyalist colleagues that he had killed the young Catholic as a birthday present for Billy Wright.

The McGoldrick murder provoked a crisis in the CLMC, which immediately distanced itself from the killing. It was put under further pressure when television pictures showed Billy Wright and Alex Kerr together on Drumcree hill, directing the loyalist protesters' violent clashes with the security forces. In ten days the RUC was to fire 6,000 plastic bullets across Northern Ireland as the Province was engulfed in a wave of sectarian rioting. Wright and Kerr had even planned to hijack a manure-spreader, use it to spray police lines at Drumcree bridge with petrol and set them alight. Hundreds of young loyalists, mainly from Wright's Portadown UVF, flocked behind the Wright–Kerr alliance. So when the

CLMC met in emergency session during the Drumcree crisis there were demands that it act against the dissident duo. A senior UVF commander, who had once worked with Kerr as a military liaison officer on the CLMC, claimed in January 1999 that the UDA led the charge against the two men: 'It was the UDA that argued we should go all the way and expel Billy Wright from the UVF and sentence the two of them to death. It's ironic that they were the ones baying for Wright and Kerr's blood even though much later down the line some of them would be linking up with Billy's new organization.'

The 'new organization' was the Loyalist Volunteer Force, a hard-line anti-peace process terror group centred around Wright, Kerr and most of the old UVF in Lurgan and Portadown. Wright's failed attempt to seize control of the UVF during the summer of 1996 was encouraged by former Progressive Unionist Party talks delegate and ex-UVF prisoner Jackie Mahood. He goaded Wright to try to stage a coup against the Shankill Road leadership. Mahood was also a close friend of the West Belfast UDA figure Jim Spence, and used that relationship to try to cultivate future links between the two groups. But Spence had doubts about the UDA getting into bed with Billy Wright. He called him 'Billy Wrong'.

Another figure who encouraged the Kerr–Wright alliance during this period was Kenny McClinton. A convicted murderer who had shot dead a Belfast City bus-driver at point-blank range on the Shankill Road during the 1977 loyalist general strike, while in the H-blocks McClinton had converted to a form of born-again Christianity. Styling himself a pastor, he adopted an extreme brand of Protestant fundamentalism with links to southern American white supremacist groups. He was also committed to the concept of an independent Ulster which would be exclusively Protestant and run as a Calvinist state. The former UDA killer linked up with an ex-UVF man from the Shankill, Clifford Peoples, who had worked for the victims' group Families Against Intimidation and Terror during the mid-1990s. McClinton and Peoples fell under the influence of another sinister self-appointed pastor. The Pastor had been a member of Tara, the secretive Protestant terror group which counted among its members the serial child sex abuser, prominent Orangeman and British intelligence agent, the late William McGrath. The trio had a vision – the foundation of an army of evangelicals who would use the gun to re-establish Protestant hegemony throughout Northern Ireland. They had no truck with the concept of compromise with republicans, nationalists and Catholics.

Although Ian Paisley was in the tradition of Bible-belt Protestantism himself, he fiercely distrusted these far-right evangelicals led by the Pastor, and the DUP was openly hostile to them.

Most of the UDA, and the entire leadership of the UVF, regarded this small bloc, and the Pastor in particular, with deep suspicion. Their wariness was justified because the Pastor was (and continues to be) a paid British army intelligence asset who has been used since the early 1970s to infiltrate, spy on and destabilize loyalist organizations. A close associate of the late John McKeag, the Pastor was run by army agents from Thiepval barracks, and he appeared and then disappeared from the scene whenever unionism underwent a periodic crisis.

He emerged from obscurity in the mid-1980s and turned up at protests against the Anglo-Irish Agreement, associating himself with the bigot George Seawright (who also worked for the security forces, passing information about loyalists, particularly the UVF, to the RUC Special Branch). Once the loyalist ceasefire was declared a decade later the Pastor threw himself into a black propaganda campaign to undermine support for the peace process. He was acting under instructions. Breaking up, weakening and atomizing the loyalist organizations would make it easier for the British to reach a settlement with republicans that could potentially elicit a violent Protestant backlash. The loyalists would be fatally weakened and unable to resist the UK government's designs.

The Pastor penned several pamphlets accusing the PUP leadership of being MI5 agents, of setting up the likes of Joe Bratty and Ray Smallwoods for assassination, and even of being in league with communists and republicans. Interestingly, the Pastor's pamphleteering was not pointed at the UDA or even the UDP. From the outset Alex Kerr and his LVF confidant, Mark 'Swinger'

Fulton, had urged King Rat to build an alliance with the UDA in opposition to the UVF. 'Swinger kept telling Billy over and over again that what the LVF needed to do was link up with the UDA,' said one of Fulton's former colleagues in February 1997. 'That was the way not only of surviving any onslaught by the UVF but forming a new loyalist army.'

To the UVF the Pastor's accusations and rhetoric sounded familiar, just like the black propaganda campaign the British security services had run in the 1970s in order to destabilize and weaken loyalism. Wright was certainly seduced by the arguments of the Pastor, McClinton and, to a lesser degree, Peoples. Although he had his own reservations about the way the peace process was developing, Wright was also attracted to the idea of an 'army of God', especially given his declarations of being a born-again Christian. The end of the IRA ceasefire and the Drumcree ban were the catalysts that produced the first major split in loyalism during the 1990s. But it is clear Wright, Kerr and their small band of followers fell for a classic British intelligence sting.

On 28 August the CLMC formally expelled Wright and Kerr and ordered the pair to leave Northern Ireland or face death. Among those loyalists who opposed the expulsion was Gusty Spence's nephew, Frankie Curry, who had committed over a dozen sectarian murders for the Red Hand Commando. Curry nicknamed 'Pigface', admired Wright and the Mid-Ulster UVF and built links with Wright's dissidents in the build-up to the Drumcree crisis. For that he was stood down from the RHC and sent into purdah by the Shankill UVF. Not only was Curry a killer addicted to morphine-based painkillers and prone to violent mood swings, he also had rudimentary bomb-making skills which he now offered on a freelance basis to any loyalist grouping willing to employ him.

In the autumn of 1996 Curry invented a new flag of convenience that would eventually be adopted by elements in the UDA – the Red Hand Defenders (RHD), a name combining Red Hand Commandos and UDA – and was designed to allow loyalists to carry out attacks without putting the mainstream organizations into the frame. Meantime, Curry successfully fooled a number of journalists into believing he was not the man behind the Red Hand Defenders and that he had no connections to the LVF. They published denial after denial by the self-confessed loyalist killer that he had any dealings with the dissidents or was aiding their cause, but the truth was that from 1996 onwards Curry sought to undermine the loyalist ceasefire and force both the UVF and UDA back to 'war'.

The irony about the rise of loyalist dissidents was that in the summer and autumn of 1996 the UDA was determined to act against them and if necessary kill those leading figures who were arguing for a return to 'armed struggle'. The organization seemed to be aware of the role of *agents provocateurs* on the fringes of loyalism, goading it and the UVF towards a return to terrorism. In a telling editorial of the *New Ulster Defender*'s autumn 1996 edition, the UDA leadership dealt with the 'sinister force' at the edge of loyalism: 'Centred in the Mid-Ulster area, but with active assistance of unsavoury elements from other areas of Northern Ireland, an unholy alliance of drug dealers, media junkies, criminal elements and, believe it or not, fundamentalist clerics have been active in trying to bring about a collapse of the loyalist ceasefire.'

Yet within three years men such as Billy Wright and Frankie Curry were adopted by the West Belfast UDA as martyrs. Moreover, leading figures in the West Belfast brigade would be rushing to the defence of Clifford Peoples and his allies in the face of UVF aggression. This cannot be put down just to the Shankill UDA's long-standing grudge against its rivals on the Shankill Road. Someone inside the UDA itself was clearly determined to pursue the same agenda as the 'unholy alliance' mentioned in the *New Ulster Defender* editorial.

In the autumn of 1996 Alex Kerr and some of his followers staged a show of strength for the world's cameras at Annahilt in County Down. A number of media organizations, including Sky television, turned up for the stunt, which had been compromised from the start. RUC officers wearing boiler suits, body armour and toting Heckler and Koch machine guns swooped down on the party of terrorists and their media entourage and arrested everyone at the scene. Kerr was among several loyalists taken into custody and was later held on remand at Maghaberry Prison.

On his release two years later, and with the LVF in disarray, Kerr protested that he wanted to live a normal life outside of paramilitarism. Yet, within months of returning to his new safe haven in Portadown, the former brigadier of the South Belfast UDA mysteriously disappeared with his family overnight. Locals on the estate where the Kerrs lived reported that removal vans had come to their door in the early hours of the morning and taken away all the family's goods. Kerr had fled to England. The new UDA leadership in South Belfast claimed that, like Ned Greer, he escaped with the aid of the RUC Special Branch.

The allegations that Kerr had a relationship with the police, and possibly at least one other wing of the security services operating out of the Mahon Road police–army base in Portadown, surprised even those in the UVF who opposed his hard-line brand of loyalism. The UVF's liaison officer on the CLMC, Kerr's opposite number, dismissed the claims that Kerr was an agent as 'black propaganda'. He said that for all Kerr's failings and his misjudgement with regard to Billy Wright, the former South Belfast brigadier was a 'true believer'. A less dramatic reason for Kerr's flight from Portadown was that he fell out of favour with the Fultons, including Swinger and his cousin Gary, now the leading lights in the LVF, once Billy Wright went to jail in March 1997. The Fultons, anxious as ever to forge an alliance with the UDA, were prepared to abandon Kerr as a gesture of goodwill specifically to the South Belfast brigade. In contrast, Kerr, isolated and demonized by the UDA, had little to offer the Fultons.

Amidst the turmoil caused by Kerr's defection to Billy Wright, his arrest and the subsequent allegations about his relations with the RUC, the UDA continued to promote its new political faces. Gary McMichael and Davy Adams travelled to the British Labour party's pre-election annual conference in Blackpool in the first week of October 1996. Again they accompanied the PUP which, unlike the UDP, had declared itself to be a socialist party. In addition, for the first time a Labour party leader's conference speech was attended by an Ulster Unionist leader. David Trimble tore up a century-old tradition of links with the Conservatives and agreed to address a Labour fringe meeting. All sections of unionism except Ian Paisley's DUP mingled with Old and New Labour delegates as the party stood on the threshold of power.

McMichael and his companions received a degree of attention and respect from Labour members for their role in securing the loyalist ceasefire. However, the attitude of rank-and-file UDP activists in Blackpool only underlined their lack of real interest in normal democratic politics. The more sombre and ideologically motivated PUP delegates met a group of UDP members from Lisburn ambling along Blackpool's North Pier. One of the PUP men said they should hurry up and get back to the Winter Gardens before security closed the doors on the arena in preparation for Blair's keynote speech. A young UDP activist replied: 'Fuck Blair's speech, we're off to the topless bar around the corner.'

The UDA's repeated bids to shoot Alex Kerr, its on-going involvement in so-called punishment beatings, drug-dealing by two of its brigades and the robbery of £1 million from a Securicor van in April 1997 provided all the ammunition their political opponents within unionism needed. On 9 September 1997 the Democratic Unionists and Bob McCartney's UK Unionist Party launched a joint bid to have the UDP expelled from multi-party talks.

The DUP and UK Unionists also argued that the UDA's activities meant that its prisoners, along with all other paramilitary inmates, should not be granted early release from prison. The slow progress over the prisoners' issue had almost shattered the loyalist ceasefire in the autumn of 1996 when both UVF and UDA inmates publicly withdrew their support for the peace process. Only a jail visit by both PUP and UDP representatives prevented further damage. Again John White was a crucial figure, influencing Johnny Adair to encourage fellow loyalist inmates inside the Maze to reverse their anti-ceasefire stance.

There was, however, a far more serious threat to the loyalist cessation at the end of a traumatic, fractured and potentially disastrous year. Using Frankie Curry's bomb-making skills the UDA in West Belfast had built a number of sophisticated under-car booby-trap devices which would be used in the event of a return to 'war'. One of their targets was the IRA's commander in Ardoyne and Johnny Adair's nemesis, Eddie Copeland. On Sunday 22 December, Copeland started his car outside his home and triggered a device which went off, leaving him seriously injured. Around lunchtime word reached the Shankill Road that Copeland was dead, sparking off widespread celebrations throughout the Shankill. Pubs flung their doors open, music blared from loudspeakers and free pints were offered to customers. One jubilant UDA man from the lower Shankill could barely disguise his glee when he telephoned one of the authors. 'Steady Eddie's dead, Steady Eddie's dead,' he whooped over a crackling mobile phone. But the euphoria was short-lived because Copeland had yet again survived a murder bid.

No one claimed responsibility for the explosion although it was clear from the outset that 'C' company members had entered Ardoyne and planted the device under Copeland's car. Thus began a policy of 'no claim, no blame' as loyalists carried out what they regarded as retaliation on republicans for the IRA's resumption of violence without public admission. UDP figures such as Gary McMichael protested that they didn't know who was carrying out the attacks, a denial that prompted a characteristically tart question from Bob McCartney: 'Well, who put the bomb there? The Tooth Fairy?'

The farce of 'no claim, no blame' continued through the first half of 1997 with an attempted booby-trap bomb attack on a nationalist in Larne, a car bomb at a Sinn Féin office in North Belfast and the murder of a Catholic man in West Belfast on 14 March. John Slane was shot dead at his home in Thames Court, near Broadway link, as he was making up bottles for his twin baby daughters. Two gunmen walked across the M1 motorway, through the security barrier at the end of Broadway, and into the small housing enclosure where the Slane family lived. They then simply walked into the Slanes' kitchen and shot their victim at point-blank range. (John Slane was the second member of his family to die at the hands of UDA assassins. His cousin, Gerald Slane, was shot dead in 1988. His murder was controversial as the intelligence provided to his killers came from the army's agent Brian Nelson. The UDA mistakenly believed Gerald was a member of the IPLO. Eight years on they made the same error about his cousin. The man the killers were sent out to shoot was an INLA activist, not John Slane.)

The UDA's rolling resumption of 'war' was complemented by growing sectarian strife on the streets, which demonstrated that, while there was an imperfect peace process, there was no harmony between the two communities. The first serious round of sectarian rioting broke out on 12 April on Belfast's Limestone Road and involved UDA members clashing with nationalists, in some cases driving them from their homes. As the loyalist marching season started the 'unholy alliance' also stepped up their activities. On 20 April a Protestant church was burned down in East Belfast and rumours were spread that Catholics from the nearby nationalist enclave had been behind it. In fact, the Pastor's boyfriend burned the church in the classic act of an *agent provocateur.*

Mainstream loyalists immediately spotted the ruse. David Ervine openly accused anti-ceasefire elements of deliberately burning down a Protestant church in order to spark off sectarian violence in the east of the city. In East Antrim however, the UDA fell for the trick. Five days later John 'Grugg' Gregg ordered a team to burn down a Catholic church in Carrickfergus.

Part of the 'unholy alliance's' strategy – the LVF's in particular – was to drive a wedge through the CLMC and separate the UDA from the UVF. Two incidents in the latter half of 1997 brought that scenario closer. On 11 June Robert 'Basher' Bates turned up, as he usually did, at an ex-prisoners' centre on the Woodvale Road. He had been part of the Shankill Butchers, and had also been responsible for the murder of several Protestants who crossed them in bars along the Shankill Road. As Bates stood outside the centre on that bright June morning a young man walked up to him and asked: 'Are you Basher Bates?' When Bates said he was, the questioner took a pistol from his coat pocket and fired into his body several times. Bates died at the scene and his killer casually walked away.

The cold-blooded nature of the murder and the sang-froid of the young assassin, still in his early twenties, demonstrated a thirst for revenge that stretched back over two decades. The killer was a relative of James Curtis Moorehead, a UDA man who had got into a row with the Shankill Butchers in a UVF-controlled pub in January 1977 and ended up in the bar's back-room being tortured, beaten and finally shot.

While serving a life sentence in the Maze for ten murders Robert Bates had announced that he was now a born-again Christian and renounced his former life. As a supposedly reformed man he got to know a number of Catholic priests from Clonard Monastery and they believed he was genuinely ashamed of and sorry for his crimes. However, others, on both sides of the peace lines of North and West Belfast, were not so forgiving. While there had been a number of unsuccessful murder bids on other members of the gang, including Eddie McElhwaine, whom the IPLO shot and wounded in Belfast city centre, no one on the Shankill ever expected that it would be a young Protestant who would slay the first of the Butchers.

Within an hour the UVF knew the identity of Bates's killer and immediately scoured the Shankill to find him, leaving the UDA in a precarious position. The young assassin had been recruited into their organization and was regarded by the West Belfast brigade as a potential asset. They felt little sympathy for Bates, given that he had killed one of their own back in the 1970s, but they did not want to start a shooting war with the UVF with whom they were still officially cooperating on the CLMC. Instead the Inner Council opted to shift Bates's killer across to South Belfast, permanently exiling him from the Shankill Road and putting him under the command of the South Belfast brigadier, Jackie McDonald, who had replaced Alex Kerr. McDonald had relatively good relations with the UVF in the south of the city, but now he had to face the prospect of UVF murder teams from the Shankill going through his territory searching for Basher's assassin.

The UVF made at least one attempt to shoot its quarry in the summer, opening fire on him and a group of friends as they stood outside a pub in Sandy Row. The incident almost led to a feud between the Sandy Row UDA and its neighbours, the Donegall Pass UVF. An eventual truce was worked out whereby Bates's killer was sent to live in the Taughmonagh estate on the edge of South Belfast, as far as possible from the Shankill. While McDonald was prepared to give the young man sanctuary, he wanted at all costs to avoid a shooting war between his brigade and the UVF, a policy he was to pursue even when the core of the UDA sought outright conflict with their loyalist rivals in the summer of 2000.

Relations deteriorated even further between the UDA and the UVF at the end of a violent marching season. Three people had been killed and several seriously injured in a spate of Drumcree-related loyalist attacks over July and August 1997, including a UDA man from Jackie McDonald's brigade, Brian 'Morty' Morton, who blew himself up on 7 July at Seymour Hill in Dunmurry while making a bomb. Morty was highly regarded in the UDA for being a pipe-bomb maker and was also second-in-command of the UDA in Seymour Hill. That he died while opening a cache of explosives made a nonsense of the UDA leadership's claim that it was staying out of the seasonal violence. Many of the pipe-bomb attacks on Catholic homes across Northern Ireland in July and August were the work of the UDA as well as of the officially off-ceasefire LVF. (There was further evidence of the UDA's improved bomb-making skills on 25 October when a device, similar to the one that almost killed Eddie Copeland, exploded under the car of a former member from Bangor, Glen Greer, and killed him. The freelance bomb-maker, Frankie Curry, had helped to make the device.)

The Apprentice Boys' annual parade through Derry city centre on the last Saturday in August to commemorate the relief of the city at the end of the siege during the Williamite wars marked the official end of the marching season. Part of the loyal order's route took them around the ramparts of the old city's seventeenth-century walls and overlooked the republican Bogside. After residents there lodged objections to the march passing their area, the RUC was forced to ban the Apprentice Boys from part of their traditional route, thus creating a potential Drumcree-style stand-off in

Northern Ireland's second city. Parallels were drawn with the Apprentice Boys' march in 1969, which many believe was the catalyst for the start of the Northern Ireland Troubles, and the world's media flocked to Derry in expectation of conflagration. In the event, although there was some rioting, and clashes between the RUC and nationalists, the violence was not on the scale of the Drumcree dispute. The supreme irony was that the worst trouble, the most vicious hand-to-hand fighting, took place after the parade left the west bank of the city and involved loyalists viciously attacking other loyalists.

Young loyalists are often inducted into paramilitary organizations through the Kick-the-Pope/Blood and Thunder marching bands. Two of the most famous are the Shankill Protestant Boys, aligned to the UVF, and the Rathcoole-based Cloughfern Young Conquerors, aligned to the UDA. The Cloughfern Young Conquerors' bass drum player was John 'Grugg' Gregg.

As they waited for their train to take them back to Belfast after the parade the two bands faced each other across the railway station. A *de facto* war between the UDA and the UVF was about to break out. Fuelled by drink and memories of previous skirmishes, the two bands set upon each other. Members shoved broken bottles into the faces of their rivals and vandalized parts of the station, including the roof, searching for anything they could use as a weapon. In the mêlée someone from the Shankill Protestant Boys managed to gouge out one of John Gregg's eyes and it fell on the blood-splattered floor while young children looked on in horror.

Although the leadership of the two organizations attempted to repair the damage, the bad feeling between the rank-and-file members smouldered on throughout the autumn and winter of 1997. Even after the UDP and PUP accompanied David Trimble into all-party talks on 17 September, to face Sinn Féin across the negotiating table, relations between the two groups remained sour. The UVF refused to turn out for a City Hall joint rally to commemorate the second anniversary of the loyalist ceasefire on 12 October. In the end only 5,000 UDA supporters attended. A day later Gary McMichael admitted that he would not be surprised if the UDA left the CLMC.

The era of staunch loyalist unity had already come to a close. None the less 1997 ended with high hopes that peace could be made permanent and an historic compromise worked out to satisfy both unionists and nationalists. Tony Blair had swept to power in May with a promise to work for a lasting peace in Northern Ireland, the marching season had not tipped the Province over the brink after all, in David Trimble unionism had a leader prepared to enter talks with Sinn Féin, and after a bloody eighteen-month hiatus the IRA had been forced to restore its ceasefire. However, in the very last days of the year, events would deliver a mortal blow to hopes for a final settlement in Northern Ireland. And once again it would be the UDA, along with some new-found allies, that would be responsible for almost bringing down the entire edifice of the peace process.

19. A Realignment of Terror

Mark Fulton's dream of a grand alliance between the LVF and the UDA, ranged not only against the UVF but the entire peace process, was about to become a reality – but not in the way he had imagined. On the morning of 27 December 1997 Billy Wright and other LVF prisoners were being taken to the Maze's visiting area for Christmas visits. Wright was going to see his girlfriend. He had started an eight-year jail sentence in March after being convicted of threatening a woman who had transgressed against the LVF in Portadown. His supporters had argued (with some justification) that the evidence against him was flimsy and designed solely to keep him off the streets during the all-party talks. As Wright was led away from the dock he shouted out that he was being subjected to *de facto* internment.

As the prison van waited to pull off, suddenly its sliding door opened. Two armed INLA prisoners, Thomas 'Crip' McWilliams and John Kennaway, who had managed to escape their wing, get through a prison fence (where a hole had previously been cut), climb over a roof and arrive in the yard where the bus was parked, picked out Wright. McWilliams fired into his body, killing him almost instantly. Mission accomplished, the INLA duo retraced their steps, climbed back into their wing on H6, boarded themselves into a cell and demanded to see a priest in order to negotiate their surrender.

The assassination of the LVF's founder was the final security blunder to occur inside the Maze during the peace process – and the most serious. Just prior to the killing, during a Christmas party for prisoners and their children, IRA double murderer Liam Averill escaped from the jail dressed as a woman. And the authorities had discovered a sophisticated, fully lit IRA escape tunnel leading out of the prison. The engines of the washing machines provided by the NIO so that prisoners could wash their own clothing had been recalibrated to work as generators to provide illumination for the tunnel.

Wright's assassination not only raised serious questions about security lapses and paramilitary control in what was supposedly western Europe's most secure prison, but it also provoked accusations that someone in authority allowed McWilliams and Kennaway to smuggle guns into the jail, break out of their wing, penetrate the security barrier under the noses of watchtowers and CCTV and walk unopposed into the forecourt to kill Wright. McWilliams's role was particularly interesting. Only twelve months earlier, during a family visit, INLA supporters had smuggled a gun to him in Maghaberry Prison, hidden in a child's nappy, so that he could kill a fellow inmate, Kevin McAlorum, a petty criminal who had murdered INLA boss Geno Gallagher during an internal feud in 1996. The plot was discovered and McWilliams was transferred to the Maze. When the INLA planned to assassinate Wright, again it concealed the weapon in a child's nappy.

Kennaway, now a republican dissident who has been threatened with death by the IRA, has told the authors there was no collusion between INLA and the prison authorities over Wright's murder. However, retired officers from the RUC's Special Branch have insisted that the government knew the guns had been taken into the INLA wing and that the republican terror group was preparing to kill Wright during the Christmas visits. Undoubtedly, loyalists of all hues believe there was some form of collusion leading to Wright being permanently removed from the political scene; at the very least it seems someone in authority turned a blind eye to the tensions in the H-block.

The impact of Wright's killing on the peace process was profound. Johnny Adair, locked up in another part of the prison, took the murder very personally. 'He had come to admire Billy and saw himself and Wright as the embodiment of loyalism,' recalled one long-time 'C' company follower in April 2003. 'I think he also thought that if this could happen to Billy inside the Maze then it could happen to him as well.' Using mobile telephones (again, provided by the prison service) Adair contacted 'C' company leaders such as Gary Smyth and Stephen McKeag, giving them the go-ahead to avenge Wright's death. He didn't have long to wait before his comrades acted. At 9 p.m., with Wright just over twelve hours dead, Stephen McKeag entered the Clifton Tavern at the top of the Cliftonville Road in North Belfast and opened fire on customers at the bar, spraying the pub with an Uzi sub-machine gun. An accomplice also tried to open fire but his pistol jammed. McKeag and his colleague then escaped from the scene in a stolen white Vauxhall car. Only one man was killed, 31-year-old Edmund Trainor. His uncle was a Second World War RAF hero who had been killed in France and whose memory was commemorated every year in a small French village. The villagers sent a message of condolence to Edmund's mother.

McKeag's weapon was part of a batch of guns the UDA had brought into Northern Ireland after the IRA bomb at Canary Wharf. Both the UDA and UVF had decided to rearm in response to the IRA's resumption of violence. The new Uzis, which could empty their 32-round magazines in about three seconds, were copied on licence or illegally in the former Soviet bloc and were bought up by criminals in England with connections to the British far right. In turn the far right, specifically Combat 18, sold the guns on to their allies in the UDA, notably 'C' company.

On this occasion 'C' company deviated from its 'no claim, no blame' policy; it allowed the LVF to claim responsibility. On that night the LVF did carry out a retaliatory strike, shooting dead Catholic doorman and convicted IRA killer Seamus Dillon at the Exit 15 nightclub near Dungannon, County Tyrone, but it played no part in the near massacre at Clifton Tavern. Even other loyalists, notably Billy Hutchinson of the PUP, suggested that it was the UDA rather than the LVF which was responsible. Hutchinson's intervention further soured relations between the two main loyalist organizations on the Shankill. John White was openly critical of Hutchinson, accusing him of siding with the UDA's enemies in Sinn Féin and the SDLP to discredit his organization.

Wright's death continued to cast a shadow over the peace process as 1998 began. The UDP suffered another stunning blow on 4 January when UDA prisoners, including Johnny Adair, voted by 80 to 40 to withdraw support for all-party talks because of 'this government's pandering to Sinn Féin/IRA'. Two days later David Trimble and the UUP's deputy leader, John Taylor, paid an unprecedented visit to UDA inmates in the Maze and met with the organization's commanders in the H-blocks, Johnny Adair and Sam 'Skelly' McCrory, along with several other of the organization's prisoners. They were unable to convince the UDA inside the Maze to support unionism's continued participation in the talks.

History says Mo Mowlam succeeded where Trimble and Taylor failed. In the official accounts of the peace process her 8 January visit is hailed as a bold initiative that saved lives. Mowlam's meeting with Adair, McCrory and others certainly produced bizarre moments: a secretary of state borrowing tobacco and roll-ups from the UDA prisoners so she could have a smoke; a cabinet minister taking off the wig which covered her chemotherapy-induced hair-loss as she got stuck into talks with Adair and his colleagues, persuading them of the necessity to call off the violence from inside the Maze. No one could doubt Dr Mowlam's sincerity and courage in facing some of western Europe's most dangerous terror-ists, but the idea that her eyeball-to-eyeball meeting with Adair and his comrades produced peace on the streets is a myth. Between 8 January and the end of the month five more Catholics were shot dead, four by the UDA.

In fact, the first Catholic to die violently in 1998, Terry Enright, a doorman allegedly shot by the LVF three days after the Mowlam Maze meeting, may also have been a UDA victim. Enright, a community worker from West Belfast, was gunned down outside Space nightclub in central Belfast. Although the LVF admitted the killing there is evidence that, at the very least, the UDA provided the intelligence for the murder; several times in the weeks up to the killing its drug dealers came into contact with Enright at the door of the club where the security man turned them away.

Four further sectarian killings in January were all the UDA's work. On the night of 19 January, just hours after the INLA killed Jim Guiney, a retired UDA member from South Belfast who was close to Gary McMichael, the UDA gunned down Larry Brennan on the Ormeau Road around 7.30 p.m. (in front of the sister of one of the authors). A Catholic taxi-driver with a Protestant girl-friend, Larry Brennan lived in the nationalist Markets area but had worked in the upper Ormeau for several years. The UDA in the upper Ormeau later justified the killing by claiming that Brennan had 'set up' Joe Bratty and Raymond Elder for the IRA, a charge his friends denied vehemently. In fact, he was an opponent of violence and had attended the Irish Congress of Trade Unions' demonstration against the IRA bomb at Canary Wharf two years previously.

On 21 January 1998 the UDA murdered 55-year-old West Belfast Catholic Benedict Hughes as he got into his car outside a vehicle respraying centre in Sandy Row. He was the only Catholic who worked at the company. Forty-eight hours later 'C' company shot dead Liam Conway, a Catholic digging gas pipelines on Hesketh Road in North Belfast.

Liam Conway was murdered hours after the UDA Inner Council officially declared a ceasefire – a declaration few inside the security forces, the UVF, or for that matter the entire nationalist community, believed was genuine. McKeag himself was hauled in to a meeting with the Inner Council to explain 'C' company's actions that day. Top Gun was unperturbed. He shrugged off the leadership's questioning by pointing out that loyalists always had a defence and retaliation clause built into their ceasefire. If republicans were attacking loyalists, as was the case with the INLA (but not at this stage the IRA), then individual UDA units had the right to strike back – a euphemism for killing more Catholics. No one on the Inner Council had the audacity to challenge Top Gun. Three murders in the space of a month forced the British government to act and the UDP was finally expelled from all-party talks.

One of the 'unholy alliance's' objectives in pulling the UDA back into terrorism was to provoke the IRA in turn and thus bring about the collapse of the republicans' ceasefire. (That one of the key characters in the loose alliance between the LVF and its cronies, and evangelical fundamentalists – the Pastor – was being handled by British intelligence agents who were hoping for entirely the opposite result – the consolidation of the republican ceasefire and the fragmentation of loyalism – was a twist the alliance's members never suspected.)

An end to the IRA's cessation would have spelt doom for the all-party talks once Sinn Féin was ejected from the discussions. The loyalist dissidents almost succeeded. The IRA was under incredible grassroots pressure to hit back at the UDA for the January slaughter. At a republican rally on the Falls Road at the end of the month speakers from Sinn Féin were heckled by a section of the 1,000-strong crowd chanting 'Retaliation'. Up until then the Provisionals had resisted the temptation to shoot leading UDA figures responsible for the sectarian onslaught. The INLA sought to exploit the IRA's reticence by going on the offensive and attacking known UDA figures such as Jim Guiney. The Provos, who were founded on the myth of being a defence force for beleaguered Belfast Catholics, were in danger of losing face to the INLA. The IRA's patience finally snapped after a UDA unit from Suffolk pulled Catholic driver John McColgan out of his taxi on 24 January and shot him at a lonely spot on Hannahstown Hill on Belfast's western edge. Three weeks later, on 10 February, the Provos singled out the man they suspected of organizing the McColgan murder, the Suffolk UDA commander Bobby Dougan, and shot him dead in nearby Dunmurry. The killing led to Sinn Féin being temporarily suspended from all-party talks ten days later with a usually cautious Gerry Adams describing himself as being 'pissed off' over the move.

The UDA now had two wings: by day, the relative moderation and rational unionism of Gary McMichael and Davy Adams; by night, McKeag and his team of assassins making a nonsense of the claim that the UDA was still on ceasefire. Straddling the two was John White. Publicly the former assassin turned peace process enthusiast continued to protest that he was for peace and compromise with nationalists. Yet more than any other figure in the UDP he exerted huge influence on the young killers, especially those belonging to 'C' company, and he had extensive knowledge about what these murder gangs were up to.

Accompanying the two faces of the UDA, two distinct subcultures were emerging. New loyalists such as McMichael and his colleagues were dressing in sharp suits, collar and tie, fluently articulating their cause, debating with Sinn Féin in public (as McMichael had done at a Liberal Democrat conference the previous year, when he took on Mitchel McLaughlin), writing cogent pieces for newspapers of record and being on the A list of receptions in Belfast, Dublin, London and Washington. But alongside the suits and the smiles the other wing of young loyalism organized itself on the lines of gangsta culture where hip haircuts, garish jewellery and designer wear were as important as guns and murder. Baseball cap and Nike trainers were the new uniform of gangs like 'C' company.

To a great extent, this development was the inevitable outcome of the UDA's post-ceasefire leadership. After October 1994 the organization continued to recruit young men from the Protestant underclass and to train them in firearms, without providing any political education or proper discipline. While these young recruits still adhered strongly to the Protestant martial music tradition and belonged to Kick-the-Pope bands, they eschewed the old-fashioned quasi-military structure of the traditional paramilitary organizations. This was a social group mixing Ulster patriotism with drug-taking, their leaders supplying them with bullets and Ecstasy tablets. Drug use created an organic link to the LVF, which had recruited many young loyalists in Mid-Ulster, and latterly North Down, involved in drug-dealing.

This struggle between would-be politicians and gunmen was not unprecedented. Throughout UDA's history tension between those seeking to build political careers and urban street-fighters, who regarded such ambitions as being beyond the station of the volunteer, was a recurring issue. Now the clash between the politicos and the young militants was to have far-reaching consequences for the future of loyalism and ultimately lead to the worst ever divide at the heart of Protestant Ulster.

By the early spring of 1998 it appeared that politics was triumphing after the UDP was allowed back into talks just in time for the make-or-break marathon discussions at Castle Buildings Stormont during Holy Week. Expulsion from the talks had been the catalyst for a change in UDA direction with John White again using his influence on Adair to get its violence turned off in Belfast. After a brief period in quarantine both the UDP and Sinn Féin were allowed back into the discussions which by then had picked up tempo and seemed headed for some agreement.

The drive for a settlement reached a climax on Holy Thursday night with the Ulster Unionists coming under pressure to sign up to a peace deal that would effectively put them into government with Sinn Féin. The up-side for unionism, however, was twofold: first, all parties, including republicans, would have to adhere to the core principle that there could be no constitutional change in Northern Ireland without majority consent; second, during the negotiations Trimble and his team had managed to whittle down and seriously dilute the number of cross-border bodies set up under the agreement. For some in the unionist community this was not good enough and smacked of a sell-out by stealth. Ian Paisley led a small band of followers up to Stormont in protest at the negotiations. Although his supporters were barred from entering the area around Castle Buildings, he and the DUP deputy leader, Peter Robinson, were allowed through the security cordon. They arrived on site to address the world's media, camped in a large tent adjacent to the talks venue. As well as journalists, the tent was packed with activists from all the parties involved in the talks, including the UDP and PUP. What happened next summed up the new divisions tearing unionism apart. The moment Paisley rose to speak in an impromptu press conference, ex-UDA and UVF prisoners turned on him. 'We don't listen to you any more,' some shouted. 'Go and fight to the last drop of someone else's blood.' 'We're sorry we ever listened to you in the first place, Ian.' As Paisley left the media facility under a barrage of abuse the loyalists started chanting, 'Cheerio, cheerio, cheerio', to the tune of the football chant 'Here we go'. One loyalist remarked to the authors: 'The Big Man is finished. He's history.' A number of UK journalists, who were mainly Westminster-based, concurred. Events would shortly prove them wrong.

Inside the media mini-village there were bizarre and unprecedented meetings between former adversaries. IRA veterans mingled with UDA and UVF men who had tried to kill them

prior to the ceasefires. But when they came across Danny
Morrison, Sinn Féin's former publicity director, a group of young
UDP members from Lisburn showed that even the mildest form
of liberal toleration had yet to permeate their ranks. 'Watch yer
arse,' they quipped as they passed him talking to journalists – a
crude reference to his latest novel which told the story of a gay
man trying to survive in homophobic Belfast. The former Sinn
Féin spin doctor turned writer was outraged but failed to win an
apology.

The UDA threw its weight behind David Trimble's decision to
sign up to the peace accord on Good Friday 1998. For Gary
McMichael much of the Agreement, with its emphasis on a voluntary coalition, constitutional checks and balances and the consent
principle, resembled the 'Common Sense' document his father had
helped draw up at the end of the 1980s. However, others in the
military leadership remained either cautious or sceptical about the
Good Friday Agreement. At least three brigadiers on the Inner
Council – Jackie McDonald in South Belfast, John Gregg in South-
east Antrim and Billy McFarland in the North-west – were lukewarm about the Agreement's merits, especially the prospect of
Sinn Féin entering a power-sharing cabinet. Other UDA veterans – crucially John White – were more enthusiastic about the
Agreement. The prisoners also backed it, with Sam McCrory
announcing from the Maze on 14 May (the day of a UDA pro-
Agreement rally in the Ulster Hall) that the UDA's 'war' was over.
Twenty-four hours later the LVF announced a ceasefire but called
for a No vote in the forthcoming referendum.

The people of Northern Ireland were to be given their chance
to endorse the Good Friday Agreement on 22 May. One of its
most controversial aspects was the early-release scheme for terrorist
prisoners and that would be one of the major points on which
the anti-Agreement unionists campaigned. The battle for hearts
and minds, particularly those of middle-class moderate unionists,
was severely damaged by the issue. The public was given a glimpse
of what was to come during two ex-prisoners' rallies – the UDA's
Ulster Hall rally and a Sinn Féin rally in Dublin. The star turn at
the packed Ulster Hall was the recently paroled Michael Stone,

the Milltown Cemetery murderer and hero to thousands of loyalists. David Trimble later confessed that his stomach lurched when all the UDA brigades, along with their relatives and supporters, gave Stone a hero's welcome. The overwhelming majority of unionists had little or no sympathy for groups such as the UDA, let alone a convicted killer such as Michael Stone. Opinion polls taken shortly after Stone's appearance, coupled with a similar gross act of triumphalism at Dublin's Royal Dublin Society, involving the murderers from the IRA's Balcombe Street gang, showed a sharp drop in Protestant support for the Agreement.

Tony Blair's personal intervention, and his appeal to middle-class Protestant Ulster for support and trust, won the day, and there was a 72 per cent Yes vote for the Agreement – almost exactly the percentage opting for the Agreement at a vote during a critical Ulster Unionist Council meeting a few weeks earlier at Belfast's Europa Hotel. That meeting had been picketed by a small hardcore of dissident loyalists, including members of the 'unholy alliance'. It was a measure of the UDA's new-found support for compromise that a larger group of loyalist demonstrators stood outside the Europa backing Trimble. This group was comprised mainly of 'C' company activists and their followers who were in a position to shout down and effectively intimidate the dissidents. David Trimble must have felt that with friends like these, did he really need any more enemies?

Gary McMichael, Davy Adams and John White were convinced that they would be rewarded at the ballot box for their efforts in securing the loyalist ceasefire and backing the historic peace accord at Easter. The trio was regarded as the UDP's safest bets for seats in a new Northern Ireland Assembly out of which a power-sharing coalition would emerge. When the elections were held on 25 June they were cruelly brought down to earth. None of the UDP's candidates was elected, although McMichael came tantalizingly close (within 300 votes) to taking a seat in the Lagan Valley constituency. The failure to win a single seat was a blow, particularly to Davy Adams, who was highly regarded both inside and outside the UDP. 'I was gutted for wee Davy,' the UVF's second-in-command said shortly after the elections. 'Not only was he a gentleman but he had a good political brain. He could have kept the UDA on the straight and narrow if he had won an Assembly seat.'

The Assembly elections demonstrated two important facts about the UDA's latest intervention in politics. First, the failure to establish an electoral pact with the PUP showed that the old divisions and jealousies between the two main unionist blocs were as deep as ever; loyalist unity had been an anomaly. Had either the UDP or the PUP stood aside and urged its supporters to back the other loyalist force in South Belfast, then the new loyalism would have secured a third seat in the Assembly. The success of the PUP in winning two seats for David Ervine and Billy Hutchinson merely exacerbated that rivalry and envy. Second, given the improved performance of Paisley's DUP, which won twenty seats, it was clear that, unlike their leadership, many in the UDA rank and file did not believe the union was safe and had voted for anti-Agreement candidates against their own party, even if they disliked Paisleyite posturing. Even where loyalism performed strongly, as with Ervine in East Belfast, the fringe loyalist parties were still far behind the DUP in terms of support. Ervine won 5,114 votes; Peter Robinson's poll-topping tally was more than double that figure.

The UDA's experiment with electoral politics is interesting in how it has contrasted with that of the IRA. On the face of it the IRA and Sinn Féin were able to run parallel terrorist and political campaigns. On its first serious outing in a Northern Ireland election, in the contest for the local assembly elections of 1982, Sinn Féin polled a highly reputable 69,191 votes and won – to the horror of many unionists – five seats on an abstentionist ticket. Both it, and the much more popular SDLP, approached the elections on the same basis: that they would not take their seats as long as there was no formal power-sharing arrangement in the Assembly. In the 1983 general election Gerry Adams took the West Belfast parliamentary constituency, beating the SDLP candidate, Dr Joe Hendron. The 1985 local government elections saw a similar good result for Sinn Féin – still horrifying for many, given that the IRA was continuing to run a bloody terrorism campaign –

with 75,686 votes. From that point, however, the Sinn Féin vote began to decline as republican voters were turned off by the continuing, bloody actions of the IRA.

Senior intelligence sources in the Irish Republic learned that part of the IRA's contribution to Sinn Féin's electoral advance during the 1980s was to pursue a twin-track strategy in which the UDA was, to an extent, a willing dupe. A couple of months before a poll – and there was almost one a year between Westminster, European, local government and local assembly elections – the IRA's Northern commander (who would later become a prominent Sinn Féin figure) would issue orders for a dramatic stepping up of attacks, preferably on local Protestant targets, particularly the RUC and UDR or loyalists. Predictably this was followed by a loyalist response, usually involving retaliatory killings of Catholic civilians. This, the IRA leadership figured, would stir Catholic voters to identify with the IRA as their protectors and to vote for Sinn Féin. Danny Morrison explained the strategy at a Sinn Féin Ard Fheis in Dublin as 'an Armalite in this hand and a ballot box in this hand'.

The policy seemed to work well enough but as IRA atrocities continued, Catholic voters waned in their enthusiasm for the Armalite side of things. In April 1992 Gerry Adams narrowly lost his Westminster seat in West Belfast in a humiliating contest with Dr Hendron of the SDLP. In the 1994 European election the Sinn Féin vote slipped to 55,215, while the SDLP's candidate, John Hume, got nearly triple that number of votes. A short while later the IRA called its first ceasefire.

The next elections – to the Northern Ireland Forum in 1996 – showed that Sinn Féin voters liked the idea of a cessation of terrorism. Their vote shot up to 116,377. In 1997 Sinn Féin polled a highly impressive 126,921 votes in the general election. Gerry Adams regained West Belfast and Martin McGuinness seized Mid-Ulster from the DUP. After another disastrous flirtation with terrorism, when the IRA ended its ceasefire between February 1996 and August 1997, Sinn Féin found its electoral ambitions in the Republic of Ireland severely diminished. With the (final) IRA ceasefire in place it made renewed and in the end successful efforts

to beat the SDLP to become the majority nationalist party in
Northern Ireland, winning four Westminster seats with 175,932
votes in the 2001 Westminster general election against the SDLP's
three seats and 169,873 votes.

During all this time the UDA's political wing, the UDP, made
virtually no inroads on the Northern Ireland political scene. In
retrospect, some UDA figures believe that not having a strong
political wing was a real mistake. The Ulster Unionists and the
Democratic Unionist Party both represent strong unionist principles and both parties have continued to hold up well against
the nationalist vote, though in recent years the political map has
shown much greater nationalist and republican gains in the mainly
Catholic areas west of the Bann. The Sinn Féin vote, some loyalists
observe, held up only because the republicans were forced to give
up their Armalites in favour of the ballot box. Any return to
terrorism by the IRA would be a death knell for republican political aspirations and is – at the time of writing – no longer an
option.

(This raises an intriguing question: in the light of the IRA
calling off its campaign, and Sinn Féin opting for an increasingly
constitutional form of politics within the borders of a Northern
Ireland still attached to Great Britain by the Act of Union, who
won the war?)

In the 1998 Assembly election the UDP's inability to win seats
merely bolstered the arguments of the sceptics and doubters who
complained that the UDA had got nothing out of the four years
of ceasefire – ignoring the fact that for a brief but bloody period
in early 1998 its actions had almost destroyed the peace process.
Furthermore, 'middle Ulster' recoiled at the sight of loyalists
growing rich on the backs of the Province's burgeoning drugs
trade. Even in greater Belfast working-class Protestants looked on
and wondered how the likes of John White acquired so much
wealth (including property in affluent North Down, beside the
retired RUC Chief Constable Sir Jack Hermon) despite having
no visible means of financial support outside the catch-all peace
process profession, 'community worker'.

(Both loyalist organizations were guilty of self-deception on a

grand scale when it came to reading the general unionist population. At the beginning of 1999 Billy Hutchinson launched an
attack on David Trimble, accusing him of endangering the peace
process by insisting on the IRA decommissioning. This was a
remarkable statement given the fact that according to one *Belfast
Telegraph* opinion poll in February 1999 84 per cent of the Ulster
public wanted the IRA and loyalists to disarm. Was it any mystery
therefore that between them the PUP and UDP failed to poll
more than 4 per cent of the vote?)

With the UDA and the LVF on ceasefire, the 'unholy alliance'
sought to exploit the annual ban on the Drumcree parade in
Portadown to destabilize the peace process. The first week of July
saw the Province engulfed in violence, particularly at Drumcree,
where loyalist gangs supporting the Orange Order continually
attacked the police and troops. The trouble subsided only on the
morning of 12 July, when loyalist thugs in Ballymoney murdered
three young Catholic kids in a petrol-bomb attack at their home.
The death of the Quinn children ended the Drumcree stand-off
which the Orange Order had threatened to escalate with a mass
loyalist rally, involving all members of the institution, marching in
their thousands to Portadown.

At this stage the UDA played no part, at least as an organization, in the Drumcree disturbances. Freelance loyalist bomb-maker
Frankie Curry though continued to provide expertise and encour-
agement to the disparate dissidents still determined to undermine
the peace and destroy the Agreement by force. On 5 September,
during a violent clash on Drumcree hill involving a small band
of loyalist hard-liners and the police, a pipe-bomb was thrown at
the security forces' line blocking the Orange Order's path to
Garvaghy Road. Muriel Landree, one of Billy Wright's closest
female followers, was later arrested for bringing the device to
Portadown. When it exploded, a piece of shrapnel pierced the eye
of Constable Frankie O'Reilly (who was, ironically, a Catholic
convert to Presbyterianism). He lingered between life and death
for over a month before dying in hospital on 6 October.

The police officer was murdered at the hands of people who
said they were fighting to save the RUC from the reforms proposed

by the former Hong Kong governor, Chris Patten. He was the first fatality of the Red Hand Defenders, a flag of convenience Curry had invented to allow loyalists from all factions to continue shooting and bombing. At the end of the month the new name was used again – this time to commit murder in North Belfast. On Hallowe'en night Brian Service was gunned down as he walked home along Alliance Avenue, the street marking the border between republican Ardoyne and the loyalist upper Ardoyne.

Shooting a defenceless Catholic such as Brian Service when the LVF was on the verge of decommissioning a small amount of weapons was designed to reignite sectarian tensions in North Belfast and to derail the LVF's ceasefire. The object of the killing seems to have been to provoke a republican response – or the threat of one – and so prevent the LVF going ahead with its plans to disarm and to thereby aid the cause of the Ulster Unionists. In the same week the dissidents, encouraged by Frankie Curry, shot up a bar on the outskirts of West Belfast. Although 'C' company played no role in the Hallowe'en shootings it kept in touch with Curry and his band of rejectionists including Clifford Peoples.

The murky world of Ulster loyalism became even more complex at the end of 1998 when another new terror group emerged from the shadows. A band of rural loyalists, with a leadership based around Stoneyford, County Antrim, claimed to have re-formed the Orange Volunteers (OV) around Drumcree. The name was the same as that of the organization founded at the beginning of the Troubles which had lain dormant ever since. Members of the original Orange Volunteers contacted the authors to say that this new grouping had no links to them. Moreover, they believed the groupuscle was the invention of elements within British intelligence, and that the security services' use of agents flying under the flag of 'Orange Volunteers' was a deliberate attempt to associate the Orange Order directly with loyalist terrorism.

The Orange Volunteer veterans' suspicions about this new movement, which carried out a series of pipe-bomb attacks on GAA halls and nationalist homes and businesses in the South Antrim/South Derry region, were confirmed by an incident at Jeffrey Donaldson's Lisburn office during the 1998 Drumcree stand-off. The Lagan Valley Ulster Unionist MP was approached by a man who wanted to talk to him about Drumcree. He suggested that what was needed was the establishment of a phantom Protestant army based around the Orange Order and its mass membership. Donaldson was immediately suspicious and, rather than treat the individual as a crank, had him followed when he left his constituency office. The man was seen driving straight into nearby Thiepval barracks – the British army's headquarters in Northern Ireland.

Others in the mainstream unionist political parties were less cautious about the emergence of this new loyalist army. In late 1999 the RUC's Special Branch had Stoneyford Orange Hall under round-the-clock surveillance, including the use of sophisticated bugging devices inside the premises. To their astonishment the officers heard a conversation between the putative head of the new OVs, a young Orangeman from County Antrim, and an anti-Agreement politician about suspected republican activists in the border area and what should be done to them. The DUP member was heard urging the Orange Volunteers to act against the republicans they mentioned. No action was taken against either the head of the OVs or the DUP member, although the latter was visited by Special Branch officers and agreed to pass the police intelligence about loyalists.

Despite clear evidence that *agents provocateurs* were busy working to force loyalists back to full-blown violence, sections of the UDA, notably the lower Shankill, were taking the bait, especially if it meant getting a chance to undermine 'those Blackneck bastards' (Shankill street slang for the rival UVF). The countdown to the biggest and most damaging feud in Ulster loyalist history had begun.

20. Under Billy Wright's Shadow

In early spring 1999, as the gates of the Maze clicked constantly with republican and loyalist prisoners walking free under the Good Friday Agreement's early-release scheme, the last UDA commanding officer in the H-blocks raised the spectre of collusion again. In an interview with veteran BBC reporter Peter Taylor for his television series *Loyalists*, Bobby Philpott, the UVF's second-in-command for Northern Ireland, said that he had received so many RUC and British army intelligence documents over the years that he had not known where to store them. His remarks tally with what other loyalists have admitted to the authors over the years. One senior member of the now defunct CLMC confessed that security files on IRA and INLA suspects were 'more common than beer mats were in pubs and clubs'. Much of these intelligence leaks came from individual soldiers and policemen who lived, socialized and often worked in loyalist areas. Sir John Stevens's inquiry team has obtained several high-grade security documents with a number of key UDA players' fingerprints on them, including Johnny Adair's.

There was, of course, another strand to the collusion, which involved highly placed agents in all the paramilitary groups – republican and loyalist – being allowed to operate freely, in some instances to kill, in order to mask their true role as traitors to their respective causes. Retired Special Branch officers have admitted that at one stage in West Belfast the RUC and other branches of the security services were running twenty-seven separate agents inside the UDA, some of whom were actively involved in sectarian terrorism while working as servants of the state.

These agents included William Stobie, the UDA's quartermaster in the upper Shankill. Stobie, who had originally applied to join the UVF but fell under suspicion of being a double agent and was rejected, ended up with the UDA's 'A' company in

Highfield – the unit which killed Pat Finucane. Stobie provided the guns used in the Belfast solicitor's murder, and on the night of the assassination he rang his RUC handlers and told them 'the team's out', although it now seems clear the UDA quartermaster did not know exactly who the team was about to shoot. Stobie signed his death warrant when he intimated that he was prepared to testify in any public inquiry into the Finucane killing, not necessarily against those who pulled the trigger but rather against the police officers who did nothing to stop it. Supporting the Finucane family's demand for a public inquiry was the last straw for the UDA.

Not for the first time, nor the last, the UDA lashed out at the media, specifically the authors. On St Patrick's Day Frankie Curry was shot dead in the middle of the Shankill, close to the spot where his uncle, Gusty Spence, and his original UVF gang from the 1960s had murdered Catholic barman Peter Ward, in 1966. The killing was an act of personal revenge although it had the sanction of Shankill UVF leaders who were fed up with Curry's clandestine aid to the loyalist dissidents. Those behind the murder were friends of William 'Wassy' Paul, whom Curry had killed in North Down the previous year in a row over control of drugs in the area. Curry's death prompted an angry response from the UDA and LVF in the Shankill. The UDA's commander of 'B' company, along with Jackie Mahood, another of the LVF's founders, issued a death threat to the authors – transmitting their coded message through BBC Northern Ireland and using the Red Hand Defenders title as a flag of convenience. Lashing out over the Curry killing, they sought to blame journalists because they had dared to tell the truth about his role in the post-Good Friday Agreement bombing campaign. That threat still remains.

Although the UDA killed no one in 1999, it was not for want of trying. Throughout the year loyalists threw 229 pipe bombs in 123 separate incidents across Northern Ireland. Gerry Adams was absolutely correct when he asserted that the LVF and the satellite dissident groups were not the only ones carrying out these attacks; the majority of the attacks were in greater Belfast and East Antrim where the UDA pursued a campaign of ethnic cleansing against Catholics living in mainly Protestant areas. Most of the pipe bombs were thrown by the UDA's junior wing, the Ulster Young Militants, in two brigade areas, North Belfast and South-east Antrim. This violence was directed by John 'Grugg' Gregg, the man who had almost killed Adams. Regardless of peace process, ceasefires and agreements, Gregg nurtured a deep and unbending hatred for Catholics, especially those who dared remain in his domain. Gregg's brigade, using the cover name of Protestant Liberation Force, had also tried to kill a Catholic builder in Carrickfergus on 12 May. They shot him but he survived his injuries.

One of those enjoying the relative peace of 1999 was Johnny Adair, who was let out on licence as part of the early-release scheme. On 30 April he and his wife, Gina, decided to celebrate his freedom by reliving his skinhead past at a UB40 concert in the Botanic Gardens in South Belfast. It seemed an odd choice for someone who once followed the neo-Nazi band Skrewdriver: UB40 was multi-racial and its music contained messages of tolerance and leftish radicalism, all of which the far-right admirers of Johnny Adair detested. However, according to friends, he adored the band's music and was determined to be among the thousands in the park by the River Lagan. It was an incredibly foolhardy decision. A number of security men at the concert had been Sinn Féin activists from the east and south of the city. Indeed, one of the chief security men on duty was Jim Clinton, the former Sinn Féin candidate from the lower Ormeau, whose wife, Teresa, Adair's comrades had murdered five years earlier. However, Clinton posed no threat to Adair and so concerned was he about the impact of Adair's presence that he called over a policeman and told him that it would be impossible to protect the UDA commander and that the police should advice him to leave. For whatever reason the officer ignored Clinton's advice and Adair was left to his own devices.

During the concert a West Belfast man in the crowd, an ordinary criminal and drug dealer with a grudge against Adair, opened fire on him, grazing him several times in the head. Appearing on television the day after the shooting, having used up another of his nine lives, a shaven-headed Adair showed off his wounds for the cameras. He and Gina alleged that the IRA was responsible, but if the Provos had really been behind the attack Adair would have been dead.

Even in death Billy Wright continued to cast a long shadow over loyalism. On 27 December 1999 his followers gathered inside Portadown FC's social club, close to where Wright once had a safe house. His cadre, known as the 'rat pack', was enjoying a drink after attending a memorial service over Wright's grave on the second anniversary of his death. As an afternoon's heavy drinking wore on a number of UVF men came into the club, including the organization's Mid-Ulster commander and local businessman, Richard Jameson. Someone in the LVF delegation challenged Jameson about a brawl he was involved in which resulted in a woman being beaten up, taunting him for being a 'woman-beater'. Jameson stormed out of the bar, but returned about an hour later, accompanied by a group of UVF men armed with baseball bats, hammers, hatchets and knives. They set upon the drunken LVF group, inflicting horrific injuries on seventeen of Wright's men, one of whom had a thumb severed. From their hospital beds the LVF men swore revenge on Jameson. The feud which had been simmering between the LVF and the UVF since Drumcree 1996 was reaching boiling point. Here, in the heart of rural Ulster, forty miles from Belfast, was the start of the split that would tear the Shankill apart.

On the night of 10 January Richard Jameson was shot dead outside his home on the outskirts of Portadown. His killer came from near Dungannon, and got the gun he used from a North Belfast loyalist family who had broken with the UVF after Wright was expelled. Following Jameson's murder the UVF and the Jameson family went ballistic. The Jamesons invited television cameras to Portadown where they defaced LVF murals and painted slogans openly accusing the organization of being drug dealers.

Despite the tensions that had been mounting with the UVF and the LVF's opposition to its pro-Agreement policy, the eruption of the feud was not universally welcomed within the LVF.

While seeking an alliance with the UDA, partly as a shield because it was outnumbered by the UVF, partly as an ally against the Good Friday Agreement, Fulton desperately wanted the rising animosity with the UVF to be defused. He had even remained on good terms with the Jamesons after Wright's expulsion. But now it was too late. The UVF was determined to avenge Richard Jameson's death and had a list of targets that stretched from North Belfast to Ballygowan and Portadown.

Some UDA brigadiers watching from the wings were deeply troubled about the looming intra-loyalist war. Jackie McDonald made it clear both to the Inner Council and the media that his brigade wanted nothing to do with an LVF–UVF shooting war. Billy McFarland, John Gregg and East Belfast's new commander, Jim Grey, shared McDonald's caution. West Belfast however, notably 'C' company, took a different view. Johnny Adair admired not only Wright but the cadre of killers with which he had surrounded himself. He regarded LVF men such as Robin Billy King and Gary Fulton (Mark 'Swinger' Fulton's cousin) as being militant loyalists. 'Adair once told me, "You can't touch the LVF, Jackie, they are the Daddies,"' Jackie McDonald recalled in June 2003. 'He wouldn't listen when I said we should have absolutely nothing to do with them.'

Adair's devotion to Wright's legacy and his organization would spell disaster for the Shankill. Throughout early 2000 'C' company and the Portadown LVF established links behind the backs of the rest of the Inner Council. Adair struck up friendships with Gary Fulton and a number of LVF supporters from North Down, including drug dealer Adrian Porter. Their alliance was strength-ened by a shared hatred of the UVF, a hatred which became more vengeful after a horrific double murder on 19 February. Two Protestant teenagers, Andrew Robb and David McIlwaine, were abducted from a party and later found stabbed to death on a rural road outside Tandragee, County Armagh. Even though neither of them played any part in it, they were killed in revenge for Richard Jameson's murder. On the Shankill the UDA accused the UVF of being 'Protestant killers'. Adair ordered UDA's headquarters to produce a news-sheet detailing the UVF's record on killing

Protestants who crossed it. The leaflet, which did not bear any organization's name, listed recent murders, including that of Frankie Curry, as well as describing the UVF's repeated attempts to murder Jackie Mahood, Clifford Peoples and Kenny McClinton and its threats to Billy Wright. Suddenly the UDA, at least on the Shankill, had become the champions of loyalist dissidents, who, back in the halcyon days of the CLMC, they favoured shooting.

The political figures who had emerged from the loyalist cease-fires watched on with alarm as the bond between Adair and the LVF strengthened. Gary McMichael faded from the scene and now spent his time penning articles for the Dublin-based hard-line nationalist newspaper (at least, as it then was) *Ireland On Sunday*. Davy Adams also retired from UDP politics, throwing himself into several community projects in the Lisburn area where he still commanded deep respect. Jackie McDonald continued to look to Adams for political advice but the centre of power was draining away from the UDP leadership and flowing into the lower Shankill. John White remained the most enigmatic of all the UDA luminaries to survive and prosper under Adair. White protested that he still enthusiastically supported the Good Friday Agreement, David Trimble and even paramilitary organizations decommissioning their weapons. By the spring of 2000 the UDA hardly resembled a 'national' organization at all but rather a series of paramilitary fiefdoms which sometimes acted in unison but more often than not did their own thing.

By mid-February the new secretary of state, Peter Mandelson, had suspended the short-lived power-sharing government that had included Martin McGuinness, the IRA's former chief-of-staff, as education minister. The issue that broke the new Executive was the IRA's refusal to disarm and Trimble's insistence on 'no guns, no government'. Shortly after Mandelson's decision to put devo-lution into cold storage, White, through one of the authors, announced that he had issued a challenge to the UDA. In the back room of the UDP's offices on the middle Shankill, sitting underneath enlarged black and white photographs of marching UDA men in their 1970s uniform of bush hats, black sunglasses and army-style parka jackets, White called on the UDA to take a leap of faith. He said he had asked the UDA to hand over some of its arms to General John de Chastelain's decommissioning body in front of the world's media. White claimed he had almost succeeded in persuading the organization that he helped turn into a killing machine back in 1972–3 into destroying some of its weapons *before* the IRA acted on its arms. He turned to the man sitting beside him for confirmation that this was true. Johnny Adair nodded in the affirmative.

What blocked the UDA being the first terrorist group to give up weapons was the on-going fallout from the murder of Pat Finucane. Since 1989 the Finucane family had campaigned vigorously for an independent inquiry into the solicitor's assassination. In January 2000 the reactivated Stevens inquiry had confirmed that it had identified six loyalists as the main suspects for Finucane's murder, and their details had since been sent to the director of public prosecutions, along with forensic evidence linking them to the killing. But Johnny Adair was adamant that a move against any of the men would scupper any chance of the UDA decommissioning. And there was more. 'If any of those men, whether it's one of them or all six, are arrested and charged then you can kiss goodnight to the peace process from our point of view,' he said.

To an extent Adair had a point. The philosophy underpinning the Good Friday Agreement was that Northern Ireland needed to draw a line under the past and move on. It was in this spirit that the people of the Province had swallowed hard and voted for an accord that freed men who had killed and maimed and gave them what amounted to an amnesty for crimes committed prior to Good Friday 1998. Moreover, when unionists recoiled at the sight of someone such as Martin McGuinness being in charge of their children's education, given his record as head of the IRA, they were chided for living in the past. Yet, while they lectured unionists about the necessity of leaving the Troubles behind, nationalists were demanding publicly funded inquiries into selected crimes from the past – crimes against nationalist victims only.

The arrest of the six UDA men, including the organization's commander in the Highfield area, Eric McKee, coincided with the emergence of a scandal involving the IRA across the Atlantic: the Provos had been caught buying scores of handguns in Florida gun shops. The operation was eventually thwarted by the FBI and several Provisionals, including West Belfast man Conor Claxton, were arrested and charged. The gun-running route had already provided the IRA with up to 100 weapons with no forensic history, which allowed it to conduct its own 'no claim, no blame' charade if it decided to kill someone. One of the 'clean' guns was used to assassinate Real IRA man Joe O'Connor in 1999. Despite the indisputable fact that the IRA Army Council had sanctioned the Florida arms-buying spree, no penalties were imposed on Sinn Féin. Indeed, most of nationalist Ireland appeared to be in a collective state of denial over the arrests in Florida.

Adair had fully supported John White's argument that the UDA should decommission first. At the joint interview in which White said he was recommending that the UDA give up some weapons, he had said: 'We have been working very hard to move things forward on the decommissioning front. The UFF respects and trusts John White. I can see what he means when he says that decommissioning is taking the war to the IRA in a different way, not through the barrel of a gun but rather through politics.' But when Adair and his cronies looked at the IRA getting away with clear breaches of good faith, they thought to themselves that they could do the same. What compounded their anger was that their colleagues in West Belfast were more vulnerable to arrest over crimes committed before Good Friday 1998 than IRA members were for committing crimes *since* then.

The UDA came extremely close to publicly decommissioning a large amount of weaponry in early 2000. Adair had spoken to quartermasters about the guns and explosives selected for destruction; White had laid out plans to invite the world's media to an undisclosed location where the weapons would either be handed over to, or destroyed in front of, a representative from John de Chastelain's office. But the arrest of the six Finucane suspects allowed Inner Council sceptics such as John Gregg to scuttle the initiative. The past crimes of the Troubles, specifically the Finucane murder legacy, had effectively scuppered a chance to move forward.

Paradoxically, while Adair was prepared to decommission weapons in order to boost David Trimble in his battle with the IRA, he continued to nurture links with the Trimble-hating LVF. Despite denials from Adair and White, there was clear evidence of collusion between the two groups during the UVF–LVF feud of early 2000. In February the Tyrone man who assassinated Richard Jameson travelled to North Belfast, his destination the home of a member of an extended loyalist family from Ballysillan who controlled guns and drugs for the LVF across County Antrim. The UVF got wind of his visit and tried to shoot him as he was being driven along the Oldpark Road. Jameson's killer survived the gun attack and was taken to Tennent Street RUC station, in a four-wheel-drive vehicle that belonged to none other than John White, who suggested that he report the murder bid to the police. The UVF was incensed and openly accused 'C' company of secretly siding with the LVF in the feud.

UVF anger intensified on 26 May when an LVF gunman shot dead Progressive Unionist Party member Martin Taylor while he was building a wall outside a house in Ballysillan. The UVF blamed the LVF-aligned family from Ballysillan for the murder. UVF members' suspicions about UDA collusion were confirmed when just a few days later the man they believed had pulled the trigger was seen walking past the PUP's headquarters on the Shankill Road, protectively flanked by Adair and White who were making their way towards the UDP's office further up. 'Adair was flaunting it in front of our faces,' the UVF's second-in-command recalled in October 2000. 'He was sending out a signal that these gangsters were under his wing. We should have realized even then that he was planning something even bigger for us.'

Two days after Martin Taylor's death White publicly offered to set up conciliation talks between the LVF and UVF. He suggested that Revd Roy Magee should be invited to mediate, but this was turned down flat by the UVF. They decided to go on the offensive and tried to kill one of the LVF's founding members, a loyalist veteran living in Ballygowan, County Down.

While Adair's ambition and burning hatred for the UVF were the main force creating the chasm on the Shankill, the twin

pressures of the anti- and pro-Agreement factions within unionism were also responsible for the widening gap in the loyalist
heartland. The UVF and many in the UDA have always been
lukewarm in their support of the Drumcree Orangemen. Leaders
suspected that anti-Agreement elements, not only inside the
Orange Order but within the unionist mainstream, were seeking
to use the Drumcree dispute as the final battleground to destroy
the Good Friday accord. On the UDA Inner Council there were
individual brigadiers who, while supporting the principle of the
right to march, also suspected a wider agenda. Jackie McDonald
was extremely wary of dabbling in Drumcree. A veteran from the
1970s, he had watched while unionist politicians first inflamed
working-class loyalists and then disowned them when these same
loyalists engaged in terrorism. 'I've been around too many corners
to allow myself to be used by outside forces,' McDonald warned
on the eve of the annual Drumcree march on the first Sunday of
July 2000.

McDonald had been sceptical too about a series of attacks on
Protestant areas in Belfast during June in the build-up to the
marching season. A 'flying squad' of two to three cars, all with
their vehicle registrations blacked out, would invade Protestant
redoubts in the dead of night. When the cars arrived a number
of young men wearing baseball caps and with football scarves
wrapped around their faces would attack several houses with bricks
and bottles. They targeted homes on the edge of loyalist areas,
such as houses in Sandy Row close to the Boyne Bridge which
connects the south-central Belfast UDA stronghold to Grosvenor
Road, the gateway to the republican west.

On 20 June, following a raft of assaults, a UDA statement was
issued from the UDP offices on the Shankill warning that the
organization would break its ceasefire if 'nationalist attacks' on
Protestant areas continued. The communiqué had been released
without the knowledge of other brigades, including Jackie
McDonald's South Belfast, and merely reflected the hidden agenda
behind this wave of supposed republican sorties into places such
as Sandy Row. Although there were clashes along sectarian interfaces, sometimes sparked off by nationalist attacks on Protestants,

the majority of the hit-and-run raids in the run-up to 20 June were the work of 'C' company. McDonald and his allies suspected this to be the case but could find no proof.

Through one of his agents, a Special Branch officer who monitored the West Belfast UDA, particularly 'C' company, learned that Adair had selected Sandy Row for special treatment because he felt it was the best way to draw South Belfast into the impending conflict with republicans at Drumcree. The tactic was a repeat of the ruse used by the Pastor when his boyfriend helped burn down a Protestant church three years earlier: attack a Protestant target and then blame it on nationalists with a view to fomenting sectarian disorder on the streets.

At this stage none of the other brigades challenged Adair's growing alliance with the LVF or the lower Shankill's new-found enthusiasm for the Orange Order's cause at Drumcree. Only McDonald was prepared to question openly the wisdom of going down such a road. 'At Inner Council meetings the only one who stood up to Johnny was Jackie McDonald,' one confidant of the South Belfast brigadier said. 'Jackie was the only one who said we shouldn't have links with the LVF. The rest of them [the brigadiers] just sat there and said nothing.'

The Orange Order prides itself on being a religious institution whose members respect their faith, the Crown and the law of the land. It based its refusal to enter into dialogue with nationalist residents' groups on the principle that it would not talk or negotiate with terrorists, pointing out that in the three main areas of contention – Derry, the lower Ormeau and Portadown's Garvaghy Road – the spokesmen heading up the nationalist groups had all served sentences for terrorist activities. But the order's stance reeked of hypocrisy when compared with its attitude to loyalist terrorists. At a controversial Orange parade that passed from the Shankill on to the Springfield Road on 24 June UDA and UFF banners were displayed by loyalist bands taking part in the procession. The order's capacity for cant and doublespeak was underlined on 3 July, in the midst of the Drumcree stand-off: twenty-four hours after the parade was again banned, up to 100 men, mostly shaven-headed, bulging out of tight white T-shirts bearing the slogan 'UFF Simply the Best', wearing earrings and marching in military-style formation, formed up outside Drumcree parish church. Accompanied by his pet Alsatian dog, Rebel, Johnny Adair led the muscle men from the lower Shankill into the field, amid the Orangemen, where a smaller group of LVF activists was waiting for them. Walking in unison, this mass of men with shaven heads was reminiscent of the skinhead surge outside the Specials concert two decades earlier. Though to one police officer standing on the front line at Drumcree bridge it brought to mind something else entirely: 'Look lads,' he was heard muttering to colleagues protected by fireproof black uniforms, helmets, body armour, visors, shields and batons, 'it's a gay male choir.'

The essential campness of their approach was lost on the militants from 'C' company who had come to join their brothers in solidarity at Drumcree. That group included the LVF's Portadown leader, Gary Fulton, and Adrian Porter from North Down, a former member of the Red Hand Commando who had defected to the dissident loyalist faction. 'C' company was there not only to show its support for the anti-Agreement fanatics in Portadown, but its presence also cocked a snook at the UVF back on the Shankill Road which was still involved in its murderous feud with the LVF.

However, even this show of UDA–LVF unity did not alert the UVF to the true intentions of Adair and his band. 'We saw it as grandstanding, Johnny having his ego massaged in Portadown. Sure they were being used but no one could imagine what was about to happen next,' said a UVF commander of thirty years' experience. Later that evening Adair, Gary Smyth, 'Winky' Dodds and others from 'C' company, including Rebel the dog, were treated to an armed display at a bonfire on the Corcrain estate. Cameras captured Adair whooping and cheering when three LVF gunmen, wearing masks and green combat fatigues, fired shots into the air. He himself was greeted like a saviour and given hero status by the embattled LVF in the heart of Portadown. Meanwhile, the Orange Order, in a characteristic display of humbug, defended Adair and his chums' 'right' to attend the Drumcree protest, even though they were openly supporting a terrorist organization.

The 2000 Drumcree dispute failed to plunge the Province into all-out chaos, but it provoked several days of sectarian rioting along interfaces in North and West Belfast. In the lower Shankill Stephen McKeag saw an opportunity to take on the force he hated almost as much as the republican movement – the police. During an outbreak of rioting close to Carlisle Circus McKeag (in what would turn out to be his last action for 'C' company) opened fire on a police patrol with an AK47 rifle. The protest by the law-abiding God-fearing Orange Order had ended with young loyalists, half-crazed through drink and drugs, shooting at police officers. How the republican strategists who first drew up the plans to turn the loyalist marching season into a *casus belli* must have enjoyed the irony.

21. The Shankill Devours Itself

From the beginning of July 2000 the phoney war between the UDA and the UVF on the Shankill (or to be more accurate, 'C' company) was conducted with flags. In commemoration of the Battle of the Somme, and the sacrifice of the 36th Ulster Division (the original UVF), the UVF placed its crimson colours strategically around the main routes – thoroughfares such as the Shankill, Shore, Ravenhill, Woodstock and Newtownards Roads – into loyalist redoubts in the city. John White and Johnny Adair took umbrage and ordered 500 UDA banners from a flag manufacturer in Taiwan. Within weeks sky blue UDA flags fluttered alongside the UVF's colours in every loyalist district. It was a prophetic struggle because less than a month later it would be the flaunting of a single flag which would finally unleash vicious in-fighting on the Shankill.

For several months there had been rumours and whispers about Adair's ultimate goal: to lead a realigned anti-Agreement mass loyalist movement. Mad Dog wanted to go one step further than 'Swinger' Fulton's dream of a UDA–LVF alliance. He saw the future of loyalism with himself as supreme leader, and only the UVF stood in the way of his naked ambition. Adair and White had been planning for a 'Loyalist Day of Culture' in the lower Shankill on 19 August. The lower Shankill UDA invited comrades from all over Northern Ireland to this show of strength-cum-Protestant festival. The UVF feared that with the influx of thousands of UDA members there was potential for trouble on a grand scale. The leaders at the Eagle (a building used by the UVF command that was once a renowned chip shop on the Shankill) sought a meeting with the UDA a few days before the festival on Saturday afternoon. Their prime concern was that LVF members would be invited to the lower Shankill. Given the UVF rank and file's hostility to the LVF, there was a serious risk of confrontation. White was asked to ensure that no LVF emblems or flags

were displayed during a march down the length of the Shankill
Road, the parade which was planned to start the day's festivities.
The Eagle leadership was repeatedly assured that the festival was
a UDA-organized event only and that no other organization's
paraphernalia would be allowed.

None of the assurances were genuine. On the eve of the festival an LVF flag was brought into the lower Shankill and secreted
in the Big Brother house, a two-house community centre in
Boundary Way that had been taken over by 'C' company and was
run as its *de facto* headquarters. The flag belonged to a loyalist
marching band from Antrim town with links to the LVF. On the
afternoon of the march, as a procession of between five to seven
thousand UDA members and their supporters made their way up
the Shankill Road for a memorial service in Woodvale Park, the
Antrim band kept its colours tightly wrapped up so no one watching the parade, least of all anyone aligned to the UVF, could see
them. The UVF had decided to film the march secretly in order
to spot any LVF elements tagging along with the UDA. They
mounted a video camera upstairs in the Progressive Unionist Party
headquarters, which faced the Rex Bar, a pub frequented by UVF
volunteers and their followers for decades.

At first all was peaceful. As the marchers returned from the
ceremony at Woodvale, making their way back towards the lower
Shankill a small knot of UVF supporters gathered outside the Rex
to watch the show of strength. As the rival loyalists passed by there
was even good-natured banter, and at one stage a UDA flute band
from the Shankill Road stopped outside the Rex and played a
number of UVF party tunes. This delighted the UVF-supporting
audience, which clapped, cheered and danced. But the good
humour was not to last for long.

Adair had organized the rally so that the last band to make its
way past the Rex would be the young LVF supporters from Antrim
town. The second they reached the Rex the tightly rolled-up LVF
flag was unfurled and waved about. The UVF followers were
incensed at this deliberate act of provocation and several of them
stormed across the road to seize the band's colours. Immediately
a vicious fist-fight broke out between the Antrim bandsmen and

the drinkers at the Rex. The men outside the pub tried to grab the LVF colours, the band members fought back. The phoney war of the flags was now the real war of the flag. The UDA entourage at the end of the rally joined in the fracas and several were badly beaten. People standing close to the parade, including journalists, were mistaken for UDA supporters and set upon by furious, and in many cases inebriated, young UVF men.

Word reached the lower Shankill that the parade had been attacked and that prompted three waves of assaults on the Rex. The first took place minutes after the bloodied and bruised remnants of the march reached the lower Shankill. An angry mob surged back up the Shankill. Sam McCrory and Tommy Potts, another of Adair's lieutenants, led the charge. (McCrory, the UDA's former commander in the Maze, had settled in Irvine, on Scotland's western coast, after his release from prison in 1999 and moved in with his boyfriend. After his partner died of an Aids-related illness he inherited a small fortune and made a new life for himself in Scotland. He had only returned to Belfast that weekend to see his old comrades for the 'Loyalist Day of Culture'.) Most of the UDA avengers carried baseball bats, clubs, knives, hatchets and hammers; at least two however – McCrory and Potts – had pistols. When the gang of about seventy to eighty UDA men reached the Rex, all hell broke loose as they tried to gain access to the pub. Since they were outnumbered and, for the time being, outgunned, customers slammed the doors shut and boarded themselves in.

Finding their way into the pub blocked, the UDA men turned on the crowd outside it. Oddly, a small contingent of police and troops, which had been drafted into the Shankill in case of any trouble, simply looked on as loyalists went about trying to slaughter each other. The fighting in the street involved young UDA activists attacking anyone – including pensioners – they suspected of UVF links. For media witnesses, many of them seasoned journalists whose careers spanned the Troubles, the ferocity of the assaults of loyalist against loyalist was both terrifying and bewildering. And all the time the UVF continued to record the mayhem from its secret vantage point overlooking the scene. Its film – as well as police footage from CCTV cameras – clearly shows Tommy Potts opening fire on the Rex. A large number of eyewitnesses also saw Sam McCrory training his gun on the remaining punters trying to scramble into the relative safety of the bar. A number of local men were wounded, including a bandsman called Dee Madine who was shot in the back. Following the shooting the mob turned its attentions on the PUP office, smashing windows and trying to force their way in. After the police restored some semblance of order and separated the two sides, the UDA gang charged back down into the lower Shankill. Loyalism's heartland was now effectively cut in two.

However, the orgy of violence and destruction was far from over on that bright August afternoon. The old skinhead *Alterkampfen*, long since morphed into the 'C' company cadre, then went about wreaking what they saw as revenge on anyone living in the lower Shankill with even a tenuous connection to the UVF. In the maze of whitewashed publicly owned houses gangs of UDA and UYM men picked out those belonging to families they believed to be UVF supporters. Thirty-six families were initially targeted. Attackers shot into their homes, broke their windows and eventually torched the interiors. One woman was evicted at gunpoint simply because her two sons, who lived further up the road, played in the Shankill Protestant Boys, the flute band associated with the UVF. In another incident a group of young UDA men burst into the home of Winston Churchill Ray, a long-standing UVF veteran and close friend of the PUP leader David Ervine. 'Winky' Ray was lucky not to be at home when the UDA men smashed down his door. Not finding their quarry inside they set about destroying his home, managing even to tear up his Orange sash and smash a picture of Sir Edward Carson, the found-ing father of twentieth-century loyalism, that was hanging on his living-room wall. Another gang then stormed into the home of Gusty Spence, the UVF veteran who had read out the loyalist ceasefire statement flanked by, among others, John White. Spence, too, was fortunate not to be home when the mob struck. He spent his summers at a caravan at Groomsport, a North Down seaside resort known as 'Little Shankill' due to its popularity with loyalists. After breaking Spence's windows and smashing down his door, the UDA men ransacked the house and stole several British military medals that the modern UVF's founder collected. Spence and his family had to stay out of their street for the duration of the feud. The destruction of their home took its greatest toll on Gusty Spence's beloved wife, Louis. After she died three years later Spence muttered that 'C' company had been as responsible for her death as the illness that killed her.

No one was safe from 'C' company's wrath, including those trying to help the evicted to get to safety. Chris McGimpsey, a hard-working and popular councillor for the Ulster Unionist Party in the greater Shankill, decided to drive into the lower Shankill and try to transport a number of women and children from the estate to their relatives' homes further up the road. When he arrived amidst the expulsions he was surrounded by a group of young men, many the worse for wear on drink and drugs, and told to get out of the area or they would torch his Jeep. Despite the threats, McGimpsey came to the aid of at least one family under attack and drove them away at top speed.

By the end of the 'Loyalist Day of Culture' there was barely anyone left in the lower Shankill with even a slight link to the UVF or PUP. But still, in the midst of this intra-loyalist form of 'ethnic cleansing', Johnny Adair was determined to throw a party. He had invited all the other UDA brigadiers to the festival in the lower Shankill and had a special platform constructed for the occasion. On to the stage stepped a number of dazed and confused UDA brigadiers, including Jackie McDonald, who had known nothing of Adair's plan to provoke all-out war with the UVF. McDonald, along with the North Belfast UDA's commander Jimbo Simpson, John Gregg and Billy McFarland, was a prisoner of the spectacle. They were joined on stage by Councillor Frank McCoubrey, a UDP member from the Highfield estate who had been elected deputy Lord Mayor of Belfast just two months earlier, and wore his red robe and gold chain of office to the event.

After a speech by John White the highlight of the festival was an armed display. Among the firing party which stepped on to the platform was a slender woman, none other than Gina Adair.

She sent the crowd around the platform wild with her mastery of the AK47 as she fired volleys into the night air. The UDA leadership and the deputy Lord Mayor of Belfast looked on in awe – albeit with their fingers shoved into their ears.

The pictures of the second citizen of Belfast in his Mayor's garb on the same platform as masked gun-toting terrorists provoked demands from nationalists and others that he be stripped of his office. Even his fellow unionists on Belfast City Council, especially the PUP's long-standing councillor Hugh Smyth, felt betrayed. When McCoubrey was first elected to City Hall in 1997 Smyth had been one of the first to show him round and explain the intricacies of council politics. Now McCoubrey was sharing a platform with men and women, some of whom were attacking Smyth's election workers and closest friends.

To be fair to McCoubrey, he – like most of the UDA brigadiers on the stage – knew nothing of the planned provocation or the attacks on the Rex that afternoon. Many in the UDA rank and file were also kept in the dark. A bus-load of about seventy UDA members and their families had travelled to the 'Day of Culture' from Derry city. For many on the Ulsterbus it was just an excuse for a day-trip to Belfast. The women accompanying the Derry UDA had decided not to attend the march at all and instead walked the short distance from the middle Shankill down into Belfast city centre for a spot of Saturday-afternoon shopping. So when the fighting broke out the Derry UDA's wives and girlfriends knew nothing about it.

The irony of the events of 19 August was underlined by the fact that the driver who took the Derry UDA to Belfast was a Catholic from the republican Bogside. He was known to all the Derry UDA and their families, often drove them around Northern Ireland to loyalist events and was on good personal terms with his loyalist passengers. When hostilities broke out on the Shankill Seamus was asleep in the cabin of his Ulsterbus, which was parked in Berlin Street, and was oblivious to the shooting and fighting raging just a couple of hundred yards away. One Derry UDA man with more than twenty-five years' experience in loyalist politics recognized the incongruity. 'Seamus was, and is, a very popular driver with us. He gets on well with the lads up here in Londonderry and no one would be allowed to lay a finger on him. But it was certainly ironic that here was a Catholic from the Bogside sleeping in the middle of the Shankill while loyalists were kicking the shit out of one another. It showed how times had changed.'

By the end of the afternoon the Derry UDA delegation had met up in the lower Shankill and was about to board the bus for home when members realized that a number of their colleagues were missing. It turned out that several young men from the North-west UDA brigade had sneaked off from the march with a number of Shankill women they had met that morning. All of them were drinking in pubs and houses in the upper Shankill, now UVF territory, following the attack on the Rex. The Ulsterbus carrying the Derry UDA had to drive up the Crumlin Road, which runs parallel to the Shankill, searching for the young activists who they feared might now be attacked by the UVF. 'In the end they were all accounted for but because they went chasing skirt they could have lost their lives,' the Derry UDA veteran recalled.

Adair was still far from finished with either the UVF or the regulars at the Rex Bar. With a characteristic touch of theatricality he staged a third and final assault on the bar as night fell. The 'Loyalist Day of Culture' ended with a huge bonfire at a piece of derelict ground in the middle of the Lower Shankill estate. The bonfire was ringed by about a dozen firework rockets timed to go off just as the conflagration was lit. A group of 'C' company gunmen was also planning fireworks to coincide with the bonfire. They were sent back up the Shankill in a car to shoot up the Rex Bar once more. When the shots rang out across the Shankill as the Rex was hit for the third time in a single day, Adair set off the fireworks. While ambulances and police Land Rovers rushed to the aid of the newly wounded the Shankill skyline was illuminated as rockets and whizz-bangs exploded into the air.

Amazingly, no one had been killed during the first day of the UDA–UVF feud, a conflict Adair hoped would involve every single brigade taking on the hated 'Blackneck bastards'. It was, however, the first of a series of major miscalculations by Adair.

McDonald, McFarland and the new East Belfast brigadier, the flamboyantly dressed and neatly coiffured Jim Grey, pulled their membership out of the lower Shankill that Saturday evening. All three had been extremely wary about joining with Johnny Adair in a crusade to realign loyalism and, unknown to Adair and 'C' company, they ordered their units to stay out of conflict with the UVF over the remainder of the weekend.

The master-plan to wipe out the UVF and form a grand coalition with the LVF sustained another blow within hours of the violence breaking out. West Belfast brigade was comprised of 'A', 'B' and 'C' companies. 'C' company was fiercely loyal to Adair and would follow him to the abyss; 'A' and 'B' companies were in more precarious positions: 'A' was based in the Highfield estate while 'B' covered the Woodvale/middle Shankill. These were areas where the UVF was stronger and where many of its most ruthless activists lived and worked. Moreover, in 'A' company's domain leading UDA figures such as Eric McKee had long-standing friendships with local UVF men. Both UDA companies were extremely reluctant to follow 'C' company's warpath. Despite this, Winky Dodds, acting on Adair's orders, told 'A' company to 'cleanse' the Highfield estate of UVF men and their families and continue the process its comrades in the lower Shankill had initiated.

The order from 'below' (the lower Shankill) led to an absurd scenario in the upper Shankill. A Highfield UDA man approached his neighbour, who was a member of the UVF. He informed him of Dodds's directive and asked the UVF man if he could break his windows and if he would not mind moving out of his house for a day or two. The two neighbours would simply pretend that the Highfield UDA had expelled a UVF family and then Dodds, Adair and 'C' company would be satisfied. The UVF leadership was having none of this charade in Highfield or anywhere else. It ordered all its members in every other part of the Shankill to stay put. 'The Highfield UDA man was told to get lost,' the UVF's second-in-command recalls. 'None of our members were allowed to participate in that farce. But his offer of a "deal" showed us that 'C' company were acting alone. Nobody else in the UDA wanted this feud. In a sense this was our trump card.'

Adair and the other masterminds of this would-be coup had also seriously underestimated the UVF's willingness to fight back. On Sunday 20 August, the day after the 'Loyalist Day of Culture', the UVF dispatched two teams to destroy the UDP's old headquarters in the middle Shankill. First, they riddled the premises with a sub-machine gun and then, twenty-four hours later, blew it up with a bomb made of Powergel. No one was injured in the late-night blast, but the use of Powergel to bring down the UDP/Loyalist Prisoners Aid centre sent out a powerful warning. 'It sent out a message that the UVF had the bomb-making capability and were willing to use it in a war of survival. That message was particularly meant for the other UDA brigadiers, to tell them stay out of this conflict,' said the UVF's second-in-command shortly after the feud began.

The UVF underscored its ability to strike back at the larger UDA less than forty-eight hours after the intra-loyalist war began. Jackie Coulter was sitting with Bobby Mahood in a Jeep on the Crumlin Road. Mahood, the owner of the vehicle, had been a member of the UVF but was long retired from loyalist politics and now ran two businesses: a pub in the upper Shankill and a taxi service for journalists from around the world visiting local trouble spots such as Drumcree. Indeed, during the 2000 Drumcree crisis Bobby Mahood had brought CNN's London correspondent, Nick Robertson, to the home of one of the authors for an interview about the impending crisis within loyalism. During a break in filming Mahood expressed his deepest concerns about the way the loyalist community was turning in on itself, possibly even sliding towards an all-out feud. On the morning of 21 August the 48-year-old would become the first fatality of the turf war he had predicted. A young UVF man, armed with a shotgun, was sent to the Crumlin Road because the UVF had heard that Jackie Mahood was in the area, holding talks with the UDA. Mistaking Bobby for his brother the gunman opened fire on the Jeep, killing both Mahood and Jackie Coulter. Ironically, the two men had been talking about ways to end the feud and mend the deadly divisions on the Shankill.

Coulter was a UDA activist but took no part in the assault on the Rex and for many years had been solely involved in prisoners' welfare, driving UDA families to the Maze. He was extremely popular among the 'C' company members and, on hearing about his murder, a mob gathered around Boundary Way to take revenge. Thirty men, including Adair, armed with knives, hammers, hatchets, baseball bats and guns charged again up the Shankill Road. Their target was the PUP's headquarters close to Agnes Street, the dividing line between the UDA and UVF zones of influence on the Shankill. The gang managed to set fire to the front of the PUP office and also smashed up a taxi firm directly across the road before returning to their lower Shankill lair.

Within hours of the double murder and the assault on the PUP HQ Adair was back behind bars, having been arrested by a large number of soldiers and police officers in the lower Shankill. Peter Mandelson's patience had reached breaking point. The instigator and chief organizer of the Rex attack was taken the short journey from the lower Shankill to Girdwood army barracks off the Antrim Road in the back of a Land Rover. From there, he was flown by helicopter to Maghaberry, an integrated prison where republican dissidents were forced to share the same facilities as their loyalist enemies. As he was being led away in handcuffs Gina Adair cried to reporters: 'My Johnny hasn't done anything.'

Mandelson based his decision to rearrest Adair and put him back in custody on a secret document drawn up by the security services. The confidential intelligence file concerned Adair's activities following his early release on licence from the Maze on 14 September 1999, after serving just four years of a sixteen-year sentence for directing acts of terrorism. In the paper, for the first time, a British minister was told how drug-dealing financed loyalist terror and Adair's lifestyle. The document's authors concluded that since his early release Adair had been

involved in the procurement and distribution of firearms and munitions; the authorization of paramilitary attempted murders and of a number of so-called punishment shootings; the instigation and orchestration of sectarian tensions and attacks in North and West Belfast during July and August 2000 and in Portadown on 3 July 2000; the planning of the paramilitary show of strength in Belfast on 11 July and of the UDA/UFF Shankill parade on 19 August 2000.

Mandelson was left in no doubt about Johnny Adair's hand in the latest disturbances to rock the Shankill. The then secretary of state would later use this file to oppose any move by the Sentence Review Commission to free Adair on appeal.

Following the August events other 'C' company luminaries either fled the Shankill or died. Under the threat of death by the UVF, and arrest by the police, McCrory fled back to Scotland on the Monday after the feud's genesis – without much effort by the PSNI (the RUC's name had just been changed to Police Service of Northern Ireland under the Patten reforms of policing) or any branch of the security forces to stop him doing so. His involvement in the Rex Bar attack was to be his last ever operation for the UDA. Stephen 'Top Gun' McKeag played no part in the feud at all. Even before the eruption McKeag had been in internal exile in the Oldpark for having crossed, first, Gary Smyth, when he intervened to save a woman being beaten up in a loyalist shebeen, and later Adair, who was intensely jealous and suspicious of Top Gun's reputation. Isolated from his former comrades with whom he had killed for the cause, McKeag degenerated into a life of hard drinking and drug-taking and had become addicted to cocaine and the morphine-based pain-killers he took for the injuries he suffered in a motorbike crash two years earlier. When he was found dead at his home in the lower Oldpark, McKeag's family initially believed he had been killed in the feud, but toxicology reports revealed that Top Gun had died from a lethal cocktail of spirits, cocaine and pain-killers. A bolt fired from a cross-bow was welded into the wall above where his body was found. Of course his funeral was a major event, with UDA teams from all over Northern Ireland paying homage. The rest of 'C' company, most of whom still held McKeag in awe, insisted that the leadership commemorate the young killer. A mural was therefore commissioned and Top Gun joined Billy Wright, Jackie Coulter, Bucky McCullough (shot dead by the INLA in 1981) and Princess Diana on the lower Shankill's walls. His face looks down on passers-by to this day.

At first, removing Adair from the streets did not seem to make a difference. Two days after the Coulter/Mahood double murder the UDA struck back, shooting dead 21-year-old Samuel Rockett, a member of the UVF, at his girlfriend's home in Summer Street, in the 'C' company stronghold of lower Oldpark. Between the end of the summer and Christmas the feud would claim three more lives, all of them beyond the Shankill, in North Belfast.

North Belfast brigadier Jimbo Simpson, had been reluctant to join the war against the UVF but some elements within his brigade were more loyal to Adair and their comrades in 'C' company than to him. Those close to the Adair faction included Andre and Ihab Shoukri, two brothers from the Westland housing estate, a Protestant redoubt on the bank of the man-made Waterworks lake off the Cavehill Road. They were rising stars in North Belfast and had attracted Adair's attention. Because of their sallow skin and foreign names they were nicknamed the 'Turks' or the 'Pakis' by other young UDA men. In fact the Shoukris' father was an Egyptian Coptic Christian who had settled in Belfast and married a local woman. The brothers and their friends admired Adair's militancy and aimed to be like him and 'C' company.

Another of those in North Belfast close to the lower Shankill UDA was 21-year-old David Greer, who the UVF believed had been involved in the attacks on the Rex Bar. On 28 October a UVF unit from North Belfast, led by an extremely volatile and violent loyalist, gunned down Greer as he walked along Mountcollyer Street in Tigers Bay. The feud had finally extended beyond the Shankill. The Tigers Bay UDA responded on Hallowe'en night, forcing its way into the home of a pensioner who had just returned to Belfast after more than a decade in South Africa. Sixty-three-year-old Herbert Rice had been a member of the UVF at the start of the Troubles and on his return to Northern Ireland joined the Progressive Unionist Party. Given his age Rice no longer took part in any paramilitary activity and was simply a soft target for young UDA men hell-bent on revenge for David Greer's death.

Within hours of Rice's murder the North Belfast UVF sought to even the score and it found itself an equally soft target. Tommy

English was a mesh of contradictions. During the run-up to the referendum on the Good Friday Agreement, English mocked Ian Paisley by going on stage at the notorious UDA rally at the Ulster Hall wearing a Paisley mask and a clerical collar. Subsequently he was a UDP candidate in the 1998 Assembly elections. He took part in several cross-border peace conferences held at the Glencree Centre for Reconciliation in the County Wicklow hills and several Southern Irish peace activists such as Paul Burton and Chris Hudson had held him in high esteem and formed a bond with him during a visit to the Somme battlefield in July 1999. Yet English was also embroiled in a number of sectarian clashes around two pressure points in North Belfast – the Limestone Road and White City/Whitewell Road. On the same night Herbert Rice died David Greer's killer (who had committed more than a dozen murders) shot English at his home in Ballyfore Gardens in Newtownabbey.

Twenty-four hours later John Gregg's second-in-command in the South-east Antrim brigade, Rab Carson, opened fire on 26-year-old UVF man Mark Quail, at his house in the middle of the Rathcoole estate. The feud was escalating out of control, Adair and company were delighted, the UVF in their Eagle HQ was getting alarmed.

Adair's influence on younger UDA men in the north-west provoked units in Coleraine and outlying areas to seek to 'expel' UVF-aligned families from Protestant housing estates. The UVF, however, fought back ferociously – some would argue indiscriminately. On 11 October, in retaliation for attacks on PUP homes in Coleraine, a UVF unit fired into the home of a former UDA prisoner. One of the bullets hit the man's eleven-year-old daughter, Charlene Daly, who spent several weeks in intensive care recovering from her wounds.

Even though the maiming of a defenceless child did not give the warring factions pause for thought, at least there were no signs that other UDA brigade areas were prepared to join the struggle against the UVF. In East Belfast individual UDA commanders had made approaches to their UVF counterparts to tell them that 'C' company would fight its own battles. On the Cregagh estate for instance, the well-maintained trouble-free area where, among others, George Best and Michael Stone grew up, the local UDA leader made it his business to have a drink in the pub with a senior UVF commander. The message was simple: there was no feud in Cregagh or any other part of loyalist East Belfast. That situation was mirrored in South Belfast where Jackie McDonald had come to an agreement with the UVF that they would not attack each other. Even in Derry city, where there had previously been short violent skirmishes between the UVF and UDA, relative calm had descended on the loyalist Waterside. Most critically of all, the UDA companies in the upper Shankill had no stomach for an outright confrontation with the UVF.

The unofficial peace pact between the UVF and 'A' and 'B' companies of the UDA on the Shankill was plain for all to see on 2 September. Every year the UVF holds a memorial parade in Woodvale for Brian Robinson, a young UVF gunman shot dead by undercover soldiers from the 14th Intelligence Unit on his way back from a sectarian murder at Ardoyne. The first Brian Robinson commemoration of the twenty-first century would provide the UVF with an opportunity to show some muscle in the face of its enemies in the greater Shankill. After forming up outside the Rex, young bandsmen, dressed in the uniforms of the 36th Ulster Division, carrying UVF and YCV banners from the First World War, made their way along the Shankill to the heart of the Woodvale.

Since this was the first major loyalist band parade since the events of 19 August, the atmosphere on the Shankill was febrile. Hundreds of British troops and police had swamped the area, blocking off the lower Shankill with armoured Saxon personnel carriers and battle-ship-grey PSNI Land Rovers. The graffiti on the walls spelt out Shankill UVF's contempt for Adair and 'C' company. Beside 'UVF – the People's Army' was the slogan 'UDA drug dealers'. A young woman from the lower Shankill, who was known to have had affairs with Johnny Adair and later with his son, Jonathan junior, was labelled a 'UDA spunk bucket'. Leaflets handed out at the Rex detailed the alleged criminality of leading figures from 'C' company, accusing them of drug-dealing, pimping prostitutes and beating up women. However, the most telling piece of graffiti was painted at the entrance of Cambrai Street, a road that links the Shankill with the Crumlin Road. It spelt out a message from the UVF to the rest of the UDA: 'B company area not drug dealers'. Jim Spence and 'B' company were in a highly vulnerable position. The huge and highly profitable social club they ran in Heather Street was in a UVF stronghold, close to where the Brian Robinson parade would take place. In order to prevent trouble breaking out the army had surrounded the social club, even though the likelihood of conflict breaking out between 'B' company and the UVF was minimal. In the end, the only shots fired that day came from a UVF gun over the memorial stone dedicated to Robinson.

By the autumn the Shankill Road resembled an armed camp with hundreds of soldiers and police officers keeping the peace between the warring loyalist factions. Agnes Street cuts the Shankill in two between the peace line to the west with the republican Falls and the Crumlin Road to the north-east. In the autumn–winter of 2000 it had become the Shankill's Friedrichstrasse. Like the thoroughfare in divided Berlin, Agnes Street was the crossing point between the UVF zone in the middle/upper Shankill and the UDA-controlled lower Shankill. No one with any connection, family or friendship, to the UDA would venture northwards beyond the semi-permanent army–police checkpoint at Agnes Street; and the same applied for anyone remotely linked to the UVF heading south down the Shankill Road. The mid-Shankill, where most of the shops, chemists, supermarkets, butchers and other stores were sited, was effectively a 'no-go' zone for those families loyal to Adair.

At the height of the feud the UVF-controlled black taxis that had traversed the Shankill from North Street in Belfast city centre for thirty years had to find an alternative route. Unable to travel in safety past the lower Shankill for fear the distinctive vehicles would be targeted by the UDA, the Shankill taxis found it was safer to use another road – the Falls. The sight of Shankill taxis packed with Protestant passengers driving through the Shankill/Falls peace line along Northumberland Street, and continuing their journey along the Catholic Falls Road was a powerful symbol of how fractured loyalism had become.

Most republicans in the city privately enjoyed the irony that the Falls was safer for large numbers of loyalists than the lower Shankill. However, the more thoughtful leadership in Sinn Féin worried that when they stopped shooting each other the loyalists would return to old ways and turn their guns back on Catholics. Only in Ardoyne, an area that suffered more than most from the attentions of the UDA and UVF, and a hotbed of nationalist sectarianism for more than three decades, did republicans openly gloat about the intra-loyalist war. 'Ardoyne supports the loyalist feud', one wag painted on a wall that could be seen by residents of the upper Shankill.

Chris McGimpsey's office, which had been equidistant between the old, now destroyed UDP/Prisoners' Aid HQ and the PUP's headquarters, was dealing with hundreds of families expelled from their homes. The majority – up to 200 – were from the lower Shankill and satellite areas such as Oldpark and had been driven from their houses at gunpoint by 'C' company teams. A smaller number – perhaps up to forty families aligned to the UDA – were expelled from their homes in retaliation by the UVF on the middle and upper Shankill. 'We have a new partition on the Shankill,' McGimpsey said less than a week after the feud erupted. 'There is effectively a new peace line dividing not Catholics and Protestants but rather Protestants from Protestants. This is [*sic*] road is dividing into separate paramilitary zones and that is a tragedy for the Shankill Road. It will be the death of this community.'

Some non-aligned people on the Shankill remarked bitterly that the feud had actually done more damage to the loyalist heartland than the IRA bomb in 1993. 'Swinger' Fulton's dream of sucking the UDA into open conflict with the UVF had turned out to be a nightmare for the overwhelming majority of people in the greater Shankill.

The divide reached even into schools and among pupils. Born-again Christian preacher Jack McKee, a man concerned about his community and deeply opposed to all paramilitary violence, got a disturbing insight into how the feud reached into the classroom.

From his pastoral work McKee found that members of the rival loyalist youth wings, the Young Citizens Volunteers (UVF) and the Ulster Young Militants (UDA), had to be let out of school from different gates at different times at the end of each day to avoid clashes. And although their hero-figure was now behind bars, the UYM pupils continued to flaunt their teachers' rules and taunt their fellow classmates by wearing T-shirts glorifying Adair with the legend 'C company – simply the best'.

In some sense the 2000 feud was part of a pattern replicated throughout the Troubles in earlier UDA–UVF conflicts. One organization, the UVF, sought a political way forward by reaching out to compromise with republicans and nationalists. The other organization, the UDA, in a bid for hegemony in the Protestant working class, became more militant, sectarian and outspoken against its rivals. It depicted the UVF as crypto-communists and/or as a crowd of 'Fenian lovers'. In this they were aided, whether they asked for it or not, by *agents provocateurs* on loyalism's fringe, men such as the Pastor who played up the allegations of communism and referred to the likes of Billy Hutchinson as a 'Godless thug'. The net result was always the same: working-class loyalism became increasingly sub-divided, marginalized and detached from political reality.

At some stage in the latest and most damaging loyalist schism the security services played a role. Despite having twenty-seven informants inside the West Belfast UDA, Special Branch did nothing to stymie Adair's plans for a final conflict with the UVF. The 'unholy alliance' was allowed to continue its black propaganda campaign against the PUP while encouraging the UDA and LVF to realign loyalism. Undercover army units still operated in the north and west of Belfast, sometimes even without the knowledge of the PSNI, and the army also had many informants inside 'C' company and thus would have been aware of Adair's designs.

Ever since the loyalist ceasefires clergymen, unionist politicians and loyalist figures tried to mediate in disputes between the two rival forces. However, now that the tension between the two organizations had erupted into open warfare, some in the UVF leadership argued that it should maintain the pressure on 'C' company and their families, that the UDA in the lower Shankill would eventually crack. During a brigade staff meeting the UVF's second-in-command pointed out that 'C' company and its friends and families were effectively trapped inside the lower Shankill estate. They had no access to the Shankill's shopping area. Even a visit to a GP risked attack from the vengeful UVF and its supporters, many of whom had been made homeless by the UDA. He suggested that if the UVF kept up the pressure and sealed off the lower Shankill then, without the unifying figure of Johnny Adair, the jealousies, resentments and suspicions that many in 'C' company bore towards each other would rise to the surface and 'C' company would implode.

In the end the more conservative and cautious UVF brigadier general, John Graham, won the argument. The UVF would agree to a negotiated end to the feud, following talks between David Ervine and Gary McMichael, who had come out of semi-retirement to offer his services to end the bloodshed. The commander who had argued for keeping 'C' company under pressure resigned from the organization's mediation team in disgust and frustration. 'I had argued for some time that these people in the lower Shankill owed no loyalty to one another. Adair was in jail, McCrory was back in Scotland, McKeag was dead. It was a house of cards and all we had to do was keep them holed up in the lower end of the road and the house would fall down.'

His words were prophetic. One of the key players in the UDA–UVF feud also hinted at the new fault-lines in the UDA. Several days after the conflict with the UVF officially ended John White, the sharp-suited respectable face of 'C' company, was asked for his thoughts about his 'comrades' in 'A' and 'B' companies. The former killer gazed up the Shankill Road and muttered: 'They're guilty. Guilty of cowardice in the face of the enemy.'

22. Turning on 'the Taigs' Again

Unionism entered the twentieth century in a position of enormous economic and political strength. The industrial revolution in the north-east had laid the foundations for partition of the island. The industries that powered the rise in living standards in the counties bunched around Belfast – shipbuilding, engineering, textiles and rope-making – were, in the main, dominated by the Protestant working class. Unionist politics had coalesced around flamboyant and able figures such as Edward Carson and could look to powerful allies in the British establishment such as Andrew Bonar Law in their struggle against Home Rule. Unity was the order of the day with a single and determined Ulster Unionist Party and, by 1912, up to 30,000 armed men under orders to thwart, by military means if necessary, the Liberal government's plans to give Irish nationalists self-rule inside the British empire.

Yet, if Carson, Sir James Craig and the other founding fathers of unionism could be raised from their graves and taken on a journey across Belfast at the start of the twenty-first century, they would see a very different city and a radically changed unionism. The blood-letting on the Shankill – the area where Carson recruited some of his most dedicated, ruthless and insanely brave foot-soldiers – was merely the violent climax of a process that had resulted in unionist communal fragmentation. Inside the Stormont Assembly there were six separate unionist parties vying against each other (seven if the soon-to-be defunct UDP is counted) as opposed to two nationalist movements, Sinn Féin and the SDLP. Within Carson's Ulster Unionist Party there were an additional two, arguably even three, distinct factions – only one of which still supported the Good Friday Agreement. The loyalist paramilitaries were broken into three rival groupings, and, even inside the relatively homogeneous UVF bitter divisions were emerging between those who backed the Good Friday accord and those who now opposed it. That anti-Agreement faction emerged on the Shankill Road in late 2000 when at least two battalions registered their hostility to the accord at a mass meeting in a local Glasgow Rangers supporters' club.

The UDA was also torn apart by the historic compromise with nationalism. While John White continued to insist he was pro-Agreement, the commanders who counted all around him were either publicly or privately in the anti-camp. More crucially still, many of those who had been at the centre of the maelstrom of late 2000 were bitter and resentful of their comrades who had failed to join them in fighting the UVF. Beneath the thin veneer of public unity the UDA was breaking apart.

The ghosts of unionism past would be pining for their graves when they saw former strongholds such as the Shankill, Sandy Row and the Newtownards Road, where communities had become disconnected from the institutions that once held the unionist working class together as a coherent united force. The Protestant churches were either empty or closing, the influence of ministers on their flock dwindling by the day. With factories shut and the staple industries all but disappeared, the skills, and with them the wage packets that sustained industrial Ulster, were lost. The respectable Protestant working class too was an endangered species, being displaced by a new underclass which coped with the pressures of modern life by relying on hedonistic props such as alcohol and drugs, paid for, in many cases, by either crime or loans from paramilitary sharks who exploited the poor and the needy.

The spirits from unionism's golden age would also have been shocked by the nihilism infecting the general unionist population, a nihilism particularly virulent among the Protestant working class and underclass. Defeatism was prevalent throughout the entire unionist community. The apocalyptic prophecies of Ian Paisley, who had predicted sell-out and nationalist victory for decades, had affected the Protestant psyche more than commentators cared to imagine or admit. Even if the Good Friday Agreement was predicated on the principle of consent, the majority of unionists came to believe that nationalists and republicans were somehow winning, that unionists were the new downtrodden people. Every concession to Sinn Féin, every incremental gain designed to entice the IRA away from violence, was therefore magnified and then dressed up to look like another milestone on the road to a United Ireland. Every sign of Catholic advancement – from education results to the growth of a new nationalist middle class – was portrayed as proof positive that the Prods were being put down.

On the issue of territory, Protestant paranoia was at its peak. Belfast in the twenty-first century is more bigoted and divided than it was before the IRA and loyalist ceasefires of 1994. At the beginning of 2000 University of Ulster social scientist Dr Peter Shirlow, himself a product of the unionist working class, carried out a survey to track social attitudes in the city from the cease-fires to the Agreement and beyond. What he found was both star-tling and disturbing. On the sectarian interfaces of North and West Belfast 72 per cent of those surveyed felt that divisions between Catholics and Protestants had worsened since the ceasefires. More depressing still was the fact that teenagers and schoolchildren, some of whom were still in their prams when the Troubles ended in 1994, were more bigoted than older people who had lived through three decades of incipient civil war. Shirlow questioned teenagers who were in Primary 3 (six- or seven-year-olds) back when the ceasefires were declared. Of the 112 surveyed, who had met the other side on cross-community holidays, summer schemes and sporting events, eighty-six said they still harboured strong sectar-ian attitudes. Furthermore, people's choice of hospitals, leisure centres, libraries, shops and social security offices were all predi-cated, first and foremost, on sectarian criteria. Among those living at the sharp end of sectarianism the peace process barely existed.

The manifestations of this mutual suspicion and immutable inter-communal loathing were all around in North and West Belfast. By the start of the new century there were twenty-six barriers – 'peace walls' – most of them erected only *after* the loyal-ist and IRA cessations. And, unlike the wall that once cut Berlin in half, the walls of North and West Belfast were, and continue to be, extremely popular among those living on either side of the divide. They were viewed as, literally, the last line of defence against the Other.

The UDA had emerged from the Protestant working class initially as a defence militia blocking off routes into loyalist areas with hijacked buses, makeshift barriers, lines of long-haired men dressed incongruously in military-style uniforms, often armed only with clubs and bats. In the mid-1970s it could arguably describe itself as a popular army that helped defeat a British government in the 1974 general strike. It could call upon thousands of men in the event of all-out confrontation with either the state to which it proclaimed loyalty or their traditional enemies across the sectarian divide. The twenty-first-century UDA, particularly in North Belfast, sought to recapture that spirit, to once again put itself forward as the defender of beleaguered Protestant communities under fire or encroachment from the nationalist foe. But for the UDA defence often meant going on the attack.

In the first three months of 2001 barely a night went by without a pipe-bomb attack on Catholic homes and areas. The onslaught began on 2 January, with bombs in North Belfast, and it continued on throughout the year. In the main almost all the sorties were UDA organized, in many cases the work of their junior wing, the UYM. The campaign was directed at two sets of Catholic targets: vulnerable families living inside Protestant-dominated housing estates in mainly loyalist rural towns, and Catholic homes contiguous to the peace walls of North Belfast. The strategy behind the first target was simply to 'cleanse' Protestant towns of their Catholics. In South-east Antrim John Gregg authorized a particularly vicious campaign against Catholics in Larne and Carrickfergus and hundreds of families were driven from their homes. Gregg, viscerally sectarian and addicted to violence, despite the peace process, feared that Protestant towns along the East Antrim coast ran the risk of becoming like places such as Glengormley and Crumlin, satellite villages of Belfast which had been transformed from solely loyalist to nationalist. He looked at where the new Catholic middle class had moved to and Protestants deserted, in turn, as evidence of encroachment. Gregg and his local commanders were determined that Larne and Carrickfergus would not go the same way.

In the campaign to reduce the Catholic population along the

East Antrim coast no one was safe, even democratically elected representatives. For instance, between 2000 and 2002 more than a dozen attacks were launched on Danny O'Connor's advice centre and at his home in Larne. A local SDLP councillor and Assembly man, O'Connor is unquestionably one of the bravest politicians in Northern Ireland. The assaults on his party office and home have included petrol and pipe-bombings and attacks with gun shots, ball bearings, stones and bottles. Despite being constantly under threat and under fire, O'Connor continues to represent his constituents and works for all sides of the community regardless of the local UDA campaign against him.

In North Belfast the pressure point areas were Tigers Bay/ Newington, White City/Whitewell Road, Westland/Cavehill and Rathcoole/Glengormley. The nightly violence along North Belfast's interfaces has often been explained as spontaneous, drink-fuelled and generally the work of teenagers from the underclass. But behind the seemingly mindless violence and sectarian nihilism was a carefully designed strategy. In areas such as Tigers Bay the UDA was responding to a localized form of Protestant paranoia. The local populace believed, rightly or wrongly, that the place would eventually be swamped by the nearby nationalist New Lodge. The contrast between the two areas could not have been greater. While the New Lodge was bulging at the seams, the demand for housing far outstripping supply as the Catholic population soared, whole streets in Tigers Bay lay virtually empty. Suspicions in Tigers Bay were bolstered by calls by articulate Sinn Féin representatives, such as Gerry Kelly, for the housing executive to extend out the peace line and build more homes desperately needed by North Belfast's growing Catholic population. The Tigers Bay UDA decided to dissuade any Catholic of thinking about moving into new housing closer than ever before to a loyalist area. One of their local commanders confirmed to the authors that the object of the pipe-bomb campaigns in 2000–2001 was to secure territory on their side of the peace line. This included intimidating out of their homes those Catholics living cheek by jowl to the peace walls at Newington.

Jimbo Simpson, the UDA North Belfast brigadier, said of the

campaign that it was merely the organization going back to its roots. 'I joined the UDA because there was no one to defend our streets from republicans in the New Lodge in the early seventies. What is going on now is the UDA doing the same thing. Stopping our area from being taken over by nationalists.' Even though Simpson was under pressure to retire due to his drinking (he was nicknamed the 'Bacardi Brigadier'), and was eventually ousted in an internal coup and replaced as brigadier by Andre Shoukri, the pipe-bomb campaign in the north of the city went on until the end of 2001.

The interface battle reached a bloody climax on 11 November when the UDA in Tigers Bay gained a new martyr. Sixteen-year-old Glen Branagh was the archetypal raw recruit to the UYM. He sported the new uniform of the junior UDA – baseball cap, Nike trainers, shaved head, single earring, designer sports shirt and tracksuit trousers. Barely educated and growing up in an environment where paramilitarism was glorified on the gable walls all around him, it was inevitable that the teenager would follow his peers into the UYM. On the afternoon of 11 November there had been a serious outbreak of rioting at the junction of North Queen Street and Duncairn Gardens, where the New Lodge meets Tigers Bay. As in all these incidents the origins of the disturbance were disputed, but what was clear was that the loyalists gathered at the entrance to Tigers Bay were outnumbered. Branagh was in the front line of the riot, close to the last lamp-post before Duncairn Gardens, a nearly empty thoroughfare of boarded-up shops and houses, a ghost street marking the border between the two rival areas. At the height of the fighting, when to the loyalists it looked as though republicans were about to invade Tigers Bay, someone from the UYM handed Branagh a pipe-bomb. Holding it at head height he tried to throw the device in the direction of the nationalist mob but it exploded, killing him almost instantly. (The Tigers Bay UDA claims that Branagh died after picking up a pipe-bomb thrown from the nationalist side, perpetuating the widely held belief in the area that he was killed defending Tigers Bay.)

Glen Branagh was still at primary school when the UDA

declared its ceasefire seven years earlier. His death not only provided the North Belfast UDA with a new icon to rally around, but also underlined the essential design fault in the Good Friday Agreement, that is that its architects failed to address the problem of on-going sectarian attitudes, especially among the young working class and underclass. In the middle of Tigers Bay a mural is dedicated to Glen Branagh's memory. Poppy wreaths are laid every Remembrance Sunday at the giant portrait of the young man in the baseball cap as well as at the lamp-post in North Queen Street, the exact spot where he fell. The mural is not just a memorial to a dead UYM volunteer, it is also a monument, just like the twenty-six peace walls in the city, to the failure of politicians to provide an antidote to the virus of sectarianism. Glen Branagh should have been a child of the peace process but he died following the path of men who spent their time, post-ceasefire, legitimizing what they had done in the past.

The new foot-soldiers springing up at all the interfaces of North and West Belfast were a very different breed from the 'army' that emerged at the Troubles' genesis. Rather than resembling the Tartan gangs, the young men who hero-worshipped Johnny Adair and his crew adopted the sub-culture of the black North American gangsta rappers. They wore chunky garish gold jewellery; they consumed and sold drugs, including cocaine. They were fascinated with guns, particularly the AK47 and the Israeli Uzi, and they revelled in their reputation for violence and cruelty. And yet, despite the drug-dealing, the machismo and the swagger, these young men saw themselves as the defenders of their community.

Beyond the claustrophobic confines of Tigers Bay, where there was (and is) undoubted support for the UDA, the majority of the Protestant community begged to differ. The prevalence of the gangsta culture both among the UYM and its elders in the UDA led to a social disjunction between the organization and the rest of their society. The lifestyles of some young UDA commanders, financed mainly through drugs, contrasted sharply with the make-do hand-to-mouth existence of thousands of others in grim loyalist housing estates across Northern Ireland. In South Belfast, for instance, a gang of three UDA local commanders came under round-the-clock surveillance from police officers on the Lisburn Road. The undercover cops noted that their targets enjoyed a lifestyle far beyond the means of ordinary Protestants. Their daily routine reflected that privileged life gained from paramilitarism and drug-dealing. It started with a work-out at a south city gym frequented by urban professionals working in law, the media, academia and so on. After the gym they would treat themselves to a massage and then on to a Turkish barber for an expensive haircut and shave. At lunchtime they would frequent many of the best restaurants on the Lisburn Road, a prosperous South Belfast thoroughfare encompassing the university district, student bedsit land, the City Hospital and ultimately the well-to-do suburbs relatively untouched by three decades of conflict. 'These guys were better off than we were,' said one of the officers involved in the surveillance. 'They lived a lifestyle that we couldn't afford, let alone the average Prod earning a few bob.'

What had happened in Rathcoole, one of the largest public housing estates in western Europe, overlooking Belfast Lough above the East Antrim shoreline, was a classic example of para-military exploitation and degeneration. The UDA was the domi-nant terror group in the area, running extortion rackets, money-lending schemes and selling drugs, and making the occa-sional strike against soft nationalist targets. Heading up this mini-republic of fear was John Gregg, a man with an awesome reputation for violence and sectarian bigotry. Gregg, or 'Grugg' as he was known to his comrades, exuded menace. He lived off his reputa-tion as the man that almost killed Gerry Adams. Aware of his infamy, down his back Gregg had a tattoo of the Grim Reaper. Even his underlings feared his wrath. Gregg was ruthless with his local units and was renowned for kneecapping anyone in the movement who transgressed him. To challenge Gregg's hegemony, either inside or outside the UDA, was a dangerous enterprise. But one man was prepared to take him on.

It was somehow fitting that the man willing to stand up to Gregg, who admired Hitler and had forged links with English neo-Nazis, was the grandson of a socialist who had been persecuted by the Nazis. Mark Langhammer's grandfather, Franz, was forced to leave his native Czechoslovakia when the Nazis invaded in 1938. He had been a socialist councillor in the Sudetenland and would have been a candidate for the concentration camp if captured. The printer went into exile, eventually settling in Northern Ireland because of the Province's then thriving textile industry. Two generations later his grandson would also pay a heavy price for his socialist convictions.

Mark Langhammer has represented the people of Rathcoole on Newtownabbey Borough Council since the late 1980s. The 44-year-old Independent Labour councillor is one of only four left-wing public representatives in Northern Ireland. As the new century began Langhammer was becoming increasingly concerned about the growing alienation and social disjunction within the Protestant working class. He believed (and still does) that the greatest failure of the Good Friday Agreement was that it left this segment of the working class behind. In the past, he argued, Protestant areas were shored up by two pillars – the churches and the trade union movement. With both these institutions in decline communities such as Rathcoole had simply atomized. A new underclass had emerged which had become, in many instances, the tools of fascism. Drug-dealing, rackets, and the sale of illegal tobacco and stolen alcohol were rife on the estate and by and large under the control of Gregg's brigade. Yet, incredibly in Langhammer's eyes, there was no permanent police station or presence in the area. In late 2001 Langhammer petitioned the now re-formed PSNI to establish a police clinic in Rathcoole where locals could articulate their concerns about the cult of criminality.

Eventually the police succumbed to his demands and in late summer 2002 a site was found, a community centre on the estate. The establishment of a permanent police presence was a threat to Gregg's empire. At the end of August the UDA reacted by painting the words 'Touts in here' outside the community centre. Both literally and symbolically, the writing was on the wall for Langhammer and his police clinic project.

On 4 September Gregg upped the ante. In the early hours of

the morning Langhammer was wakened by a loud explosion outside his home in Whiteabbey, on the northern outskirts of Belfast. A UDA team had detonated a pipe-bomb under the councillor's Ford Mondeo while he and his family were sleeping. The message was crude but effective: abandon your plans for a police presence in Rathcoole. The bomb attack was both pointed and poignant. In the days leading up to the explosion Langhammer had been preparing to commemorate his cousin who was killed in the terrorist attacks on the twin towers of the World Trade Center; Michael Stewart had been on the ninety-first floor of the North Tower when the first hijacked jet slammed into it. The two men had grown up together, played in the same football team and belonged to the same Boys Brigade unit and, in Michael's honour, Langhammer had persuaded Newtownabbey Borough Council to dedicate a park bench to his memory. It seemed cruelly appropriate that the socialist councillor, whose grandfather fled from the Nazis and whose cousin died at the hands of Islamo-fascists, would himself come under fire from fascists at home.

Throughout 2001 Gregg's UDA brigade and its neighbours in North Belfast were also engaged in a series of sectarian murders. On the night of 11 April young Rathcoole loyalists under Gregg's command had kicked and beaten to death a Protestant man, mistaking him for a Catholic. Forty-nine-year-old Trevor Lowry died in intensive care two days after being assaulted by the gang at Harmin Parade in Glengormley. He was a quiet harmless man who spent a lot of time visiting the nearby Belfast Zoo on the slopes of the Cavehill mountain. A memorial plaque, which includes a tribute to his love of animals, still stands near the zoo's elephant house. No one claimed responsibility for Trevor Lowry's brutal death but PSNI officers pointed to young UDA men who, having beaten him viciously, escaped across fields towards the Rathcoole estate.

The flag of convenience, the Red Hand Defenders, was flown twice in July 2001. For the first time it was 'stolen' by the UVF in Antrim town when it murdered 19-year-old Catholic Ciaran Cummings, early on 4 July as he waited at a roundabout for a lift to work. The UVF killed him in retaliation for the murder of a

Progressive Unionist Party activist in Antrim the previous year. At the end of the month the mysterious RHD emerged once more after another teenager, Gavin Brett, was shot from a passing car while standing with friends near St Enda's GAA club on the Hightown Road at Glengormley. Gavin was a Protestant but was shot because the UDA team sent out to 'stiff a Taig' assumed that the group of friends standing outside the GAA club were all Catholics. This time the real culprit was the North Belfast UDA which, under Andre Shoukri, had decided to raise the stakes in the sectarian territorial battles raging along three interfaces in the north of the city during the summer.

The RHD label was deployed again on three occasions in the autumn and winter, both by the UDA and the LVF. On 28 September the LVF, under the command of Robin 'Billy' King, the terror group's last leader in the H-blocks, shot dead the *Sunday World* journalist Martin O'Hagan close to his home in Lurgan, County Armagh. The gun had been supplied by the loyalist family from Ballysillan which had control over a number of LVF weapons. This same family was behind the murder of Catholic drug dealer and career criminal Frankie Mulholland, who was shot on 3 December while sitting in his car outside a petrol station in the upper Crumlin Road. The motive was not just sectarian, however. His killers had previously been 'business partners', using Mulholland to distribute drugs brought into Northern Ireland by loyalists within Catholic areas of Belfast. They believed Mulholland had double-crossed them in a major drug deal and consequently they took their revenge.

In general republicans were loath to react to the UDA's new offensive. The INLA however, historically the most unstable republican faction, carried out a retaliatory strike, albeit on a soft and available loyalist target. On 30 October INLA had shot dead 30-year-old Charles Foliard outside his Catholic girlfriend's home in Strabane, a County Derry border town where the republican terror group has traditionally been strong. In fact Foliard had left the UDA several years earlier and turned his back on loyalist violence.

The UDA's final victim of the year, once again under the mask of the RHD, was its former quarter-master in Highfield who had provided the guns that were used to shoot Pat Finucane. Billy Stobie had been a long-time RUC Special Branch agent and on the night Finucane was murdered telephoned his handlers to tell them 'the team's out'. Stobie had no direct knowledge about who the 'team' was about to kill but it is undoubtedly clear that his handlers failed to act on the information and to alert their colleagues in both Special Branch and CID around North Belfast, actions that could have saved the solicitor's life. Stobie signed his own death warrant in the spring of 2002 when he appeared on Ulster Television and seemed to back the Finucane family's decade-long campaign for a public inquiry into the murder. To the UDA this was tantamount to treason. The 51-year-old loyalist was taking his dog for his early-morning run outside his home on Forthriver Road in the Glencairn estate when his killers struck. The murder conveniently removed a key figure in the Finucane saga, who was due to be interviewed by the Stevens inquiry team and had offered himself up as potential witness in any future inquiry.

Like the IRA informer Eamon Collins, Stobie was the victim of his own misjudgement. He could have been moved from the greater Shankill and relocated in England if he wished but fool-ishly decided to stay in Belfast, believing his high profile would protect him from the UDA. 'Billy Stobie could have stayed in the Shankill and been left alone had he not spoken out on Ulster Television and backed the public inquiry. He betrayed his comrades by doing that and for that reason he paid for his treason,' said one unapologetic West Belfast UDA figure after Stobie was killed.

Stobie's death, and the appearance of Ken Barrett on a BBC *Panorama* documentary, discussing his role in shooting Finucane, reignited the collusion controversy. Barrett did not fire the fatal shots that killed the Belfast solicitor. In fact, the killer was another prominent UDA figure who would play a central role in the new feud brewing under the surface of the organization. For some time before the *Panorama* revelations Ken Barrett had been in hiding in England under the protection of the Stevens inquiry detectives. He was not tracked down by the BBC, but rather handed to them via the Stevens team. Barrett, like Stobie, had also been providing information to Special Branch about the UDA from the late 1980s.

In response to demands for a public inquiry, the UDA in West Belfast hinted that it had information that could blow the cover of one of the British state's most important agents inside the IRA. Both it and the UVF believed – incorrectly as it turned out – that they knew the identity of the British agent codenamed Stakeknife, involved in the murky incident in 1987 when the UDA decided to kill a senior IRA member living in the Springhill estate, upon whom it and the UVF had been spying, but was steered instead towards ex-IRA pensioner Victor Notorantonio, by its West Belfast intelligence officer, Brian Nelson, who was working on the instructions of his army handlers.

In 2003, when former FRU soldier 'Martin Ingram' (as the army whistleblower called himself) said Stakeknife, the ex-head of the IRA's internal security squad, was none other than Freddie Scappaticci, the UDA and UVF men who had been involved in the Springhill plot were flummoxed. Scappaticci had never lived in Springhill and, at the time of the loyalist surveillance, was across the border in Dundalk. The loyalists have since concluded that their original target, saved by Brian Nelson, was an agent working in the highest ranks of the IRA's Belfast brigade.

Throughout the summer of 2001 there were widespread sectarian clashes in North Belfast ranging from the Protestant Twaddel Avenue/Ardoyne Road to Tigers Bay/Whitewell Road. Rioting broke out on the Twelfth (of July – loyalism's most sacred day) at Ardoyne shops after a small number of Orange bands was allowed to march up the Crumlin Road. Among those caught on camera standing beside teenage rioters on the Ardoyne side was Sean Kelly, the Shankill bomber, a sight that incensed everyone in the loyalist stronghold. Over the next eighteen days there were several incursions into Protestant areas including a mass republican attack on Twaddel Avenue in which houses were vandalized, windows smashed and cars destroyed. By 27 July shots were being exchanged across the interfaces, with the UDA firing at Ardoyne and the INLA returning fire, directing its shots at the smaller loyalist Glenbryn estate.

Glenbryn had become one of the most dangerous and contentious zones anywhere in Northern Ireland. Local loyalists believed the sorties from Ardoyne were designed to force the remaining Protestants living there to move out and, as they had done in the nearby Torrens area, allow nationalists to take over the territory. However, Catholics in Ardoyne saw a new factor at work. The nationalists believed the main reason for the escalation of trouble on the Ardoyne Road, which links the large nationalist area with Glenbryn, was the loyalist feud. In response to the mass expulsions from the lower Shankill in the previous summer, the UVF expelled a smaller number of UDA-aligned families in the middle and upper parts of the road. A group of these families, some with direct 'C' company connections, were rehoused in Glenbryn.

Ardoyne residents labelled these imports 'the new kids on the block' and blamed them for stoking up tensions. The Glenbryn UDA was an adjunct of 'C' company and took its orders directly from the lower Shankill. One of the first things the 'new kids on the block' did when they arrived in Glenbryn was to festoon their part of the Ardoyne Road with UDA flags and posters of Johnny Adair. This handful of loyalist extremists would not take any apparent aggression from Ardoyne lying down, but through their obstinacy they would create a trap for themselves which the republican movement would exploit around the world.

23. Terror at Holy Cross

The trigger for the blockade outside Holy Cross Girls' Primary School was an incident on 19 June 2001. Shortly after twenty past two in the afternoon three young men were putting up UDA and UFF flags on the upper Ardoyne Road close to the school when a white Vauxhall Cavalier car raced out of Ardoyne and came towards them at top speed. The car collided with their ladder and the man who had been hanging one of the flags on a lamp-post crashed to the ground. The loyalists retaliated by taking the two broken ends of the ladder and smashing the car windscreen. The republicans from Ardoyne then chased the Protestant trio through Glenbryn Parade, where they were confronted by other loyalist residents. After a brief fist-fight the republicans got back into their vehicle and escaped to the Crumlin Road via Wheatfield Gardens. The skirmish had brought residents from both sides of the Ardoyne Road on to the streets and within minutes a danger-ous stand-off emerged between the two communities. It took eight police Land Rovers to separate the growing crowds on either side of the dividing line. But the police operation was bungled because their lines were pushed so far up the Ardoyne Road that it left one Protestant street, Glenbryn Park, surrounded by nation-alists. At this stage the houses in Glenbryn Park came under attack.

Unfortunately the row, and subsequent mini-riot, took place at school closing time, leaving the children inside Holy Cross cut off from their parents and families, given that the school is located on the Protestant side of the invisible line dividing the Ardoyne Road. It is a matter of deep dispute why a flare-up between young loyalists and republicans led, by the end of the day, to a blockade outside Holy Cross. From all the available evidence it seems that it was not the UDA's original intention to bar the children access to their school along the Ardoyne Road. Instead it appears that once the stand-off began some of the main organizers of the loyalist protest decided to use the location of Holy Cross as a weapon in their fight to secure their territory. By the end of June, for instance, Jim Potts (whose brother, Tommy, was filmed firing on the Rex Bar the previous summer at the start of the feud with the UVF) was calling for a permanent peace line to cut the Ardoyne Road in two, ensuring no encroachment by nationalists into Glenbryn. But in an interview with one of the authors in the UDA's York Road headquarters he also suggested that the peace-line gate could be opened every weekday morning and afternoon to allow the pupils to get to and from Holy Cross.

Tensions along the Ardoyne Road reached boiling point the day after the flags incident when Billy Hutchinson arrived with a view to defusing the situation. He even crossed the line to attempt to negotiate with Sinn Féin's Gerry Kelly. Just as things were calming down Hutchinson was approached by two men, one of whom was Paul Carson, the leader of the INLA in Ardoyne. In front of the television cameras Carson lunged at Hutchinson and tried to head-butt the PUP Assembly man. Hutchinson managed to dive sidewards to avoid the blow. Only the end of the school year provided a respite, albeit a temporary one, for the children caught in the middle of the maelstrom. A failure to reach agreement between the Glenbryn residents and the Holy Cross girls' families and the school's board of governors ensured that when the children went back up the Ardoyne Road on 1 September the blockade would begin again.

Over the ensuing three months the loyalists living in Glenbryn, supported by the UDA's muscle, would attempt to prevent young girls, aged as young as four, from going to school. The loyalist protesters had to contend with a gauntlet of heavily armed and armoured RUC officers who, dressed all in black with their faces covered by balaclavas up to their eye-lines, resembled Ninja warriors. Hundreds of British troops from Scottish and Welsh regiments were also drafted in to back up the police. The security forces were expecting a violent response to Chief Constable Sir Ronnie Flanagan's promise that his officers would ensure the girls got to school. 'C' company would fulfil that promise.

On day one of the new term a young drug dealer from the

upper Shankill paid a debt to 'C' company in an unusual and deadly way. He owed the lower Shankill five hundred pounds for drugs he had borrowed and then sold on to his friends. The dealer faced two options: be shot or carry out an attack for the UDA. He took the latter option and 'C' company ordered him to go to the Glenbryn protest and, as the Holy Cross children walked up the Ardoyne Road under the protection of RUC riot shields, he was to hurl a pipe-bomb at police lines. The bomb exploded, seriously injuring a young Welsh soldier who spent several weeks in intensive care, at one stage almost dying, before recovering from his wounds. 'C' company activists were then involved in orchestrating a riot with the RUC 'Ninjas' that led to almost a dozen Glenbryn residents being beaten or struck with plastic bullets. In some cases those injured had taken part only in peaceful protests.

The longer the stand-off continued the more desperate the loyalist tactics became, and the worse was the image they presented to the rest of the world. Chants of 'scum', threats to parents, the hurling of missiles, including balloons filled with urine, all directed towards innocent schoolchildren, were broadcast around the planet. Sinn Féin was able to exploit the Holy Cross dispute to its fullest potential. The Glenbryn protesters' behaviour, particularly those with 'C' company connections, was a propaganda gift for the republican movement, which at the time was fielding questions about what two IRA men and a Sinn Féin activist were doing in Colombia with the drug-dealing South American Marxist guerrilla group, FARC. Republicans portrayed the loyalist blockade as the twenty-first-century equivalent of the white racists in the USA's southern states blocking black schoolchildren from attending racially integrated colleges during the early 1960s. In Ardoyne murals showed terrified and screaming Holy Cross children alongside black school kids walking into class under the protection of the US national guard while being bayed at by menacing racists. The harrowing images of tearful children running past loyalist mobs diverted attention away from Sinn Féin and the IRA's difficulties in Latin America. Now the loyalists were seen as the aggressors, the nationalists once again as victims.

But the Glenbryn residents had real and understandable

grievances. They were outnumbered, under constant republican attack and fearful that they would be forced to move out so their area could be taken over by republicans. They were infuriated that, when the protest at Holy Cross became internationalized in the autumn with the arrival of foreign news crews, among those put forward to champion the Catholic children's human rights was Brendan Mailey, a convicted IRA killer, although this was probably unintentional on the republicans' part as the ex-prisoner's children attended the school. The Glenbryn loyalists also pointed to the murder the previous December of Protestant taxi-driver Trevor Kells, who had been shot dead by an unnamed republican group close to the 'border' between Glenbryn and Ardoyne and whose killers had made off towards the republican stronghold. All these factors had raised the collective blood of Glenbryn to boiling point.

Their ire was further fuelled by the killing, during the Holy Cross dispute, of a Protestant teenager in White City, another sectarian interface area in North Belfast. Thomas McDonald was run down by Alison McKeown after he allegedly threw a brick at her car while she was driving past the loyalist White City to the Catholic Whitewell Road. The RUC expected the UDA to avenge the young man's death. A few weeks later it shot dead Catholic postman Danny McColgan who was a soft target since he worked inside Rathcoole sorting office. (In a tasteless postscript to the McColgan murder loyalists daubed 'Postman Splat' on a wall along the Shore Road not far from the young man's home.)

At the height of the terror outside Holy Cross, police leave throughout the entire greater Belfast region was cancelled and every available officer was forced to work twelve-hour shifts. There were now more British soldiers deployed on the streets of North Belfast than even during the year leading to the ceasefires of 1994. The dispute also drained the resources of an already hard-pressed police force faced with dwindling numbers due to retirement and high levels of sickness, the latter a *de facto* protest against Chris Patten's policing reforms. Policing Ardoyne and ensuring the children were able to attend their lessons was costing the taxpayer around £50,000 per day.

Holy Cross threatened to spark off a wider conflagration that could suck the paramilitaries back to 'war' and destroy the already fragile peace process. It also poisoned relations between many working-class loyalists and the police service they claimed to support. During the security operation at Holy Cross scores of Glenbryn residents lodged complaints alleging police brutality with the Police Ombudsman Nuala O'Loan. Among those beaten in the first week of rioting were a blind man and a twelve-year-old. It prompted the UDA to issue an unprecedented threat to police officers living in the city. One of Jimbo Simpson's last acts during his reign as North Belfast brigadier was to send out a chilling warning that if the 'heavy-handed RUC tactics' against loyalists continued on the Ardoyne Road, then they and their families would be targeted. The UDA in North Belfast insisted that targeting meant peaceful protests outside the doors of policemen and women who lived in Protestant parts of North Belfast. More disturbing still was the threat that if loyalists were continually beaten and abused 'the loyalist people will make their families pay the price'.

Loyalism, principally the UDA, was lashing out in all directions during the autumn–winter of 2001. 'C' company made constant threats to some of the Holy Cross parents, focusing on a number of outspoken and courageous women such as Isobel McGrann, one of the mothers who had first pointed out to the media the presence of the 'new kids on the block', the Shankill feud exiles, who were responsible for the new mood of militancy in Glenbryn. A number of women living on the lower Ardoyne Road moved themselves and their children out of the area altogether after receiving repeated warnings over the phone that they would be shot by the Red Hand Defenders. 'C' company, masquerading as the RHD, even tried to close down Holy Cross with a series of coded claims about bombs being left on school premises. In response the RUC bugged every public call box in the upper Shankill area, including a number in the Crumlin Road and Ballysillan areas. The bugging operation produced results when Gary Smyth was recorded ringing the media on behalf of the fictitious RHD claiming loyalists had left a car bomb outside Holy

Cross. He was arrested, charged with issuing terrorist threats and reunited with his old comrade Johnny Adair, in Maghaberry Prison. On top of helping to bring global opprobrium on to the entire loyalist community, 'C' company had lost another prominent figure.

Some inside the UDA watched developments on the Ardoyne Road with increasing concern. While they were sympathetic to the Protestant residents' grievances, they were politically astute enough to realize that loyalism was taking a battering in the propaganda war. The pressure on Sinn Féin and the IRA over Colombia, and previously its gun-running in Florida, had eased considerably as camera lenses were trained on the narrow ground separating Ardoyne from Glenbryn and the morally black and white narrative of baying loyalist protesters and crying Catholic schoolgirls.

The final bewildering paradox of the Holy Cross struggle, a battle that the loyalist residents could never win once children were placed in the front line, was that it was Johnny Adair who ordered the demonstrations to stop. While in Maghaberry Adair became a model prisoner, determined as he was to convince the Sentence Review Board to overturn Peter Mandelson's decision to re-imprison him after the UVF feud. Adair covered up his bulging muscles and UFF tattoos with the uniform of a prison orderly and took up a post washing windows, brushing floors and fetching hot water for fellow inmates, including Catholic criminals. Signing up to the prison's 'progressive regime', Adair avoided confrontations with Catholic and republican dissident inmates inside the Roe House complex at the top-security jail. He even began to earn himself privileges such as extra family visits, more credits to the tuck shop and telephone cards. None the less he was still regarded as a hate figure by both republicans and Catholics inside the prison.

Adair and convicted Catholic fraudster Stephen McEntee first clashed when they were both prisoners in Maghaberry. Their personal feud started over a row about cleaning up crumbs from a toaster on their wing. In his position as Roe House orderly Adair was in charge of hygiene in the communal kitchen. McEntee had just finished making toast when Adair came in and ordered the North Belfast man to tidy up after himself. The young Catholic prisoner had nursed a personal grudge against Adair ever since his girlfriend's home had been among the houses on the lower Cliftonville/lower Oldpark interface attacked by 'C' company pipe-bombs during sectarian disturbances the previous summer. He told Adair to 'fuck off' and challenged the man who had terrorized an entire population to a fist-fight. Adair declined but made a number of threats to McEntee who, in turn, warned the UDA commander that he would get him.

After his release in the spring of 2002 McEntee approached *The Sunday World* newspaper and confessed that he wanted to kill Adair. Following his threat, which many readers of the tabloid initially thought was some sort of macabre joke, the police questioned McEntee and a file was sent to the director of public prosecutions. McEntee's promise to murder Adair when the loyalist icon was released from Maghaberry proved to be genuine, if foolhardy and suicidal. He made at least two forays into the lower Shankill in the summer searching for Adair's home. On one occasion he was accosted by Adair's followers on the Shankill Road and almost beaten to death before the police arrived and the gang that had set upon him scattered. Following the beating McEntee remained defiant: 'I don't care, I'll fucking get him.'

When Adair was finally released from jail in June 2002 he had more than Stephen McEntee on his mind. His first major action was to close down the Holy Cross protest, a move prompted by a series of discussions with John White and a familiar figure from loyalism's past – Andy Tyrie. Despite being in long-term 'retirement' from the UDA, from time to time Tyrie was brought back into the organization as a political adviser and had been wheeled out of retirement during the referendum on the Good Friday Agreement. White had used Tyrie to explain to sceptics within the UDA that the Agreement reflected not only many of the core values of 'Common Sense', but also the organization's early document, 'Beyond the Religious Divide'. For all his faults in the eyes of the young militants who replaced him, and even if his military record was unimpressive, Tyrie had been a winner on the political front. He had been one of the main strategists on the UWC strike committee which had defeated the Sunningdale Agreement. Tyrie claimed that the Good Friday Agreement was a watered-down version of Sunningdale, that the All-Ireland bodies, whittled down by David Trimble's negotiating team at Castle Buildings, were a shadow of the Council of Ireland in 1974, which nationalist politicians had boasted would be the Trojan horse towards Irish unity. But Tyrie's recall in the Holy Cross dispute was merely the political gloss over a more direct and brutal directive: Johnny Adair would personally discipline anyone connected to 'C' company or the UDA who persisted in orchestrating violence on the Ardoyne Road.

On the eve of the new school term, in September 2002, Adair, White and Tyrie held talks with leading loyalists at the Glenbryn community centre. During the meeting Adair 'read the riot act' to the core protesters according to one of his closest comrades. His own brother had been jailed after one disturbance outside Holy Cross but Adair, once again under White's influence, was determined to shut down the protest some of his most loyal followers had helped to start. 'Johnny basically told them that he didn't want anything else to happen that would damage the loyalist cause,' his colleague said. 'He told them to knock it in the head and when Johnny tells you something you don't challenge him.'

His somewhat surprising intervention at Glenbryn was connected firstly to a new-found sense of political direction inside the UDA and to his own personal ambitions. Since Adair's release White had been trying to persuade him that he should stand as an independent candidate if and when new Assembly elections were called in Northern Ireland. The founder of the UFF genuinely believed that Adair, now the most famous face of Ulster loyalism, could galvanize the indifferent and alienated mass of young Protestant working-class males. For a short period between the summer and autumn of 2002 Adair was being won round to the idea that he could challenge the hated PUP for a seat in North Belfast. The notion of Johnny Adair MLA (Member of the Legislative Assembly) was a fanciful if intriguing prospect. Thousands on the Shankill and beyond blamed him for provoking the feud with the UVF and thus tearing loyalism's heartland apart. Those with no links to, or love for, loyalist paramilitaries might not have been able to do much about challenging Adair's hegemony on the streets, but in the ballot box they had repeatedly rejected the terror group's public representatives. It was the Protestant people's secret revenge.

Since the Holy Cross dispute began mainstream unionist politicians had been working behind the scenes not only to end the disgraceful scenes outside the school but to restore some political direction and unity to loyalism. Unionist political leaders who vowed never to sit down in government with what they deemed 'unreconstructed terrorists' (that is, Sinn Féin) were at the same time holding secret talks with loyalist terrorists. In October 2001 David Burnside, British Airways' former press officer and now Ulster Unionist MP for South Antrim, was exposed for holding private talks with members of the UDA Inner Council. Among those Burnside met was Jackie McDonald, the South Belfast brigadier, who was regarded as a moderating force on the Council.

We did talk to him and it was a discussion about the way things were going in the Province. We listened to his analysis and the view that Trimble had been very naïve, that like Tony Blair he had taken his eye off the ball. He [Burnside] told us unionists needed to slow down the progress that Sinn Féin was making. To be fair he did call for loyalist violence to be brought to an end but he said he understood the frustrations of people although violence was not the solution,

McDonald recalled. Under fire from nationalists who accused him of hypocrisy, Burnside defended his talks. 'I did my best to convince them that their actions were not doing anything for the unionist or loyalist cause. I gave them my political analysis and how I saw the situation at present. And I also asked them to observe a proper ceasefire and call off their violence,' he told the authors.

As Vanguard's press officer during the 1974 strike, Burnside had many encounters with the UDA and UVF members on the UWC. To be fair to him, so had his opponent inside the UUP, its leader,

David Trimble. Indeed, long after Burnside had gone to London to make a name in PR, Trimble continued to, indirectly, offer the UDA political guidance by advising Tyrie and John McMichael. Tyrie revealed that Trimble, then teaching constitutional law at Queen's University, had had a major input into the UDA's 'Common Sense' document. It was therefore no surprise that Trimble, and a small group of advisers around him, went further than Burnside in early 2002 in their contacts with the UDA. The Trimbleites proposed the establishment of a Loyalist Commission, a new, more political, version of the old CLMC, which would seek to rebuild bridges between the warring loyalist factions. More critically still, it would offer political advice and guidance to the paramilitaries. Its main aim, however, was to bring loyalist violence to a halt both within Protestant communities and along the interfaces with Catholics.

Trimble's project was entirely separate from Burnside's secret talks with the UDA leadership. The Ulster Unionist leader hoped that out of the commission would emerge serious and open loyalist decommissioning, something which the UVF and sections of the UDA had rejected since Good Friday 1998. John White immediately signed the UDA up to the body but caused friction with the UVF straight away by suggesting that the LVF also be admitted into the fold. The UVF objected to the LVF's inclusion and warned that they would play no part if the smallest loyalist grouping was brought on board. Several senior UVF commanders refused to sit on the body predicting that it was a waste of time parleying with the UDA. The same UVF leader who resigned from the post-feud negotiations was deeply sceptical about the commission's efficacy. 'I watched the way the UDA was going once Adair got out of jail again. I told the brigade staff that all we had to do was sit back and watch them as they tore each other limb from limb.'

However, the innate caution of the UVF's 'brigadier general' reigned supreme and the organization decided to send two 'military' representatives, including its Shankill battalion commander, to the inaugural meeting at a church hall in East Belfast. The Progressive Unionists, including David Ervine and Councillor

Hugh Smyth, also attended. The majority of the UDA's delegates came from brigade areas which had played little or no part in the Shankill feud, such as Jackie McDonald, Billy McFarland and East Belfast supremo, Jim Gray. John White insisted on being part of the delegation along with Adair – a duo whose presence must have stuck in the UVF/PUP group's collective craw.

One of the first results the Loyalist Commission achieved was to persuade the UDA to restore their ceasefire (effectively admitting it had broken it in the first place). The British secretary of state, Dr John Reid, who had replaced Peter Mandelson, had finally bowed to the inevitable in early June by declaring that the UDA cessation was effectively over. Yet, within a matter of weeks, Dr Reid was holding face-to-face talks with the same men he accused of returning to open sectarian warfare. The Loyalist Commission organized a meeting between the Glaswegian-born, Celtic-supporting, former communist New Labour minister at a church mission hall on the Newtownards Road. For the benefit of television cameras the UDA envoys selected to talk with the secretary of state as they strolled to the church hall together and their arrival looked like an out-take from Quentin Tarantino's *Reservoir Dogs*, where the killers walk with a casual swagger in their sharp suits, white shirts and funereal black ties. Johnny Adair led the way in a light blue tight-fitting shirt and fat-knotted Italian tie. He was followed by Andre Shoukri, who went for an open-necked shirt and a suit. Shoukri, with his slicked back hair, tall gait, Mediterranean looks and passing resemblance to the French footballer Eric Cantona, was an unlikely sex symbol not only among the ranks of female loyalist groupies, but also among many women who would never dream of dating a self-proclaimed terrorist. Among the other UDA men to press Dr Reid's flesh was Jim Gray, the floppy-haired blond East Belfast UDA brigadier who looked more like an ageing New Romantic than the leader of a terrorist empire.

The discussion was organized principally to allow the Northern Ireland secretary to allay loyalist fears about any secret deals between the British government and Sinn Féin. Early on the secretary of state disarmed the loyalists by asking if they minded if he smoked, a far cry from the politically correct health-obsessed lifestyles of London's New Labour luminaries. He then managed a joke about being a Celtic supporter amid a knot of Rangers fans. Dr Reid defended his meeting by pointing out that he had insisted from the outset that all loyalist violence had to come to a permanent and complete end; otherwise the government would not engage with loyalist political representatives.

The display of unity as Adair, Shoukri, Gray and company strolled across the Newtownards Road on that summer's afternoon was a mirage. Just as the stage-managed welcome home party that had met Adair as he walked out of Maghaberry the previous month, wearing his trademark baseball cap and designer label red and white T-shirt, had been a façade. The Inner Council had gone out of its way to portray the UDA as united and whole when Adair re-emerged from prison, and Jackie McDonald, Billy McFarland, John Gregg and Jim Grey had all been outside the Maghaberry car park to greet the mercurial loyalist commander. The rest of the Inner Council had hoped that they could now bring Adair under control and, through the Loyalist Commission, give the UDA a new coherent political direction. The old Ulster Political Research Group (UPRG) was resurrected in place of the defunct UDP. Ex-UDP councillors such as Tommy Kirkham in Rathcoole, and community workers such as Frankie Gallagher from East Belfast, a close friend of Michael Stone, were put forward as the UPRG's new faces. Sammy Duddy, the UDA's former press officer and ex-editor of *Ulster* magazine, was brought out of retirement too in order to clean up the organization's severely soiled public image. On the eve of the Twelfth, UDA veterans spoke confidently about a fresh sense of unity and co-operation between the brigades.

Duddy's re-emergence prompted the resurrection of entertaining stories about his 1970s drag act as 'Samantha'. In a series of interviews in 2002 Duddy talked openly about his past life in stockings and suspenders and even threatened to bring 'Samantha' out of retirement. His candour was in sharp contrast to his earlier attitude to anyone writing about him being a drag queen. When the New York-based author Jack Holland first exposed 'Samantha' in the late 1970s he received a thinly veiled death threat written on UDA-headed notepaper from the organization's old Gawn Street headquarters. Holland, who died in May 2004, had the warning framed in his office in Brooklyn.

Back in the 1980s Duddy had produced a booklet of poetry, *Concrete Whirlpools of the Mind*. The poems were heartfelt and strikingly devoid of any sectarian anti-Catholicism, bemoaning the effects of violence on young men drawn into the conflict. In the foreword, Andy Tyrie wrote: 'After fourteen years of bloody fighting it is refreshing to read the reflective thoughts of an Ulster poet who has had his fair share of sorrow and tragedy. He paints a sometimes depressing picture of the unwanted truth concerning our troubled times. And it is indeed a true picture.' Duddy described his collection of twenty-three poems thus: 'There is nothing sectarian about them. I am trying to get across the message that violence for the sake of violence is futile.'

Sadly Duddy's fine sentiments had no effect on his contemporaneous or future colleagues. Behind the smiles and the outward displays of comradeship there were simmering tensions, jealousies and, in Adair's case, a destructive desire for absolute power. For instance, Adair loathed Jim Gray, blaming his brigade for the torture killing of UDA assassin Geordie Legge the year before. In Adair and 'C' company's eyes Legge had credibility because of his reputation as an 'operator' – a killer, in layman's terms. He had been responsible for several sectarian murders in East Belfast before the ceasefires and had personally killed Ned McCreery. But during the peace process Legge began to speak out about the lifestyles of, and wealth accumulated by, the new UDA leadership in the east of the city.

Legge's open criticism of the leadership in East Belfast posed a dangerous threat to Gray and his empire. On the morning of 6 January 2001 Legge's body was found in a field off the Clontonacally Road near Carryduff in County Down. The 37-year-old veteran of the UDA's 1990s terror offensive had been abducted the night before while drinking in the Bunch of Grapes on the Newtownards Road, the same pub where Jim Craig had been shot dead.

The manner of Legge's death showed how desperate the East Belfast UDA was to stamp out internal criticism of their leaders: his head had been virtually severed from his torso and there were numerous stab wounds on his body. He had also been severely beaten during a captivity detectives estimate lasted at least six to eight hours. Adair never forgave the East Belfast UDA for Legge's murder.

There were other factors behind Adair's secret bid for total control of the UDA beyond a visceral and personal search for revenge. Against the wishes of the other five UDA brigadiers, Adair, along with John White, continued to solidify his alliance with the LVF. The unity between 'C' company and the smaller faction was epitomized in a new mural drawn in the lower Shankill that summer. It depicted the two emblems of the UFF and the LVF flanking the legend 'Brothers in arms' on a wall close to Adair's home in Boundary Way. The other brigadiers' suspicions about Adair's true plans were heightened when he established a new company attached to the West Belfast brigade, 'D' company, comprised of Adair followers living beyond the lower Shankill. Estimates of 'D' company's strength varied between 100 to 400 but the fact that most of its members came from North Down and the fringes of East Belfast alarmed men such as Jim Gray. They became more and more convinced that during the summer of 2002 the Adair–White axis was in the process of building a parallel organization that would eventually take over the entire UDA.

A pointed media campaign, fuelled by leaks from sources Adair had sanctioned, undermined a number of the brigadiers, in particular John 'Grugg' Gregg. In early September stories appeared in several newspapers – broadsheet and tabloid – alleging that Gregg was under death threat from his own comrades. The pretext for the briefing campaign against Gregg was a double shooting he had ordered. Three UDA men from the Woodvale area including a recently released prisoner, Geordie Courtney, had gone to Gregg's home in Rathcoole to complain about the treatment of one of their comrades who had incurred the local UDA's wrath for continuing his friendship with Joe English, the former UDP talks delegate. The UDA man had just moved into Rathcoole and was beaten up for his links with English, who remained in internal exile for speaking out against drug-dealing on the estate. Gregg was furious about the men's threatening behaviour. He complained to leading figures in the West Belfast brigade about this personal slight and claimed it had broken the standing orders of the Inner Council which stipulated that no individual member could threaten any brigadier in any part of Northern Ireland. In the last weekend in August he had the three men shot in the legs.

After the shooting there was consternation on the Shankill which, naturally, Johnny Adair sought to exploit. Internally he depicted Gregg as out of control, as someone with a ferocious and irrational temper, who had ordered scores of his own men kneecapped for the most trivial of reasons. Adair started to use words like 'thug' and 'bully boy' about a man he once regarded as a loyalist icon for coming close to killing Gerry Adams. The anti-Gregg media briefings reached the point where Adair supporters were claiming openly that the Rathcoole UDA veteran was about to be replaced as South-east Antrim brigadier. There were also reports, the origins of which could be found on the Shankill, that Jim Gray's days as East Belfast brigadier were also numbered.

White and Adair were by now acting independently of the Inner Council in their dealings with the media and the political mainstream. Adair caused a sensation just prior to the marching season when, through White, he offered to hold talks with Belfast's first Sinn Féin Lord Mayor, the recently elected Alex Maskey, to discuss how tensions could be defused along the interfaces during the summer. Adair's willingness to speak to the veteran Sinn Féin councillor was an illustration of the absurd times. Here was the loyalist leader, who had repeatedly sent murder teams out to assassinate Alex Maskey and associates such as Alan Lundy, now prepared to do what other unionists regarded as unthinkable: sit down to tea and buns with a republican Lord Mayor. To his great credit, Maskey, a man still bearing the scars of 'C' company murder attempts, immediately accepted the offer to talk, although subsequent events would tie up Adair and White in more pressing matters.

The other brigadiers were not only astonished by Adair's statement, they were outraged. Now in anti-Agreement mode, the remaining members of the Inner Council said that under no circumstances would they meet with Alex Maskey or any other Sinn Féin representative. Adair countered that with the exception of Gregg, the other brigadiers had done next to nothing to bring the 'war' to Sinn Féin doorsteps during the 1990s. His 'comrades', who had greeted him so warmly on his release from Maghaberry, began to wonder about Adair's sanity. None the less, during Inner Council meetings in early summer, only one brigadier, Jackie McDonald, was prepared to challenge the lower Shankill man's erratic and at times inexplicable behaviour. 'Jackie was the only one with the balls to stand up to him,' one UDA veteran remembered of the period prior to the new feud. 'It was Jackie who led the way in opposition to Johnny. Without McDonald, Adair would have got his own way entirely.'

Yet the incident that detonated the second loyalist feud in less than two years came as a result of the UVF: it was the UVF's revenge on Adair and all the others they blamed for the 2000 feud on the Shankill that unexpectedly led to the vicious internal war for control of the UDA. Despite the uneasy truce between the UVF and the UDA, the UVF insisted that its war against the LVF was far from over. The UVF refused point-blank to allow the LVF to join the mediation process that had kept the peace between the two bigger loyalist organizations. The process had worked so well that both larger groups had gone to extraordinary lengths to prevent another shooting war on the Shankill. In mid-May 2001 the UVF had even kneecapped one of its members who had left a pipe-bomb at the home of a UDA man he held responsible for much of the violence outside the Rex during the so-called 'Loyalist Day of Culture' the previous August. Although the bomb failed to kill or injure anyone at the house in Snugville Street off the Shankill Road, 'C' company vowed to retaliate unless the UVF disciplined its 'volunteer'. The UVF was put in a difficult position as its man had planted the pipe-bomb without the sanction of an organization that prided itself on its centralism and military-style code of conduct. They were left with little choice but to shoot their man in the leg to placate 'C' company and stave off any danger of a fresh round of feuding.

However, as far as the UVF was concerned, if the LVF was brought into the mediation procedures, all bets were definitely off. In March 2001 the UVF's satellite organization in North Down, the Red Hand Commando, shot dead 34-year-old Adrian Porter at Conlig, near Bangor in County Down. Porter had been a close friend of the Fultons in Portadown and appeared with Johnny Adair and company at their infamous march to Drumcree hill in 2000. He was also the titular head of the LVF in the North Down region and a prime target for the UVF/RHC, who had blamed Porter for a booby-trap bomb attack in Bangor on a van belonging to Progressive Unionist Party member Sandy Rice, which had left him crippled. The RHC chose a former Royal Marine to carry out the Porter assassination. The ex-soldier riddled Porter's home in Breezemount Park with automatic gunfire giving the LVF man little chance of survival. The same assassin was selected to take out another LVF-aligned figure in nearby East Belfast. This murder was particularly clinically executed. On 13 September 35-year-old LVF brigadier Stephen Warnock was sitting in his BMW car outside Regents House Grammar School in Newtownards; his three-year-old daughter was sitting in the back. A motorbike pulled up alongside the vehicle and the pillion passenger sprayed Warnock with bullets. Warnock owed a North Down businessman £150,000 from a drugs deal, but had refused to pay up, so the businessman had hired in the RHC's top assassin in the region. Although Warnock's daughter miraculously escaped injury, she had to be taken to hospital suffering from severe shock.

Instantly Adair saw an opportunity to exploit the confusion regarding Warnock's death, for which neither the RHC nor the UVF was admitting responsibility. Twenty-four hours after the murder Adair went to the Warnock family home in the Gransha area of East Belfast, close to where Stephen Warnock had been murdered. He managed to convince Warnock's colleagues in the

LVF, and their satellites in North Down's drug-dealing fraternity, that Jim Gray's brigade had carried out the killing, assuring them that 'C' company had intelligence that the East Belfast UDA was responsible. Within hours of the meeting friends of Warnock took what they believed was direct revenge for the killing. After the UDA brigadier had paid his respects to the Warnock family a lone gunman approached Gray and shot him straight through the face as he sat in his car. Incredibly, Gray survived the shooting, although surgeons had to work for more than twelve hours to save his tongue and rebuild his shattered face.

The other five brigadiers were no longer in doubt about Adair's intent. Gray had hardly been anaesthetized when the UDA found out that, although Warnock's gang had carried out the murder bid, it had been acting at Adair's prompting. They looked at one another and wondered who would be next. Although divided geographically, and in the case of Gregg and McDonald, temperamentally (McDonald being a more moderate voice on the Inner Council), the four brigadiers knew they had to band together if they were going to survive. The attempted murder of Gray, and the PR onslaught on Gregg, were mere precursors to a *coup d'état*.

In a sense they were reacting to the perennial problem that afflicted the UDA – the cult of the personality. Throughout its history there has been the recurring theme of a charismatic, often militant, figure emerging and becoming the personification of the UDA. Tommy Herron, Andy Tyrie, John McMichael, Jim Craig and Tucker Lyttle – all in their different and inimitable ways were personalities that became almost too big for others in the organization to bear. Each time one of these figures was removed – either killed or, in Tyrie's case, 'retired' – collective leadership was restored. By the late summer of 2002 Johnny Adair had come to believe that he was the godhead of the UDA, the physical embodiment of its killing machine, the UFF. He drew legitimacy for this claim from the man he perceived as the UFF's founder, John White. In a telling interview with one of the authors just before his and White's official expulsion from the UDA, Adair identified himself and his mentor as the alpha and omega of UDA terrorism.

'In the 1970s the Catholics of Belfast couldn't sleep soundly in their beds because of John White,' Adair said. And he emphasized that he had followed in White's footsteps, turning himself into a nightmare for the entire Catholic population.

24. The Final Conflict

The final straw for Adair's fellow brigadiers was the contempt with which he treated a crisis meeting in Sandy Row held shortly after Warnock's death and Gray's shooting. At this stage there were still some voices on the Inner Council which were reluctant to act against the lower Shankill team. Adair was summoned to the talks to explain himself. He arrived with a huge entourage of 'C' company hardmen who blocked off either end of Sandy Row to ensure no hit teams could arrive to assassinate their leader. The meeting failed to produce a satisfactory outcome, with Adair protesting his innocence regarding Gray and seeking to influence Jackie McDonald and the others by warning them not to strike back at the LVF. McDonald's anger deepened when he discovered that Adair later met the LVF in another part of Belfast and relayed to them what had gone on in the internal UDA meeting. McDonald had reached the end of the line. 'There is no way back for him,' he told the authors, 'not if he came on bended knee.'

In October 2002, following a meeting in Sandy Row, the five brigadiers decided to expel both White and Adair from the UDA. The duo were informed of their expulsion in a fax sent to the Big Brother house, the 'C' company-run 'community centre'. White had invited in the cameras and as the statement was printed, Adair ripped it from the machine and tore it up in front of the media.

The lower Shankill leadership opted to tough out the crisis and adopted a casually indifferent attitude to the expulsion order. Banners were painted and strung up across the lower end of the Shankill Road: 'West Belfast UDA – business as usual'. Adair's followers were holed up inside the lower Shankill once more. They gathered in the Big Brother house every morning for tea, coffee and a cholesterol special – a traditional Ulster fry served up by Maureen Miller, a long-time 'C' company devotee. The atmosphere resembled that of a bunker in wartime, with Adair directing operations and holding private talks in quiet corners with men from other parts of Belfast who had snippets of information about the intentions of his new enemies.

From mid-October until Christmas the feud that had been brewing inside the UDA since Adair's release was no more than a tense stand-off. On the Taughmonagh estate in South Belfast Jackie McDonald's men went to extraordinary lengths to protect themselves from 'C' company. The Taughmonagh UDA even deployed an air-raid siren which would be set off in the event of 'foreign' cars being spotted driving around the estate. Adair's men launched a number of gun attacks against Sammy Duddy's home in Rathcoole, during one of which they shot dead his pet Chihuahua. On the other side, John White appeared to be the most vulnerable target given that he was still living in his luxury home outside Carrickfergus, right on the fringes of 'Grugg' Gregg's territory. The stresses and pressures of siding with Adair had taken their toll on his private life. Unable to cope any longer with yet another feud, White's wife had taken their children and fled. And the former UDP chairman also had to abandon one of his beloved pets, a Vietnamese pot-bellied pig he had bought for his children.

Like the dark lord Sauron, Adair stalked about his private kingdom of Mordor, growing increasingly paranoid and suspicious about whom he could trust in his dark little kingdom. His doubts about key figures in the Lower Shankill led to a second round of 'cleansing', with six families forced out of the estate at gunpoint. They even included his old pal Winky Dodds, his wife Maureen (who had worked for UDA Prisoners Welfare) and their entire family. Despite having suffered a stroke earlier in the year, Winky was cast into the ranks of Adair's unforgiven. Adair had been incensed over the desertion of Alan McClean, Winky's cousin and a 'C' company veteran, who had taken off with a considerable portion of the lower Shankill's war chest and handed it over to the North Belfast brigade. When Dodds expressed doubts about going on the offensive, and Adair learned that he continued in contact with McClean, Mad Dog acted against his old comrade.

Further up the Shankill 'A' and 'B' companies showed no

willingness to take on the rest of the UDA either. They did, however, turn out for an impressive Remembrance Sunday march up the Shankill Road, which was as much about demonstrating the strength of Adair's faction as it was about commemorating Britain's war dead. Around 300 to 400 of Adair's allies from all over Northern Ireland turned up at the lower Shankill, including a number of leading figures from Woodvale and Highfield. Adair was not fooled by 'A' and 'B' companies' attendance at the Poppy Day rally. Cynical as ever, he later quipped: 'They've sat on the fence so long they've got splinters right up their arses.' For once, however, the Highfield and Woodvale UDA companies would prove Adair wrong, although in a manner he could never have imagined.

'C' company's plans for total domination sustained another severe blow just before Christmas when the LVF announced that it would take no part in any internal UDA feud. By this time the LVF was a weakened and fragmented organization having lost some of its key militants either at the end of UVF gun barrels or in a series of arrests in Northern Ireland and England. Gary Fulton was in an English jail, his cousin Swinger had killed himself in prison and the leadership had switched from Portadown to Lurgan, where Robin 'Billy' King was unenthusiastic about taking on the likes of the South Belfast UDA on top of having to contend with the ever present UVF threat. Moreover, the LVF had come to the conclusion that Jim Gray's UDA brigade had played no part in the Stephen Warnock killing. The joint UDA–LVF mural Adair had ordered for a lower Shankill wall contained a hollow and meaningless message. One of the 'brothers in arms' had deserted the other in his hour of need.

The glue holding together 'C' company, and its satellite 'D' company, was a toxic compound of old loyalty to Adair and greed. The lower Shankill controlled large amounts of cash and drugs with some unit/team commanders earning up to £60,000 per week. Adair had been careful to nurture some of the most militant of the UYM. He built up a praetorian guard of young men in their early twenties, many of whom were primary school pupils when their hero was directing the UDA's terrorism across

Northern Ireland in the early 1990s. His new assassins, the third generation, included Alan 'Bucky' McCullough, whose father, William, had been shot dead by the INLA in 1981. The 21-year-old looked upon Adair as a father figure and was one of the few prepared to follow his leader to the bitter end. The old cadre that remained with Adair also included the two Millar brothers, Herbie and Sham, a duo he could always rely upon. He hoped he could also rely on William Mo Courtney, a veteran of the organization and one of the most fearsome UDA figures in the lower Shankill, who had, among other things, been questioned about Pat Finucane's murder, and had thrown himself into the front line in the clashes with the UVF outside the Rex Bar two years earlier.

During the week before Christmas Adair made a number of lightning visits to loyalist pubs in North Belfast, walking into bars with the swagger of a gun-fighter entering a Western saloon looking for trouble. It was a characteristically brazen stunt by the man who some were convinced really did have nine lives. As the feud reduced to a series of half-hearted gun attacks and attempted abductions, Johnny Adair decided to throw a party for local children. On the eve of the bash he gave one of the authors what was to be his first and last interview during the feud. He arrived at the Big Brother house wearing a black Diesel sweatshirt and black gym shorts. Despite the bone-chilling December, Adair was sweating profusely: he had just finished his early-morning muscle-building work-out. Inside a festive Big Brother house, festooned with tinsel, multi-coloured lights, mini-Christmas trees and messages of peace and goodwill to all men, Adair seemed oblivious to the death threats springing up across the walls of other loyalist redoubts beyond the Shankill. One warning, directly from Gregg, read: 'Daft dog and White beware. The Reaper is coming for you.'

'They're just criminals, extortionists and bully boys who, when the Troubles were at their height, did nothing to bring the war to republicans,' Adair shouted, bringing his enormous hands down on a table laden with plates of food, tea cups and sauce bottles.

He then vowed that the Adairs would have a normal family Christmas: 'I am not going anywhere. The IRA and INLA tried to kill me. I survived fifteen republican murder bids and have bullet fragments in my head and side. So I'm hardly worried about a couple of bully boys who sat on their hands and did nothing when loyalists from the West Belfast brigade were taking the war to the IRA.' At this, a gaggle of young men in tracksuits, baseball caps and the short, black woollen caps known as monkey hats cheered.

'Grugg' had promised that Adair would be dead for Christmas. 'If I was to wait for these people to do anything I would die of old age,' Adair said. Cue more whoops and sniggers from his acolytes. With the light from golden tinsel reflecting on his bald head, he added, after sipping a mug of tea:'And no, I'm not playing Daddy Christmas tomorrow. I'll just be giving out the presents. I won't be dressing up.'

Surrounded by fawning supporters, including Mo Courtney, who guarded the door to the Big Brother house, Adair seemed confident, almost cocky. There would be no compromise with the UDA leadership, he said. It was a clash of wills, a fight to the death. He also repeated that he had been prepared to decommission UDA weapons in order to shore up David Trimble's position within unionism and put pressure on the IRA to follow suit. 'It was the West Belfast brigade who were willing to decommission, yet it was the other brigadiers, the so-called peace makers, who were the ones that opposed that move. I am not the big bad wolf of the peace process.' During the interview he also confirmed that it was he who had personally persuaded the militants at Glenbryn to call off their protests outside Holy Cross. He did not, of course, elaborate on the manner of his persuasion.

Among those cheering and laughing at Adair's every word were men from Holywood and Bangor ('D' company), as well as Ian Truesdale, a North Belfast businessman who had thrown in his lot with the 'C' company brigadier. The encounter with Adair ended when two PSNI cars pulled up at the end of Boundary Way. They had come to inform Truesdale that his house and his wife's Crumlin Road hairdressing business had just been shot up by the North Belfast UDA. As he sat on Adair's right hand, Truesdale hardly imagined that within days one of the first of

'C' company's serious actions in the new feud would tragically affect his own family.

From the outset of his war with his former allies, 'C' company team commanders were under severe pressure from Adair to 'get results'. One of those still loyal to him recalled Adair's attitude once he and White had been expelled. 'Johnny would ring you up or call at your door at all hours of the day. He kept saying, 'We need a result, we need a result.' It was like the old days again. He was relentless. He couldn't sit still.'

'C' company got its result on Boxing Night, their victim a young man with no connections to the UDA or any other loyalist faction. Jonathan Stewart, whose only crime was to be the nephew of one of Adair's foes, Alan McClean, was shot dead at a house party in Manor Street as he was standing in the kitchen drinking with another man. The lower Oldpark UDA had got wind that Stewart was at a party in their area and believed, mistakenly, that he was there to spy for the rival faction. A lone gunman wearing a Puffa jacket, the hood pulled up to conceal his face, burst into the house, ran towards the kitchen and shot the 22-year-old man dead in front of his girlfriend, Natalie Truesdale. The couple's love spanned the murderous divide within the UDA and now her fiancé had paid the ultimate price.

Ian Truesdale, the man sitting on Adair's right hand in the Big Brother house the day before the children's Christmas party, was Natalie's father, and her mother had been shot during the attack on her hair salon. Also among those supporting Adair when he gave his tough-talking interview was 23-year-old Wayne Dowie, the man later charged with killing Truesdale's future son-in-law.

Alan McClean's wife, Maureen, was the first one to speak out against 'C' company for slaying her nephew. Clutching a photograph of Jonathan and Natalie taken during a holiday in Tenerife two months earlier, she condemned Adair's men as 'scumbags and cowards'. She denied that Jonathan Stewart had anything to do with loyalism. 'He told Natalie he wanted nothing to do with it. He wanted to keep well out of that kind of thing.'

The murder caused widespread outrage in North and West Belfast and was seized upon by the mainstream UDA as evidence of 'C' company's callous irrationality. After Boxing Day there was little prospect of mediation between the warring factions. Sammy Duddy, a spokesman for the Ulster Political Research Group, the body allied to the anti-Adair UDA leadership, said the murder made it impossible for dialogue to start, adding:

There is no appetite to talk to these people especially after what happened on Friday morning. This young lad had no links with any paramilitary group. He wouldn't even have joined the Boys Brigade. He just happened to be in the wrong place at the wrong time. They singled him out simply because of who his uncle is. His uncle is hated by 'C' company because he would not support Johnny Adair.

Adair's men had crossed the line. There was indeed no turning back.

In the midst of the feud Adair briefly turned his attentions to the man who had publicly sworn to kill him, the Catholic fraud-ster Stephen McEntee. 'C' company spotters had come across McEntee drinking inside several city centre pubs in December. When they got word that he was enjoying a beer in the Morning Star, a popular pub in Pottingers Entry, one of the oldest streets in central Belfast, they decided to act. While McEntee was supping his pint a man came into the bar wearing white gloves and a baseball cap pulled down over his face. McEntee remembered that the man stared straight at him for a few seconds and then went outside. Rather than heed the obvious warning, McEntee went on drinking until twenty minutes later, when another man wearing a hooded fleece jumper came into the bar. He got to within three yards of McEntee, pulled out a pistol, pointed it at his head and tried to fire it. Fellow drinkers and bar staff dived for cover. But McEntee's life was saved as the weapon jammed, even after the gunman casually slapped the chamber of the revolver three times to try to clear it. Failing to unjam the pistol's chamber, the gunman fled.

Despite his narrow brush with death Stephen McEntee, still obsessed with killing Adair, remained defiant. At a secret location in Belfast, he told the authors that 'I don't give a fuck about it.

I'll get him in the end.' After the fallout from the Boxing Day murder, McEntee would have to go back into jail to 'get' Mad Dog.

A few days before Christmas Adair and his chums enjoyed some diversion from the pressure of living under a collective death threat. They hired in a troupe of female strippers from the North Belfast-based strippogram agency Angels, for an evening's entertainment at the Big Brother house. Angels specialized in long-legged multi-pierced dancers dressed up in the uniforms of the old Royal Ulster Constabulary. Their stage show at the Big Brother house involved one of the thigh-booted strippers in surplus RUC hat, shirt, coat and baton 'arresting' Adair. The erotic dancer even managed to slap on a pair of handcuffs. Within a matter of weeks he would be restrained again – and this time it would be for real.

Throughout the 'phoney feud' between Adair's faction and the rest of the UDA, he had always maintained that he commanded support far beyond his traditional stronghold. His opponents never doubted his boast, seeking out anyone they regarded as 'spies' in their camps. And, just as Adair turned on those he felt he could no longer trust, the other brigadiers watched a number of their men who were regarded as unreliable or as dangerously close to the 'C' company leader. One of those they suspected of passing on intelligence about the movements of UDA members in South Belfast was Roy Green, a 32-year-old former associate of Adair. Green was followed around Belfast and was spotted in pubs in the city centre meeting with 'C' company figures, so on 2 January he was summoned to a meeting at a house close to the Kimberly Inn in Ballynafeigh. As he arrived in Kimberly Street a gunman emerged from a nearby house the UDA had taken over and shot him several times in the head. Roy Green lay dead outside the pub where Tucker Annett had been killed. The UDA leadership accused him of 'acts of treason', code for aiding and abetting the cause of Johnny Adair.

There was a widespread assumption, both inside and outside loyalism, that once Adair was removed from the lower Shankill scene the slights, grudges, rivalries and jealousies lurking beneath 'C' company's outer image of unity would bubble up to the surface. He was the bolt that held the killing machine together; pulling out that vital part would result in the entire mechanism collapsing. Eight days after the Green murder the new secretary of state, Paul Murphy, authorized Adair's arrest. A large contingent of police and troops swooped once again on Boundary Way and lifted Adair from his home, despite the protests of Gina and his supporters gathered nearby at the Big Brother house. In the words of John White, the UDA's embattled West Belfast brigadier was said to be 'philosophical' about his re-incarceration. Yet, even while he was held in Maghaberry, Adair continued to implore his young lieutenants on the outside, including 'C' company's new commanding officer, 21-year-old Alan 'Bucky' McCullough, to 'get results'. He was frustrated by the lull in attacks on his enemies since he had been put back behind bars.

On 1 February the Adair faction appeared to contradict the theory that with its leader back in jail 'C' company would fail to function as a killing machine. John Gregg was a regular visitor to Ibrox, Glasgow Rangers' 40,000-seat stadium in the heart of Govan, the former shipbuilding district of the city. He often travelled over for home games, along with other leading UDA men such as Michael Stone, who was pictured beside several Rangers stars at hotels and bars after matches. Gregg even had a conviction for violent conduct outside Ibrox during a Rangers–Celtic Old Firm tie. Feud or no feud, big 'Grugg' wasn't to be deterred from watching his beloved Rangers. Through Adair, Alan McCullough knew this as well, and between them they prepared a hit team to wait for Gregg as he arrived back in Belfast.

On that Saturday night Gregg and his second-in-command in South-east Antrim, Rab Carson, were travelling home on the Stena HSS ferry from Scotland. A taxi took them from the port of Belfast, under the M3 motorway and towards the M2 and Rathcoole, via the city centre. As their car passed close to the M3 bridge two gunmen from 'C' company jumped out of another car and raked the taxi with gunfire. Gregg and Carson were killed; two other men, including the driver, were injured. The assassins were two brothers in their early twenties who had been in thrall of Adair while they were children. Adair had told McCullough to pay them £100 each for the hit. When news broke late on Saturday night that one of his most feared rivals had been killed, Adair was said to be jubilant inside Maghaberry. The Gregg killing and the removal of his replacement, Carson, seemed to be a devastating blow to the UDA mainstream. 'C' company had ruthlessly raised the stakes in the internal shooting war and demonstrated its ability to strike at the very top of the Inner Council. But Gregg's assassination proved to be the turning point – and the undoing of the lower Shankill gang.

To many loyalists, including those in the greater Shankill with long-standing ties to Adair and his comrades, the Gregg murder was a step too far. 'Grugg', despite his reputation for brutality towards his own men, had been the man who shot Gerry Adams and gone to jail for his efforts. The remaining four brigadiers had to act decisively to bring the feud to an end otherwise their fate would be the same as Gregg's. Their strategy in winning the internal war showed that some on the Inner Council, not least Jackie McDonald, were more tactically astute than their opponents realized.

By contrast John White was starting to believe in his own propaganda. Twenty-four hours after Adair had been rearrested White claimed that his ally still commanded huge support throughout the UDA in Northern Ireland. He was particularly confident that the entire West Belfast brigade would run to 'C' company's aid. 'West Belfast is 100 per cent behind Johnny Adair,' White said. He had learned nothing. From his bitter comments about 'A' and 'B' companies during the feud with the UVF it was clear that he realized then that their 'loyalty' was highly conditional and their willingness to fight other loyalists virtually non-existent, but he had managed to forget this very quickly.

The Inner Council's game-plan to break 'C' company was a combination of carrot and stick. On the eve of John Gregg and Rab Carson's funerals members met in Rathcoole to discuss their move. The word had already gone out from Jackie McDonald and the new leadership in North Belfast to Highfield and Woodvale, telling the leaderships of 'A' and 'B' companies that they wanted to avoid mass bloodshed. Among those McDonald and his allies struck a deal with was Billy Twister McQuiston, a former UDA prisoner in the Maze and a popular loyalist figure in the Highfield estate. They offered an outer core of 'C' company members still in the lower Shankill a way out. They agreed on a plan that would allow the bulk of 'C' company to defect back to the mainstream organization. Heather Street Social Club would be used as a 'clearing house' for 'C' company renegades prepared to desert the Adair–White axis, and 'A' and 'B' companies would coordinate the surrender from Heather Street, contacting their comrades in the lower Shankill by mobile phone or through relatives. The 'stick' part of the strategy would be a mass incursion into the Lower Shankill estate involving up to several hundred UDA men loyal to the leadership. Their target would be an inner core, based around Boundary Way.

Even before the brigadiers started to bombard 'C' company members with inducements and threats, nerves in the lower Shankill had started to break. Over the weekend of Gregg's death, Adair's followers were rattled by media leaks of a planned invasion by up to 10,000 UDA men from across Northern Ireland. The first major defection was also the most important. On Tuesday, forty-eight hours before Gregg's burial, William 'Mo' Courtney switched allegiances to the UDA leadership. Before fleeing the lower Shankill Courtney went to the house of Gina Adair's mother on the pretext of dropping around for a cup of tea and a chat. Once inside her home he threatened Gina's mother and questioned her about where her son-in-law might have hidden the 'C' company war chest. It is unclear if Adair's mother-in-law knew where any of the loot was but Courtney did make off with some cash and a number of weapons from a nearby hide and handed both money and guns to the leadership faction's base in Heather Street. Courtney was seen by Adair as one of his closest and most reliable comrades and his switch of allegiance was a stunning blow for 'C' company given that, as one of his former friends said, Mo 'knew every brick' in the lower Shankill. By the morning of the Carson and Gregg funerals things were falling apart there and the telephone traffic between the two ends of the road had reached fever pitch.

John Gregg was buried with full paramilitary honours on 6 February 2003 at a funeral attended by members of every loyalist faction, as well as Protestant clergymen and local community leaders. (Only a handful of UVF leaders refused to join the delegation. One prominent UVF man told the authors he would not pay his respects because he blamed Rab Carson for murdering Mark Quail, a UVF member killed during the summer 2000 feud.) After Gregg was buried and darkness fell the UDA leadership put its plan into action. Mobiles buzzed the length and breadth of the Shankill as leaders in Woodvale and Highfield implored 'C' company members to come over to the mainstream side.

Throughout the early evening the 'A' and 'B' company commanders directed dozens of their old chums in 'C' company to come forward. They arrived in small groups of two and three, always accompanied either by wives and girlfriends or mothers, sisters and brothers to ensure their safety. Those who surrendered brought with them plastic bags and holdalls full of cash and guns belonging to the lower Shankill unit – the price for being allowed to return to the UDA fold. Black humour prevailed in the bizarre atmosphere of the Heather Street club. One of those present at the surrender described the scene: 'People at the top table were setting their watches to which time exactly this one or that from 'C' company would arrive and hand over the guns and money. Others inside Heather Street were taking bets on who would be next through the door.'

Back down in the lower Shankill panic, fear and paranoia were palpable as those loyal to Adair and White looked around them and saw the mass desertions. In the midst of the confusion there was another Romeo and Juliet moment. Adair's eldest daughter, sixteen-year-old Natalie, had been engaged to a young man from further up the Shankill Road whose family were aligned to the UVF. On hearing that the Lower Shankill estate was about to be invaded, the man's mother drove down the road at top speed. She arrived at Gina Adair's door in Boundary Way and implored her to let Natalie stay with her family if the Adairs were about to flee. Gina, and the core of 'C' company gathered in the street, strongly objected. A group of men set upon the woman's car, smashing it with baseball bats, and Natalie Adair's future mother-in-law was forced to flee in fear of her life. Natalie would have to leave her home without seeing the man she loved.

Shortly afterwards, at about 1 a.m., around 100 men, including about a dozen with firearms, arrived in the estate in a mass convoy. Immediately they started breaking windows, kicking down doors and beating up anyone on the streets remotely connected with Adair's faction. The hand-to-hand fighting between the UDA mainstream and about twenty of those still loyal to Adair lasted for ten to fifteen minutes. At one stage armed UDA men got hold of Gregg's assassin and bundled him into the boot of a car. The plan was to take him away, torture and then kill him, but he was rescued by police officers, who arrived just in time to pull him from the back of the car. During the skirmishes shots were fired at police lines from both sides. Through the chaos and the confusion it became clear that the Adair faction had been routed, reduced in numbers to just over a dozen.

One experienced police officer who had spent years observing the rise of Adair's gang said that night that he was witnessing the end of an era. He even compared the demise of 'C' company to Francis Ford Coppola's classic gangster film *The Godfather*. Except, he said, in this case it was 'the victory of the five families over the Corleones'.

Incredibly, no one was arrested during the brief but bloody internal UDA battle for control of the lower Shankill. The security forces merely acted as a buffer zone between the factions and provided armed escort for the flight of the Adairs. Left behind was not only Gina's mother, still terrified over her ordeal at the hands of Mo Courtney, but also Johnny's beloved pet Alsatian dogs, Rebel and Shane. Under police protection the pathetic caravan of former 'C' company gunmen, John White, Gina, the Millar brothers and several young children made their way to the port of Larne. Within a few hours they were on a ferry to Cairnryan and ultimately the watchful eye of the Dumfries and Galloway police.

Their stay in Scotland would be a short one since the UDA's Scottish brigade had sworn allegiance to the leadership back in Belfast. Even their old friend Sam 'Skelly' McCrory, now living in Irvine on the western Scottish coast, wanted nothing to do with them. The remnants of the Adair faction were weakened and isolated like never before. Around midnight a bitter John White telephoned one of the authors from a hotel outside Stranraer where the group was staying before heading south for England. His voice cracking, the stress and shock of the routing still obvious from his tone, White said that 'for several years now I've believed privately that the UDA was finished. I'm certainly finished with loyalist politics and the UDA for good after spending so many years in jail for the organization, after working hard for the cease-fires.' He then said that he had spoken to Adair by telephone and made an astonishing claim: 'Johnny told me that he is finished with the UDA and is also finished with loyalism. All he is concerned about is the welfare of Gina and his children.'

Back in Belfast those who had so recently incurred Adair's wrath were jubilant. Maureen Dodds was spotted driving around the Lower Shankill estate in a people carrier, seeking out houses boarded up since the feud began. 'I'm down here to get our house back and if I can't get it back I will move into one of their houses,' she shouted.

Back in December 1998 an anonymous balladeer had lavished generous praise on Johnny Adair in the pages of the *New Ulster Defender*:

> When they turn the pages of history
> And remember deeds so bold
> When they mention Ulster's heroes
> Let his name be written in gold.
>
> There is none more so deserving
> Than the man from West Belfast
> Fighting to maintain our freedom
> Striving onward to the last.
>
> Just a lad of sixteen summers
> Born to fight and born to lead
> And like the few who went before him
> One of Ulster's dying breed.

> Leading us by his example
> Fearless in the face of fear
> Always there when he was needed
> *It's alright, Wee Johnny's here.*

> Now we grow a little older
> And look back on times of strife
> Let us not forget our leader
> As we soldier on in life.

Over the days and weeks after the defeat of 'C' company, the UDA leadership would do everything it could to forget its former hero as it sought to stamp its authority on the troublesome lower Shankill. The imagery of Adair – the shaved head, the muscular frame, the earrings, the cheeky grin and the tattoos – was erased from its walls. Stencils of his face were defaced, posters ripped up and torn down. Banners that had been strung across the Shankill Road calling for his release were removed. For the benefit of television cameras the mural he had ordered to be painted close to the Big Brother house, portraying eternal friendship between the UDA and the LVF, was vandalized by none other than Mo Courtney. Even more menacing murals from the Adair era, such as the Grim Reaper armed with a Kalashnikov, dancing on the graves of three Ardoyne republicans – Eddie Copeland, Stephen Larkin and Shankill bomber Sean Kelly – were covered with bright green paint. There were changes inside the Big Brother house, too, with the removal of the gaming machines that were once fed constantly with money earned through drugs and extortion. Security grilles were taken off another nearby community house once used by Adair and White. The arch at the entrance of Boundary Way, constructed out of concrete-filled oil drums and covered in UDA logos and pro-Adair graffiti, was torn down. The atmosphere in the area was reminiscent of that in an Eastern bloc capital just after the fall of communism. There were still traces of the old order, but signs everywhere that a new regime was displacing it for ever.

Within weeks desolation and defeat were all that remained

around Adair's home at number 100 Boundary Way. The 12-foot security gates leading to an alleyway at the back of the house lay open, and on a windswept rain-soaked March afternoon, Spanish and French tourists were able to walk straight into Adair's back garden. The fountain was overflowing and a lone Chinese figurine stood upright beside the wooden fence. Inside the house the back kitchen looked as if it had been stripped bare; the only sign of life was a half-empty bottle of milk lying in the kitchen sink. Outside, the mournful tinkling of a set of wooden wind chimes seemed to beat out the message that an era in Ulster loyalist history had come to a close.

Epilogue – Fallen Idols

Having destroyed the imagery of Johnny Adair in February 2003, seven months later the UDA leadership sanctioned the erasure of another loyalist icon from the lower Shankill. On 1 September the painters started to wipe out the portrait of Billy 'King Rat' Wright, a mural commissioned by Adair following the LVF founder's assassination in the Maze. Painting over Wright marked the end of a turbulent chapter in the UDA's history and sent out a powerful signal that the epoch of collaboration with the LVF and smaller loyalist micro-groups was over. It was also an olive branch to the UVF, which had insisted in the Loyalist Commission that the Wright mural must go as part of a deal with the UDA to clean up Protestant housing estates, to, in effect, 'demilitarize' the walls in working-class areas such as the Shankill.

But another mural in the lower Shankill has proved to be more problematic for the UDA command. Barbara McCullough has only to look out of her living-room window to be reminded of the price her family paid for involvement with the UDA. From the sofa in her Denmark Street home she can see a painting of her dead husband, commemorated as a UDA martyr. William 'Bucky' McCullough was involved in the organization at its inception, had a reputation as a ruthless gunman and was frequently questioned about UDA murders and armed robberies. He had once taken part in a grenade attack on the Gem Bar on the New Lodge Road. On 16 October 1981, as he left home to take one of his daughters to school, two INLA gunmen pulled up on a motorbike and the pillion passenger opened up from close range just as McCullough got into his car. He was hit twelve times and died minutes later as doctors fought to save his life. Instantly McCullough became an icon.

Yet the INLA may have singled out the wrong man when they gunned down McCullough. According to testimony from an INLA supergrass, Robbie McAllister, the real target that day was Tommy 'Tucker' Lyttle, the West Belfast brigadier and Special Branch agent. When McAllister (who later retracted his evidence) suggested to the INLA's most ruthless assassin, Gerard 'Dr Death' Steenson, that they had got the wrong man, he replied: 'It didn't matter. He was in the UDA anyway.' The INLA had been able to track McCullough's movements and find out his address thanks to someone inside the UDA – Jim Craig. In its detailed 'collusion memo', outlining Craig's relationship with two ex-Official IRA racketeers, his secret meetings with an IRA member from Unity Flats and his introduction to INLA activists such as Steenson, the UDA's Special Assignments Section openly accused Craig of setting up McCullough for assassination.

The murdered UDA man's youngest son, Alan, was just a baby in his mother's arms at the time of the killing. It was a bitter irony that twenty-two years later he would suffer the same fate as his father, even down to the detail of being betrayed by fellow loyalists.

Alan McCullough was the last lower Shankill commander loyal to Johnny Adair. He was so in awe of Adair that he even forgave Mad Dog for once ordering 'C' company to beat him up. A few months before Adair's release from Maghaberry, and the onset of the internal UDA feud, McCullough was still only a foot-soldier in Johnny's army. Prior to his incarceration over the Holy Cross bomb-warning, Gary Smyth was the anointed head of the lower Shankill unit. Smyth contacted Adair in jail to tell him that two of his younger members, one of whom was Adair's own son, Jonathan, had broken a golden rule: they had assaulted clients using the 'dope flat'. A young Catholic schoolboy, still in the uniform that marked out his religion, travelled to buy drugs on Shankill Way. As he was leaving the estate with his purchase, he was set upon by Alan McCullough and John Adair Junior who beat him to a pulp, stole his watch, mobile phone, money and the ten-deal of hashish he had just bought from the 'C' company-controlled drugs base. The schoolboy, lucky to escape with his life, ran from the area up the Antrim Road. Incredibly, when he told his mother about his ordeal, she got into her car and drove to Boundary Way to seek a meeting with John White in the 'Community House' directly facing the Adairs' home. White assured the Catholic mother that 'something would be done' about the boy's assailants.

When Smyth informed Adair about the incident he was furious and ordered that the pair be 'dealt with'. Mimicking the *modus operandi* of the British army, the UDA had 'provost marshals' in every brigade area, sadistic men who dished out internal discipline to members who transgressed the movement's tenets. The golden rule in the Lower Shankill was to do nothing that would disrupt business and drive potential customers, regardless of their religion, away from the 'dope flat'. Tommy Potts, the West Belfast brigade's provost marshal, dished out a severe beating to McCullough and Adair junior.

Despite the hammering, McCullough was highly regarded by Adair and, on his release from prison, Mad Dog had him elevated to overall command of 'C' company just before the second feud erupted. He was therefore forced to flee Northern Ireland on the UDA's own 'night of the long knives.' Exiled to Bolton with the core of the Adair faction – Gina and her children, the Millar brothers, Wayne Dowie and a handful of others – young 'Bucky' pined for home. Life for the group the UDA contemptuously dubbed 'the Bolton wanderers' was now shapeless and grim.

Adair's people fled to north-west England because of links forged between Adair, dissident loyalists in Mid-Ulster and English neo-Nazis based around Bolton. For decades the British far right had sought to promote the loyalist cause, often to the embarrassment of some loyalist leaders in Belfast. Disgusted with the UVF and UDA ceasefires, perceiving them as going soft on the IRA enemy, neo-Nazis in groups such as Combat 18 fluctuated to Billy Wright's LVF. A number of Wright's followers had neo-fascist and racist sympathies and, during the Drumcree disputes from 1997 to 1999, invited to Portadown delegations from Combat 18 in the Bolton/Oldham area. The Lancashire fascists were billeted in homes on loyalist estates in the build-up to the annual Drumcree parade, which was banned from passing through the nationalist Garvaghy Road.

When Wright was assassinated in the Maze at Christmas 1997,

he became an icon not only for loyalists but also for their Combat 18 sympathizers. One of those who travelled to Northern Ireland before and after Wright's murder was a tattooist from Bolton. Such was the demand for tattoos of Wright's image that the body artist financed his annual summer trip to Portadown by tattooing Billy Wright's face on to hundreds of loyalist bodies, male and female.

The Bolton fascists might have lost one Ulster-born hero but after 1999 they gained another – Johnny Adair. Against the advice of his mentor, John White, Adair courted the English fascists and even wore an England shirt during the Euro 2000 tournament which had been given to him by the Bolton Combat 18 delegation. On the day the first loyalist feud erupted in August 2000 a small delegation of Bolton Combat 18 was there as 'C' company fired the first shots at the Rex Bar.

It was natural therefore for the remnants of 'C' company, or at least those still loyal to Adair, to flee to the Lancashire town in early 2003. But homesickness got the better of Bucky McCullough. He phoned Mo Courtney and offered him a deal: if the new UDA leadership on the Shankill allowed him to come home unharmed, he would supply Gina Adair's address and also disclose the whereabouts of a large drugs haul 'C' company had smuggled into Northern Ireland in late 2002. To demonstrate his bona fides McCullough even raked Gina's rented house with a machine gun given to him by the UDA mainstream.

Believing that he had been forgiven by the UDA, and that he would be accepted back into the fold, McCullough returned to Belfast on 28 May and agreed to go to a meeting with two UDA commanders on that same day. The men who turned up at his mother's door in Denmark Street assured Barbara that her son would be safe with them. They took McCullough for a meal at the Hilton Hotel in Templepatrick near Belfast international airport, during which they discussed the 'Bolton wanderers' and the location of the drugs and money they believed the exiles controlled. After dinner the two men drove McCullough up a back road towards Belfast, stopped the car and, after a brief struggle, shot him in the head and buried him in a shallow grave at a remote spot in Mallusk.

After the burial his killers spread rumours that were soon picked up by the press and police that McCullough's body had been dumped in the Waterworks, a man-made lake contiguous to the Westland estate in North Belfast, a UDA stronghold. Police divers searched the lake for days while the duo destroyed forensic evidence and established alibis for themselves. Two men have since been charged with McCullough's murder, one of whom is Johnny Adair's old pal Mo Courtney, the other Ihab Shoukri, who, at the time of his arrest, was out on bail awaiting trial for the possession of a handgun during the feud with 'C' company.

The McCullough killing squashed any hopes the 'Bolton wanderers' might have harboured about making deals to return home. Those who have been close to the exiles for two decades say the majority are deeply homesick and have offered money to be allowed back. They are now isolated because their former friends in the fascist underground in Lancashire have also abandoned them. Even Bolton City Council has turned on the Adairs, refusing to grant Gina and her family a council house. Myths abound about the 'Bolton wanderers' having large amounts of money secreted away either in England, Northern Ireland or even Spain. The reality is that most are broke and are living more frugally than they ever had before. Before their flight, using torture and intimidation, the UDA discovered where most of the proceeds of drugs, racketeering and prostitution were hidden.

Unable to return home, the exiles are likely to stay put in Bolton for the foreseeable future. Given loyalism's innate thirst for revenge it is likely that there will be further incidents in the Lancashire town, where most residents don't know anything about Ulster's paramilitary underworld. Meanwhile, relatives of many of the 'wanderers' remain on the Shankill Road, effectively living as hostages who would suffer if the exiles decided to strike back at the mainstream UDA.

The rout of the Adair faction boosted hopes of a new era of stability and unity within the UDA. Having scored a famous victory over 'C' company, the leadership enjoyed another triumph over an even more dangerous adversary – the press. A few weeks after the shooting stopped the UDA managed to persuade the Loyalist Commission to back its demand that Protestant shop-keepers and their customers stop buying the campaigning tabloid *The Sunday World*. The loyalists had had an attack of moral indig-nation over a series of – largely accurate – articles exposing the crime-financed lifestyles of individual UDA brigadiers. Retailers in loyalist parts of greater Belfast were threatened, van-drivers transporting the paper into areas such as the Newtownards Road and Rathcoole were warned to stop delivering *The Sunday World* 'or else', and leaflets and posters were circulated calling on Protestants to boycott the tabloid.

Regardless of its tattered reputation within the unionist commu-nity, the UDA was still able to exercise muscle and influence the editorial policies of an authentic voice of the people in Northern Ireland. The episode proved that the UDA was, and is, not to be underestimated.

To underline its hegemony the UDA leadership organized a show of strength several weeks after the flight of the Adairs. The event was held in the Taughmonagh Social Club, under the control of Jackie McDonald's South Belfast brigade. Ostensibly, there was to be a battle of the bands, with flute bands from across Northern Ireland taking part. However, McDonald used the competition to press home to every brigade area the bands came from the message that collective responsibility had been re-established. During a break in the music a masked man, waving an AK47 rifle in the air, marched into the function room. The crowd of about 500 went ecstatic when the six brigadiers filed in behind the gunman and took their places on the stage. A UDA veteran who attended the social night said Jackie McDonald looked triumphant as the audience burst into applause. 'Personally, I thought it was as much a celebration of what Jackie had done for the UDA, than the leadership's victory over Adair and White. And he deserved it, Jackie McDonald in my opinion saved the UDA.'

There were some positive post-feud developments emerging out of the UDA's inclusion in the Loyalist Commission. The summer of 2003 proved to be the most peaceful marching season in almost a decade and the UDA undoubtedly played its part in helping to ensure that the 'mad months' of July and August were unseasonably quiet. One of the key figures in this enterprise was Billy 'Twister' McQuiston who, along with his West Belfast IRA counterpart, Anto 'Spike' Murray, guaranteed that the interfaces through North and West Belfast remained peaceful during potentially dangerous marches such as the Orange Order parade along the Springfield Road in late June.

In other parts of Northern Ireland individual UDA units tried to rebuild the organization's tarnished public image. In Lisburn ex-UDA prisoners set up a project in which leaders work with up to 400 teenagers and attempt to wean them off drugs, alcohol and the cult of paramilitarism. The energies of former UYM members are no longer directed towards intimidating Catholic families in the town, dealing drugs, clashing with the UVF or menacing people in general. Instead the older UDA men have established an army of volunteer street cleaners, graffiti expungers and community workers. As part of a scheme to warn youngsters about the perils of paramilitarism, Lisburn UDA even came up with a plan for ex-prisoners such as Adie Bird to take their charges into the now-empty Maze prison and show them around the H-blocks.

However, others within the organization returned to type. In the first week of September 2003 the UDA's new brigadier in North Belfast, 33-year-old William 'Bonzer' Borland, the successor to the jailed Andre Shoukri and his brother, Ihab, ordered a wave of attacks on Catholic houses in the mixed Deerpark Road area, which backs on to the Glenbryn estate. The convicted racketeer even employed his girlfriend to turn up at the residents' doorsteps urging them to leave the Deerpark Road. Catholic families and some of their Protestant friends paid a heavy price for Borland's desire to make his mark while his comrades were locked up in prison. Almost every window in Catholic-owned homes was smashed, cars were damaged, and in the first week of the terror three families were driven out. They included a Protestant pensioner and her bedridden disabled daughter who fled Deerpark after they spoke up for their Catholic neighbours. As she left her home for the last time 83-year-old Jane Thompson compared the North Belfast UDA to the Nazis. 'I am ashamed to be Protestant,' she said. 'This is the way things started in Nazi Germany with people being picked off one by one.'

Her remarks sum up how a once popular mass loyalist army degenerated into disparate, and often rival, localized factions. Borland's reign of fear and his ambition to be top dog in North Belfast are typical of the central problem afflicting attempts to give the UDA a meaningful political purpose. The federal nature of the movement, geographic sectarian differences, clashing personalities, serial criminality and the laws of Ulster social gravity continually pull the UDA back into the sectarian quagmire.

The post-feud UDA was faced with a choice: to dissolve its paramilitary wing and evolve into an Ulster-wide community welfare organization, or to stay in the shadows of Northern Ireland political life, waiting for another call to arm if the union and the state itself reach terminal crisis. The detritus on the streets, the familiar slogans of bigotry on the walls, the boarded-up houses, the broken glass and the removal vans ferrying vulnerable Catholic families along the Deerpark Road, just a small corner of North Belfast, the most bitterly contested area of western Europe, are all indicators that the UDA seems genetically programmed to take the latter option.

Meanwhile, now that one of his oldest comrades, Gary 'Smickers' Smyth, has been freed from Maghaberry, Johnny Adair is more alone than ever before. After Smyth was warned that he would be killed if he returned to the lower Shankill, he beat a path to Gina Adair's door in Bolton. Adair faces a similar option when he is freed in January 2005: flee to Bolton or face death. It remains unclear which road the man who ran the UDA's pre-ceasefire terror campaign will travel.

From behind bars Adair has warned that on his release he is going to confront the 'traitors' who conspired against him. 'In ten months' time I will be out. The clock is ticking and the tables are turning,' he says. He insists that he has no intention to flee Northern Ireland once the gates open. Already he has made plans to build a new power base in the Ballysillan area, linking up with two brothers, prominent in violent loyalist circles, who were founder members of the LVF in Belfast and, if they can be believed, have promised Mad Dog sanctuary in their corner of Ballysillan. The brothers are among the few people left in the greater Shankill to give succour to Gina Adair. They often pick her up at Belfast international airport and drive her the short distance to Maghaberry to visit her husband.

When Adair gets out, his enemies on the UDA Inner Council face a grim choice. The potential alliance of the Ballysillan brothers and Adair has created unlikely allies on the Shankill Road. In the early 1990s, thanks to Adair, the UDA was at war with the UVF. Four years on, the two organizations have drawn closer and put their past differences aside. The UDA knows that if Adair establishes any kind of foothold in North Belfast he will use it as a launch pad for revenge attacks on the men who organized the expulsion of his family from the lower Shankill. The UDA figure under greatest threat is Adair's old mate Jim Spence, whom Adair has targeted as a 'coward and tout' in a carefully orchestrated media campaign. Meanwhile, the UVF is also seeking revenge. It blames the Ballysillan brothers for the murder of its members by the LVF during the on-going feud. Both organizations have discussed a joint purge against the Ballysillan/North Belfast LVF in a bid to destroy Adair's base before he even gets control of it. One long-term observer of loyalist paramilitary feuding on the Shankill Road sums up the new alliances taking shape in Protestant Ulster's urban heartland cynically but succinctly: 'The Blacknecks [the UVF] and the Wombles [the UDA] realize they now have a common enemy. If the brothers are prepared to give Adair shelter the two organizations have only one option – to destroy them and their stronghold before Johnny gets a foot in the door.'

It may be still too soon to write off Johnny Adair as a force within loyalist terrorism. His destiny lies in the hands of his former comrades and their new-found friends in the UVF.

Back on the Lower Shankill estate there is one mural the UDA has not dared destroy or erase – the painting celebrating the violent life and squalid death of Stephen McKeag. Because he had fallen out of favour with Adair even before the UVF feud, and because of his legendary status as a UDA assassin, the mural remains. When McKeag died of a drug overdose in September 2000 tributes poured in from all over Northern Ireland. Two days after he was found, fifty-nine separate death notices appeared in the *Belfast Telegraph*; the following day a further 120 were printed. They lavished praise on the UDA's serial killer and expressed a deep sense of loss. The short verses and terse expressions of grief illuminate how a fractured, sectarian community copes with the atrocities and pain that its 'own' has inflicted on the 'other' – sentimentality and denial.

The majority were brief valedictions, signing off with the 'C' company slogan, 'Simply the best'. A large number were as sugary and pious as Hallmark cards. 'Do you make them laugh in heaven, does your big smile make them cheer, do you make the sunshine brighter like you did when you were here?' one asks. Another, from an 'Uncle Davy', recalls McKeag as, 'Happy, smiling, always content, loved and respected wherever he went; Always willing, helpful and kind, what a beautiful memory he left behind.'

Epilogue to the Paperback

The organization Johnny Adair once effectively headed was pulled in different directions after 'C' company scattered across the Irish sea. After the last outbreak of feuding ended Jackie McDonald, the strongest figure on the Inner Council, began to lead the UDA into secret talks with both the British and Irish governments about ways in which the organization could be reformed into some kind of community/political group involved in purely legal activity. Seeing the huge amount of money from America, the European Union and both Irish and British governments that was flowing into the coffers of 'community' organizations in nationalist areas, the UDA began demanding that it too receive a slice of the peace cake.

So, despite the fact that UDA members were engaging in bank robberies and extorting money from businessmen and women in greater Belfast, throughout 2004 there seemed to be no end to the British or Irish governments' willingness to placate, financially and politically, the organization's new leadership. In June 2004 the authors discovered that Irish taxpayers were funding a scheme to train Ulster Political Research Group members in the art of political spin doctoring. Through the Armagh-based North/South Ministerial Council the Irish government provided money to pay for a consultant who ran a course for the UPRG's fledgling politicians. The Republic's Department of Foreign Affairs even appointed an Irish official to work one day per week throughout the summer with the UPRG.

A series of leaked emails from the North/South Ministerial Council revealed that the two governments were aware of the outrage that funding and training the UDA's political wing could provoke if it came to light. In one email from an NSMC official a senior civil servant, based at Stormont, is advised to 'drop the reference to the number of officials attending the meetings', i.e. the talks between the Council and the UPRG. In another communication with a colleague the same NSMC official admits that the council 'has no mandate in legislation to support such encounters'. In two emails the official uses the term 'Jesuitical' when making a distinction between actual contacts that did take place between officials and the UPRG and the claim that these civil servants were 'not acting in their capacity as Secretariat staff'. This 'Jesuitical' relationship between the governments and the UDA's political wing was further illuminated in a parliamentary answer to Lord Laird of Artigarvan, the Ulster Unionist peer who first highlighted the links. 'There has been no contact between the NSMC Joint Secretariat and the UPRG,' read a statement from Secretary of State Paul Murphy. 'Staff of the Secretariat, acting in their capacity as officials of the Irish Government and the Office of First Minister/Deputy First Minister, have helped facilitate meetings between members of the UPRG and a number of external organizations.' In a revealing background note in Hansard the Northern Ireland Secretary referred to the ongoing links between the Irish president's husband, Martin McAleese, and the UPRG, which had 'taken place with the knowledge of the Taoiseach's Department and the Department of Foreign Affairs [DFA], and a number of meetings have been facilitated by DFA staff seconded to the NSMC Secretariat'. Once more it seemed like a case of making a Jesuitical distinction where officials 'facil-itating' meetings was not quite the same thing as actually having the meetings themselves, but the reality was still that they were finding a way of meeting, negotiating with and funding the UDA's political allies.

Martin McAleese had played a low-key role in what the Department of Foreign Affairs in Dublin referred to as 'parallel diplomacy' in the North. He had the specific task of 'reaching out' to working-class Protestants. Though from a Belfast Catholic background, Mary and Martin McAleese seemed to get along swimmingly with the new UDA leadership, repeatedly inviting its members to visit them in their official residence, Áras an Uachtaráin, the stately Georgian house in Dublin's Phoenix Park that was once the home of the Viceroys who oversaw British rule in Ireland. The UDA men were wined and dined in a bid to demonstrate the caring, sharing face of modern Catholic Ireland. Jackie McDonald even played golf with the President's husband on some of Ireland's most expensive courses, like the exclusive K Club in Kildare and Ballybunion in Kerry, a favourite of President Bill Clinton's.

By the end of 2004 groups of UDA men, who previously only expected to visit Dublin in order to plant incendiary bombs, were taking coach tours to play golf and enjoy lavish hospitality. The trips were kept quiet by both sides and there seemed to be a growing acceptance among the UDA that this was the way of the future – helped by the prospect of massive UK and Irish government grants to help ease them into more peaceable and legal activities.

However, an organization like the UDA was not going to transform itself after a spot of golf and fine food. In the autumn of 2004 Jackie McDonald led members of the senior ranks of the UDA/UPRG, including the organization's political leadership of Tommy Kirkham and Frankie Gallagher, in talks with the Northern Secretary and his senior officials, aimed at securing public funding to the tune of £70 million to pave the way for its agreeing to decommissioning weapons and turn to purely legitimate pursuits. McDonald's view was that the UDA should put violence in the past. The only trouble was that while he was taking politics, other UDA units, notably Andre Shoukri's North Belfast Brigade, were getting back to what they knew best – terror and intimidation. Shoukri had been freed from jail in early 2004 and resumed his role as North Belfast Brigadier. His units also continued to be openly involved in the drugs trade.

In early 2005 a Presbyterian Minister with decades of experience working in Protestant working-class districts announced that she was a victim of a protracted UDA terror campaign. In UDA eyes the Reverend Ruth Pettigrew's 'crime' was to help and counsel the family of the murdered Adair ally Alan 'Bucky' McCullough. First, her car was petrol-bombed outside her home off the Shankill Road. Then UDA members informed her that they would shoot her if she continued to support the McCullough family.

The UDA had concluded, wrongly, that the McCulloughs were refusing to withdraw charges against two senior loyalists because of the continued help, welfare and advice the minister was offering them. They believed, incorrectly, that the Reverend Pettigrew was advising them to hold firm and stick to the statements to the police, which claimed that two key UDA members took Alan McCullough from his home prior to the murder. The intimidation had already worked on someone outside of the McCullough family circle who was paid £10,000 to withdraw his statement against the two charged with the murder – Ihab Shoukhri and 'Mo' Courtney.

Towards the end of 2004 any hopes Johnny Adair may have harboured about re-building a power base in loyalist Belfast were sunk following the arrest of a prominent LVF boss from Ballysillan. The man, a kingpin of the only LVF stronghold in North Belfast, was arrested after a raid on a house in Ligoneil during which drugs, guns and cash were uncovered. Since the LVF's foundation in 1996 he had been on close personal terms with Adair and his faction. Although his gang took no part in the 2002/2003 intra-UDA feud, there were fears in the Greater Shankill that the LVF boss would offer Ballysillan as a refuge for Adair.

Indeed in November 2004 the PSNI got wink of intelligence that Sam McCrory and Gary Smyth had been to the area. When detectives raided a house the pair were supposed to have been seen entering, they found a loaded pistol and ammunition, minus the duo. Given McCrory's liking for the quiet life in western Scotland it is unclear why he returned to his native Shankill. However, Smyth is known to be fanatically loyal to the former UDA chief.

Shortly before his release from Maghaberry Jail the UDA leadership vowed to take out Johnny Adair for good. 'If you journalists go to a house to interview Johnny by the front door at the same time there'll be a team going through the back door to kill him,' a member of the Inner Council told the authors.

That threat to his life, along with the arrest of the Ballysillan

LVF boss and the disintegration of his faction of the LVF (made all the more vulnerable by a fresh bout of feuding with the larger UVF at the beginning of 2005), left Adair with only one option – an escape to the grim streets of Horwich, Bolton.

In the days building up to his release on Monday, 10 January Adair received a visit from two senior detectives from the Police Service of Northern Ireland. They told him that the UDA had arranged for at least two separate hit squads to track the dethroned loyalist commander from the moment he left Maghaberry to when he arrived at one of Belfast's two airports. The officers informed Adair that they could not guarantee his safety if Adair chose to fly out of either of the two civilian airports in the city. There was only one alternative for Adair – to be flown by British military helicopter from RAF Aldergrove to Manchester airport. Mad Dog would fly into exile at the taxpayers' expense.

Shortly after his flight into exile Adair left the prospect of him returning to Northern Ireland hanging in the air. 'The mystery of not knowing what a man can do, can drive another man paranoid and crazy,' he said from his new home, sounding like some retired Western gunfighter hinting at a return for one last act of vengeance.

Others from the Adair faction had already returned to Northern Ireland albeit with their tails between their legs. Big Donald Hodgen paid the UDA £50,000 for safe passage and a quiet life on the Co Down coast; Jackie 'Fats' Thompson and Sham Millar have also slipped quietly back to the province, both men also living on the Down coast, far removed from the Shankill.

Some on the Shankill were convinced that Adair's return could happen at any time. Just over a fortnight after Adair's release and enforced exile to Bolton his successor as master of 'C' company declared a state of emergency in Adair's former stronghold, the Lower Shankill estate. The man had become increasingly paranoid because the spectre of Mad Dog's return was haunting him. He was starting to see the ousted loyalist icon everywhere and he had heard rumours that Adair and his old chums, Gary Smyth and Sam McCrory, were on their way back to their native city. Reports had filtered through earlier in the week that the trio were preparing to pose in paramilitary regalia down in the Lower Shankill for a Sunday tabloid. It would be a show of defiance, sticking two fingers up to the current UDA leadership that had expelled them following the feud two years earlier. On Friday, 28 January 2005 the 'C' company chief sent out edicts to junior UDA members, the Ulster Young Militants, ordering them not to partake in their normal weekend activities – heavy drinking and drug-taking. Instead UYM members in west Belfast were drafted into the estate where Adair once reigned supreme, their 'mission' to guard every street corner, entry point and gable end.

For twenty-four hours the UYM sentinels, backed up by a smaller number of armed UDA veterans, patrolled the estate waiting for Mad Dog to return. But their all night sit-out was for nothing; Adair was still in Bolton with his wife Gina and his children. Indeed he was highly amused when he learned that the 'C' company chief, his second-in-command and the UYM had sat up around the clock like modern day Gary Coopers anticipating the arrival of the bad guys riding into town.

A few weeks later Adair managed to sneak in for the photo-call in which he posed in the strongholds of his old enemies and announced that it was 'an act of defiance to the UDA. They won't keep me out.' Adair also travelled to the LVF power base of Portadown where he was pursued by up to forty Belfast UDA members who stormed into a hotel and conducted a room to room search for him.

This anger about Adair's presence in Northern Ireland underlines the fear that remains that he could make a comeback. Meanwhile Adair broods on the personal betrayals he suffered in late 2002/early 2003 and plots his next move. He vows that he will come back to Belfast and face his former comrades. He delivers attacks on the current UDA leaders denouncing them as 'pimps, rapists and gangsters'. He insists (with some justification) that it was he rather than the present Inner Council that 'took the war' to the IRA and forced them into a ceasefire.

Behind the characteristic bombast though is a man who knows his enemies are legion and his friends are few and when he assesses his position the prospects of resuming his former activities in

Belfast look bleak. Hodgen, Thompson and Millar have retired from terrorism and are anxious not to draw any attention to themselves or their families. McCrory has a good life on the Ayrshire coast in Scotland. The LVF meanwhile is in disarray and its members are unlikely to rush to his aid.

And even if he survives a UDA onslaught, Adair knows that there are UVF members on the Shankill who blame him for the August/September 2000 feud that tore the loyalist community apart.

And yet, Fortune had smiled on Adair in the past. A crisis in the peace process, a breakdown in the IRA ceasefire, the flaring of serious sectarian violence on religious interfaces, the discrediting of a leadership perceived to be too close to the Irish State, are X factors that could play into Adair's hands. If Protestants feel mortally threatened by the actions of the British and Irish governments and the IRA – as they have done so many times before; if his opponents are undermined or undermine themselves, there could be an opening for his return. And in the early days of 2005 such possibilities are not as unthinkable as they might have been only a short time before.

At the end of 2004 the media raised expectations to fever pitch that the DUP and Sinn Féin would form a power-sharing government at Stormont. 'Imminent' and 'historic' IRA declarations about open decommissioning of weapons and even the disbandment of the IRA was widely touted. The historic break never came. It later emerged that while the Sinn Féin leaders were engaging both governments and, by proxy, the DUP in political talks in Belfast, they were simultaneously engaged in talks with hard-line elements in the IRA about a 'limited' return to war. There would be no bombs as it was still too close to the Madrid and 11 September bombings, the IRA explosions would undoubtedly come at a severe price in the form of restrictions from the United States. Instead the IRA – and Sinn Féin leadership – came up with a massive 'spectacular': an IRA operation, involving dozens of volunteers, which saw them virtually sealing off the Northern Bank's headquarters in Belfast and removing £26.5 million from its vaults.

IRA volunteers had been quietly carrying out big robberies

and hijacking cigarette trucks before and after the establishment of power-sharing government, but this was on an entirely new scale. The IRA, it emerged, was also recruiting and training dozens, maybe hundreds, of young men in Catholic areas. Loyalists who had been anticipating a gradual drift into some kind of peaceful new era, were now facing the prospect of a resurgent IRA. There was growing disquiet that the IRA was drifting back to war.

The McDonald-Shoukri leadership was then hit by a double whammy in the shape of a spectacularly misjudged statement by President Mary McAleese. On the eve of her participation in the ceremony to mark the sixtieth anniversary of the release of the remaining inmates at the Auschwitz-Birkenau death camp in southern Poland, the President appeared to compare the Protestants of Northern Ireland with the Nazis. In an interview on RTÉ radio, Mrs McAleese said the Nazis had given to their children an irrational hatred of Jews 'in the same way that people in Northern Ireland transmitted to their children an irrational hatred, for example, of Catholics, in the same way that people give to their children an outrageous and irrational hatred to those who are of different colour and all of those things'. Two days later the President attempted to apologize: 'What I said I undoubtedly said clumsily. I should have finished out the example and it would have been a much better interview had I done that. That was certainly my intention. It was never my intention going into it simply to blame one side of the community in Northern Ireland.'

From a southern diplomatic perspective, years of patient and quiet diplomacy to try and win the loyalists over had been scuppered. There was outrage among Protestants and her remarks were denounced by the Democratic Unionists Party and the Ulster Unionist Party. The Orange Order scrapped plans to meet the President in March. The most important effect of the Protestant-Nazi comparison was that the UDA leadership could no longer associate itself with an Irish president: there would be no further UDA social trips to Dublin.

Two weeks later the IRA began issuing threatening statements hinting further at a return to war. The entire political and security situation in the North began to appear, yet again, unstable. From a position where a more moderate UDA leadership was at last considering a new path, the North was again in turmoil. For the first time in ages, republicans began organizing riots as PSNI officers attempted to raid the homes of suspects in the northern Bank raid and investigated the murder of a Catholic man from the Short Strand, Robert McCartney, by members of the IRA.

At the time of writing the prospects for the summer of 2005 are bleak, with the probability that street protests will lead to sectarian disorder that could climax in fatalities. This could provide Johnny Adair with the pretext for turning up and presenting himself as the defender of the loyalist working and under-classes as he did at Drumcree in the mid 90s. And a return by Adair, though horrifying to the bulk of rational loyalists, is being talked about. The best hope of stopping Johnny Adair's ambition is that the loyalist people, as evidenced by their refusal to back both paramilitary-linked parties at the ballot box, appear mightily fed up with their very own defenders.

February 2005

Appendix

Before his murder in October 1988 the UDA had been spying on Jim Craig's extortion activities and on his contacts with known republicans (see Chapter 8, page 156). What follows is the text of a UDA document that was circulated internally in the weeks after his death. Its title is Collusion. *Its author is unnamed. For legal reasons certain names from the document have been replaced by letters and some small cuts have been made.*

The rank and file first became aware of contact between loyalists and republicans in the late seventies following the shooting of Joe McKee [shot dead by the UDA in June 1979] in a butcher's shop in Castle Street. A series of meetings took place on the subject of why McKee had been shot. The Woodvale Defence Association, which organised the shooting, had been given a photograph and informed that McKee was an active member of the Provisional IRA. The photograph and the information had been handed over to the WDA by Jim Craig. But apparently the man shot was not in PIRA: he was in the Official IRA.

Three leading officers in the WDA were ordered to go to the Royal Bar in Ann Street to discuss the matter. Among those at the meeting on the republican side were 'A', 'B' and 'C', a man called 'D' and another man, with only one eye, who answered to a nickname 'E'. At the time of the meeting 'D' was on the run from the security forces and the one-eyed man has since been shot dead. At the date of this meeting all these people were members of the Official IRA.

Among those present on the loyalist side were Jim Craig, Bucky McCullough, the three WDA officers and Tommy McCreery. From this meeting it emerged that Craig knew some of the republican side from jail and from before the present troubles (witness available).

This was the start of a liaison that was to bring about racketeering, extortion and collusion, leading to the death of leading loyalists. The people involved in this and subsequent meetings became so confident that they invited each other to pubs and clubs in their respective areas. The republicans drank in such places as the Loyalist Club, Royal Bar and Top House bar. Loyalists in return visited and drank in such places as the Lagan Social Club in the Markets, the Trocadero and Manhattan bar. All this took place with the knowledge of Andy Tyrie. It should also be pointed out that some of those involved on the republican side were later to become members of the INLA and IPLO.

The most dangerous development of all was the relationship between Craig and McCreery on the one hand, and 'A' and 'B' on the other. At first this relationship was confined to building site extortion and tax exemption racketeering but it was later to have lethal consequences for Bucky McCullough, the first of the collusion victims [Billy 'Bucky' McCullough was shot dead by the INLA at his home in Denmark Street on the Shankill in October 1981].

The allegations about Craig's involvement in McCullough's murder are well known; it will be sufficient here simply to name the people concerned. Firstly, Mrs McCullough's allegations about missing money is now known to be quite true – it has been confirmed by leading Shankill Road officers during a thorough investigation. Craig, who was on remand in the Crumlin Road jail, was informed of what was happening. From evidence we now possess, it is known that Craig's contact people for the McCullough killing were 'C' and a man called 'F'. Both live in Unity Flats, an area which figures later in the Craig saga.

After Craig's trial collapsed and he was released, he resumed his partnership with McCreery, 'A' and 'B'. Around this time he also engineered the removal of John McClatchey as west Belfast UDA commander. It was Craig's information on site income which was to prove McClatchey's downfall.

Also around this time, in 1982, a mysterious person called Joe began making contact with Craig through phone calls to Shankill Road HQ. When Craig was told Joe had called, he passed it off by saying Joe was a screw who helped him and Tommy McCreery when Craig was arrested for the hooded witness trial.

It emerged, however, that Joe was one 'G' of [address given], member of PIRA. This came to light after Snow Hamilton [a Shankill UDA member] was sent to meet Joe on the basis that he was a screw. This is also believed to be the same man who supplied Tommy McCreery with poison for use against the supergrasses. After taking delivery of the poison McCreery was stopped and searched by police and held in Castlereagh for several days.

Meetings with Joe were only attended by Craig or McCreery, and took place in the Capstan, Royal and King Arthur bars. All this went on with Andy Tyrie's [knowledge]. Tyrie also called off the proposed shooting of 'A', claiming 'A' was working on intelligence with McCreery. PIRA contacted Craig after Gerry Adams was shot and asked him what was going on and what about the agreement regarding top men. It is believed Joe made the call. Craig was stupid enough to tell other people about the call (witness available). Tyrie knew about this.

Lennie Murphy

The people who know about Murphy's death have no doubt who set him up. Craig and McCreery set him up using David Thompson, a Ligoniel Protestant married to a Catholic, as a contact man. In 1987 Davy Payne claimed the machinegun used in the shooting had been dug up in Silverstream and that 'I' had burned the van used. 'I' belonged to McCreery's team.

Craig himself provided the most damning evidence telling a number of people of his part in the killing. These included A. Fee [Artie Fee, a Shankill UDA man], T. [Tommy] Lyttle, and S. [Snow] Hamilton, among others. Letters from a republican source in Ligoniel to Ohio Street confirmed meetings between McCreery and Thompson and both their parts in the killing. Craig conned UDA people in Glencairn into showing him where Murphy lived and where he parked his car (witness available).

Two points have not as yet been clearly established:

Did UDA people actually shoot Murphy or did they just set him up? Collusion of this kind is, by definition, murder.

Did the UVF leadership at that time have knowledge of, and give their approval to, the shooting of Murphy? One source we have spoken to claims UVF leader 'J' knew, though we have not been able to confirm this. Confirmation can only come from McCreery.

All through the 80s the Craig–McCreery–'A'–'B'–'G' relationship continued, though some people began to get worried. McCreery complained to Tyrie that Craig was divulging all the information to 'G' and getting nothing in return. McCreery also revealed that PIRA had asked for a meeting with Tyrie who refused, suggesting to Craig and McCreery that they ask McMichael instead.

McMichael blew his top when this was suggested to him and told Craig to drop all contact with republicans. But McMichael was not aware that the contact had moved up the scale to a far more dangerous level. Recent press stories about a video-tape of Craig talking to a top PIRA officer can be confirmed. Craig and McCreery had a meeting with 'K' [Andersonstown address given], PIRA northern command intelligence. This meeting was videoed in the Capstan Bar in 1985 or 1986.

Despite McMichael's warning, Craig continued to meet PIRA and INLA–IPLO people. Although the row before Christmas 1987 probably hastened McMichael's death it in itself did not bring it about. McMichael had confided in close colleagues that he knew Craig had warned the PIRA that 'L' [name of Belfast IRA officer commanding] was a UFF target. McMichael had also told UFF intelligence to drop info that Craig could pick up – the idea being to watch for the info coming back.

There is no doubt that 'L' and 'M' [another senior IRA man in Belfast] were both warned about the UFF targeting them. Last but not least, McMichael had re-opened the issue of alleged UDA–PIRA collusion in Lennie Murphy's murder.

Within two days of John McMichael's murder sources close to senior UDA officers indicated loyalist involvement. Rumour became rife, not least because his office in UDA HQ in Gawn Street was ransacked and orders issued that the office should be locked and no one allowed admittance. Contrary to public belief, there was no UDA inquiry into McMichael's death; when the

Chief Constable [Sir John Hermon] said at a press conference on December 31, 1987 that there was loyalist involvement, Tyrie claimed it was a mix.

If it was a mix it was a good one. Inner Council members who were not happy about the affair decided to make their own inquiries. For obvious reasons these early inquiries had to be very discreet, but after the leadership changes in March 1988 things began to come together.

The breakthrough came in the summer when a council member was contacted by some UDA people in England who claimed to have some information about McMichael's death. A meeting was arranged in England, at which it soon became clear that what was being said came from Northern Ireland sources using the English UDA people as a means of relaying vital information about McMichael's death.

By this stage it had been established that Craig had supplied the colour, make and number of McMichael's car, as well as information on a place (not his home) where it would be parked for a certain period. It was decided to watch Craig as closely as possible, not because we did not believe what we were told, but because we wished to catch him out ourselves.

Within limits, Craig had been under almost constant observation and investigation since last Christmas. The results of this surveillance make interesting reading. All of Craig's taxi journeys were monitored and the drivers questioned. The areas he was dropped off at include Lower Ormeau Road, Markets, Short Strand and United Flats. He used the central Information Agency in Ormeau Avenue and Apollo Road, off the Boucher Road, as meeting places with PIRA people. He nearly always used taxis for these journeys, getting out of the taxis to sit in other cars, telling the taxi drivers to wait for him as he was only collecting money off builders.

A short piece in the Who column of the Sunday World, asking how a leading Shankill Road loyalist was able to walk freely about the United Flats complex came as no surprise to our investigators. They had twice observed Craig going into the flats, meeting a girl, and being taken to two separate addresses.

In February of 1988 Craig was in a car stopped by a security force patrol in Dunmurry. The other occupant of the car was 'N', a top Provo Craig met in Crumlin Road jail [the man named in the document is now a prominent Sinn Féin member]. 'N' is the boyfriend of another leading Provo 'O' [the name, address and telephone number of this woman who is also now prominent in Sinn Féin are given]. Craig was also observed meeting 'P' in the Short Strand area – 'P' has Provo form.

Probably his last act of treachery was to tell leading Market Provo 'Q' that a Protestant builder 'R' was carrying out work for the security forces up the country. Craig had fallen out with 'R' after 'R' refused to pay him for the [name of pub in County Antrim]. 'Q' unknowingly let this slip to a source friendly to the UDA. Craig's meeting with 'Q' was observed and a warning has been passed to 'R'.

Although there is nothing to link Craig with the death of John Bingham, coincidence is stretched to the limit regarding the deaths of Frenchie Marchant, George Seawright and Fred Otley.

On the day of Marchant's death Craig had arranged to meet him. Instead of Craig getting out of the car outside the Eagle [the name of the UVF offices on the Shankill Road] to meet Frenchie he got out outside Inter-city furniture shop at the corner of Conway Street and stood talking for five minutes. Inside that five minutes, fifty yards away Marchant was murdered by PIRA (witness available).

On the day George Seawright was murdered, Craig brought two other UDA men to a meeting in Shankill leisure centre car park (witnesses available). While they were sitting in the car park Seawright was shot fifty yards away (witnesses available).

Fred Otley was shot at about 9.45 a.m. in his shop at the corner of Agnes Street and Shankill Road. During the shooting Craig was sitting in Mikhala's café twenty yards away across the Shankill Road (witness available). Others can be the judge of whether these three events were coincidence.

Another example of Craig's dealings with republican paramilitaries came about when he claimed his wife, Mary's, brother was picked up in a bar in Donegall Street, taken to New Lodge Road, stripped, beaten and questioned about Craig.

Craig further claimed he was being blamed for the shooting of a milkman called Dandy [Trevor 'Dandy' Close, shot dead by the UDA in North Belfast in May 1983] who was an INLA member, on the Cliftonville Road. Craig was able to arrange a meeting in the Europa Hotel at which 'S' [INLA brigade staff member], 'B' and 'A' were present. Two west Belfast senior officers were sent to observe the proceedings after the top rank officers declined to attend. The two west Belfast officers were disgusted at what went on (witness available). The INLA delegation said at the end of the meeting they were now satisfied Craig had nothing to do with the shooting but then put forward two UVF men's names as being those responsible. (It must be stressed here Craig was alone with the INLA people half an hour before our people arrived). The INLA asked if these names could be confirmed – at this point our people got up and left.

After Craig's death Tommy McCreery asked for a meeting with the inner council. At this meeting McCreery confirmed the Craig meetings with Joe and 'G' of PIRA. He told of receiving the poison from the PIRA. He told of arranging a meeting in the King Arthur bar at which he accused the PIRA of setting him up. This was after his release from Castlereagh. Most important, he told the council he had informed Andy Tyrie that Craig had set up Bucky McCullough. McCreery also was emphatic that Tyrie knew all about these Provo and INLA contacts.

McCreery denied having any part in Lennie Murphy's murder. On-going investigations have revealed that Artie Fee told 'T' [another UDA man] in the Crescent bar that Craig had told him about his part in the Murphy. Fee went so far as to say he would have shot Murphy himself if asked. Craig did not have to go to PIRA. Spud Murphy [a former UDA commander on the Shankill] also informed the investigators that he was taken to a building site on the Cliftonville Road by Craig and Craig informed him the site was jointly run by himself and the INLA.

Glossary

DUP – Democratic Unionist Party: hard-line mainstream unionist party set up by Revd Ian Paisley and Desmond Boal in 1971

INLA – Irish National Liberation Army: formed in 1975; paramilitary wing of the Irish Republican Socialist Party (IRSP)

IPLO – Irish People's Liberation Organisation: breakaway faction of the INLA; disbanded in 1992

IRA – Irish Republican Army: main republican paramilitary group

IRSP – Irish Republican Socialist Party

LVF – Loyalist Volunteer Force: anti-peace process faction of the UVF led by Billy Wright of Portadown

PUP – Progressive Unionist Party: the political party originating in and allied to the UVF

PSNI – Police Service of Northern Ireland

RHC – Red Hand Commando: UVF satellite organization formed in 1972

RHD – Red Hand Defenders: post-ceasefire flag of convenience for the UDA and the LVF

RUC – Royal Ulster Constabulary: Northern Ireland's police force from 1 June 1922 to 4 November 2001; replaced by the PSNI

SDLP – Social Democratic and Labour Party: party of mainstream middle-class nationalism

UDA – Ulster Defence Association: largest loyalist paramilitary group

UDP – Ulster Democratic Party: formed in 1989; the political party originating in and allied to the UDA; formerly ULDP

ULDP – Ulster Loyalist Democratic Party: political party set up by the Ulster Defence Association in 1981 and chaired by John McMichael; became the UDP

UUP – Ulster Unionist Party: party of mainstream middle-class unionism

UVF – Ulster Volunteer Force: loyalist paramilitary group formed in 1966 and named after the previous UVF which opposed Home Rule over fifty years earlier

UYM – Ulster Young Militants: the youth wing of the UDA

YCV – Young Citizens Volunteers: the youth wing of the UVF

Index